THE DISCERNING TRAVELER'S GUIDE TO THE MIDDLE ATLANTIC STATES

The Discerning Traveler's Guide to New England

THE

DISCERNING TRAVELER'S GUIDE TO THE MIDDLE ATLANTIC STATES

DAVID AND LINDA GLICKSTEIN

Drawings by Jane Adams Stauffer
Maps by David Glickstein

St. Martin's Press
New York

Drawings by Jane Adams Stauffer
Maps by David Glickstein
Design by Chris Welch

Library of Congress Cataloging-in-Publication Data

     The discerning traveler's guide to the Middle Atlantic States / David and Linda Glickstein
         p. cm.
    ISBN 0-312-05857-8
    1. Middle Atlantic States—Description and travel—Guide-books
    I. Glickstein, Linda. II. Title.
    F106.G575 1991
    917.404'43—dc20   90-28615
                             CIP

First Edition

10 9 8 7 6 5 4 3 2 1

To Dorothy and Bernard Schiro

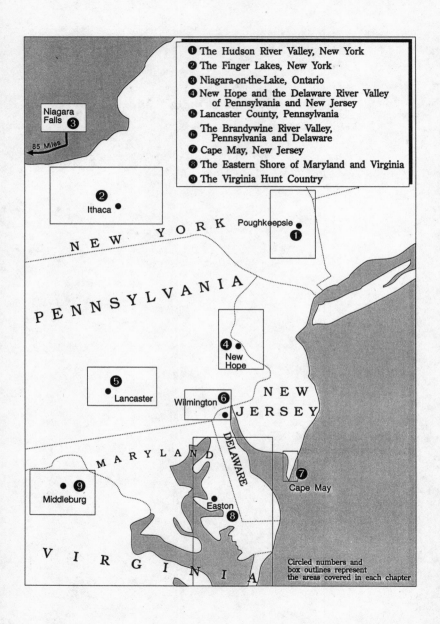

1. The Hudson River Valley, New York
2. The Finger Lakes, New York
3. Niagara-on-the-Lake, Ontario
4. New Hope and the Delaware River Valley of Pennsylvania and New Jersey
5. Lancaster County, Pennsylvania
6. The Brandywine River Valley, Pennsylvania and Delaware
7. Cape May, New Jersey
8. The Eastern Shore of Maryland and Virginia
9. The Virginia Hunt Country

Niagara Falls 3

85 Miles

NEW YORK

2 Ithaca

Poughkeepsie 1

PENNSYLVANIA

4 New Hope

5 Lancaster

Wilmington 6

NEW JERSEY

DELAWARE

MARYLAND

9 Middleburg

Easton 8

7 Cape May

VIRGINIA

Circled numbers and box outlines represent the areas covered in each chapter

CONTENTS

ACKNOWLEDGMENTS

We want to thank Joshua Baskin, our first editor at St. Martin's Press, who convinced us to undertake the writing of this book. Anne Savarese, our editor at St. Martin's, has guided us through the details of making this book a reality.

In researching these destinations we particularly want to thank those who went out of their way to help us learn about their communities by giving us tours and steering us to craftspeople, historians, stores, and cultural events that we might not have discovered on our own: Carl Glassman, Linda Castagna, Mike and Suella Wass, Charles and Sherry Rosemann, Margie Rumsey, Jack and Dee Dee Meyer, Allan Smith, Dorothy Graybill, Debbie David, Bob and Jane Stauffer, Tucker Withers, Roma Sherman, Sandra Cartwright-Brown, and Pamela Goold. We also want to thank editors Linda and Bill Spink for their help in the formative years of the newsletter; Harry Solomon for his critical appraisal of the newsletter, particularly the layout and maps; and Loren Jones for his suggestions on improving the maps.

We owe our greatest thanks to our families and friends, who provided encouragement and lent a hand of support.

INTRODUCTION

Five years ago we began publishing "The Discerning Traveler,"® a unique travel newsletter that covers destinations primarily in the New England and Middle Atlantic states. The newsletter developed as a natural extension of our interest in traveling, which we have done at every opportunity over the past twenty-five years. When we stayed at small inns, hotels, and bed-and-breakfast homes, the owners often took time to recommend restaurants, craft studios, pleasant walks, and unusual shops to visit. Most of these places were not mentioned in the collection of guidebooks we brought along, so we started to build our own storehouse of knowledge. Soon our files bulged with clippings and notes, and our journals recorded our adventures. We developed a knack for designing trips and helped our friends plan theirs.

We started the newsletter to give a larger audience of travelers a practical, easy-to-use guide that would help them develop the same appreciation of a place as the people who live there have. As we gather information for the newsletter, we talk with innkeepers, guests, and craftspeople, stay at different types of lodgings in the area, and eat a wide variety of meals. (We've often referred to our research methods as "poking with a purpose.") Our newsletter, and consequently this book, is far more personal than most other guides, since what is included is based almost exclusively on our own experiences.

For each issue of the newsletter we spend up to two weeks in a particular area. We stay at the inns, eat at the restaurants, and visit the attractions we write about. We drive the back roads and walk the side streets to find the best markets, roadside stands, crafts, shops, regional theater, museums, and historic sites. We look for, and usually find, that elusive something that can turn even a weekend getaway into a treasured experience. No one pays to be included in either the newsletter or this book.

The Discerning Traveler's Guide to the Middle Atlantic States is not a guide to every city, town, and village in the region; other guides are available for that purpose. Instead, we have selected nine of the most popular Middle Atlantic and Canadian issues of "The Discerning Traveler"® newsletter. Each has been updated and expanded, with new entries, maps, and illustrations. Places that no longer meet our standards or have gone out of business have been eliminated.

Travelers using this guide will find virtually all the information necessary to experience the heart and soul of the Middle Atlantic region: the seaside resort of Victorian Cape May, New Jersey; the beautiful hunt country of Northern Virginia; the Hudson River Valley and Finger Lakes regions of New York state; historic towns along the Delaware River in Pennsylvania and New Jersey; the Brandywine River Valley of Pennsylvania and Delaware; the Amish community of Lancaster County, Pennsylvania; the Eastern Shore of Maryland and Virginia; and Niagara-on-the-Lake in Ontario, Canada. The last chapter of the book is a selection of romantic hideaways scattered throughout the Middle Atlantic area.

Each chapter includes a short history of the region and first-hand reviews of accommodations, ranging from small historic bed-and-breakfast inns to larger, full-service resorts. Restaurant reviews cover inexpensive regional and ethnic cuisine as well as gourmet restaurants of the highest caliber. The shops and craft studios we visit are, for the most part, small and family-owned. We describe museums and historic sites, walks and hikes, cruises, bicycle touring, downhill and cross-country skiing, horseback riding, and much more. To help you plan your trip, we supply a map of each area, a three- to five-day itinerary, our recommendations of what to see and do, and a detailed budget for two people. Each chapter also features a tested recipe that uses the ingredients or is influenced by the traditions of the region. For travelers who want more detailed information about their destination, we include short reading lists.

We have made every attempt to verify prices, hours, and dates of operation at the time this book went to press. It always is wise to call ahead, however; many of the attractions, restaurants, and inns are small and subject to changes in management, prices, and policies.

We appreciate any comments you might have, good or bad, about the inns, restaurants, and attractions reviewed in this book. Write to us at The Discerning Traveler, 504 West Mermaid Lane, Philadelphia, Pennsylvania 19118.

We wish you happy, healthy travels.

—David and Linda Glickstein

ONE

THE HUDSON RIVER VALLEY, NEW YORK

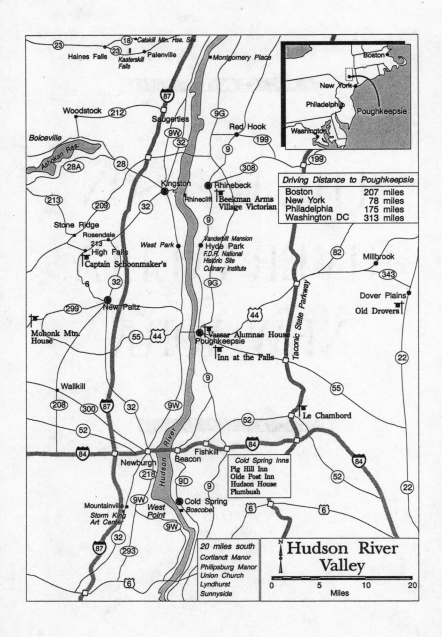

Driving Distance to Poughkeepsie

Boston	207 miles
New York	78 miles
Philadelphia	175 miles
Washington DC	313 miles

Hudson River Valley

N

0	5	10	20

Miles

The inspiration for this chapter came from an exhibition of Hudson River painters at the Metropolitan Museum of Art in New York City. We admired the romanticism of these great nineteenth-century landscape painters: Asher B. Durand, Thomas Cole, John Kensett, Jasper Cropsey, Frederic Church, and others. Keeping their vision in mind, we traveled through the region that these artists depicted, shutting out the fast-paced world of today, to experience the Romantics' nineteenth-century vision of man in nature.

We searched out the places they painted. The Catskill Mountain House, a grand hotel of the late nineteenth century, was torn down some years ago but the views of the valley remain one of the most awe-inspiring wonders in the Northeast. You can still hike to Kaaterskill Falls, another favorite landscape scene. Olana, Frederic Church's extravagant Moorish structure set atop a hill overlooking the valley, is preserved as it was when Church painted there.

The past and the present peacefully co-exist in the valley today. Thirty-five properties have been designated as National Historic Landmarks. Countless others are protected as historic sites. Up and down the river there is a growing awareness that this valley is too precious to lose to pollution and industrial decay. The river is getting cleaner and the shad are returning. Plans for the creation of a Hudson River Greenway, a network of parklands, historic sites, recreational and environmentally protected areas, are well underway.

The great river estates are being preserved and opened to visitors. Franklin Delano Roosevelt's home and the Vanderbilt Mansion in Hyde Park, and Montgomery Place farther north are examples of ones that you can visit. Other grand estates once thought to be white elephants are now owned by schools and seminaries. The Culinary Institute of America is flourishing in one; Bard College has one; the Reverend Sun Myung Moon has another for his flock; others are still owned by the families that built them. New wealth is moving into the valley, buying up and restoring these architectural gems of America's past. These estates were designed to take advantage of the water views, so they can best be seen from the deck of one of the boats that cruise or sail the river.

Agriculture is alive and thriving in the valley. Specialty farms are now growing exotic produce as demanded by today's sophisticated palates. The old orchards, many still owned by the original families, grow countless varieties of apples. In close proximity to the orchards a new breed of vintners are carrying on the tradition in the oldest wine district in the United States.

As you explore the river valley, step back to a slower and gentler way of life as romanticized by the Hudson River painters.

Hudson River Valley Association. Call or write for general information about the entire region. Guidebooks and products made in the Hudson River Valley are for sale here. Items for a remembrance of your trip include herbs and jams from Grieg Farm in Red Hook. 72 Main Street, Cold Spring, NY 10516; (914) 452-4910 or (800) 232-HRVA.

Historic Hudson Valley. Five properties owned by Historic Hudson are Sunnyside, Union Pocantico Church, Philipsburg Manor, Van Cortlandt Manor, and Montgomery Place. When you purchase an admission ticket to one of the sites, you receive a Hudson Valley "Passport" that provides a 20 percent discount on admission to the other sites. Admission to each of the properties is $5 for adults, $4.50 for senior citizens, $3 for students under 18 and full-time college students. Children under 6 free. A $3 donation is requested at Union Pocantico Church. 150 White Plains Road, Tarrytown, NY 10591; (914) 631-8200.

SPECIAL EVENTS THROUGHOUT THE YEAR

Events at the Wineries.   Concerts, grape stomping, dinners, special tastings are held at many of the region's twenty wineries. Hudson River Region Wine Council; (914) 265-3066.

May.   Candlelight Tours at Boscobel Restoration. Garrison-on-Hudson; (914) 265-3638.

May.   Shad Festival. Outdoor grilling, exhibits. Hudson River Maritime Center, Kingston; (914) 338-0071.

Mid-June Through October Weekends.   Antique Air Shows. Stunt flights with old planes. Old Rhinebeck Aerodrome, Rhinebeck; (914) 758-8610.

July.   Aston Magna Music Festival. Sixteenth- and seventeenth-century baroque chamber music concerts played on period instruments. Bard College, Annandale-on-Hudson; (914) 758-7425.

Early August.   Stone House Day. Visit authentically furnished houses from the late seventeenth century. Huguenot Street, New Paltz; (914) 255-1660.

August.   Dutchess County Fair. 4-H exhibitions, midway, amusements, food. Rhinebeck; (914) 876–4001.

October.   Fall concerts in color. Chamber music. Union Church of Pocantico Hills, North Tarrytown; (914) 631-8200.

December.   Candlelight Tours. Each weekend at a different site: Philipsburg Manor, Montgomery Place, Sunnyside, Van Cortlandt Manor. Hot cider, music, bonfires, house tours; (914) 631-8200.

WHERE TO GO, WHAT TO DO

Getting Out on the River

To fully experience this valley and especially to see the grand old estates, save some time to get out on the river. We have picked a selection of cruises for every taste and budget, from a twenty-eight-foot sailboat to a passenger ship holding 300. Write or call for the exact schedules.

Hudson Highland Cruises.   The *Commander* has full-day and half-day cruises. It leaves Haverstraw at 10 A.M. and puts in at West Point at 12 P.M. Passengers may disembark here and pick up the boat on its return to Haverstraw, arriving back at 4:30 P.M. Or, board at West Point at 12:30 for a 1½-hour cruise.

Operates Monday through Friday, late May through October. Full-day trips: adults, $12; seniors and children, $10. One-and-a-half-hour trips: adults, $6; seniors and children, $5. Box 265, Highland Falls, NY 10928; (914) 446-7171.

Hudson River Cruises.   The 300-passenger *Rip Van Winkle* leaves from the Kingston Rondout Landing. Full-day, sightseeing, lunch, dinner, and rock'n'roll cruises are offered on different days.

Operates May through October. Fares $12 (sightseeing cruise), $20 (full day), $15 (lunch), $25 (dinner). 20524 North Ohioville Road, New Paltz, NY 12561; (914) 255-6515.

Hudson Rondout Cruises.   The ninety-passenger *Rondout Belle* leaves from the Kingston Rondout Landing. This boat stops to let its passengers visit the historic Rondout Lighthouse with much of its early twentieth-century furnishings still intact. Sightseeing, lunch, dinner, and brunch cruises, are available.

Weekend cruises May through October, 11 A.M. and 1 P.M. Daily cruises June through September, 11 A.M. and 1 P.M. Adults, $10; seniors, $8; children, $6. This price also includes admission to the Maritime Museum in Kingston. Dinner cruises, $22–$30; Champagne brunches, $16–$25. 11 East Chestnut Street, Kingston, NY 12401; (914) 338-6280.

Sailing on the River–Shearwater Cruises.   For a personal and up-close view of the river, take a two-hour cruise with Marty Ward on her Sabre 28 or Bristol 24. Leave from Staatsburg, six miles south of Rhinebeck. You'll pass the estates that dot the east shore and the Esopus Lighthouse (the one with the *trompe l'oeil* cat in the window). Marty told us, "I let guests participate as much as they'd like. Some like to raise the sails, others want to just motor." Champagne and hors d'oeuvres are complimentary; a lobster lunch is about $5 extra.

Weekends only, May, June, September, and October; daily, July and August. Two-hour cruises (two to six people): adults, $25; children, $10. Four-hour cruises, $180. Eight-hour cruises, $295 (up to six people). Sailing lessons and bare boat charters available. Shearwater Cruises and Sailing School, RD#2, Box 329, Rhinebeck, NY 12572; (914) 876-7350.

It was hard for us to know where to start our exploration of the valley. With so many historic towns, sites, and drives, we have selected a collection of things to do and see, starting on the East Bank at Tarrytown and continuing north to just south of Hudson. Then we crossed the river to the West Bank and included selections from West Point in the south to Haines Falls in the north. We discovered there is a lifetime of exploring in this valley.

TARRYTOWN

This area is easy commuting distance from New York City and can become congested. The historic houses and sites listed below are little oases in a sea of twentieth-century development and traffic. When you visit these properties, try to remember that the surrounding landscape was once like Montgomery Place, eighty miles to the north.

Sunnyside. What child hasn't grown up on the stories of *Rip Van Winkle* and *The Legend of Sleepy Hollow?* Consequently, a visit to Washington Irving's home is particularly meaningful. The guide, dressed in period costume, recounts tales of Irving's life. The bed in his study is where Irving slept; his nieces, who took care of the house and organized his social calendar, lived in the upstairs bedrooms. While you can't sit in the chair where he spent hours looking at the river, you can sit outside on the porch and enjoy the same views across the three-mile expanse of the Hudson. (This is the widest part of the river, known as the Tappan Zee.)

Open daily except Tuesday. April through December, 10 A.M. to 5 P.M.; January through March, Saturday and Sunday only. Adults, $5, seniors $4.50, children $3. Historic Hudson property. Off Route 9, Tarrytown, NY 10591; (914) 591-8763.

Lyndhurst. While you'll need to imagine the knights, the sixty-seven-acre estate set on the banks of the Hudson provides the ideal setting for fairytale imagination. This gray-white marble Gothic castle that seems to grow out of the earth is a bit startling to find on the banks of the Hudson River. What a place to study the elements of Gothic architecture: turrets, parapets with crenelations and merlons, a tower, arched doorways, odd-shaped windows, and vaulted ceilings. Take time to wander the sweeping lawns, enjoy the massive copper beech trees and the elegant thread-leaf maples, and stroll through the rose garden with its 127 varieties.

This property was once the home of Jay Gould, one of the so-called robber barons, who amassed his fortune in railroads at the end of the nineteenth century. It now is owned by the National Trust for Historic Preservation.

Open May through October, and December, Tuesday through Sunday, 10 A.M. to 5 P.M. January through April, and November, weekends only, 10 A.M. to 5 P.M. Adults, $5; seniors, $4; children, $3. Free for members. 635 South Broadway, Tarrytown, NY 10591; (914) 631-0046.

Philipsburg Manor.   The waterwheel at this eighteenth-century mill is operating again. You can see the entire milling process from harvesting the grain to adjusting the stones to sifting the flour. (Bags of flour can be purchased.) Colonial-costumed guides explain the workings of the farm and guide you through the manor house. To make the manor historically accurate, the cows and the sheep are breeds that might have been here 200 years ago.

At the grain harvest in early July, we tried using the sickles in the wheat fields and found it is mighty hard work.

Open daily April through December, 10 A.M. to 5 P.M.; Saturday and Sunday in March, 10 A.M. to 5 P.M., Adults $5, seniors $4.50, children $3. Historic Hudson property, Route 9, North Tarrytown, NY 10591; (914) 631-3992.

Union Church of Pocantico Hills.   Here is a little gem often overlooked by the harried traveler. Down the road from the entrance to Pocantico Hills (the Rockefeller family compound that someday will be open to the public) is a little stone church with a rare set of eight Chagall stained-glass windows and a Matisse rose medallion window. There is nothing else like it in this country. The windows are Biblical scenes from the Old Testament in those glorious Chagall shades of blue and yellow. Chamber music concerts are held Sunday afternoons in April and October.

Open April through December, Wednesday, Thursday, and Friday, 1 to 4 P.M.; Sunday, 2 to 5 P.M. $3 donation. Historic Hudson property: from Route 9 turn east on Route 448 to the stop sign. North Tarrytown, NY 10591; (914) 631-8200.

CROTON-ON-HUDSON

Van Cortlandt Manor. This is the best place in the valley to see a demonstration of open-hearth cooking using Colonial implements and following the original recipes. Breads, pies, butter, cookies, and roasts are all prepared in front of the visitors. After seeing the women stirring pots and raking embers, we can understand why burns were a leading cause of death during this period of history.

The owner of the home was Pierre Van Cortlandt, the state's first lieutenant governor. Fine examples of period furniture are displayed in the room settings. After a tour of the house, we walked through extensive eighteenth-century herb gardens to the Ferry house where travelers on the old Albany Post Road stopped for refreshment or overnight lodging.

Open daily except Tuesday, April through December, 10 A.M. to 5 P.M. Saturday and Sunday in March, 10 A.M. to 5 P.M. Adults, $5, seniors $4.50; children $3. Historic Hudson property. Off Route 9, Croton-on-Hudson, NY 10520; (914) 271-8981.

GARRISON AND COLD SPRING

Cold Spring. Highlights not to be missed in this charming river town of 2,000, just ninety minutes from Grand Central Station, include the views of the river from the Chapel of Our Lady and the gazebo at the river's edge. There are about a dozen antique stores, a neat bookshop, three B&Bs, great hiking, fine restaurants, and Dixieland jazz on the weekends. Frankly, we are amazed that the town hasn't been spoiled by hordes of tourists. Just to the south, practically within walking distance, is the impeccable restoration of Boscobel.

Shopping tip: The U.S. distributors of Alan Paine, manufacturer of top-quality English men's sweaters, has its headquarters in Cold Spring right across the road from the chapel. A tiny mill outlet stocks the sweaters at attractive prices. We promised not to give prices, but we did stock up; (914) 265-3939.

Boscobel Restoration.   There are restorations and there are *restorations.* This is one of the best. From the formal gardens with carefully pruned ornamental trees, to the breathtaking vistas of the Hudson River, to the meticulously restored and maintained Federal mansion filled with an outstanding collection of New York Federal furniture, this is a definite must for interested visitors. Lila Acheson Wallace, co-founder of *Reader's Digest,* rescued Boscobel from the wrecking ball in 1955. The building was taken apart board by board, placed on trucks and moved fifteen miles north to its present location. Not only is the structure original, but the furnishings, which had been dispersed over the years, were sought out by curators, purchased, restored (when needed), and placed, based on original inventories, in their original rooms.

Open daily except Tuesday. April through October, 9:30 A.M. to

Boscobel is a meticulously restored and maintained Federal mansion that offers breathtaking views of the Hudson River.

4:15 P.M.; March, November, and December, 9:30 A.M. to 3:15 P.M. Closed January and February. Adults, $5; seniors, $4; children, $2.50. Route 9W, Garrison-on-Hudson, NY 10524; (914) 265-3638.

HYDE PARK

Franklin Delano Roosevelt National Historic Site. After our visit we came away with a personal view of Franklin Roosevelt—a man who, though confined to a wheelchair throughout his presidency, led this country through the Great Depression and World War II. We got the impression that his wife, Eleanor, never felt comfortable here, as she regarded the house as the exclusive domain of her mother-in-law. Pointing out the two large leather chairs next to the fireplace in the library, the guide said, "One was Franklin's and one was for his mother." Where did Eleanor sit?

A visit to the presidential library is fascinating whether you are coming for scholarly research (which we weren't) or just as interested travelers. This is a good rainy-day excursion—we could have spent hours looking at the photographs and accompanying commentaries telling of world events during his presidency and displays such as Franklin's hand-controlled Ford Phaeton. On our way to Hyde Park we listened to the cassette of excerpts from David Brinkley's book, *Washington Goes to War.* This lively account of the events in Washington leading up to the war made our visit more meaningful.

Open daily, 9 A.M. to 5 P.M. Adults, $3.50. Free to senior citizens, Golden Eagle cardholders, and visitors under 16. Route 9, Hyde Park, NY 12538; (914) 229-9115.

Val-Kill. This modest home, built on the Hyde Park estate in 1925, was Eleanor Roosevelt's retreat. She lived here from the time of Franklin's death in 1945 until her death in 1962.

As we walked the trails, toured the buildings, and saw the film about Eleanor's life, we could imagine how happy she must have felt in this private oasis.

Open daily, 9 A.M. to 5 P.M. April through October. Thursday through Monday, November through March, 9 A.M. to 5 P.M. Admission included with ticket to FDR home. Get a map from the FDR library. Hyde Park, NY 12538; (914) 229-9115.

Vanderbilt Mansion. If you have seen The Breakers in Newport, Rhode Island, you might think this Vanderbilt mansion was a poor cousin. If you haven't, you will be amazed at how these Vanderbilts lavishly spent their fortunes. The fifty-four-room Italian Renaissance house was completed in 1899 at a cost of $3 million and employed a full-time staff of sixty.

Compare the stark simplicity of Eleanor Roosevelt's bedroom to Mrs. Vanderbilt's ornate, French-inspired queen's boudoir. On a nice day save some time to wander the spacious, well-landscaped grounds planted with dozens of varieties of fine old specimen trees and offering panoramic views of the Hudson River and the Shawangunk and Catskill mountains.

Open daily, April through October, 9 A.M. to 5 P.M.; November through March, Thursday through Monday, 9 A.M. to 5 P.M. Adults, $4, seniors and students free. Route 9, Hyde Park, NY 12538; (914) 229-9115.

RHINEBECK

This intact nineteenth-century town is best explored on foot. Besides the renowned Beekman Arms (see *Where to Stay,* page 27, and *Where to Dine,* page 41) there is a Victorian B&B, a movie theater that offers an excellent selection of foreign and Hollywood classics, the Dutchess County fairgrounds, and the aerodrome. Other restaurants in town include Le Bistro for French food, La Parmigiana Trattoria for pizza cooked in a wood-fired brick oven, Foster's for large burgers, and Schemmy's for an old-fashioned ice cream soda.

Old Rhinebeck Aerodrome. Here is your chance to play the Red Baron by taking a ride in an old biplane at this living museum of antique aircraft. Weekends during spring, summer, and fall, daredevil owner Cole Palen and other pilots bring out the old World War I aircraft to perform mock air duels. Three hangars filled with planes that date back to the early 1900s are also on the property.

Open daily mid-May through October, 10 A.M. to 5 P.M. Shows at 2:30 P.M. on Saturday and Sunday. For the airshow: adults, $8;

children ages 6 to 10, $4. Weekdays: adults, $3; children, $1.50. Rides are given in an open-cockpit biplane before and after the air show. Three miles north of town, off Route 9. Stone Church Road, Rhinebeck, NY 12572; (914) 758-8610.

ANNANDALE-ON-HUDSON

Montgomery Place.   This is as close as most of us will ever come to experiencing what it was like to live on the great river estates. The 434-acre property was owned and occupied by the same family throughout its 200-year history. The rooms, some of which are still under restoration, reflect the various furniture styles of the past 200 years. There is a bit of every kind of furniture here. The magnificent exterior (which, when we visited, was still undergoing restoration) was of more interest to us. The shop is designed so that visitors can watch the master carpenters and masons at work on the mansion.

The natural woodland trails developed in the 1800s have been restored to their original appearance and provide wonderful hiking and picnicking opportunities. Fruit from the 5,000 apple, pear, and peach trees, still under active cultivation, is sold at the roadside stand. You can also pick your own.

Open daily except Tuesday, April through October, 10 A.M. to 5 P.M. and until sunset summer weekends. November, December, March, open weekends only. Closed January and February. Adults, $5; students under 18, $3. Historic Hudson property, Box 32, Annandale-on-Hudson, NY 12504; (914) 758-5461.

HUDSON

Olana.   Frederic Church was one of the most successful nineteenth-century landscape painters. After purchasing 126 acres on a hilltop overlooking the Hudson, he improved the landscape by planting thousands of trees, creating a reflecting pond, and laying out curving roads that took advantage of the spectacular vistas, which he painted time and time again. After dismissing the architect, Church designed the Moorish-inspired thirty-seven-room mansion himself. Perched 500 feet above the river, it is most unusual. The house is jammed with furnishings from his travels, as well as many of his paintings.

Open May through Labor Day weekend, Wednesday through Saturday, 10 A.M. to 4 P.M.; Sunday, 1 to 4 P.M. After Labor Day through October, Wednesday through Saturday, 12 to 4 P.M.; Sunday, 1 to 4 P.M. As tours are limited to twelve persons, we suggest making advance reservations. Adults $1, children 50¢. Grounds are open year-round. Route 9G, Hudson, NY 12534; (518) 828-0135.

WEST POINT AND STORM KING MOUNTAIN

West Point Military Academy. If you haven't yet visited this American landmark, do so when you come to the valley. The views from Trophy Point of the Hudson Highlands are some of the best to be had. There is an outstanding, newly constructed military museum. We suggest taking the guided bus tour, as the walking distances are extensive. The guides, many of whom are wives of officers, tell personal stories about life at the academy. The public is invited to see the parades. For a listing of dates for the sporting events and parades, send a stamped self-addressed business envelope to the visitor's center.

Open daily, 9 A.M. to 4:45 P.M. Free admission. Guided bus tours last one hour and leave every twenty minutes starting at 9:30 A.M. (11:30 on Sunday). Adults, $3. For information about sports events call the Army Ticket Office, (914) 446-4996. Route 9W, West Point, NY 10996. For other information, (914) 938-2638.

Storm King Art Center. We had a grand time walking about the hillsides and meadows of this 350-acre manicured park and coming across another masterpiece at every turn. Works by such greats as Alexander Calder, Louise Nevelson, Isamu Noguchi, David Smith, and Henry Moore are included among more than 130 large sculptures scattered throughout the grounds. What an idyllic way to learn to appreciate these mostly contemporary (post-1945) works of art! When most art museums mount a new exhibit, rooms are repainted, lighting is changed, and walls are moved. When a special exhibit is mounted at Storm King, thousands of yards of soil are moved and the landscape is changed to accommodate the large sculptures. There are picnic tables on the grounds.

The museum is open mid-May through October, Wednesday through Monday, 12 to 5:30 P.M. The park is open April through Thanksgiving, daily, noon to 5:30 P.M. Adults, $5; seniors and children, $3. New York Thruway, exit 16. Take Route 32 north to Old Pleasant Hill Road, Mountainville, NY 10953; (914) 534-3115.

KINGSTON

The Rondout area of lower Kingston was a hub of commercial and passenger travel in the eighteenth and nineteenth centuries. Side-wheel passenger steamboats stopped here. The Delaware and Hudson Canal, which carried coal to fuel the fires of industrial America and bluestone (slate) to build the urban sidewalks, terminated here. Today the area is undergoing major renovation. Stores and restaurants including Mary P's (see *Where to Dine,* page 42), have opened in the former nineteenth-century shops that serviced the riverboats. Two Hudson River cruise boats, *Rip Van Winkle* and *Rondout Belle,* leave from here. There is a fledgling trolley museum that operates streetcars out to Kingston Park, a good spot for a picnic. You'll also find a maritime center with exhibits and an 1899 steam tugboat named *Mathilda,* which is currently under restoration.

Hudson River Maritime Center. Open daily except Tuesday. Early May through late October, 11 A.M. to 5 P.M.; Saturday and Sunday, 10 A.M. to 5 P.M. Adults, $2.50; seniors, $2; children, $1. One Rondout Landing, Kingston, NY 12498; (914) 338-0071.

Trolley Museum. Open weekends and holidays Memorial Day to Columbus Day, daily during July and August, 12 to 5 P.M. Adults, $1.50; children, $1.

89 East Strand, Kingston, NY 12401; (914) 331-3399.

BOICEVILLE AND PHOENICIA

These towns are a bit off the river, but worth the trip for the *bread alone.*

Bread Alone Bakery. Those of you who frequent the green-markets in New York City at 57th Street or Union Square may already have tasted these loaves that have been much touted by food critics and now by us. Seven varieties of crusty, moist, dense bread are made with organically grown, stone-ground flour from North Dakota. The loaves rise for a minimum of six hours and are then cast onto the floor of an enormous French-designed wood-fired brick oven.

The bread may be purchased at the bakery, which is on the right side of Route 28 just before you get to Boiceville, as well as in area markets. Open Monday through Friday, 8 A.M. to 11 P.M.; Saturday, 9 A.M. to 5 P.M. They will ship UPS. (914) 657-3328.

Town Tinker Tube Rental. Last season over 30,000 people floated down the Esopus River. You can rent tubes, life jackets, helmets, and even sneakers here for a 1¾-hour float down the river.

There are two river runs to choose from. The more experienced, who can handle one- to three-foot waves, can take the trip (class 2) that starts two and a half miles above Phoenicia. The novice will want to take the trip that goes two and a half miles downstream from Phoenicia. On weekends the Catskill Mountain Railroad, a very short railroad of just over two miles, provides the return transportation.

Open May through September, daily 9 A.M. to 6 P.M. Standard tubes, $7; tubes with seats (this saves your bottom from scrapes on the rocks), $10; life jackets, $2; creek sneakers, $2; bus or train transportation, $3. Appropriate for children over 12. Box 404, Phoenicia, NY 12464; (914) 688-5553.

HAINES FALLS

During the mid to late 1800s, landscape painters came to Hunter Mountain, Kaaterskill Falls, Kaaterskill Clove, and the Catskill Mountain House. As discerning travelers we've had to do a lot of hunting to make the connection between what the painters painted and what you can see today.

Catskill Mountain House. To get to the site of this former 300-room hotel you will need the following directions, as there are no signs until you get to the exact site.

From Saugerties, take exit 20 on the New York Thruway. Go north on Route 32 for six miles and on Route 32A for another two miles. At Palenville turn left on Route 23A. The road curves up, and each hairpin turn brings waterfalls and vistas. Follow Route 23A for five miles to Haines Falls. At Haines Falls turn right onto Greene County Route 18 and follow this road for 2%o miles to North Lake State Campground.

From North Lake follow the paved park road around the lake to the group picnic area. Park your car at the end farthest from the picnic shelter. Look for the path that leads up a hill. In about five minutes you will arrive at a clearing 2,000 feet above the valley and will see the signs marking the spot of the Catskill Mountain House. As you approach the edge of the cliff, you have no idea of the magnificence that awaits. The view is spectacular.

From here, the valley is spread out in front of you. We felt as if we had found one of the unheralded treasures of the Northeast. If you take no other walks during the course of your stay in the Hudson River Valley this is the one that you must take.

Kaaterskill Falls. As you wound your way along Route 23A, you passed the falls. To hike to the upper falls, turn right just past the entrance booth of North Lake State Campground and follow the road to the end. Follow the dirt path, about a thirty-minute level walk, to the head of the falls. This also was one of the spots frequently painted.

To view the falls from the bottom, take a trail that leads off 23A. As you drive back toward Palenville, the trail starts at Horseshoe Curve, about one mile before you get to Palenville. The walk to the falls is a steep ten-minute climb.

WINERIES

Spectacular vistas, gourmet picnics, art galleries, bistros, cafés, chamber music, and some mighty fine wines await the smart traveler who seeks out the wineries of the oldest wine-growing district in the United States. You won't find the slick multimillion-dollar operations of the Napa Valley, but you probably can talk to the owners and winemakers and taste some exceptionally fine wines.

You will find here not only the traditional native Labrusca, Concord, and Niagara grapes, but also the vinifera varietals of Chardonnay, Riesling, and Cabernet Sauvignon, among others. The oenophile can easily spend a weekend touring and tasting from among the twenty or so wineries that make up the Hudson Valley wine district. For a full listing, description, and directions to each property, call the Hudson River Valley Association, (914) 265-3066; in New York State, (800) 237-7898.

For a taste of the region we offer this sampling.

Benmarl. We tasted some of the twelve different table wines produced on this 100-acre vineyard, where grapes have grown for more than 150 years. A favorite is an aged, full-bodied dry Estate Red. Mark Miller, a highly respected and vigorous promoter of the valley's wines, has a unique club for Benmarl wine enthusiasts (membership fee is sponsorship of two vines). Besides offering the usual events for members—barrel tastings, formal dinners and special tours—an annual grape-stomping party is held to produce a wine aptly called Ped Red.

Open daily, 11 A.M. to 4 P.M. Art gallery, concerts in June and July. Bistro, Friday through Sunday, 11 A.M. to 5 P.M. On Route 9W, two miles south of Marlboro. Turn west on Conway Road one mile; (914) 236-4265.

West Park. As ardent fans of California Chardonnays we were skeptical until we sampled a bottle of this New York wine. Vintner Louis Fiore enters his Chardonnay in the Sonoma County wine competition. He isn't satisfied with being the best in New York; he wants to compete with the "big boys" out west. West Park has hundreds of acres overlooking the Hudson River, and is a perfect spot to take West Park's gourmet picnic basket for a lazy afternoon.

Open May through January, Friday through Sunday, 11 A.M. to 6 P.M. Gourmet picnic basket (about $25 for two) includes smoked trout, pâté forestier and canard à l'orange, Brie and Jarlsberg, fruits, breads, cold salads, and a half bottle of Champagne, Beaujolais, or Chardonnay. On Route 9W five miles north of Mid-Hudson Bridge; (914) 384-6709.

Baldwin. We tasted the chilled strawberry wine, made from 100% local strawberries, at the DePuy Canal House and were impressed. The apple wine and the Landot Noir have won major awards.

Open late May through October, Thursday through Monday, 11 A.M. to 5 P.M. Route 302 north to Pine Bush and Route 52, then follow signs; (914) 744-2226.

WHERE TO STAY

COLD SPRING, HOPEWELL JUNCTION, AND DOVER PLAINS

Old Drovers Inn, Dover Plains

Almost 250 years of continuous use has imparted a warm glow of welcome to this historic inn. Four gracious guest rooms beckon travelers to stop and rest. For a romantic getaway, especially in cold weather, this is ideal.

Innkeepers Alice Pitcher and Kemper Peacock have admirably continued the preservation of this museum-quality gem. On the first floor there is a quiet, formal library. The front-hall lounge has a couch facing an old wood-burning fireplace. While sitting here, notice the antique chest whose legs have had to be drastically altered to compensate for the sagging floor.

Three of the four guest rooms have working wood-burning fireplaces. The largest and the most sumptuous is the Meeting Room, which has a barrel-shaped ceiling, two double beds, a fireplace, and two wingback chairs. An antique writing desk, bureau, and window seats that were filled with more than a dozen current upscale magazines create a cozy, inviting hideaway.

The second-largest room is the Cherry Room, which has much larger windows than those in the Meeting Room plus two double beds, lined chintz draperies, a fireplace, and two wingback chairs.

The Sleigh Room has a double sleigh bed, fireplace, and two easy chairs. We appreciated the thick terrycloth robes as well as the high-quality soap, shampoo, and conditioner in the baths. Be fore-warned that all of the baths have tubs only except for the Meeting Room, which has a combination tub and shower. The evening turndown service includes a plate with an apple, chocolate thin mints, chocolate truffles, and an old glass milk bottle filled with cold water.

A thermos of juice and freshly brewed coffee is set out for early-rising guests in the first-floor Federal Room, where breakfast is served starting at 9 A.M. The walls of this room are decorated with murals painted in 1941 of the inn, West Point, and Hyde Park. Start with a glass of freshly squeezed orange or grapefruit juice and homemade breakfast breads. This is followed by a choice of ome-lets with wild mushrooms or cheddar cheese, French toast ba-guette, Belgian malted waffles, shepherd's eggs on hashed browns, or Southern-style grits. Bacon, sausage patties, and Canadian bacon are also served.

Four rooms, all with private bath, $110–$170. 15% service charge additional. Full breakfast included. Children welcome, $30 additional. No pets. Located about seventy-five miles north of New York City off Route 22, between Wingdale and Dover Plains. Old Drovers Inn Road, Dover Plains, NY 12522; (914) 832-9311.

Pig Hill Inn, Cold Spring

Everything is for sale here except the inn itself. Each of the eight rooms has an inconspicuous card listing the prices of all the furni-ture and art in the room. As an example, the total cost for room 8 was $12,000, which included a $3,000 love seat, a $1,450 armoire, and a $1,850 sampler.

The inn's eclectic style artfully combines antiques from Chippen-dale to chinoiserie. The front room is an antique store.

The guest rooms, located on the second and third floors, have four-poster or brass beds, pine armoires, painted rockers, chintz curtains, prints, oil paintings, and lots of pigs in every shape and form. There is even a Pig Hill watch. To add to the ambience, fireplaces or stoves are found in six of the eight rooms.

Out back is a rock garden, a delightful spot to catch up on your reading.

Breakfast of eggs or waffles, sausage, tomatoes, and more can be enjoyed in the downstairs dining room, in the privacy of your room, or outside in the rock garden.

Eight rooms. Four with fireplace and private bath, $140. Two with fireplace and shared bath, $115. Two with shared bath, $90. Midweek rates are lower. Children welcome, $25 for a cot or crib. No pets. Full country breakfast included. 73 Main Street, Cold Spring, NY 10516; (914) 265-9247.

Plumbush, Cold Spring

Owner Gieri Albin and chef Ans Benderer are both Swiss by birth. Over fourteen years ago they opened their well-regarded restaurant (see *Where to Dine,* page 39) in this large Victorian-era home. A few years ago they decided to convert the unutilized second floor into three quiet guest rooms.

Care was taken in selecting the Victorian furnishings for these rooms. In the Marchesa Suite the slanted walls are papered with a flowered print; the Victorian sofa and chairs are upholstered in pink that compliments both the walls and the colors of the Oriental rug. A white brass bed adds to the light feeling of the room.

The other two rooms with appropriate regional names, Washington Irving and Hendrick Hudson, are a bit smaller. A sitting room with a television and Victorian sofa and chairs is for the use of the overnight guests.

Do remember that while these rooms are pleasant, the primary focus of attention is downstairs in the first-class restaurant. For those who desire a leisurely dinner without the drive home, Plumbush might suit you just fine.

Two rooms, with private bath, $95. One suite, $125. Continental breakfast is included. Not appropriate for children. No pets. Route 9D, Cold Spring, NY 10516; (914) 265-3904.

Hudson House, Cold Spring

This beige clapboard three-story structure with a balcony circling the second floor started life in 1832 as a steamboat stop between New York City and Albany. The views across the river to Storm King Mountain and West Point are particularly memorable. Whether you have a room with a view or not, you are only 100 yards from the water.

The rooms are all similarly decorated with twin, double, or queen-size beds, flowered wallpaper, pine headboards, and country curtains that match the dust ruffles. There are large cookie-cutter decorations mounted above each bed. The inn has the added advantage of a full-service bar and restaurant. However, we felt that rates were high for what we consider a fairly standard room, albeit one with a view.

What is an outstanding value is the Sunday brunch that includes poached salmon, shrimp cocktail, roast beef, chicken, ham, muffins, fruits, and desserts.

Fifteen rooms and suites, all with private bath. Non-riverview rooms, $125; riverview rooms, $150; suites, $175–$225. Monday through Thursday rates, $95, $125; suites $125–$175, continental breakfast included. Lunch and dinner served daily. Children welcome, cots $15 additional. Pets with permission. 2 Main Street, Cold Spring, NY 10516; (914) 265-9355.

Olde Post Inn, Cold Spring

The premier attraction at this 1820 inn is the Friday and Saturday night jazz concerts held downstairs in the old tavern, which seats fifty-five. The talent is either local or groups that come up from New York City. If you are staying at the inn there is no cover charge; otherwise it's $4.50 per person.

Innkeepers Barbara and Jim Ryan, both teachers, are around on the weekends and during the summer. At other times Barbara's sister Mary Leber, who lives at the inn, is in charge.

On the first floor there is a living room and a breakfast room.

The best rooms are the two on the third floor. These rooms have slanted ceilings and skylights. One is a double and one has twin beds. These two rooms share a hall bath. On the second floor there are four additional rooms that all share the second-floor hall bath. Three of these rooms have double beds and one has twin beds.

A continental breakfast of juice, a piece of melon or other fruit, and croissants or muffins is served.

Six rooms share two baths. Monday through Thursday, $60. Friday through Sunday, $75. Children over 12 permitted. No pets. 43 Main Street, Cold Spring, NY 10516; (914) 265-2510.

Le Chambord, Hopewell Junction

In response to the growing number of weekday business travelers who are tired of impersonal chain motels, innkeeper Roy Benich built Tara Hall in a wooded area behind the 1863 Georgian Colonial inn and restaurant. This new building has an additional sixteen attractively decorated mini-suites, each fourteen by twenty feet complete with remote-control color television, reproduction four-poster queen-size beds, Victorian couches, and wall-to-wall carpeting. This building also has a small conference room.

Above the restaurant on the second and third floors are nine rooms furnished comfortably with a collection of assorted antiques. We stayed in room 9 on the third floor. Our room was of an ample size, filled with old pieces, but we felt that it needed some redecorating.

When you make your reservation you might want to know that room 1 is the largest room, room 2 is the most traditionally feminine, room 3 has an attractive antique bed, and rooms 3, 4, 6, and 8 face east and get the morning light.

The continental breakfast is served by Roy, a man who wears many hats. Formerly the maitre d' at Tavern on the Green in New York City, Roy now oversees his restaurant and inn. In addition, he is an art dealer with an extensive collection of oil paintings that grace the walls of his restaurant.

After we enjoyed a leisurely breakfast of fresh fruit salad, juice, croissants, and banana bread, Roy gave us a tour of his paintings and entertained us with fascinating stories of his art finds.

The new, enlarged complex along with the first-rate restaurant makes this a good choice for a small business meeting, a family reunion, or a getaway for a couples club.

Nine rooms in the inn, all with private bath, $105. An additional sixteen rooms in Tara Hall, all with private bath, $105. Phones and televisions in all rooms. Continental breakfast included. Children over 12 welcome. Third person in room, $25 additional. No pets. Located one mile east of the Taconic Parkway. 2075 Route 52, Hopewell Junction, NY 12533 (914) 221–1941.

POUGHKEEPSIE AND RHINEBECK

Inn at the Falls, Poughkeepsie

This contemporary, spotlessly clean, two-story structure is a cross between a B&B and a hotel. It is nestled in residential suburban Poughkeepsie along the banks of the Spackenkill River.

The individually controlled air-conditioned and heated rooms are extra large. The luxuriously appointed rooms have king- and queen-size canopy or brass beds. The suites are even more sumptuous with small kitchenettes, Jacuzzis, two televisions, and three telephones (one is on the wall next to the toilet). The dramatic, contemporary suites with black baths, black Jacuzzis, walk-in showers, and full-length mirrors are the most popular ones with honeymooners. The more traditional country rooms and suites decorated with wicker and chintz are also very attractive.

No matter which room you choose you'll be pampered with a color television, terrycloth robes, fine soaps, shampoo, mouthwash, and toothpaste. There is even a safe in each room that is wired to an alarm at the front desk.

A continental breakfast of baked goods, bagels, toast, coffee, and juice is served either in the two-story living room overlooking the river and the falls or is brought to your room starting at 6:30 A.M.

(a boon for early risers). During the week, guests are mostly business people visiting the IBM plants in the area. Weekends attract couples, honeymooners, and families. Because of the large size of the rooms, the suites are well suited for families.

A nice touch is evening turndown service in which towels are changed, ice is placed in the bucket, and mints are put on your pillow.

Note: Half the rooms overlook the river and the other half overlook the parking lot. There is no difference in price whether you reserve a room with a river view or a parking-lot view.

Twenty-two rooms, all with private bath and queen-size, king-size, or two double beds, $107. Two mini-suites, $117. Twelve suites, five with Jacuzzis, $137. One suite, $150. Continental breakfast included. Children welcome. No additional charge. No pets. From Route 9 take Route 113 east for four miles. At the stop light, take the diagonal right to the inn. 50 Red Oaks Mill Road, Poughkeepsie, NY 12603; (914) 462-5770.

Vassar College Alumnae House, Poughkeepsie

This is an old Tudor-style stone inn built in the 1920s with massive doors, thick walls, stone floors, large fireplaces, and high first-floor ceilings. At one end of the entrance hall is a large reception room that is often used for weddings, recitals, and meetings. At the other end of the entrance hall is the oak-paneled dining room serving moderately priced meals. The recently redecorated library is located off the first floor and has a nice collection of books to peruse.

Most of the furnishings in the rooms have been donated by Vassar alumnae. The double rooms, some with double canopy beds and others with twin beds, are clean, spacious, and furnished with a desk, easy chair, and lamp. There is a telephone but no television or air-conditioner.

For the female traveler on a budget, there are single rooms available in the women's wing. These small, pleasantly furnished rooms share a couple of bathrooms down the hall.

Sparsely decorated third-floor single and double cubicle rooms are also available. In the heat of the summer, these rooms can be uncomfortable.

During the week a breakfast of hard-boiled eggs, cereal, rolls, juice, and fruit slices is available. On the weekend, brunch is served.

Thirteen rooms (four with double beds, nine with twin beds), all with private bath, $60. One suite (for up to four persons), $75. Thirty-five rooms (women's wing and cubicle rooms $32.50 per room, single occupancy), with bath down the hall, $35. A discount is available for Vassar alumnae, and students. None of rooms are air-conditioned but fans are available. Children welcome. Third person in room, $7.50 additional. No pets. Continental breakfast is included. Sunday brunch, 11 A.M. to 2 P.M., $10. From Route 9 take Route 44/55 to Raymond Avenue. Enter from College Avenue. Vassar College Alumnae House, Poughkeepsie, NY 12601; (914) 437-7100.

The 1814 American Gothic Delamater House at Beekman Arms drips with gingerbread trim.

Beekman Arms, Rhinebeck

This grand old village inn has been a haven for guests since before the birth of the nation. Innkeeper Chuck LaForge eliminated one of his dining rooms and converted the space into a splendid common room. Leather sofas, easy chairs, a wall of books, games, and puzzles provide a comfortable socializing spot that previously was missing.

Although we adore the old rooms in the main inn, we don't recommend them to light sleepers as many lack air-conditioners and tend to get noisy. However, room 36 on the third floor is quiet and was recently redecorated with a television, air-conditioner, and two phones (including one in the bathroom—the current rage in higher-priced establishments). An electric pants press is in all of the inn rooms as well as the two rooms above the former firehouse. (This is a fascinating gadget you may have seen in the Hammacher Schlemmer catalogue and have always wanted to try.) We stayed in one of the firehouse rooms and left the next day with freshly pressed pants.

Old-house buffs will want to stay a block away in one of the seven rooms at the Delamater House. This magnificent 1844 American Gothic, one of the finest restored and preserved houses in the Hudson River Valley, drips with gingerbread trim. The best room here is 52, called the Wicker Room, with a queen-size bed set in a bay window, white wicker sofa, rocking chairs, and wide-board pine floors. The New York firm of Brunschwig & Fils has redecorated the hallway, sitting room and room 52 using their custom fabrics.

Behind the Delamater House is a new section called the Courtyard. Here are the largest rooms, with working wood-burning fireplaces, four-poster beds, televisions hidden in armoires, and especially large work surfaces great for the business traveler or for people like us who like to spread out.

For firehouse buffs, the upstairs of the old town firehouse (minus the old firepole) has been converted into two exceptionally large rooms. The drawback to these rooms is the steep stairs you need to climb.

We don't recommend the 1950s-style motel units located at the end of the parking lot unless you have to stay in the area and can't be choosy about accommodations. All of these rooms have telephones and most have televisions. A new acquisition is The Gables, a Victorian house located next to the Delamater House. The Gables has four rooms with reproduction antiques. It is designated for non-smoking adults only.

Fifty-nine rooms, all with private bath. May 15 through October and all weekends, $62–$99. Midweek and off-season, $52–$99. Coffee and doughnuts are provided for guests staying at the Delamater House, the Carriage House, the Gables, and the Courtyard rooms. Full breakfast is available at the inn. Children welcome except in the Delamater House and The Gables. Pets welcome in the motel-style rooms and the firehouse rooms. Two-night minimum stay on seasonal weekends. Route 9, Rhinebeck, NY 12572; (914) 876-7077.

Village Victorian Inn, Rhinebeck

Imagine you have enough money and patience to restore that perfect Victorian house the way it should be. You could search out the antique shops for period furniture in mint condition, purchase authentic wallpaper, refinish the wood floors and cover them with Oriental rugs, install modern fixtures in the bathrooms, and keep the rooms white-glove clean. Innkeeper Judy Kohler had the dream and the resources. All that's missing to make it properly Victorian is lots more picture frames, froufrou and *chotchkes* (for the uninitiated, that's Yiddish for trinkets or ornaments)—and those will come with time.

The proper living room with its decanter of fine sherry has a collection of upholstered chairs and couches. It's a wonderful jumble of flowered wallpaper, flowered easy chairs, fringed lampshades, even an antique doll carriage. As an anachronism there is a large-screen television.

Upstairs, the larger rooms have king-size fishnet canopy beds. The blue room, decorated with blue-patterned wallpaper and comforter, two ornate white wicker chairs, a bureau, and a huge antique armoire, is our choice for that special occasion. Our room had an elaborately carved queen-size bed that, like all the beds in the inn, was covered with eight or nine pillows in fabrics to coordinate with the comforters. Each bathroom has thick fluffy towels that match the color or motif of the room. Early risers will especially like the rose room, as the morning sun streams in.

Breakfast consists of fresh orange juice, muffins (we had raisin bran banana), eggs any way you like, sausage, and bacon.

Five rooms, all with private bath: $145 for rooms with queen-size bed, $195 for rooms with king-size bed. Full breakfast included. Children over 17 permitted, third person $40 additional. No pets. Two-night minimum stay on weekends and holidays. Located two blocks from Route 9 at the corner of Livingston and Center Street. 31 Center Street, Rhinebeck, NY 12572; (914) 876-8345.

HIGH FALLS AND NEW PALTZ

Captain Schoonmaker's B&B, High Falls

Imagine a rushing waterfall right outside your window, a stocked trout stream, a stone house built before the American Revolution, and rooms overflowing with Americana. In the living room we found a painted armoire artfully propped open with an antique wooden lamb set on wheels. Inside, stacks of old quilts were signs of a collector's passion. By the open fireplace, infants' old-fashioned leather boots and shoes were arranged on blocks. In other parts of the room were teddy bears, pottery jugs, old spindles, hat boxes, and baskets filled with magazines and books about the area—all providing a richness of visual detail.

Relax in this room or in the dining room by another open fireplace where guests enjoy wine, cheese, and lively conversation in the late afternoon.

Our room was in the adjacent barn by the waterfall—a setting where we, and probably you, have always dreamed of living. We could lie in bed and listen to the water rushing over the rocks or go out on our private porch for a close-up view. Beds are covered with old quilts; the original, rough wood beams are exposed; antique bureaus, wooden trunks, chairs, and couches fill the room.

A second building called the Towpath is in the town of High Falls, about a mile away. This converted old building once housed the company store for the Delaware and Hudson Canal Company. It is now the site of a number of antique shops as well as four delightful guest rooms. A favorite is the former summer kitchen with a working fireplace.

Innkeepers Sam and Julia Krieg will also accommodate guests in six additional rooms in the main house; the most popular of these has a fireplace and is in the part of the house built in 1760. These rooms are filled last because, as Julia said honestly, "Guests like their privacy and so do we." As Julia finished showing us around our room, she told us that breakfast was at 9 A.M. promptly—a soufflé was on the menu.

Breakfast here is a seven-course gourmet repast. Ours started with a warm, poached pear served with whipped cream, followed by a large loaf of fresh-baked bread. Next, fresh from the oven, came a steaming puffed herb soufflé accompanied by locally made sausage links. The feast continued with a chocolate peanut-butter bundt cake, a flaky apple strudel, and an apricot pecan Danish.

Neither Sam or Julia is at home during the day; Sam teaches biology in New Paltz and Julia is a third-grade teacher. Best time to call is before 9 A.M., in the late afternoon, or in the evenings.

Fourteen rooms. $75 for rooms with shared bath, $85 for rooms with private baths and/or with fireplaces. Full breakfast and wine and cheese in the late afternoon included. Children welcome Sunday through Thursday, no extra charge. Third adult in room, $20 additional. No pets. From New Paltz take Route 32 north eight miles to Route 213 west. Go 2⁶/₁₀ miles to the B&B, located between Rosendale and High Falls. Route 213, Box 37, High Falls, NY 12440; (914) 687-7946.

Mohonk Mountain House, New Paltz

By all accounts in today's world of sleek, expensive upscale resorts, the Mohonk Mountain House probably shouldn't exist. It's an anachronism . . . maybe. This massive stone Victorian-era castle is one of the last of the great mountain resorts from the nineteenth century, with 283 rooms, 151 working wood-burning fireplaces, and 200 balconies. Set atop the Shawangunk Mountain ridge on 7,500 acres, Mohonk is unlike any other resort you'll visit. Even more unusual in this era of takeovers and mergers is that the entire complex has been under the same family ownership since its founding 120 years ago.

A number of the rules are delightfully puritanical. There is no smoking in the grand dining hall, six comfortable parlors, or reading library. Jackets are required at dinner for all males over the age of twelve. There is no bar or cocktail lounge. Drinks have to be specifically ordered at lunch or dinner.

A staff of more than 750 is employed at Mohonk—the maintenance standards are very high. Furnishings are Victorian and are in good repair. In fact, this happens to be the largest intact collection of Victorian furniture in the country still in use for its intended purpose. In 1986 the entire 7,500 acres including all the structures, even the 100 wooden gazebos, were declared a National Historic Landmark, thus preserving this unique experience for future generations.

The scenery is stunning. From one side of the house (as it is affectionately called by the staff) the vistas face the west; the Rondout Valley 1,200 feet below is dotted with generations-old farms, and beyond you see the Catskill Mountains. The eastern side of the house looks onto the more intimate, glacial Mohonk Lake and its surrounding rock formations. Flower gardens, ornamental shrubs, and specimen trees surround the buildings.

Miles of hiking and horseback riding trails wind through the property. There is golfing on the nine-hole Scottish-designed course, fishing, boating (no motors), and swimming in the lake in summer, skating in winter, tennis on real clay courts, and what appears year in and year out to be the guests' favorite pastime: rocking in hundreds of wooden rocking chairs.

Structured special-interest programs are held weekends throughout the year. A sampling of the thirty-seven include mystery weekends, stress management, running and fitness, chamber music, cooking, and painting. This is an ideal spot for kids, as there are separate programs for different age groups.

When you arrive, your name is checked at the gatehouse. As we wound our way, slowly and quietly as the signs instructed, up the mountain past the mature woodlands and the vistas of the valley below, we thought about the thousands of guests from times past who have made this same trip by horse-drawn carriage. This is indeed a place to get away from the pressures of one's daily life.

283 rooms. All rates are for two persons and include three meals and afternoon tea. The food is wholesome and plentiful but not gourmet. Regular guest rooms, $230–$302. Special tower rooms with balconies and wood-burning fireplaces $325–$369. Rooms with a basin only, $190. Fifteen percent gratuity is additional. Children 4 to 12 welcome; $50 additional. Third adult in a room, $60 additional. Call or write for a brochure, which lists special weekends, activities, and packages, and includes fine old photographs. Lake Mohonk, New Paltz, NY 12561; (914) 255-1000 or (212) 233-2244.

WHERE TO DINE

FINE DINING

Culinary Institute of America, Hyde Park

On a high bluff overlooking the Hudson River in a former Jesuit seminary are 1,800 budding chefs in starched white uniforms and tall toques, eagerly learning their trade from ninety top culinary professionals. These students participate in a rigorous twenty-one-month academic and hands-on program by chopping, deboning, sautéing, baking, tasting, sniffing, and serving. Dine at the cutting edge of the culinary arts in one or more of the four public restaurants and watch close-up as tomorrow's chefs learn the fine details of their craft.

How to Get Reservations. Needless to say, the restaurants at the Culinary Institute have become a favorite destination of gourmets.

Securing a reservation, especially for weekend dining, has become difficult. We visited the reservations office and talked with the unflappable women who answer the phones. Here are the tips we were able to glean: At 8:30 A.M. on the first working day in March, June, September, and December you can make reservations for the Escoffier, American Bounty, and St. Andrew's Café restaurants. For example, if you call September 1 you can make reservations for October, November, or December. In the course of that first day, the Institute receives more than 1,300 telephone requests for reservations.

The Caterina de Medici room accepts reservations starting at 8:30 A.M. on a Tuesday for the week beginning on Monday three weeks hence. Lunches are often booked by groups.

For reservations: (914) 471-6608, 8:30 A.M. to 5 P.M., Monday through Friday. A credit card is required to hold a reservation. Should your plans change, be sure to cancel your reservation to avoid a charge. Route 9, Hyde Park, NY 12538. They don't keep a waiting list, so you may find a cancellation if you call at the last minute.

Escoffier. The atmosphere is subdued elegance; the service is formal and very French, with lots of tableside service. The raspberry and light-pink room with thick, comfortable upholstered chairs and tables correctly set with ten pieces of flatware overlooks the Hudson River and the Catskill Mountains.

In the adjacent dining room, only an arched twelve- by eight-foot glass wall separated us from the spotless kitchen. Students worked at their assigned stations stirring pots of simmering sauces, peeling and chopping vegetables, sautéing and broiling meats and fish—all under the watchful and encouraging eyes of their chef-instructors.

Artichoke hearts with mushroom-escargot duxelles in asparagus sauce, cucumber and dill cream soup, entrecôte with onions and Dijon mustard, a selection of French cheeses, strawberry-orange compote in pastry, and profiteroles with chocolate sauce completed our classic French lunch. A highlight was a continuous offering of flaky, buttery rich croissants.

The à la carte menu includes hors d'oeuvres such as preserved duck salad with walnuts, salmon mousse in a zucchini tulip, ratatouille timbale, and entrées like beef filet with marrow and walnuts, strips of veal and filet of sole with dill cream, pork medallions in grain mustard sauce, and savarin of scallops with oysters and petits legumes. The dessert cart, filled with creations from the patisserie, was very tempting.

Lunch is served Tuesday through Saturday, 12 to 1 P.M.; $11.50–$16, or $20 prix fixe. Dinner, 6:30 to 8:30 P.M. Entrées, $16.50–$24 or $40 prix fixe.

American Bounty. A cornucopia of breads, wooden boxes filled with fresh fruits and vegetables, and students preparing meals in full view behind the glass-enclosed kitchen greet arriving diners.

Be careful not to eat too much of any one bread so you can sample the endless variety throughout your meal, such as Navajo fried, cottage cheese dill, banana nut, and spicy Cajun.

We started with marinated grilled gulf shrimp in papaya salsa, tequila, lime, and cilantro. Other appetizers available the night we dined were a rich, creamy mussel and saffron soup, three preparations of smoked scallops, shrimp and trout, crabcakes with a smoked-pepper butter sauce, and grilled California quail on wilted spinach with sweet potato fries.

One of our entrées was rolled veal stuffed with shrimp served with a colorful medley of vegetables and pasta. Our other entrée was roast duck and duck sausage accompanied by a smoky lentil sauce, parsnip purée, and haricots verts. We felt the sausage was outstanding but the duck, always a good test of a restaurant, was too fatty.

Desserts are all-American: apple pie, a warm pecan tart with Jack Daniel's pecan ice cream, chocolate seduction (a chocolate concoction so rich that it gives you chills when you eat it), and the house specialty, fresh fruit cobbler for two served with Wild Turkey sauce.

Lunch served Tuesday through Saturday, 12 to 1 P.M.; $11.50–$14.50. Dinner, 6:30–8:30 P.M. Entrées, $14.50–$21.

Caterina de Medici. At this restaurant everyone arrives for lunch or dinner at the same time, which gives this forty-seat restaurant the familial feeling of an upscale trattoria.

Start with the antipasti from the cart, a salad of homemade mozzarella, a tartlet of fontina cheese and onions, smoked pork

*Students prepare and serve meals at American Bounty Restaurant,
Culinary Institute of America.*

with a three-bean salad, or boned frog's legs served with rice. Lentil soup or beef broth with tortellini is next, followed by pasta. Choose from the innovative agnoletti filled with shrimp or the traditional linguine with a classic meat sauce.

For the secondi piatti we had a choice of four: grilled Cornish hen, roast leg of lamb with cabbage and chestnuts, veal scaloppine with a wild mushroom cream sauce, or stuffed calamari, mussels, clams, scallops, and shrimp in a fish broth. A mixed salad is served after the entrée, followed by a choice of fruit or gelato.

Lunch served Monday through Friday. One seating only, 11:30 A.M.; $15 prix fixe. Dinner, 6 P.M., $20 prix fixe.

St. Andrew's Café. Wild mushroom ravioli, 117 calories; salad, 30 calories; beef tenderloin with bleu cheese, 174 calories; two rolls and butter, 252 calories; a glass of white wine, 113 calories; apple strudel, 198 calories. The total for the four-course dinner: 884 calories.

The purpose of the St. Andrew's Café is to serve nutritionally sound, tasty, and well-prepared dinners of about 800 calories. The food is surprisingly good. From a purely hedonistic viewpoint, it doesn't have the same appeal as eating buttery rich croissants, prime sirloin steak with lots of marbling, and chocolate cake made with egg yolks and heavy cream. But in the new era of more healthful eating, we applaud the school.

Here's a sampling of the type of foods served: poached salmon on spinach pasta and saffron sauce; scallops, shrimp, and lobster Newburg served with vegetables and toasted quinoa; and loin of pork with honey and thyme glacé served with red cabbage.

At the end of your meal, fill out a card indicating what you've eaten. In a few minutes you will get a detailed computer printout listing the amount of protein, fat, carbohydrate, sodium, and so on in each food you've eaten.

The café is now located in the new nutrition center. The bookstore and retail shop, which sells breads, cakes, and charcuterie prepared by the students, is housed in the building that formerly was the St. Andrew's Café.

Open Monday through Friday only. Lunch, 11:30 A.M. to 1 P.M.; $6–$8. Dinner, 6 to 8 P.M. Entrées, $9–$11.

Depuy Canal House, High Falls

"I've always thought that there are no boundaries as to the way food can be prepared," commented owner/chef John Novi as we watched him prepare our dinner on a Thursday evening. This famous and highly respected restaurant has been under John's direction for over twenty years. Here you will not only find a great chef but also an avid environmentalist, historian, artist, and teacher who invites you into his eclectic kitchen to chat while he's cooking your dinner. You will not easily find another restaurant serving the combinations of tastes, textures, visual artistry, and personal rapport that you find here.

John converted the 1797 stone building, located next to lock 16 of the former Delaware and Hudson Canal, into seven small dining rooms and a basement cabaret, all decorated with hundreds of bits and pieces of Americana. We were seated by one of the large, open wood-burning fireplaces. The tables are set with bluestone (slate) place mats to remind diners of one of the principal commodities carried on the old canal.

If your appetite runs to steak and potatoes, it's best to go elsewhere. We began with complimentary hors d'oeuvres of farmstead cheese in phyllo, and chicken and apple on Belgian endive. We had an unusual soup of porcini mushrooms and veal broth covered with edible Vietnamese rice paper and decorated with puréed eggplant. An alternative appetizer was a Russian zakuska (fresh beef and ginger ground together, then wrapped around a slice of banana, baked and covered with teriyaki sauce and sprinkled with white sesame seeds and cilantro).

The second course is pasta or a second appetizer. Our favorite is the fresh meaty portobello mushrooms served on a Madeira beurre blanc. Three small scoops of cranberry, lemon, and pear sorbets were served as an intermezzo.

For our entrées we happily let ourselves be guided by headwaiter Michael Ryan, a culinary school graduate who has enthusiastically worked with John for over fifteen years. The grilled, fresh-water striped bass was served on puréed salsify and decorated with cellophane noodles, asparagus, and pickled beets. Our loin of rabbit was quickly seared and served with wild rice and choucroute.

A salad of baby greens is garnished with popcorn, a signature here. The salad is served along with a fresh fruit bowl and a platter of three cheeses.

A tray of eight desserts was brought to our table. John's mother created the Italian ricotta cheesecake. Michael saw us eyeing the meringue with fresh raspberries so he added a few and a scoop of whipped cream to each of our dessert plates. A second dessert was an intensely rich rum-soaked chocolate cake with very fudgy icing.

The selection of wines is extensive and reasonably priced. The knowledgeable sommelier will steer you eagerly through the maze of choices. The meal was topped off with fresh-ground espresso made from roasted beans imported from Italy.

Dinner is served Thursday, Friday, and Saturday 5 to 10 P.M. Sunday brunch, 11:30 A.M. to 2 P.M. and dinner, 3 to 8 P.M. Closed January through February 13. Four-course dinner includes hors d'oeuvres, soup or zukuski, entrée, Coheerie salad, fresh fruit bowl, coffee or tea, $42. The eight-course dinner includes all of the above plus an appetizer or pasta, sorbet, cheese tray and dessert, $55. A light three-course dinner of hors d'oeuvres, soup, appetizer, or pasta (entrée size), coffee or tea is $30. An a la carte menu is also available. High Falls, NY 12440; (914) 687-7700.

Old Drovers Inn, Dover Plains

The dark, low-ceilinged, wood-beamed tap room with its great stone fireplace is one of the coziest and most intimate dining spots we've seen.

Both lunch and dinner are served to inn guests as well as to the general public under the watchful eyes of restaurant manager Charlie Wilbur (who has been an Old Drovers tradition for more than twenty-five years) in the low-beamed tap room with its massive fireplace, which oozes atmosphere. Lighting is supplied mainly by candles set inside etched hurricane lamps.

The inn is justly famous for the double-size drinks served in hand-blown Lenox crystal glasses, accompanied by stuffed eggs and hickory-smoked salt, cheddar cheese soup, and browned turkey hash (see *Recipe,* page 44). The blackboard menu is hung on hooks by your table. We started with gravlax attractively formed into a large rose shape and poached sea scallops in a light cream sauce served with crisp potato baskets.

The lamb chops are in a class by themselves. Two double-thick chops trimmed of excess fat were perfectly grilled and served with Charlie's tomato chutney. Other house specialties are breast of Muscovy duck, grilled veal chop, and the traditional browned turkey hash served with mustard sauce. For dessert we'd stick with the peppermint-stick-candy ice cream, specially made for Old Drovers at a local dairy, or with traditional favorites such as pecan or key lime pie.

Lunch, Monday, Thursday, Friday, Saturday, 12 to 3 P.M.; $7.75–$15.50. Dinner, Monday and Thursday, 5:30 to 9 P.M.; Friday, 5:30 to 9:30 P.M.; Saturday, 3 to 10 P.M.; Sunday, 12 to 8:30 P.M. Dinner entrées, $15.50–$27.00. 15% gratuity is added to the bill. Located off Route 22, about seventy-five miles north of New York City. Old Drovers Inn Road, Dover Plains, NY 12522; (914) 832-9311.

Plumbush, Cold Spring

Host Gieri Albin and chef Ans Benderer must be doing something right—they are now in their fifteenth year in this ornate, nineteenth-century Victorian structure. The charm of the original house has been retained. The rich dark oak-panelled bar's walls once graced a French chateau as did those in the adjacent small oak-panelled room. In here a gas-burning fireplace sets the mood. The floors are dark wood; a candle burns on each of the four tables; the open corner cupboards are filled with quality pieces. The setting is utterly romantic.

Some diners prefer the small porch room; others like the airy yellow room with coordinated wallpaper and swag draperies; still others like to dine more informally on the stone terrace overlooking the gazebo in the park-like surroundings.

Formal tableside preparations are the norm here. The classic trout au bleu (which must be absolutely fresh and alive minutes before being poached in a court bouillon) is a signature item. The duck, another specialty, is crisp on the outside, moist on the inside, and has the fat removed. Each evening, veal, a popular choice, is served in a different preparation.

The Swiss-influenced desserts are not too sweet. A fine Sacher torte and Swiss apple fritters, a long-time favorite, are as good as they were ten years ago.

Lunch, Wednesday through Saturday, 12 to 2:30 P.M.; $7.50–$10.95. Sunday brunch, 12 to 2:30 P.M.; $15.95. Dinner, Wednesday through Saturday from 5:30 P.M., Sunday 2:30 to 8 P.M.; entrées from $24.95 or prix fixe $32. Route 9D, Cold Spring, NY 10516; (914) 265-3904.

Le Chambord, Hopewell Junction

Are you in a fine restaurant or a fine art gallery? Close to a quarter of a million dollars worth of paintings hang on the walls in the two dining rooms. The visual display of these works added greatly to our enjoyment of the dining experience.

Each evening there is a five-course dinner special. The night we dined, the five-course dinner began with a green salad garnished with walnuts and raisins, followed by a superb pasta with a mushroom cream sauce that tasted as though it was made with morels. Fried catfish came next, followed by the entrée of sliced roast lamb. The dinner also included a selection from the dessert tray and coffee.

If your appetite doesn't warrant this many courses, we suggest you steer toward that night's specials. We ordered the poached salmon, swordfish, and scallops served on a bed of braised fennel. The fish was napped with a tomato-onion cream sauce and was served in a flaky, buttery puff-pastry shell. We felt this was a much finer preparation than that from the prix fixe menu.

Other entrées included venison with blackberry sauce, veal chop with French morel mushrooms, rack of lamb, and broiled lobster with a Champagne leek and mushroom sauce.

The people at the table next to ours had saved room for one of the dessert specialties, an almond pastry shell with vanilla whipped cream and fresh raspberries. From the sounds of appreciation we knew it was a success.

Lunch, Monday through Friday, 11:30 to 2:30 P.M.; $9.95–$16.95. Dinner, Monday through Friday, 6 to 10 P.M.; Saturday, 6 to 11 P.M.; Sunday, 3 to 9 P.M. Entrées, $16.95–$25.95. On Route 52, one mile east of the Taconic State Parkway; (914) 221-1941.

Beekman Arms, Rhinebeck

This inn and restaurant claims to be the oldest in continuous operation in America. Choose the dining room by the feeling you want. The dark wine cellar has high-backed booths and low, exposed overhead beams. The Colonial tap room with its well-cared-for wood glows with the patina of age. The popular sun-filled greenhouse room with hanging plants and a green and white awning provides a stark contrast to the Colonial dining rooms; smoking is not allowed in this room.

The moderately priced menu has a choice of eighteen entrées. The venison, a house favorite, comes from a local farm. Prime rib has been a house specialty for as long as we can remember. For the most interesting preparations look to the blackboard, for it's here that the chef's creativity is given free rein. Recent winners have included grilled tuna with peppers and mushrooms served with a salsa vinaigrette, sautéed sweetbreads, Oriental stir-frys, and the Mexican dishes.

Appetizers on the more unusual side include beggar's purse (curried shrimp, apples, and currants wrapped in phyllo pastry), grilled duck sausage, and warm goat cheese salad with poached pear, watercress, and spiced walnuts.

The sumptuous Sunday brunch has been voted best in the region. At the center of the banquet room is a waterfall of fruit surrounded by tables laid for a truly grand buffet.

Open daily for breakfast, lunch, and dinner. Lunch, 11:30 A.M. to 3 P.M.; $5.25–$9.95. Dinner, 5 P.M. to 10 P.M.; entrées, $10.50–$19.75. Sunday brunch, 10 A.M. to 2 P.M.; $14.95. Route 9, Rhinebeck, NY 12572; (914) 876-7077.

INFORMAL DINING

Mary P's, Kingston

The large semicircular bar with overhead televisions at the entrance to Mary P's didn't give us a clue about the food. We hadn't heard of the restaurant, and it wasn't listed in any guidebook that we owned. But the menu had the right feel, and the location on the water couldn't be better.

In warm weather, diners flock to the outside deck overlooking the Rondout Creek. The dining room adjacent to the bar area is nothing to rave about, but the value received does make this a bargain. The menu goes on for pages and pages, listing dishes made with homemade pasta (19), seafood dishes (25), chicken (10), veal (10), and steak dishes (6). That's enough of a selection for anyone!

The last page of the menu lists complete dinners that include soup, salad, entrée, dessert, and coffee. We started with ravioli soup and a bowl of thick vegetable soup. The pescado à la Veracruz was a large plate overflowing with shrimp, scallops, and white fish in a tomato sauce served over linguine. The calamari Livornese also served over linguine had a spicy tomato-based sauce more to our liking. The portions were so ample that we had the leftovers packed up for another day.

Our choice for dessert was an outstanding tiramisu (very popular at present). Chef Tarcisio makes his by sprinkling sponge layers with dark rum. Mascarpone, zabaglione, and whipped cream are folded together and layered between rum-soaked sponge cake. This makes a light "non-caloric" heavenly dessert.

Open daily. Lunch, 11:30 A.M. to 2:30 P.M.; $3.25–$9.50. Dinner, 4:30 to 11 P.M.; to 9 P.M. on Sunday. Dinner specials, $12.95–$14.95 for a complete dinner. Dinner entrées, $7.95–$24. 1 Broadway, Kingston, NY 12401; (914) 338-0116.

Good Enough to Eat, High Falls

Here's a story with a different twist. A restaurant that made its reputation serving large country breakfasts and home style meals on Amsterdam Avenue on New York City's trendy Upper West Side has opened a branch in the country.

Varnished wooden picnic tables set on a red-stained stenciled wood floor, a few country quilts, a piano player in the bar, and a philosophy of serving an abundance of wholesome foods has paid off for the owners.

Dishes such as grilled hamburger on a homemade kaiser roll with jalapeño jack cheese, fried chicken wings, baked ziti, lemon Parmesan chicken, Cajun pork chops, and sautéed catfish were some of the dishes that poured forth from the kitchen.

The desserts are the kind you see at country fairs with blue ribbons attached: triple-layer chocolate cake, sour cream blueberry pie, bread pudding, spice cake, and assorted brownies.

Dinner Monday through Thursday and Sunday, 5:30 to 10 P.M.; Friday and Saturday until 11 P.M.; entrées, $7.50–$15.50. Saturday and Sunday brunch, $3.75–$8. High Falls, NY 12440; (914) 687-9003.

Painter's Tavern, Cornwall-on-Hudson

This storefront small-town eatery serves a creative menu in an "arty" environment. The walls are covered floor to ceiling with large pieces of contemporary art; the paintings, masks, and sculptures are all for sale. The majority of diners are young. The beer list sports over fifty different varieties from the four corners of the earth, including a personal favorite, Samuel Smith's Nut Brown Ale.

The small, open kitchen turns out a remarkable menu: fajitas from the Southwest, negamaki yakatori from Japan, California carbonara, and Cincinnati chili. (If you didn't know, over 100 Cincinnati restaurants specialize in chili.)

On the lighter side are sunburgers (vegetarian hamburgers made with soybeans), steak, chicken, and sausage grills with a list of toppings that range from jalapeño cheddar to sun-dried tomatoes to all but the kitchen sink. Salads like dream spinach, warm Oriental shrimp, hot taco Mexican chilicheese, and California field give a sampling of the types of choices.

Open daily, 11 A.M. to 10 P.M., $3.75–$16.50. Idlewild Avenue, Cornwall-on-Hudson, NY 12520; (914) 534-2109.

Cold Spring Depot, Cold Spring

Collectors of train stations-turned-into-restaurants will love this one. The inside of this brick station has character: straight-backed wooden booths, a potbelly stove, old trunks, a hand cart, wooden barrels, and overhead fans. Just as you settle into the nostalgia of the turn-of-the-century, a train whizzes by the window. In nice weather you can sit outside even closer to the tracks and listen to the Dixieland jazz band that plays on Sundays from 2 to 6 P.M.

We were more than satisfied with the Depot sandwich of turkey, bacon, tomato, and melted Swiss and the mussels marinara. Dinner includes heartier fare, such as barbecued baby back ribs, chicken, prime rib, along with the same overstuffed sandwiches on the lunch menu.

Open daily, noon to 10 P.M.; to 11 P.M. on Friday and Saturday. Lunch, $3.95–$9.95. Dinner, $4.95–$16.95. One Depot Square (at the foot of Main Street), Cold Spring, NY; (914) 265-2305.

RECIPE

Browned Turkey Hash

This typically American dish is hearty and economical. It has been on the menu at Old Drovers for as long as anyone can remember. Here it is served with a zesty mustard sauce.

Hash

1½ cups medium-diced cooked
turkey, white meat
2½ cups medium-diced cooked
turkey, dark meat
1 cup finely diced boiled
potatoes

4 tablespoons finely chopped
onions, optional
salt and pepper to taste
¼ to ½ cup clarified butter
¼ teaspoon paprika
chopped parsley

Mix turkey, potatoes, and onions in large bowl. Add salt and pepper to taste. Heat ¼ cup butter in a well-seasoned 7-inch frying pan until it begins to brown; stir in paprika. Quickly add turkey mixture and pack it firmly on bottom and sides of pan. Cover and reduce heat to medium. Cook 5–7 minutes or until edges brown, adding more butter if necessary. Turn out onto a heated plate. Garnish with chopped parsley.
YIELD: 4 servings.

Mustard Sauce

3 cups chicken stock
½ cup beef consommé
2 tablespoons dry mustard,
  such as Coleman's

½ cup Dijon mustard
4–6 tablespoons softened butter
4–6 tablespoons flour

In a saucepan over medium heat, combine chicken stock, beef consommé, dry mustard, and Dijon mustard. Beat with a whisk to blend. Thicken with equal parts butter and flour, cooking and stirring until the consistency of heavy cream. Serve very hot on top or on the side of the hash.
YIELD: 1 quart.

ITINERARY

Start at the east side of the Bear Mountain Bridge and follow Route 9D north. On a cliff above Garrison is a castle with pointed red turrets that served as the inspiration for the Wicked Witch's castle in *The Wizard of Oz*. We suggest you spend your first night in the Cold Spring area.

DAY ONE. After exploring **Cold Spring** head south to the restoration at **Boscobel**. This Federal-period house and gardens have views that are not to be missed. Drive north, stopping for lunch at the **Cold Spring Depot** or for a more leisurely lunch, make reservations at the **Culinary Institute of America**. Continue to Franklin's home and library at **Hyde Park** and Eleanor's retreat at **Val-Kill**. As a contrast to the simplicity of FDR's home you will want to see the **Vanderbilt Mansion**. Dine in one of the Culinary Institute's restaurants or drive north to the **Beekman Arms** in Rhinebeck.

DAY TWO. Cross the Bear Mountain Bridge. Take Route 9W north to **West Point** for a tour. Have lunch at the Academy if you are taking a cruise up the Hudson on the ***Commander.*** Otherwise take Route 218 north to Cornwall-on-Hudson. This narrow road twists along the face of Storm King Mountain, affording spectacular views of the river. Lunch at **Painter's Tavern**. Then follow signs to **Storm King Art Center** to see the finest collection of post-1945 sculpture in a landscaped setting. Dine at **Plumbush, Le Chambord**, or **Old Drovers Inn**.

DAY THREE. We suggest you spend the next two nights in the **Rhinebeck** area or in **High Falls**. Visit a few of the wineries. You can also get lunch at **West Park** and **Benmarl**. Beyond **New Paltz** is the **Mohonk Mountain House**. To see the house, the lake, and the views on a clear day is a sight not easily forgotten. Admission to the grounds is free if you have lunch here or you can pay a hikers fee. From Mohonk it is five miles by a country road to the village of **High Falls** and the **DePuy Canal House**, the premier dining experience in the entire valley.

DAY FOUR. Pack a lunch. From **Rhinebeck** take Market Street to River Road (County 103). Tour **Montgomery Place** in Annandale. The River Road meets Route 9G beyond Bard College. Continue to **Olana** to see Frederic Church's unusual home. Cross the Hudson and take Route 23A along twisting roads to **Palenville** and **Haines Falls**. Follow our directions to the site of the **Catskill Mountain House**. Return to Kingston and the **Rondout** area to see the **Maritime Museum** and take a cruise on the ***Rondout Belle.*** Dine at **Mary P's** on the waterfront. If tubing on the Esopus is a priority, you will need to adjust your plans for the day. From Haines Falls take Route 23A to Route 214 to **Town Tinker Tubes** in **Phoenicia**. Return on Route 28 to Boiceville, stopping at **Bread Alone** (we suggest you take some bread home). Return to Kingston for dinner, or if you are staying in High Falls, go to **Good Enough to Eat**.

DAY FIVE. Head south to the **Tarrytown** area, where you will visit a number of historic sites. **Van Cortlandt Manor** is in **Croton-on-Hudson** and **Philipsburg Manor, Sunnyside, Lyndhurst**, and the **Union Church** are nearby. Read the descriptions, as you won't have time to visit them all in one day. From here it is easy to make your way home.

Getting to the Area

To get to Cold Spring from New York City, take the Taconic State Parkway north to I-84 west, Route 9D south to Cold Spring. Or take the Palisades Parkway north to Bear Mountain Bridge, then Route 9D north. From Connecticut take I-84 west to Route 9D south.

BUDGETING YOUR TRIP

To help you get the most for your money, here are some travel suggestions at three budget levels (cost per day at peak season with two people sharing a room, including tax, 15% gratuity at meals, and service charges). Prices are approximate and intended for planning purposes only. Lodgings are categorized by price. Meal prices at lunch include an average entrée and beverage. Dinner prices include an appetizer, entrée, beverage, and dessert. Wine or alcoholic drinks are not included. Admission prices vary widely based on activities.

Staying and Dining at Expensive Lodgings and Restaurants: From $270 to $470 per day for two.

Lodging: Pig Hill Inn $147; Hudson House $131–$236; Old Drovers Inn $132–$204; Village Victorian Inn $152–$205; Plumbush $132; Mohonk Mountain House $402–$443 for tower rooms, $276–$310 for standard rooms (includes all meals).

Dining: Breakfast: included except at Beekman Arms ($10). Lunch: Escoffier $50; American Bounty $50; Plumbush $45; Le Chambord $50. Dinner: Escoffier $100; American Bounty $70;

DuPuy Canal House $130; Old Drovers $100; Plumbush $80; Le Chambord $80.

Admissions: Shearwater cruise $50; Boscobel $10; Historic Hudson properties (three of the five) $26; Hyde Park $7; Vanderbilt Mansion $8; Storm King $10; West Point Tours $6.

Staying and Dining at Moderately Priced Lodgings and Restaurants: From $160 to $230 per day for two.

Lodging: Beekman Arms $65–$104; Le Chambord $110; Captain Schoonmaker $89; Plumbush $100; Pig Hill Inn $95–$121; Inn at the Falls $117–$123.

Dining: Breakfast: included except at Beekman Arms ($10). Vassar Alumnae House $5. Lunch: $29–$30 at Mary P's, St. Andrew's Cafe, Beekman Arms, Cold Spring Depot, and Good Enough to Eat. Dinner: Beekman Arms $65; Caterina de Medici $50; St. Andrew's Cafe $45.

Admissions: Cruise on the *Commander* $12; Hyde Park $7; Vanderbilt Mansion $8; Boscobel $10; Historic Hudson properties (two) $18; Storm King $10; West Point $6.

Staying and Dining at Less Expensive Lodgings and Restaurants: From $110 to $150 per day for two.

Lodging: Captain Schoonmaker's $79; Alumnae House $37–$79; Old Post Inn $79.

Dining: Breakfast: included. Lunch: $15 at Painter's Tavern. Dinner: $35–$40 at Mary P's, Good Enough to Eat, or Painter's Tavern.

Admissions: Cruise on the *Rondout Belle* $10; Hyde Park $7; Boscobel $10; Vanderbilt Mansion $8.

SUGGESTED READING

Here are a few titles that we have found particularly helpful.

The Hudson River Valley, Tim Mulligan. New York: Random House, 1985; $8.95. Mulligan is one of our favorite travel writers. His descriptions and vignettes of the people who lived in the grand Hudson River estates are outstanding.

The Hudson Valley and Catskill Mountains, Joanne Michaels and Mary Barile. New York: Harmony Books, 1988; $14.95. A compilation of things to see, where to stay, where to dine. The book is organized by counties.

American Paradise: The World of the Hudson River School. New York: The Metropolitan Museum of Art, 1987. This complete catalog of the exhibition at the Metropolitan includes essays and high-quality color photographs of the paintings.

Charmed Places: Hudson River Artists and Their Houses, Studios, and Vistas, Sandra Phillips. New York: Harry Abrams, 1988. This catalog of a traveling exhibition tells about the history of the Hudson River painters and where they painted. It is filled with color plates of their paintings and photographs of their homes.

A Hudson Riverbook. William Gekle. Wyvern House, 1978; $5. A longtime resident of Poughkeepsie records his thoughts on the exploration of the Hudson, its history and ecology, and the grand estates along the river. This book is available at the Historic Hudson's gift shops.

TWO

THE
FINGER LAKES,
NEW YORK

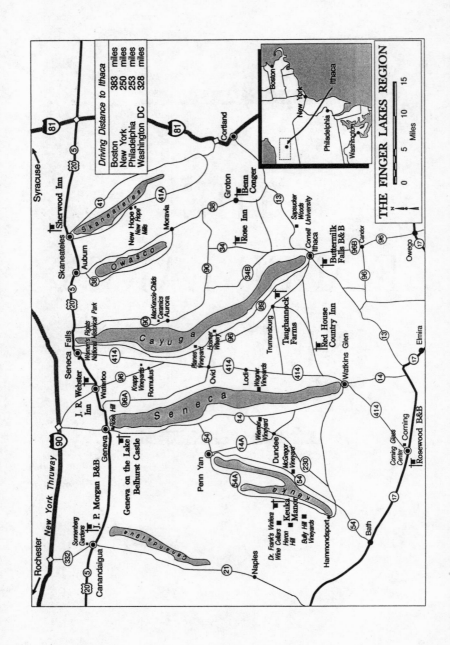

THE FINGER LAKES REGION

Driving Distance to Ithaca	
Boston	383 miles
New York	250 miles
Philadelphia	253 miles
Washington DC	328 miles

Boston
New York
Philadelphia
Washington

Ithaca

Miles
0 5 10 15

N

Miles
0 5 10 15

Rochester
New York Thruway
Syracuse
81
90
332
20
5
Canandaigua
Sonnenberg Gardens
Naples
21
Canandaigua
J. P. Morgan B&B
Geneva
Geneva on the Lake
Belhurst Castle
Seneca Falls
Waterloo
J. R. Webster Inn
Foot Hill
96A
96
Romulus
Knapp Vineyards
Penn Yan
54
54A
Dr. Frank's Vinifera Wine Cellars
Keuka
Heron Hill
Bully Hill Vineyards
Manor
Hammondsport
Keuka
Dundee
14A
Wiemer Vineyard
McGregor Vineyard
230
54
Bath
54
17
Corning
Corning Glass Center
Rosewood B&B
414
Watkins Glen
14
Seneca
Wagner Vineyards
Lodi
Ovid
414
Women's Rights National Historical Park
414
Seneca Falls
Cayuga
MacKenzie-Childs Ceramics
Aurora
89
Planes Vineyard
Hosmer Winery
Trumansburg
Taughannock Farms
89
96
Red House Country Inn
13
Elmira
17
Sherwood Inn
Skaneateles
20
5
Auburn
38
41
Skaneateles
41A
New Hope
New Hope Mills
Moravia
Owasco
38
34
90
34B
Rose Inn
Groton
Benn Conger
13
Sapsucker Woods
Cornell University
Ithaca
Buttermilk Falls B&B
96B
Candor
96
Owego
17
Elmira
81
Cortland
Syracuse

As far as the eye could see, bunches of grapes, taut with flavorful juice, soaked up the sun's rays. The rows of vines extended down the hill toward the blue water. On the other side of the valley, lush green fields and forests reached down to meet the water. The Riesling grapes and the scenery made us think of the Rhine River Valley in Germany. The white Chardonnay and the dark Pinot Noir grapes made us think of the Champagne region of France. We observed this intoxicatingly beautiful vista from a hillside above the western shore of Lake Keuka in the Finger Lakes.

Six long narrow lakes named for the Indians that inhabited the region (Cayuga, Seneca, Skaneateles, Owasco, Keuka, and Canandaigua) lie side by side, ranging in length from eleven to forty miles and varying in depth from 177 to more than 600 feet. These six fingers span a distance of sixty miles. Four smaller lakes lie slightly farther to the west. Indian lore explains the creation of the Finger Lakes by saying that a great spirit placed both of his hands upon the land and left his imprint. A more scientific theory is that Ice Age glaciers gouged out this remarkable topography.

At the southern edges of the lakes, the land is studded with miles of easily accessible, well-maintained trails that follow the deep gorges and breathtaking waterfalls (one of these is higher than Niagara Falls). Along the hillsides of the lakes are miles of vineyards. Between the lakes are colorful valleys of rolling farmland where dairy herds are raised, and fields of buckwheat and fruits are grown.

This area of New York was involved in the Revolutionary War. In the late 1700s George Washington sent John Sullivan to this region to invade the Indian country, as the Cayuga and Seneca tribes, among others, were honoring old alliances with England. Sullivan's army destroyed countless Indian settlements along the lakes and burned their fields and orchards. In lieu of payment for their wartime service, the Revolutionary veterans received parcels of land from the United States government.

The frontier communities that sprang up along the lakes were built on the sites of the former Indian settlements. The roads and highways followed the Indian trails. The names of the towns (Ithaca, Ovid, Cato, and Sempronius), odd-sounding to us today, came from a surveyor who was a classical scholar.

The region flourished. Water power came from the many waterfalls. Transportation along the rivers, and later the Erie Canal, gave shippers access to New York City and the rest of the world. Industry expanded when the railroads came to the area. Immigrants came from Southern and Eastern Europe to work in the factories. They joined the New Englanders and Pennsylvanians who had come earlier to farm the land. French and German winemakers migrated when they discovered the region's similarity to their old-world climate.

The curious traveler is rewarded with unexpected vistas and experiences. Picturesque nineteenth-century small towns and villages dot the landscape. As you drive along the roads, a large waterfall, a majestic lake vista, or a herd of cattle contentedly grazing on a hillside framed by a weathered red barn suddenly come into view. The rich ripe fruitiness of an elegant Chardonnay, an award-winning ice wine, or a smooth Riesling surprises and pleases the palate. The solitude of hours spent fishing on the lakes is indescribably delicious. The dining opportunities range from elegant, intimate inns to a nationally known vegetarian restaurant. There is much to discover in the Finger Lakes region.

Finger Lakes Association.   309 Lake Street, Penn Yan, NY 14527; (315) 536-7488 or (800) 548-4386. Send $2 for the travel guide, which lists the exact dates for special events.

SPECIAL EVENTS THROUGHOUT THE YEAR

June through August.   Rochester Philharmonic Orchestra. Classical and Pops concerts in outdoor pavillion in Canandaigua. Box office: 108 East Avenue, Rochester, NY 14604; (716) 222-5000.

Hangar Theatre. Dramas, musicals, comedies. Box office: De-Witt Mall, Box 205, Ithaca, NY 14851; (607) 273-2432. Theater: Cass Park, Route 89, Ithaca; (607) 273-7890.

June through September.   Auto racing at Watkins Glen. Watkins Glen International, Box 500, Watkins Glen, NY 14891; (607) 535-2481.

July through August.   Taylor Vintage Summer of Song. Free professional outdoor concerts. Friday evening in Hammondsport, Saturday evening in Trumansburg; (607) 569-2111.

Mark Twain, A Musical Drama. Musical dramatization of the life and works of Mark Twain. Box 265, Elmira, NY 14902; (607) 732-2152.

Early July.   Classic boat show and race. Hammondsport to Penn Yan. Hammondsport, NY; (315) 536-7891.

Last week of July.   Hill Cumorah Pageant. Dramatization about the founding of the Mormon Church. Free. Outdoor theater. Palmyra, NY 14522; (315) 597-5851.

Late July.   Mennonite relief sale and quilt auction. Bath, NY; (607) 776-2609.

Late August through Labor Day. New York State Fair. Displays of agriculture, livestock, arts and crafts, industry. Syracuse, NY; (315) 487-7711.

Late September. Buckwheat Harvest Festival. Music, entertainment, tours of Birkett Mills. Penn Yan, NY; (315) 536-7434.

WHERE TO GO, WHAT TO DO

CORNING

Corning Glass Center. You will need a few hours to even begin to see all that is available in this complex. Within the center there are three areas: the Steuben Factory, the Corning Museum of Glass, and the Hall of Science and Industry.

At the Steuben Factory, the only place where Steuben pieces are hand-blown, you can watch the entire process as craftsmen transform the molten glass—forming, grinding, polishing, and engraving. There is a factory store; however, the prices for these fine pieces aren't any less than they are at their Fifth Avenue store in New York City. There aren't any seconds, as imperfect pieces are destroyed.

The Museum of Glass exhibits pieces of glass ranging in age from more than 2,000 years old to contemporary, and representing every imaginable type of glass made. You may want to take a quick walk through the entire exhibit so that you can better judge how long to spend in each area; otherwise, you could get tired before you're halfway through.

The Hall of Science and Industry is a hands-on exhibit. You'll see a mirror 200 inches in diameter, a movie about 3-D television of the future, an exhibit showing how glass can bend without breaking, and much more.

For bargains, go to the Corning Consumer Products Shop to purchase Corningware, Visions, Pyrex, Corelle dinnerware, and Revereware at reduced prices.

Open daily, 9 A.M. to 5 P.M. Adults, $5; seniors, $4; children, $3.

This complex is the perfect place to visit on a rainy or snowy day. Centerway, Corning, NY 14831; (607) 974-8271.

Rockwell Museum of Western Art. The third floor of this museum has one of the best collections of Western art of the period from 1840 to 1920 in the eastern United States. In the recently renovated museum we saw paintings by George Catlin, Alfred Miller, Charles Russell, and Albert Bierstadt; bronzes by Frederic Remington; Navajo weaving, antique firearms, and Native American artifacts.

The second floor has more than 2,000 pieces of multi-colored Steuben glass produced from 1903 to the 1950s by the Frederick Carder Studio (Carder was the co-founder of Steuben Glass Works) and a comfortable seating area to rest tired feet.

Open September to June, Monday through Saturday, 9 A.M. to 5 P.M. and Sunday, 12 to 5 P.M. July and August, Monday through Friday, 9 A.M. to 7 P.M.; Saturday and Sunday, 9 A.M. to 5 P.M. Adults $3, seniors $2.50, children under 18 free. Cedar Street at Denison Parkway (Route 17), Corning, NY 14830; (607) 937-5386.

Market Street. After visiting the Steuben factory, stroll along this wonderfully restored living museum of Victorian and early twentieth-century commercial architecture. Stop for lunch at Donna's (corner of Cedar and Market streets) to get the flavor of the town. See contemporary glassblowing at Vitrix Glass Studio (77 West Market Street, 607-936-7807), Noslo Glass Studio (88 West Market Street, 607-962-7886), and Bacalles Glass Engravers (10 West Market Street, 607-962-3339). The Ice Cream Works (Baron Steuben Place, Market Street, 607-962-6553) has an old-fashioned ice cream soda fountain, in case you need a snack.

ITHACA

Cornell University. The university sits on a hill within walking distance (a steep climb) of the downtown shopping area. The setting on a hill that overlooks the long blue lake, with mountain streams rushing through deep gorges, plunging waterfalls, and gardens surrounding ivy-covered stone buildings, makes this one of the most beautiful college campuses we have visited.

Just below the campus is Collegetown. Stores and restaurants that appeal to student tastes and pocketbooks are found here. We've found a good Israeli restaurant called King David (208 Dryden Road, 607-273-5030) in this area.

Next to Cornell is the residential area of Cayuga Heights. Many of the large, old, stately homes have views of Lake Cayuga. Carl Sagan lives here in a house perched at the top of Ithaca Falls. Worth exploring, but best done on foot, is Cascadilla Park Road—a street that is just as crooked as Lombard Street in San Francisco. The street, located between Stewart and University avenues, is only wide enough for one car. As you walk down the street you will see lovely, landscaped homes tucked into every twist and turn, and water rushing in the adjacent Cascadilla Gorge.

Sapsucker Woods. Cornell's ornithological laboratory is world famous. We sat in front of a row of large picture windows, peering through binoculars, watching the action, and listening to the sounds transmitted by microphones strategically located at the feeding stations along the shore of the ten-acre pond. The day we stopped, a giant blue heron was conveniently perched in a nearby tree. Cornell has an extensive collection of bird and animal sounds on tape, which visitors can listen to in the laboratory. The 3,000-book reference library is open Monday through Friday. The trails at Sapsucker Woods are open year-round. The best times to come are in the late spring and early summer when the wildflowers are in bloom and the birds are most active. We all know the saying, "The early bird catches the worm." If you are an avid birder, come early in the morning.

Open Monday through Thursday, 8 A.M. to 5 P.M.; Friday, 8 A.M. to 4 P.M.; Saturday and Sunday, 10 A.M. to 5 P.M. Free. Route 13 north of Ithaca to Sapsucker Woods Road, Ithaca, NY 14850; (607) 256-5056.

Cornell Plantations. The 3,000 acres consist of formal gardens, herb gardens, an arboretum, and natural areas. The extensive wildflower garden is at its height in late spring. The arboretum is best seen by driving on Plantations Road (pick up a map at the gift shop).

Garden gift shop is open April through December, Monday through Friday, 8 A.M. to 4 P.M.; Saturday and Sunday, 11 A.M. to 4

P.M. From Route 13 in Ithaca, take Route 79 east, bear left on Route
366. Turn left on Judd Falls Road. Take first right after the stop
sign. One Plantations Road, Ithaca, NY 14850; (607) 255-3020.

Herbert Johnson Museum of Art. This bold, contemporary
concrete building designed by I. M. Pei is a landmark on the Cornell
campus. Go to the top floor for a spectacular view of Lake Cayuga
and an overview of Cornell and Ithaca college. This is considered
one of the finest university museums in the country; the permanent
collection is particularly strong in Asian, American, graphic, and
contemporary arts. Check the local listings, as fifteen or more
shows are held each year. We are especially fond of the Giacometti
sculpture *Walking Man II,* which is part of the permanent collection.

Open Tuesday through Sunday, 10 A.M. to 5 P.M. Free. Located
on the corner of Central and University avenues on the Cornell
campus. Ithaca, NY 14853; (607) 255-6464.

Natural History Tour. Dr. Ron Schassburger, who earned his
doctorate studying wolf utterances, takes small groups on half-day
tours in his van to learn about the natural history of the valley. On
the tour we first went to Sunset Lookout at Lake Cayuga, then to
the geology museum at Cornell. We drove through the arboretum
at Cornell Plantations and walked through the wildflower garden.
The highlight was our visit to Sapsucker Woods and a stop at Ithaca
Falls. As we were not particularly interested in the geology museum and the collection of rocks displayed in the outdoor park, we
would rather have spent more of the time visiting the falls—but we
aren't giving the tour. It is a delight to visit an unfamiliar area with
a knowledgeable resource person at your side.

The tour lasts four and a half hours and includes a light box
lunch. Times are flexible. Adults $35; children $17.50. Dire Wolf
Natural History Tours, Biology Department, Ithaca College, Ithaca,
NY 14850; (607) 273-6316.

Farmers' Market. If you are near Ithaca on a Saturday morning (9 A.M. to 1 P.M.), do not miss the farmers' market. People come
not just to buy produce (much of it organic) and crafts, but also to
visit and picnic along the lake. Farmers pull in with their pickup
trucks full of produce, flowers, honey, and herbs. There may be
singing or folk dancing. It's a weekly social event as well as a good

place to pick up bread and produce. To get to the market, take Route 13 to Buffalo Street and follow the traffic toward the lake.

If you're interested in purchasing a Windsor chair look for Ed Rumsey, who can usually be found working in one of the central stalls. He makes authentic side chairs, armchairs, children's chairs, and settees. His mother runs Buttermilk Falls B&B, where many of his chairs are found around the dining room table and look as if they've been there for a long time. Ed can be reached at 721 East Shore Drive, Ithaca, NY 14850; (607) 272-3020.

Wegmans and Tops. Servicing the diverse Cornell community are two large competing grocery chains with an abundance of high-quality gourmet and international items. Both are open twenty-four hours a day, seven days a week. The stores provide numerous complimentary consumer-oriented booklets on such topics as cholesterol-lowering food choices and the sodium content of many foods on the shelves, and have one-hour photo labs as well. Kids love to visit the make-your-own-sundae sections. If you need a fast lunch, salad bars and hot pizza are available. There is even an eating area in the stores. Memories of our childhood came back as we found a bin of fireballs in the bulk foods department at Wegmans. Located next to each other on Route 13 in the middle of Ithaca.

SENECA FALLS

Women's Rights National Historical Park. The first women's rights convention was held here in 1848. This was the beginning of the American suffrage movement. The focus of this small historical park, still in the early stages of development, is to explain the history of the women's movement and the history of its founders. A film and interpretive exhibit tells about one of the early leaders, Elizabeth Cady Stanton, who was instrumental in writing the Declaration of Sentiments. This document listed many of the rights that were denied women of the time, such as the right to vote and the right to own property. In addition to informal discussions with the National Park Service guides, tours of the restored Stanton homestead and other places of historical significance in the town are available.

Open daily, 9 A.M. to 5 P.M. Tours of Stanton's home are given May through September 9 A.M. to 5 P.M. Walking tours of Seneca Falls given during July and August. Free. 116 Fall Street, Seneca Falls, NY 13148; (315) 568-2991.

The Women's Hall of Fame. What do Mary Cassatt, Pearl Buck, Margaret Mead, Harriet Tubman, and Sally Ride have in common? Each is an honoree whose achievements have been given national recognition in the Women's Hall of Fame. Surrounding the hall are forty-four large panels with brief biographies and photographs of the women being honored. Panels are grouped by area of achievement: the arts, science, humanitarianism, education, athletics, and government. The hall has recently received funding for several projects, but more funds are needed to animate the exhibitions and keep this worthy organization expanding. Pamphlets discussing ten of the women are available free of charge. Professionally produced tape tours will enhance your visit to this small museum.

Open May through October, daily, 10 A.M. to 4 P.M.; the rest of the year Wednesday through Sunday 10 A.M. to 4 P.M. Free. 76 Fall Street, Seneca Falls, NY 13148; (315) 568-8060.

GENEVA

Rose Hill Mansion. Two-story Ionic columns support the massive central portico of this imposing white Greek Revival twenty-room mansion. Flanking the central portion are balanced wings, each supported by smaller Ionic columns. This national historic landmark is one of the finest examples of Greek Revival architecture in the U.S. Funds for the restoration were made possible by the grandson of Robert Swan, the former owner of this mansion, who helped to revolutionize farming in this country. Swan installed ceramic tiles in his marshy land to drain off the excess water, which greatly increased his crop yield. As a result of his experimentation other farmers were able to increase their yield as well. The mansion interior is furnished with high-quality Empire-style furnishings.

Open May through October, Monday through Saturday, 10 A.M.

to 4 P.M.; Sunday, 1 to 5 P.M. Adults, $2; youth (ages 10–18), $1.50. Route 96A, one mile south of junction of Routes 5 and 20. Box 464, Geneva, NY 14456; (315) 789-3848.

CANANDAIGUA

Sonnenberg Gardens.   Garden enthusiasts will not want to miss visiting and strolling through this fifty-acre estate with nine formal gardens, greenhouse conservatory, ponds, sculptures, and a forty-room mansion. On a beautiful day, Sonnenberg (the name translates to mean "sunny hill") is a very special place to visit. The gardens were begun by Mary Thompson in 1900 as a memorial to her late husband. After years of decline, the gardens were restored and opened again in 1973. Depending on your mood, visit the ornate Italian garden, the rose garden, a garden planted only in shades of blue and white, a temple niche, a pansy garden, a moonlight garden, a Japanese garden, or the rock garden with its water cascade. Light lunches and gourmet desserts are served in the former peach house and in the outdoor garden café. Two-hour tours are given, or you can stroll as you wish. Be sure to visit the restored mansion and browse through the Lavender and Old Lace gift shop.

Open daily, mid-May to mid-October, 9:30 A.M. to 5:30 P.M. Adults, $5; seniors, $4; children, $2. Free tours at 10 A.M., 1 and 3 P.M. Light lunches available, 11:30 A.M. to 3:30 P.M. 151 Charlotte Street (off Route 21N), Canandaigua, NY 14424; (716) 924-5420. Call for special events at the garden.

OTHER PLACES TO VISIT

New Hope Mills, New Hope.   This is one of the oldest commercial water-powered mills in the country still in operation. Since this is a working mill, visitors to the store can only peek into the grinding and sacking room to watch its operation. For a sight reminiscent of a bygone era, walk across the bridge to view the wheel, the water running over the dam, and the red clapboard mill.

Buttermilk pancake mix is the biggest seller at the New Hope water-powered mill.

We heard stories about the mill and the battles that Leland Weed, the miller here for thirty-five years, waged with the government as he fought to continue producing his additive-free flour. The mill, now run by his sons, ships quantities of flour overseas and to health food stores. The biggest sellers are the buttermilk pancake mix and the oat bran pancake mix. White, whole wheat, buckwheat, pastry, and cornmeal flour, all free of chemical additives, can be purchased here. Local innkeepers say that they used to purchase the buckwheat hulls from the mill to use as a garden mulch. Now, this former "waste product" is in demand by the Japanese, who use it as stuffing for pillows.

Open Monday through Friday, 9 A.M. to 4 P.M.; Saturday, 9 A.M. to 12 P.M.; to 3 P.M. in the summer. Pancake mixes and flour are also available by mail order. Located on Route 41A in New Hope. New Hope Mills, R.D. #2, Box 269A, Moravia, NY 13118; (315) 497-0783.

Robinia Hill Deer Farm, Moravia. Deer farming is a new industry in this country. Five hundred fallow deer, which are smaller than the white-tailed variety, are organically raised on this farm. Visitors can tour the farm and hear Peter Duenkelsbuehler call his herd. (The deer actually come when he calls.) Hides, antlers, and frozen venison can be purchased. Depending on the month that you come, you will see different aspects of the deer farm: in May, the antlers are shed; June and July, fawning and the growth of new velvet antlers; August, bucks shed their velvet; September, antlers are cut; October, rutting season; November, round-up for tagging.

Call for appointment and directions. Tours, $3. Peter Duenkelsbuehler, R.D. 2, Moravia, NY 13118; (315) 496-2121.

MacKenzie-Childs Ceramics, Aurora. This factory produces glazed terra-cotta ceramics unlike anything we'd ever seen before. Pastel colors and patterns are mixed and matched in a whimsical jumble, creating a fanciful, surreal feeling. No matter what your level of interest, ask to see the two designer rooms located in the original, pale-yellow, French Victorian farmhouse with pink and blue trim. The rooms have been decorated using the complete line of Mackenzie-Childs ceramics and furniture. If this piques your interest, browse through the seconds shop for a teapot, plate, door knobs, or placemats, or take the informative sixty-minute tour of the factory to see the entire process.

The seconds store and showroom is open Monday through Saturday, 10 A.M. to 4 P.M. Tours of the factory are given Monday through Friday at 2 P.M. Adults $4, children $2. Located on Route 90 one mile north of Aurora. Aurora, NY 13026; (315) 364-7131.

Misty Meadow Farm, Romulus. It's hard to imagine that cute and cuddly little piglets will, in about six months, weigh in at over 600 pounds! On a tour of this family-run farm that raises about 1,200 pigs a year, we got a chance to hold a squirmy four-week-old piglet in the nursery. We saw the breeding pens and the finishing barn where boars and sows are grown to market size. If you wish, you can feed the full-grown sows and boars. In nice weather, the guides give hay rides. A farm kitchen serves pork barbecue, Cajun pork, Yorker porkers, and boneless spare ribs. If you don't want to "pig out" on pork, ice cream and homemade cookies are also sold.

Open July through Labor Day, Tuesday through Saturday, 11 A.M. to 3 P.M. Tours at 11 A.M., and 12, 1, and 2 P.M. Adults, $2.50; children, $1.25. June and Labor Day to mid-October, open Saturday, 11 A.M. to 2 P.M.; tours at 11 A.M. and 1 P.M. Located off Route 89 along Cayuga Lake. 2828 Vineyard Road, Romulus, NY 14541; (607) 869-9243.

THE FALLS

The spectacular Finger Lakes scenery is studded with waterfalls, especially at the southern edges. Ithaca alone has three mountain streams, one of them 140 feet high, within walking distance of the central business district. Smaller waterfalls are tucked here and there "showing off" along the roadsides and in the backyards of private homes. You should plan to take some of the trails that follow the edge of the falls. For us, this was one of the highlights of our trip to the Finger Lakes. How many other places can you go swimming at the base of a falls? Camping and picnicking facilities are at the state parks listed below. The entrance fee is four dollars per car before Labor Day or when there is swimming, and three dollars at other times. The same fee will cover admission to more

Ithaca Falls is one of three waterfalls within walking distance of Ithaca's central business district.

than one park if you visit them in the same day. For more information about camping: Finger Lakes State Parks, Taughannock Falls State Park, RD #3, Box 283, Trumansburg, NY 14886-0721; (607) 387-7041. Camping reservations can be made through Ticketron.

Watkins Glen State Park.   A path follows the gorge, going over, under, and through the spray. It is the oldest and best known of the Finger Lakes state parks. The entrance is in the village of Watkins Glen; (607) 535-4511.

Timespell. At night, a sound-and-light show dramatizes natural and human history from forty-five million years ago to the present in the Watkins Glen gorge. At the end of the show, the upper falls are illuminated. Two shows are given nightly from mid-May to mid-October; one at dusk the rest of the year. Adults, $4.50, seniors and children $4. Box 6, Franklin Street Watkins Glen, NY 14891; (607) 535-4960.

Buttermilk Falls State Park.   Pick up a map at the lower falls to get the route to the upper falls. You can walk around a lake which, when we visited, had an active beaver colony. If your time is limited, drive to the upper falls as the most spectacular part of the trail starts here. Located off Route 13 about two miles south of Ithaca; (607) 273-5761.

Robert Treman State Park. Be sure not to miss the upper part of the park. An old, three-story, water-powered grist mill, built in 1839 and used until 1917, is open to visitors. A fifteen-minute walk along the gorge trail takes you to 115-foot Lucifer Falls. The lower part of this state park is located a mile or two below Buttermilk Falls on Route 13. To get to the upper park, turn right onto Route 327 and follow signs; (607) 273-3440.

Taughannock Falls State Park. Though hard to believe, the 215-foot drop of Taughannock Falls is higher than Niagara Falls. This is the most spectacular of all the falls. Be sure to at least drive to the upper lookout for a glimpse, as you do not need to walk more than a few steps to view the falls. There is no admission to get to this lookout. You can also take a three-quarter-mile walk to the base of the falls. Located on Route 89, eight miles north of Ithaca; (607) 387-6739.

THE WINERIES

The hills around the Finger Lakes, especially the western side of Keuka Lake around Hammondsport, have been producing grapes for more than 100 years. The climate here is similar to that found in the German Rhine and the French Champagne districts. The deep waters of the lakes temper the climate: The lakes take a long time to warm up in the spring, which helps to retard spring growth until danger of frost is past. The reverse is true in the fall; the lakes retain their warmth to provide protection for the last of the ripening grapes on chilly autumn nights.

What has changed in recent years are the types of grapes being grown. The region is no longer producing only the Concord, Delaware, and Niagara grapes made famous by the large, well-known Taylor/Great Western winery. The past two decades have seen the establishment of small family-owned and -operated wineries growing the vinifera grape. Excellent Chardonnay, Riesling, late harvest, and true ice wines are being produced. Sparkling wines using the Chardonnay and Pinot Noir grapes and the time-consuming *méthode champenoise* are starting to be released by the vintners; they are showing promise.

More than forty wineries now operate in the Finger Lakes region. We have listed those whose wines we have tasted and found exceptional, those whose tours are worthwhile, or those that have outstanding views or cafés. Ask to taste some of the older vintages, even if you pay an extra fee. It's well worth it. Remember that these are, for the most part, small wineries with a limited production. You are not in the Napa Valley at the large commercial multimillion-dollar reception areas. You will be tasting young wines, especially the Chardonnays and Rieslings, that need three years in the bottle to achieve their rich fruitiness, body, and finish. Hide some of the wine you purchase in a cool, dark place and forget about the bottles for a while. You will be pleasantly rewarded.

Cayuga Lake

Knapp Vineyards.   April through December, Monday through Saturday, 10 A.M. to 5 P.M.; Sunday, 12 to 5 P.M. January through March, 10 A.M. to 5 P.M. 2770 Ernsberger Road (County Road 128), Romulus, NY 14541; (607) 869-9271.

Plane's Cayuga.   Mid-May to mid-October, 12 to 5 P.M. daily. Off season, 12 to 4 P.M., weekends only. 6800 Route 89 at Elm Beach, Ovid, NY 14521; (607) 869-5158.

Hosmer.   May through October, Monday through Saturday, 11 A.M. to 5 P.M.; Sunday, 12 to 5 P.M. April, November, and December, weekends, 12 to 4 P.M. 6999 Route 89, Ovid, NY 14521; (607) 869-5585.

Seneca Lake

Hermann Wiemer Vineyard.   May through October, Monday through Saturday, 11 A.M. to 4:30 P.M.; Sunday, 12 to 5 P.M. Route 14, Dundee, NY 14837; (607) 243-7971.

Wagner Vineyards. Monday through Saturday, 10 A.M. to 4 P.M.; Sunday, 12 to 4 P.M. Route 414, Lodi, NY 14860; (607) 582-6450. Ginny Lee Café open mid-May to mid-October (see *Where to Dine,* page 96).

Keuka Lake

Dr. Frank's Vinifera Wine Cellars. March through December, Monday through Saturday, 9 A.M. to 5 P.M.; Sunday, 1 to 5 P.M. Route 76, six miles north of Hammondsport off Route 54A, Hammondsport, NY 14840; (607) 868-4884.

Heron Hill Vineyards. May through November, Monday through Saturday, 10 A.M. to 5 P.M.; Sunday, 1 to 5 P.M. Route 76, three miles north of Hammondsport off Route 54A, Hammondsport, NY 14840; (607) 868-4241.

Bully Hill Vineyards. April through October, Monday through Saturday, 10 A.M. to 4:30 P.M.; Sunday, 11 A.M. to 4:30 P.M. North of Hammondsport off Route 54A, NY 14840; (607) 868-3610. Champagne Country Restaurant open May through October (see *Where to Dine,* page 97).

McGregor Vineyard Winery. May through November, Monday through Saturday, 10 A.M. to 6 P.M.; Sunday, 11 A.M. to 5 P.M. Eight miles north of Hammondsport off Route 54. 5503 Dutch Street, Dundee, NY 14837; (607) 292-3999

THE LAKES

All of the major lakes have cruises that operate from mid-May to mid-September or later. If the weather is pleasant, a cruise can be an enjoyable and peaceful way to see the lakes. All lakes have lunch or dinner cruises. While the food on the cruises will be fine, do not expect a gourmet meal.

Lunch cruises cost about $15 for adults, $12 for children. Dinner cruises range from $20–$30 for adults, $16–$20 for children. Each company listed here has a wide selection of tours and menus.

Lake Skaneateles

Mid-Lakes Navigation Co. This four-hour mailboat cruise that goes around Skaneateles Lake delivering mail in the summer is the most interesting. One-hour sightseeing cruises, two-hour luncheon cruises, three-hour dinner cruises, and four-hour Sunday excursion cruises depart from the town dock.

Mid-Lakes also offers three-day canal cruises on the Erie Canal departing from Albany, Syracuse, and Buffalo. Newly built canal boats that accommodate up to six people can be rented by the week for cruising the Erie Canal.

Lake cruises depart from Skaneateles, mid-May to mid-September. 11 Jordan Street, Box 61, Skaneateles, NY 13152; (315) 685-8500.

Lake Seneca

Captain Bill's Seneca Lake Cruises. One-hour lunch, cocktail, dinner, and teen cruises are offered mid-May to mid-October. Ticket office is at the foot of Franklin Street, Watkins Glen, NY 14891; (607) 535-4541.

Keuka Lake

The Keuka Maid. Morning, lunch, brunch, and dinner cruises are available May through October. Departs from Hammondsport. Box 648, Hammondsport, NY 14840; (607) 569-2628.

Lake Canandaigua

Canandaigua Lady. Enjoy lunch, afternoon, dinner, or moonlight cruises on a replica of a nineteenth-century sternwheeler, powered by paddlewheels, from June to mid-October. Departs from Canandaigua. Box 856, Canandaigua, NY 14424; (716) 398-3110.

WHERE TO STAY

Rose Inn, Ithaca

The fan-shaped Palladian windows that surround the double Jacuzzi in the bridal suite overlook the gardens, a stand of aged white pines, a fifty-year-old apple orchard, and fields of corn beyond. Pick a fine bottle of New York State Hosmer or Plane's Riesling or Chardonnay kept chilled in the refrigerator. Don a thick terrycloth robe and settle into the Eames chair by the fireplace. After you're thoroughly relaxed, dress for dinner and descend the Honduran-mahogany circular staircase—the centerpiece of this 1850s Italianate mansion that sits, along with several classic eighteenth-century barns, on twenty acres of photogenic farmland just outside of Ithaca.

So began our introduction to one of the premier country inns in the Northeast. Innkeepers Charles and Sherry Rosemann are consummate professionals. Charles attended hotel management schools in Germany, and has managed five-star hotels in the United States.

The Rosemanns' attention to detail is exceptional. The well-decorated rooms surround two sitting areas where the telephones are located. In one there is a refrigerator stocked with wines and Champagne. In the bathrooms are French soap, shampoo, conditioner, shower caps, shoe polisher, Vitabath, bath sheets rather than standard-size towels, and quality adjustable shower heads—the type found in designer catalogues. Padded satin hangers are in the closets.

A broad range of rooms meets the needs of different budgets. Four of the rooms and suites have Jacuzzis. A Victorian rose-patterned sofa back is used as a headboard on a king-size bed in one room; another uses the frame of a fireplace as a headboard; and yet another has a circular shower built into an existing closet. However, no matter which room you choose, try to include a dinner with your stay—it is outstanding in every respect (see *Where to Dine,* page 85).

The elegant attention to detail continues at breakfast. We started with a mixture of fresh-squeezed juice from California Valencia and Israeli blood oranges. During the fall season, you will be served a glass of apple cider made from the Rosemanns' apples. The coffee is a mixture of Kona, Colombian, and Amaretto. Raspberries and blueberries were served with crème fraîche and brown sugar. The entrée might be smoked salmon arranged in the shape of a rose served with bagels and cream cheese, or German apple pancakes served with their own apple butter.

Thirteen rooms, all with private bath, $100 to $150; three suites, all with a Jacuzzi for two, $175 to $250. A full breakfast is included. Children over 10 permitted. Third person in room, $25 additional. No pets. Two-night minimum stay on weekends. Located on Route 34, nine miles north of the city. 813 Auburn Road, Route 34, Box 6576, Ithaca, NY 14851-6576; (607) 533-7905.

Benn Conger Inn, Groton

If you are a wine connoisseur or a bibliophile, we could not think of a better place to hole up or get snowed in for a long weekend. This Greek Revival mansion, which sits on a hill two blocks from the town center, was built in 1921 for the president of Smith-Corona. The typewriter factory is now closed—not good for the town, but great for those seeking a quiet refuge. Innkeepers Alison and Peter van der Meulen have an exceptional 5,000-bottle wine cellar (it has won a *Wine Spectator* award of excellence for a number of years), an extensive record collection, and wide-ranging library. Peter is in charge of the kitchen and Alison is the dinner hostess.

A large entry hall with a polished wood floor welcomes guests. To the left is an intimate bar and library with a stately cherrywood-burning fireplace. To the right are the dining rooms (see *Where to Dine,* page 86).

In cool weather our top choice is the Oaksford Suite. There is a queen-size, eighteenth-century cast-iron French bed and, in the adjoining private living room, two comfortable easy chairs and an

The Benn Conger Inn has an intimate bar and library with a fireplace.

antique Kerman Oriental carpet in front of a wood-burning fireplace. We stayed in the Dutch Schultz Room with a queen-size sleigh bed that disappears in the sixteen- by twenty-five-foot space (that's just the main room!). The walk-in closet (the envy of all city dwellers), separate dressing room, water closet, and bathroom complete the suite. Future plans for this suite include putting in French doors to the balcony and putting in a Jacuzzi. The Cornell Room has a queen-size canopy bed and a private porch room with a futon couch, rocking chair, and overhead fan. The Daley Room, a corner room with a double armoire, is the smallest.

On the second-floor landing at the top of the stairs is a sitting area with a window seat that overlooks the front of the inn, a television, and a large collection of books. The property includes eighteen acres of woodlands and trails for hiking and cross-country skiing. A trout stream is nearby.

The breakfast specialty is Danish Aebleskiever, round pancakes cooked in an unusual cast-iron pan and filled with apples or fresh preserves.

Open year-round. One room and three suites (one with a fireplace), all with private bath, $75 to $150. A full breakfast is included. Children welcome. Third person $25 additional. No pets. 206 West Cortland Street, Groton, NY 13073; (607) 898-5817.

Buttermilk Falls Bed and Breakfast, Ithaca

Since the inn is located just 100 yards from the base of Buttermilk Falls, guests can enjoy an early morning hike up into the gorge along the rushing waterfalls. Especially in the spring and early summer, you can lie in bed and be lulled to sleep by the cascading waterfall.

The living room has a pair of highback loveseats, a gas fireplace, and a collection of old games and puzzles. A long cherrywood table in the dining room seats twelve on Windsor chairs that are made by Margie Rumsey's son, Ed. If you have an interest in purchasing one, you can often find him demonstrating his craft at the Ithaca Farmers' Market on Saturday mornings.

The latest addition to the house is the large first-floor room complete with wood-burning fireplace, king-size bed, and double Jacuzzi; a pair of sleigh seats have been made into benches for this room. One of the smaller second-floor rooms has a vibrating massage bed. Another room is an efficiency apartment with a king-size bed and a small kitchen. For a family there is a two-room suite in another building on the property.

Breakfast is exceptional. We started with a blend of orange juice, bananas, and fresh ginger. Hot popovers (don't be late!) were served with homemade strawberry, elderberry, and spiced peach preserves. Whole-grain oat cereal came with a choice of toppings: peaches, pineapple, nuts, prunes, and Brown Cow yogurt.

Margie, an enthusiastic booster of Ithaca, has a well-stocked library on the area and has a seemingly encyclopedic knowledge of the Finger Lakes. On Saturday morning she is apt to scoop her guests up into the van and take off for the Farmers' Market (see *Where to Go, What to Do,* page 59).

Innkeepers often have accommodations for themselves in the basement or in the attic. Margie's is one of the most unusual. During pleasant weather she often climbs the apple ladder propped next to the large maple to sleep under the stars in her open-air tree house.

Six rooms and suites, four with private bath, $65–$185. Full breakfast is included. Children welcome. Third person in room $25 additional. No pets. Located just off Route 13, 3½ miles south of

Ithaca. 110 East Buttermilk Falls Road, Ithaca, NY 14850; (607) 272-6767.

Taughannock Farms Inn, Trumansburg

Surrounded by the 600-acre Taughannock State Forest, this 1873 Victorian home sits on a hillside with commanding views of Lake Cayuga. Converted to a restaurant and inn by the Agard family in 1945 (it's still owned and operated by members of the same family), Taughannock Farms has become a popular dining spot for Cornell grads over the years.

The rooms on the second floor and the two cottages are comfortably furnished. Several offer enchanting views of the lake. The Northlake Room has an exceptional view of Cayuga; twin beds, an adorable ladies' chair, and a clawfoot bathtub and marble sink. The premier room is the light-filled Garden Room. The three exposures in this room afford a view of the lake and the hillside in back of the inn. A fishnet canopy queen-size bed, lovely plaster work on the ceiling, matching wallpaper and draperies, along with a bath lined with old fireplace tiles, make this a choice for honeymooners. The second-floor parlor overlooks the lake and is decorated with Victorian couches, children's furniture, and an authentic working Swiss music box from the 1890s along with eighty of the original "digital discs." Two guesthouses (each with two bedrooms) near the property, one adjacent to the Taughannock Falls trail, are available for private getaways.

Open Good Friday through Thanksgiving. Five rooms, with private bath, $75–$100. Two guesthouses, $110–$125. Expanded Continental breakfast is included. Children welcome in the guesthouses. No pets. Route 89, Taughannock Falls, Trumansburg, NY 14886; (607) 387-7711.

The Red House Country Inn, Burdett

"Watch out for the flock of wild turkeys that hang out just down the road from the inn," Joan Martin added as she finished giving us driving instructions to this secluded mid-1800s farmhouse inn, located off a dirt road in the middle of the 13,000-acre Finger Lakes National Forest. She and Sandy Schmanke run a comfortable, friendly inn. Also living on the property are twenty-seven chickens, five goats, and five dogs. (Some are grand champion Samoyeds, distant relatives to Alaskan huskies.) The entrance to the inn is through a gift shop filled with craft and country items. One of the first things we were shown was the guest kitchen and the stash of coffee and tea. Should you decide not to leave the seclusion of the National Forest, you're welcome to use the kitchen facilities. In the winter Joan and Sandy will prepare a hearty country dinner such as a roast game hen or baked ham and gratin potatoes, by prior arrangement.

On the first floor are two dining rooms set with lace tablecloths and breakfast china. The side tables are brimming with glassware, punch bowls, and silver coffee and tea pots. Dried flowers, baskets, planters, ceramics, craft items, and paintings give the inn a warm, lived-in feel. A decanter of sherry sits in the living room along with a piano, pump organ, guitar, and a banjo which the innkeepers, with the least bit of encouragement, enjoy playing.

The blue room is the largest, with a high four-poster queen-size Charleston rice bed, rocking chair, convertible sofa, and secretary with a glass case that contains a collection of porcelain birds and vases. Another favorite is the room next door with its own fireplace. All the rooms are decorated with Amish quilts that come from the area around Penn Yan.

Breakfasts are a highlight and include juice, fresh fruit salad, locally grown seedless grapes in season, scrambled eggs, sausage, muffins, scones, and toast.

The eighteen- by thirty-six-foot swimming pool, complete with diving board, lounge chairs, and wet bar, keeps guests close by on summer days. Outdoor enthusiasts enjoy the twenty-eight miles of maintained trails for hiking and cross-country skiing.

Six double rooms (one with a fireplace), $47–$75, and one single room, $39, share four baths. A full breakfast is included. Two-night stay on weekends. Children over 12 welcome. No pets. Located in the National Forest about twelve miles northeast of Watkins Glen and eighteen miles northwest of Ithaca. Call or write for exact directions (a necessity). Finger Lakes National Forest, Picnic Area Road, Burdett, NY 14818; (607) 546-8566.

Rosewood Inn, Corning

This 1855 Victorian sits on a tree-lined street of large homes just two short blocks from the restored nineteenth-century Main Street of Corning. Since the inn is within walking distance of the world-renowned Corning Museum of Glass, visiting scholars who like the homey feel of a bed-and-breakfast often stay here.

Each room is decorated in a different theme. In the Frederick Carder Room (Carder was one of the founders of Steuben Glass), we found a display of colored glass and books about his work. Attached to this room is a small, private solarium with two stained-glass windows and a display of early glass-blowing tools that Carder might have used. In the twin-bedded Herman Melville Room, the walls are decorated with an old harpoon, a pair of binoculars, prints, and wood carvings of the sea. Naturally, there is a copy of *Moby Dick* by the bed. The Jenny Lind Room has what else but a Jenny Lind (spool) bed, violin, and sheet music from the Swedish Nightingale's era. The Charles Dana Gibson Room has a matching, three-piece Eastlake bedroom set and is decorated with the artist's illustrations.

A second-floor sitting area for guests has a television, and telephone. Notice how wooden organ pipes have creatively been turned into shelving.

A separate building has two suites, each with its own private entrance. The Patterson Suite has a gas fireplace, queen-size canopy bed, a daybed, phone, and television. Next door is the Pullman Suite. While we felt that the railroad decorations didn't match the quality found in the main part of the inn, this suite has a kitchen and phone, making it an ideal choice for a family or for a longer stay.

A full breakfast of fruit, juice, granola, and a hot entrée is served family style at 8:30, with early coffee ready at 7:30.

Four rooms and two suites, with private bath, $78–$100. Rollaway bed, $15. Full breakfast included. Children of all ages welcome.

No pets. Parking is provided behind the inn. 134 East First Street, Corning, NY 14830; (607) 962-3253.

Lake Keuka Manor, Hammondsport

With 165 feet of lakefront, this former guest cottage, also known as "Limbo," is the ideal hideaway for lake people. It was built by William Tuttle, who invented the eyelash curler. Cars are left at the top of the hill. To get to the waterfront lodge guests ride on a thirty-foot-high, four-passenger tram. This is all part of the adventure. Pile your luggage in the little open-air car and push the button.

This is the kind of place where we'd be happy to be stranded. Swim off the dock. Bring your fishing rod and tackle as Keuka Lake has plenty of trout, bass, pike, and landlocked salmon. You can cook your catch of the day in the large picnic-barbecue pavilion. Innkeeper Bob Childs has a state-of-the-art digital stereo system with a large library of compact discs. Two fireplaces keep the chill off on cool evenings. Books are scattered throughout the house with the emphasis on music (Bob's interest and former profession) and architecture (Bob's wife Ayse Child's profession).

You will want to spend most of the time in one of the two common rooms, outside on the patio, or on the deck by the lake. Floor-to-ceiling sliding-glass doors open onto the stone patio, so even if the weather is inclement, the views are terrific. Ayse's Turkish heritage is reflected by the fine Turkish carpets and antique kilims that cover the teak parquet floors in one of the common rooms. The baby grand is Bob's. As a graduate of the Westminster Choir College, he can be persuaded to play solo or with musically accomplished guests. In the late afternoon, guests can taste one or two of the local Keuka Lake wines as well as cheese made at the Steuben Cheese Company in nearby Prattsburg.

While the downstairs common rooms are spacious, the bedrooms are quite small—if room size is a priority, this is not the place for you. Two rooms have great views of the lake and two have no view as they face the steep slope that the house backs into.

Breakfast changes every day. Ours included scones accompa-

nied by locally produced jams, honey, and jellies; three-minute
eggs; grape juice from a local winery; coffee and brewed Turkish
tea. In warm weather, breakfast is served outdoors on the patio by
the lake.

Bob takes guests out on afternoon cruises and waterskiing.

Open April through November. Four rooms, all with private
bath, $75–$95. Breakfast and a wine-tasting is included. Two-night
minimum. Children over 10 permitted. No pets. 626 West Lake
Road, Route 54A, Hammondsport, NY 14840; (607) 868-3276.

J.P. Morgan House, Canandaigua

The early eighteenth-century brick and stone farmhouse, expanded over the years by a series of wealthy owners, was converted to a secluded hideaway by John and Julie Sullivan. A
2,000-foot gravel driveway edged with venerable maples contrasts
with the surrounding fields of hay and corn. Many inns have
friendly dogs who greet visitors; here you will find a dozen or so
curious free-range chickens that also provide your morning eggs.

For a special occasion when you want total privacy and lots of
space, take the 600-square-foot master suite. It is luxuriously furnished with French antiques, a king-size bed, thick beige wall-to-
wall carpeting, and a circular couch set in front of a fireplace. Two
other second-floor rooms each with French doors open onto small
balconies that overlook the tree-lined entrance drive. The room
with the king-size bed and the antique furniture is particularly
appealing.

The second-largest room is the Victorian Suite on the third floor,
decorated in shades of wine with a king-size bed, lace bedding, and
Victorian furniture. This suite also has a view down the drive and
French doors opening onto a small balcony. An arched doorway
leads into the nineteen-and-a-half-foot-long bathroom with hardwood ginger-colored floors and a Jacuzzi with green marble facing.
We were charmed by a small room with a built-in Dutch bed and
a split Dutch door, just right for a single person.

The rooms on the first floor give guests ample space for relaxing. In cool weather, curl up with a book on the semicircular couch

in front of the fireplace. In warmer weather we far prefer the glass-enclosed porch room with views over the fields.

With advance notice and a minimum of six people, you can have a private dinner at the inn. A sample menu might include shrimp cocktail, homemade soup, salad, two double lamb chops or a tenderloin, and two vegetables. Dessert is usually fresh berries and shortcake.

John takes breakfast seriously. It starts with fresh-squeezed orange juice and coffee made from fresh-ground coffee beans. Nibble on the bowl of fresh fruit and on homemade muffins while your choice of blueberry buckwheat pancakes served with real maple syrup, French toast made with bread baked at the local Trappist monastery, or eggs (from the cooperative hens out back) is prepared. If you happen to visit in August or September you will probably be served a wedge of the local Irondequoit melon, which tastes similar to canteloupe but is far sweeter.

Following breakfast you might consider a game of tennis on the Sullivans' court or ask to have arrangements made for a hay or sleigh ride.

Two suites, $150, $175; two rooms with private baths, $85, $90. Two rooms with shared bath, $95, $105. One small single room with shared bath, $60. Children welcome. Rollaway bed $20. No pets. Full breakfast is included. From Canandaigua go east on Route 5-20, left at third light on County Road 10, right at stop sign. 2920 Smith Road, Canandaigua, NY 14424; (716) 394-9232 or (800) 233-3252.

Geneva on the Lake, Geneva

Built as a private residence between 1910 and 1914, Geneva on the Lake was patterned after an Italian Renaissance villa. The building was used as a monastery from 1949 to 1974. Following this it was converted into apartments and then changed in 1982 to a European vacation resort that caters to group conferences during the week and tourists on weekends.

Accommodations here have the feel of a garden apartment. All the rooms include a kitchen, television, and telephone. Flowers and a bottle of New York State wine will be in your room on arrival. *The New York Times* will be at your door in the morning.

The basic suite has a pull-down queen-size Murphy bed. The deluxe suites have a separate bedroom and a living room and dining area. Three of the suites have fireplaces. The rooms are all similarly furnished with quality hotel furnishings. Some have Stickley reproductions. Our favorite is the dark wood–paneled Library Suite complete with shelves lined with old books, a coffered ceiling, and a fireplace. If a lighter-colored, brighter suite is desired, pick the classic two-bedroom suite with fireplaces, canopied bed, and balcony.

Marble statuary are placed among the clipped hedges of the well-cared-for symmetrical Italian gardens, at the end of which is a seventy-foot swimming pool. Small sailboats (catamarans) and canoes can be rented at the inn's dock. With advance arrangements, an instructor can be provided. Bicycles are available for rental.

The resort hotel has theme weekends that cater to singles, such as a mystery weekend, a vineyard and culinary arts getaway, a ski weekend, and a Parents without Partners weekend. Various package plans are also available.

Twenty-nine suites all with kitchens. Mid-May through October: studio, $169–$199; one- and two-bedroom suites, $230–$322. During the rest of the year: studio, $149–$179, one- and two-bedroom suites $210–$302. Continental breakfast included. Children welcome: ages 4–9, $17; 10–15, $29; Adults $52. No pets. Two-night stay on weekends during the summer. Located south of Geneva on Route 14. Box 929, Geneva, NY 14456; (315) 789-7190 or 800-3GENEVA.

Belhurst Castle, Geneva

If you've dreamed about staying in a castle and can't make it to Europe, this could be a good substitute. The turreted, ivy-covered, red Medina-stone structure sits on a bluff overlooking Lake Seneca.

It was built in 1885 as a private residence. From 1933 until the early 1950s it was a speakeasy and gambling casino. The first floor of the castle is used for the many dining rooms (see *Where to Dine,* page 93). The massive curving staircase leads to ten rooms and two suites on the second and third floors. Most of the rooms have queen-size beds, two easy chairs, and high ceilings. All of the rooms on the second floor have gas fireplaces. A feature unique to this castle is the spigot in the second-floor hall lounge that dispenses complimentary wine for the room guests.

For a romantic weekend, we would choose one of the two spacious suites without hesitation. The Tower Suite on the third floor has twenty-foot ceilings in the living room. The grand wood-paneled bath with a domed ceiling has a bidet and large Jacuzzi for two set into a raised wooden platform. A private curving staircase in the bedroom leads to the top of the turret. Bring a glass of wine and relax in the two chairs placed here to take advantage of the great views of the lake. On nice days you can sit on the private balcony that is off the living room.

The Dwyer Suite on the second floor is located in what, in former years, was the gambling hall where the high rollers tried their luck. From the high four-poster bed that you need a step-stool to get into, you can look at the lake through four stained-glass windows. The living room has a fireplace and three additional stained-glass windows. The bath has a bidet but no Jacuzzi.

All of the rooms have telephones and televisions. A path leads from the edge of the property to the dock on the edge of Lake Seneca where guests may swim or fish. Sailing or fishing boats can be rented nearby. A public golf course is about a mile from the castle.

Ten rooms and two suites, all with private bath. May through October: doubles, $90–$125; suites, $175 and $225. During the rest of the year: doubles, $75–$95; suites, $125 and $175. Breakfast available but not included in the room rate from May through October; continental breakfast included from November through April. Children welcome—no additional charge. Third adult $15 additional. No pets. Located south of Geneva on Route 14. Box 609, Geneva, NY 14456; (315) 781-0201.

James Russell Webster Mansion Inn, Waterloo

Curious visitors are not welcome here. If you want to look around, you will need to call for an appointment and pay a fee, as the inn feels like a museum. "This is not an inn for everyone," owner Leonard Cohen told us repeatedly. "I spend as much time as necessary speaking to prospective guests on the phone, making sure that they understand our philosophy of innkeeping and the rules of the house before I take a reservation." Some of their rules include removing your shoes, no matter what time of year, as you walk through the door; deciding to have dinner at their home at least a week in advance; and prepaying your room, breakfast, and dinner before you arrive. "This way we never have a problem with no-shows," Leonard said.

This 1845 Georgian mansion is located along busy Main Street in this small Finger Lakes town, population just over 5,000. Barbara and Leonard Cohen devote themselves exclusively to taking care of their two guest rooms and to creating sumptuous "haute cuisine" dinners.

Our favorite room is the twenty-five- by forty-foot Palladian Suite. Its living room has fourteen-foot ceilings and a floor of stark black-and-white checkered harlequin tiles reminiscent of Vermeer paintings. As the floors are tile, do bring wool socks or slippers— even in the summer, our feet were chilly. In the adjoining room is an eighteenth-century Philadelphia mahogany canopy double bed. The high Georgian, intricately carved Colonial doors that lead to the backyard are from an English military academy. A Baccarat chandelier hangs overhead.

The second suite, the Noah Webster, is actually a large room with a canopy bed, fireplace, and sitting area. This room has a warmer feel, as the floor is carpeted. Baths in both of the rooms have green marble on the floors and walls. The sinks are made of porcelain and decorated in gold.

And there are cats: over 600 in glass, porcelain, bronze, clay, wax, and stone placed in groupings throughout the inn. They constitute a major cat figurine museum. The Cohens also have about half a dozen real ones that are kept in their quarters.

The Cohens feel strongly that guests who stay here should also dine here at least one of the nights of their stay. Either a continental or a full breakfast is available to houseguests but must be preordered. The continental includes fruit, juices, cheeses, and homemade pastry. The full breakfast could be eggs Benedict; sourdough French toast with sausages; eggs Florentine; or bagels, cream cheese, and smoked salmon.

One large room and one suite, each $300. Breakfasts per person, from $10. Two-night stay on weekends. Not appropriate for children. No pets. 115 East Main Street (Routes 5 and 20), Waterloo, NY 13165; (315) 539-3032.

Sherwood Inn, Skaneateles

This village inn is ideally located across the road from the town park and the banks of the Skaneateles Lake. In our estimation this is one of the prettiest towns in the Finger Lakes region. The lobby has a large fireplace, Oriental carpets, and Stickley furniture. The night we were there the tavern was crowded—it seemed to be the gathering spot for the town's thirtyish professional crowd. The formal dining rooms are to the left of the lobby (see *Where to Dine,* page 95).

The management's policy is to keep the doors of the guest rooms open until their occupants arrive. The rooms are spacious. Many have old or antique furnishings, and are decorated in Colonial style using Williamsburg patterns or in Victorian style with bolder wallpapers and Stickley furniture. We were told that rooms 20 and 28, located over the tavern, had been recently insulated; the day we stopped, we could still hear a faint drum beat from below. The management compensates by charging a lower rate for these rooms.

This is a fine choice for overnight accommodations if you are exploring the northern end of the Finger Lakes or if you are taking the summer mailboat cruise on Skaneateles Lake. As a number of the rooms are suites or have a convertible couch, this is a good choice for a family. However, before you decide on a lake-view room you should consider that Route 20, a main highway that has heavy truck and automobile traffic, passes directly in front of the inn. If you are a city person this should make you feel right at home; if you are a light sleeper, we suggest a room in the rear of the inn. Keeping the windows shut and the air-conditioner turned on will help reduce the traffic noise.

Eleven rooms, all with private bath, $66–$82.50; six suites, $77–$99. Tax is included in the rates. Continental breakfast is included. Children of all ages welcome. No pets. Located on Route 20. 26 West Genesee Street, Skaneateles, NY 13152; (315) 685-3405.

WHERE TO DINE

Rose Inn, Ithaca

Escoffier, the king of chefs, once wrote, "It is far better to serve a short, well-balanced, perfectly executed menu that the guests can unhurriedly enjoy." And enjoy you will, dining in one of the four common rooms in this remarkable 1850s Italianate mansion situated on twenty acres of photogenic farmland a few miles north of Ithaca. Do a Few Things Perfectly is the motto that innkeepers Charles and Sherry Rosemann strictly adhere to as they plan their dinner selections.

The policy at this bed-and-breakfast country inn that serves classic French cuisine is that you select both your appetizer and entrée before arriving for dinner; the inn sends you a menu when you make a reservation. You may be seated in the center hall surrounded by the famous circular staircase of Honduras mahogany, in the parlor, or in one of two intimate dining rooms. Fine linens, fresh flowers, candles, china, and silver flatware frame your meal.

As a first course we sampled the sinfully rich, intensely flavored lobster bisque made with chunks of lobster and heavy cream. The artichoke-heart strudel served on puréed tomato is excellent and somewhat lighter than the bisque. A third appetizer, which melts in your mouth, is the tender smoked oysters in beurre blanc sauce served in a flaky puffed-pastry shell. The salad, one of the very best we've had, is an artistic presentation that included Boston lettuce, radicchio, artichoke hearts, hearts of palm, red and yellow peppers, tomatoes, and sprouts.

If you like duck tender with no excess fat, then request it when making your reservation. After the duck is cooked, the skin is crisped under the broiler, and a honey-almond topping is applied. It was so good that we've chosen it as the featured recipe for this chapter (see page 98). All the grilled meats and fish are cooked outdoors year round on several charcoal grills. The rack of lamb for two is grilled with a garlic and herb marinade. The large veal chop is served with a classic Madeira sauce and topped with sliced, sautéed wild mushrooms. (The night we dined, it was served with cremini mushrooms.) The scampi is sautéed just right with tomato, curry, and cream, and flambéed with brandy. The harmonious colors of the steamed broccoli, cauliflower, and slivered carrots artfully arranged in a crisp potato basket was the ultimate vegetable combination. The small, thoroughly researched, reasonably priced wine list is designed to complement the entrées.

Desserts the night we dined included a rich chocolate pot de crème. The cornucopia-shaped pizzelle filled with local raspberries set on crème Anglaise that had been painted with a fresh strawberry purée created a beautiful picture.

One of the joys of staying here is that you can savor an after-dinner drink, such as a 1984 late-harvest Riesling from the Wagner vineyards, and not have to think about driving home. If you appreciate fine dining, this is an experience that you should not miss.

Dinner, Tuesday through Saturday, 7 P.M. Twenty-four-hour advance reservation required. $50 per person prix fixe. Box 6576, 813 Auburn Road, Route 34, Ithaca, NY 14851-6576; (607) 533-7905.

Benn Conger Inn, Groton

New innkeepers Alison and Peter van der Meulen have redecorated the four dining rooms with bright chintz draperies and swags. "Our aim is to create an elegant but relaxed feeling, like dining in your own private club," said Alison.

This was our introduction to dining at the Benn Conger Inn, a Greek Revival mansion built in 1921 as the home for the president of Smith-Corona, at one time the major employer in this small Finger Lakes town. The inn is in an isolated, beautiful spot in the country, the kind of place you might never find unless you knew where to go.

With a cellar of more than 5,000 bottles, the twelve-page wine list is one of the finest in the area and has received a *Wine Spectator* award of excellence. Peter is in charge of the kitchen, and Alison orchestrates the service at the well-spaced tables in the four dining rooms. In cooler weather a wood fire burns in the marble fireplace in the main dining room and another fire is kept burning in the intimate library. The plant-filled conservatory, which has Palladian windows and French doors, is popular in the summer. For a private dinner ask to sit in the Morning Room, which has chintz shades and has a country French feel.

The menu changes frequently to accommodate the seasons and the availability of fresh ingredients. We started with the éclair of wild mushrooms and local goat cheese. A shoulder lamb chop was grilled and served with roasted garlic and topped with a generous portion of freshly made, bright-green pesto. The salmon filet was grilled with basil butter and topped with toasted pine nuts. A fine Alsatian cream sauce of mustard, onions, and white wine was served with the grilled center-cut pork chop. Other popular entrées are grilled lamb with a raspberry mint sauce, lamb Wellington, grilled swordfish marinated in lime and cilantro, and black pasta served with a lobster, shrimp, and crab sauce.

Desserts we sampled included a fresh blueberry cobbler and a classic profiterole filled with vanilla ice cream and served with dark chocolate sauce. Handmade chocolate truffles are presented with the check at the end of your dinner.

After dinner we retired to the library and sampled a Poire William from the outstanding collection of ports, brandies, and eaux-de-vie. We feel that the outstanding collection of books guests can peruse while enjoying a pre-dinner aperitif or an after-dinner liqueur gives this inn a warm, personal ambience rarely found in other restaurants.

Dinner served nightly to inn guests. For the public, Wednesday through Sunday from 6 P.M. Reservations required. Entreés, $12.-95–$19.95. 206 West Cortland Street, Groton, NY 13073; (607) 898-5817.

Taughannock Farms Inn, Trumansburg

This restaurant sits in a prime location: a large, lovely 1873 Victorian home on a hill overlooking Cayuga Lake. Since 1945, faithful guests keep returning for the complete "soup to nuts" American cuisine. There are three dining rooms. The most popular is the one with the view over the lake; it is built on three tiers so that almost every table has a good view of the lake and the surrounding countryside.

Dinner starts with relishes and the restaurant's well-known homemade orange date bread and pan rolls. This is followed by a choice of appetizer or soup. A house specialty is Nancy's whimsical chilled soups, such as the strawberry blueberry buckle we sampled. Entreés might include roast turkey with all the trimmings, roast Long Island duckling, slow-roasted prime rib, and a Friday night special of lobster Newburg. An interesting salad to try is spinach, citrus, and grapes served with a Roquefort dressing. There are about twenty desserts, including a traditional hot fudge sundae topped with Spanish peanuts, peppermint ice cream pie in a chocolate crumb crust, a gooey rich Southern pecan pie, and other fresh pies baked every day at the inn. This is not a restaurant for "grazers" or folks with small appetites.

Open from Good Friday through Thanksgiving. Dinner, Monday through Saturday, from 5 P.M.; Sunday dinner 1 to 8 P.M. Complete dinners $16.50–$24.95. Route 89, Taughannock Falls, Trumansburg, NY 14886; (607) 387-7711.

Abby's, Ithaca

For the past six years, Abby's has been Ithaca's dining location for trendy cuisine. It is located in an out-of-the-way strip mall. The open room has gray pinstriped walls and is decorated with post-

Impressionist oil paintings and graphics. Dinners are influenced by the cuisines of California and Northern Italy. We were impressed to learn that Abby's uses a number of local sources for ingredients: New York State chèvre and feta as well as Finger Lakes wines.

The bread is a highlight of the frequently changing menu. This is the tastiest and crustiest sourdough bread that's available in the area. All of the pasta is made at the restaurant. Tagliatelle is served with pesto. Sweet potato ravioli is served with almond cream sauce. Spinach lasagna is made with wild mushrooms and Parmesan, Romano, and mozzarella cheeses. Each evening a different thin-crust pizza is on the menu. One favorite has a topping of sliced pears, Saga blue cheese, toasted walnuts, and wild cherries. Other specialties are mesquite grilled salmon with a choice of three sauces: beurre rose, sorrel cream, or tarragon-lime; rack of lamb with a mustard and herb crust; and cassoulet with moulard duck confit. A mixed green salad included tatsoi, an Oriental green, and was dressed with toasted hazelnuts, garlic croutons, and a Champagne vinaigrette.

The desserts included peach and blueberry cobbler, lemon cheesecake, strawberry trifle with mascarpone, and Belgian chocolate pecan pie. We enjoyed the sourdough bread so much that we purchased a loaf for snacking on the road.

Dinner daily 5 to 11 P.M. Entrées $9.50–$20. 309 Third Street, Ithaca, NY 14850; (607) 273-1999.

Joe's, Ithaca

The hottest dining spot in Ithaca, this red-sauce Italian restaurant is a downtown fixture. After fifty years of family ownership, it closed in the early 1980s, then reopened with an Art Deco scheme; a Wurlitzer jukebox plays in the crowded bar. Joe's is known for its pasta, low prices, and large portions. There is almost always a wait for dinner. On Monday a family special offers a penny a pound for children's dinners, and the joint is jumpin'. We "carbed out at Joe's," as the locals say, with toasted ravioli, pesto pizza, garlic chicken strips, chicken breast stuffed with provolone and prosciutto, and Joe's red platter loaded with lasagna, veal Marsala, eggplant parmigiana, and a side order of spaghetti. All dinners come with a large bowl of salad. You definitely get your money's worth at this crowded, noisy, popular place.

Dinner daily, 4 to 10 P.M.; to 11 P.M. on Friday and Saturday. Entrées, $7.25–$13.95. 602 West Buffalo Street, Ithaca, NY 14850; (602) 273-2693.

The Station, Ithaca

Rail buffs will love the Station. There's lots and lots of railroad memorabilia, including photographs, paintings, signs, lanterns, and models. This is one of the best theme restaurants we've seen. You can eat in the old station or in one of the old cars—they're the ones with velvet upholstery that even smell authentic. When it comes time to order your dinner, the server gives you a punch and a ticket. We suggest sticking with traditional dishes such as the prime rib, filet mignon, tournedos, or lamb chops—then sit back and imagine yourself in a bygone era.

Dinner, Tuesday through Saturday, 4 to 9:30 P.M.; Sunday, 12 to 9:30 P.M. Dinner entrées, $9.75–$16.25. 806 West Buffalo Street, Ithaca, NY 14850; (607) 272-2609.

Moosewood Restaurant, Ithaca

Many people know this restaurant from its popular cookbooks; over 1 million copies of the *Moosewood Cookbook* have been sold. After sixteen years, this well-known vegetarian restaurant is still going strong. It is located in downtown Ithaca in a former school building, called the DeWitt Mall, that also includes an eclectic mix of shops and apartments. It is owned and operated by a cooperative whose eighteen members take turns planning menus, cooking, cleaning, waiting tables, and so on. The quality is, not surprisingly, inconsistent. With lots of people cooking, some are bound to be better than others.

The menu is written on a blackboard and changes daily. We stopped by on a Sunday night when ethnic dinners are featured. The food was good, but not outstanding. The cooks had prepared Hungarian specialties that included potato cheese soup and barley vegetable soup. Main courses were scrod topped with sour cream and paprika, a vegetarian stew, and strudel filled with cheeses, cabbage, and red peppers, topped with caraway seeds. Desserts that night were spiced brandy peaches, chocolate frosted layer cake, rice pudding, and vanilla ice cream with plum sauce. The wine list seemed to be a good value and included local selections at little or no mark-up ranging from $5 to $11 a bottle. The hearty breads are still baked down the hall at the Somadhara bakery.

Lunch, Monday through Saturday, 11:30 A.M. to 2 P.M., $4–$4.50. Dinner Sunday through Thursday, 5:30 to 8:30 P.M.; Friday and Saturday, 6 to 9 P.M. Entrées $8.50–$9.75. No smoking. No credit cards. 215 North Cayuga Street, Ithaca, NY 14850; (607) 273-9610.

Village Tavern, Hammondsport

Paul Geisz, a retired Philadelphia detective and his wife, Mary Ann, successfully operate a casual, fun neighborhood tavern in this lakeside community. The menu is heavy on seafood: poached salmon, blackened redfish, mussels diavalo, and broiled haddock. Twice a week the owners drive five and a half hours to the Philadelphia wholesale markets and load up on fresh fish and produce. There are also steaks, pork chops, and Italian specialties. The night we dined the featured special was a seafood diavalo—a huge platter of clams, shrimp, mussels, scallops, and lobster tail in a spicy red sauce. Dinner comes with beer bread and a tossed salad.

We salute the owners for featuring the local Finger Lakes wineries. Sixteen wineries are represented, including twenty selections available by the glass. As this was the hometown of Glenn Curtis, inventor of the flying boat, the walls are covered with photos of early flying machines. Maps of the region as well as beer plaques complete the decoration.

Open daily during the summer: lunch, 11 A.M. to 2 P.M.; $2–$8 dinner, 5 to 9 P.M. Open Wednesday through Sunday the rest of the

year. Entrées, $7–$14. On the Square, Hammondsport NY 14840; (607) 569-2528.

Lincoln Hill Inn, Canandaigua

The Rochester Philharmonic plays during the summer at the large outdoor Finger Lakes Performing Arts Center that's located a stone's throw from this restaurant. If you come on a night when there's a performance, you will undoubtedly encounter a crowd.

The downstairs rooms have exposed brick walls, a Colonial fireplace, crooked windows, and slightly tilted wide-board floors that date back to 1804. A mural of early Canandaigua Lake, done in a primitive style, covers the wall of the cocktail lounge. You may want to order a glass of wine here so that you can, as we did, study the mural in detail. There are fifteen wines available by the glass; unfortunately, only one is local (Widmer Chardonnay).

We visited on a warm night, so we chose to dine on one of the three porches. Appetizers included mushroom caps casino, coquilles Saint-Jacques, and French artichoke hearts. The refreshingly different salad of tender greens, mandarin oranges, and walnuts came with an orange poppy-seed dressing. There are about twenty entrées. One of the lower priced, chicken breast stuffed with spinach, herbs, feta, and ricotta cheese, was tasty and attractively cut into pinwheel circles. The broiled fresh seafood combination included a lobster tail.

Dinner Monday through Saturday, 4 to 10 P.M.; Sunday, 3 to 8 P.M. Closed Monday during the winter. Entrées $9.95–$28.95. 3365 East Lake Road, Canandaigua, NY 14424; (716) 394-8254.

Geneva on the Lake, Geneva

The intimate Lancelotti dining room with its medieval tapestries, marble floor and fireplace, baby grand piano, and inlaid ceiling overlooks the formal Italian gardens and Lake Seneca. This room is the centerpiece of the twenty-nine-room copy of an Italian Renaissance villa (see *Where to Stay,* page 80). We like the table for two in the smaller side room that's set in front of the window. This table gives a clear view down the middle of the formal gardens. However, the adjacent main dining room is far more ornately decorated.

A limited menu of traditional meals is prepared on the weekends when the dining room is open to the public. Veal medallions are sautéed with large shrimp in a sauce of Dijon mustard, heavy cream, mushrooms, and brandy. Mesquite-grilled tenderloins are served with classic béarnaise sauce. On Sunday evening, beef bourguignon is prepared along with coquille Saint-Jacques and chicken Veronique (chicken breasts sautéed in white wine, cream, and topped with grapes). For a special dessert, try the baked Alaska for two that's flamed with brandy. The bananas Foster is popular, as are the seasonal strawberries Romanoff. The wine list features the better local growers: Heron Hill, Wiemer, Wagner, Frank, Plane's, and Knapp.

Mid-May through October, dinner, Friday and Saturday, 6:30 and 8:30 P.M.; Sunday, 6 to 6:30 P.M. Other times of the year, Friday and Saturday at 7:30 P.M.; Sunday 6–6:30 P.M. Entrées, $17.50–$32. 1001 Lochland Road, Route 14S, Geneva, NY 14456; (315) 789-7190.

Belhurst Castle, Geneva

This ivy-covered, turreted red Medina stone structure overlooking Lake Seneca was built in 1885 in the heavy Richardsonian Romanesque style. The massive wood-and-stone interior reminded us of a castle in Wales or the Scottish Highlands and called for a slab of rare roast prime rib of beef, roast potatoes, and a bottle of burgundy. The menu lists twenty-eight entrées. The châteaubriand for two is served with both a sauce béarnaise and a sauce bordelaise. There are five veal dishes, roast duck, poached or broiled salmon, and several shrimp and crabmeat dishes. There are combination dinners of chicken and scallops, veal and shrimp, and sole and shrimp.

As the restaurant is large, try to come in the quieter, cooler season when you can relax near a glowing fireplace in the dark, wood-paneled library and have a leisurely dinner. If you are driving through and prefer to stop for lunch, ask to sit in the former solarium, an oval-shaped room with windows all around. This a popular stop for bus groups; a hot buffet is served at lunch. If you are on a budget or like to eat early, consider the early-bird limited menu dinner.

Lunch daily, 11:30 A.M. to 2 P.M. except January through mid-March; buffet, $6.70. Dinner Monday through Saturday, 5 to 9:30 P.M.; Sunday, 3 to 9 P.M. Sunday brunch, 11 A.M. to 2 P.M., $11.95. Dinner entreés $15.95–$23.95. Early-bird dinners Monday through Saturday, 5 to 6 P.M., and Sunday, 3 to 5 P.M., $9.95. Route 14S (just south of Geneva on the Lake), Geneva, NY 14456; (315) 781-0201.

James Russell Webster Mansion Inn, Waterloo

For $85 each, a maximum of twelve people can be served what Barbara and Leonard Cohen call "haute cuisine" in the dining room of their 1845 Georgian mansion. Only one entrée is served each night; the first person to call for reservations usually gets to make this choice.

All of the diners sit together on Philadelphia Queen Anne chairs around a Chippendale table. Antiques in this room include a marble statue of a Greek slave, a Chinese ebony and jade screen, and Empire-period sideboards. The room is lit with a five-candle candelabra. New Age music plays in the background. In the summer, dinners are served in the enclosed candlelit porch room off the rear courtyard.

Barbara does all the cooking and Leonard serves. A typical dinner begins with a plate of crudités: olives stuffed with horseradish cheese and pistachio nuts, and assorted artfully cut raw vegetables served with a rich blue-cheese dressing. The second course is a Caesar salad, which is not prepared tableside. The Cohens don't have a license for hard liquor, so they serve all their guests a Wagner or Glenora Seyval Blanc. For the kind of money you're spending on dinner, we recommend that you bring your own favorite wine or a bottle of Champagne.

The pièce de résistance is the one-and-a-half-pound lobster stuffed with Alaskan king crabmeat. Another choice is fresh salmon with sorrel sauce or, in the winter, duck with sauerkraut and apples.

Depending on Barbara's mood, you might have cheesecake with a strawberry-raspberry glaze, a latticed blueberry or peach tart, or a chocolate fudge cake with whipped cream.

The Cohens want you to feel like a guest when you come for dinner. They do not want money to change hands when you are in their home. Therefore, when you make a reservation, your meal is charged to your credit card.

Dinner, 7:30 or 8 P.M., one seating, twelve people maximum. $85 prix fixe. No tipping. Reservations usually are required a week in advance. 115 East Main Street, Routes 5 and 20, Waterloo, NY 13165; (315) 539-3032.

Sherwood Inn, Skaneateles

A traditional dining room in a traditional village inn is what we found on a recent visit to beautiful, historic Skaneateles. Since 1807 there has been an inn at this location, across the street from the lake. Sit by the fireplace in the spacious lobby and listen to the baby grand piano. Men, wear your blue blazers and gray slacks, as the patrons here seemed to dress more conservatively than in Ithaca.

The dinner menu features prime rib, sliced flank steak seasoned with peppercorns and garlic, and baked shrimp stuffed with crab-meat and wrapped with prosciutto. Other choices include chicken breast dipped in cashew nut butter and grilled swordfish. Appetizers include clams casino, escargots, and New York State goat cheese marinated with roasted peppers, herbs, and olive oil. The desserts include homemade pies and tarts, different kinds of cheesecakes, and, for a special occasion, a hot fudge sundae made with Häagen-Dazs ice cream.

If you are not in the mood for a complete dinner, go to the tavern, have a drink or two, and meet the town's young professional crowd. We can vouch for the hot chicken wings as well as the pita bread and hummus dip. Try a burger topped with onions and peppers, or a hot open-faced tuna salad sandwich with provolone. The onion soup topped with croutons and Swiss cheese, served with a spinach salad, goes well with a draft beer or a glass of Finger Lakes Riesling. On Sunday evenings a jazz group plays in the tavern.

Lunch, Monday through Saturday, 11:30 A.M. to 4 P.M.; $4.95–$7.95. Sunday brunch, May–October, 11 A.M. to 2 P.M., $10.95. Dinner, 5 to 9 P.M. daily. Entrées, $10.95–$16.95. Tavern fare, 5 to 9 P.M. $4.95–$7.95. 26 West Genesee Street, Route 20, Skaneateles, NY 13152; (315) 685-3405.

Doug's Fish Fry, Skaneateles

The line stretched out the door along Jordan Street, so we just joined in. Signs above the counter proclaimed, "We fry in pure peanut oil and filter it every day, sometimes twice a day. Then we change it before it needs it." Another sign reads, "I have no waitresses, reservations, credit cards, or coffee. There's no reason for it and there's no rule—it's just my policy."

Having served more than one million fish sandwiches since he opened the restaurant in April 1982, Doug Clark speedily demonstrated his winning technique of mass feeding as we lined up and placed our order. We polished off a large filet of fish sandwich along with a first-rate serving of onion rings and a cup of thick seafood chowder. We'll be back again.

Open Monday through Saturday, 11 A.M. to 9 P.M., Sunday to 10 P.M. Fish sandwich, $2.76; fish dinner, $4.35. 8 Jordan Street, Skaneateles, NY 13152; (315) 685-3288.

LUNCH SPOTS

Ginny Lee Café at Wagner Vineyards

This is the best of the summer lunch cafés. Sit under the canopy or on the deck and enjoy the view of the hills and Lake Seneca. Have a fruit and cheese platter, a Greek or shrimp salad, or a roast beef or turkey sandwich. The creamy peach pie is excellent. Wagner wines and exceptional grape juice are served by the glass.

Open mid-May to mid-October. Monday through Saturday, 11 A.M. to 4 P.M.; $4.75–$6.25. Sunday brunch, 10 A.M. to 2 P.M. (reservations needed); $9.95. Route 414, Lodi, NY 14860; (607) 582-6574.

Wild Winds Farm

This country café is in a scenic spot off a country road. It is set on a farm with flower and herb gardens, walking trails, a maple-sugaring house, and barnyard animals. We had heard so many good things about the restaurant and the foods that were beautifully decorated with edible flowers, that we had high expectations. When we visited, however, the management of the restaurant had changed: A single edible marigold decorated our plate. Burgers, all-natural hot dogs, marinated chicken breast sandwiches, and quiches were served. The strawberry shortcake was made the old-fashioned way with biscuits and real whipped cream.

Open Memorial Day through October, Tuesday through Sunday, 12 to 2 P.M.; $1.95–$6.25. Dinner, Friday and Saturday from 6 P.M. Entrées $15–$19. County Road #36, Naples, NY 14512; (716) 374-5523.

Champagne Country Restaurant at Bully Hill Vineyard

The walls are covered with owner Walter Taylor's art; the views of the lake and the hillside are spectacular. In an adjacent building is a grape museum and a gallery of Walter's art. Homemade spaghetti with meatballs, fresh fettuccine du jour, stuffed grape leaves, Welsh rarebit, and sandwiches are on the menu. Large portions are served.

Open daily May through October, 11:30 A.M. to 3:30 P.M.; $3.25–$6.75. Greyton Hoyt Taylor Memorial Drive, Hammondsport, NY 14840; (607) 868-3490.

RECIPE

Honey-Almond Duck

We've tried countless ducks in many fine restaurants. None had quite hit the mark until we tasted the duck at the Rose Inn: The meat is moist, there isn't a layer of fat, and the skin is crisp and flavorful. Sherry Rosemann serves this incredible duck at the inn by special request. It is surprisingly easy to prepare.

One 5-pound duck, thawed   *½ cup sliced almonds*
  ½ cup honey   *2 tablespoons Dijon mustard*
  ¼ cup orange marmalade

Preheat oven to 250° F. Put the duck breast side up in a roasting pan just big enough to hold it snugly. Do not use a roasting rack. Cook for 5 or 6 hours at 250°. Let it cool. Drain off the fat. Remove the backbone and the rib cage, leaving only the leg and wing bones. Cut the duck into quarters. Scrape off any bits of fat that still remain on the skin.

Lightly grease a 9- by 12-inch pan with oil or vegetable spray. Put the pieces of duck, skin side up, on the pan. Cook at 450°–500°F for 10 to 15 minutes until the skin is crisp.

In a small bowl, mix the honey, marmalade, almonds, and mustard for the glaze. Spoon over each piece of duck. Cook at 400°F for 6 to 10 minutes until the almonds are toasted.

YIELD: 3 servings.

Note: To make three generous portions, Sherry takes the meat from a quarter of the duck and adds it to the other three portions. She serves the duck with a savory herb stuffing; it's also good served with wild rice. To make the rice more flavorful, cook the duck giblets to make a soup stock. After deboning the duck, add the carcass to the stock and continue cooking. Use this broth instead of water to cook the wild rice.

ITINERARY

Touring some of the wineries, taking a boat trip on one of the lakes, and hiking among gorges and waterfalls in the state parks are highlights of a visit to the Finger Lakes. This itinerary is a sampling of all that this area has to offer. From one end of the region (see map, page 52) to the other is about a two-hour drive. Depending on how much time you have to spend in the area, you may find it desirable to stay in two different parts of this region.

DAY ONE. Drive along the western shore of Lake Cayuga to the **Taughannock Falls** overlook. Continue along the Cayuga Wine Trail (Route 89) visiting **Hosmer, Plane's**, and **Knapp wineries**. Stop at **Misty Meadow Farm** if you want to visit a pig farm. Drive to **Wagner Vineyard** and dine outdoors at the **Ginny Lee Café**. Take a walk along the gorge at **Watkins Glen State Park** or drive back to Ithaca to **Buttermilk Falls** or **Robert Treman State Park**. Dine elegantly at **Rose Inn** or casually at **Joe's**.

DAY TWO. Spend the day in Corning. Start at the **Corning Glass Center**. Walk along the restored **Market Street** and visit the **Rockwell Museum**. Enjoy a fine wine with your dinner at **Benn Conger Inn**, or dine in Ithaca at **Abby's** or at **Moosewood**.

DAY THREE. If you are a birder, get up early for a walk in **Sapsucker Woods**. Drive north on Route 90, stopping at **MacKenzie-Childs** pottery factory in Aurora. Continue to Seneca Falls to the **Women's Rights National Historic Park** and the **Women's Hall of Fame**. Continue to Skaneateles, where you may want to take the lunch cruise on the lake. Otherwise, have lunch at **Doug's Fish Fry** or at the **Sherwood Inn**. Explore the back roads, stopping at **Robinia Deer Farm** or at **New Hope Mills**. Dine in the Ithaca area at **The Station** or at **Taughannock Farms Inn**. If you are staying in the Geneva area, dine at **Belhurst Castle, Geneva on the Lake**, or the **James Russell Webster Mansion Inn**.

DAY FOUR. Visit **Rose Hill Mansion** outside of Geneva. Then drive to Canandaigua to stroll through **Sonnenberg Gardens**. Have lunch at the café or continue to Naples to **Wild Winds**

Farm. The **Keuka Wine Trail** on the west side of the lake, especially the view from **Heron Hill**, is spectacular. If you have time, other wineries between Keuka and Seneca Lake to visit are **McGregor** and **Wiemer**. Dine casually at the **Village Tavern** in Hammondsport.

Getting to the Area

Because this chapter covers a large area, the directions to the part of the Finger Lakes region where you are going may vary.

To Ithaca: From New York City take I-80 west to I-380 north to I-81 north. From Pennsylvania take I-81 north to Route 17 west. At Owego take Route 96 north to Candor; then Route 96B to Ithaca.

To Geneva: Follow the above directions but exit Route 17 (beyond Elmira); take Route 14 north to Geneva.

BUDGETING YOUR TRIP

To help you get the most for your money, here are some travel suggestions at three budget levels (cost per day at peak season with two people sharing a room, including tax, 15% gratuity at meals, and service charges). Prices are approximate and intended for planning purposes only. Lodgings are categorized by price. Meal prices at lunch include an average entrée and beverage. Dinner prices include an appetizer, entrée, beverage, and dessert. Wine or alcoholic drinks are not included. Admission prices vary widely based on activities.

Staying and Dining at Expensive Lodgings and Restaurants: From $240 to $510 per day for two.

Lodging: Rose Inn (Jacuzzi suites) $193–$275; J. P. Morgan House (suite) $160–$187; Geneva on the Lake (1 and 2 bedrooms) $246–$345; Belhurst Castle (suites) $187–$241; James Russell Webster Mansion Inn $321; Buttermilk Falls B&B (Jacuzzi suite) $204.

Dining: Breakfast: included except at Belhurst Castle $15;

James Russell Webster Mansion Inn $20–$30. Lunch: Sherwood Inn, Belhurst Castle $20. Dinner: Rose Inn, $100; James Russell Webster Mansion Inn $170; Geneva on the Lake $80.

Admissions: Corning Glass Center $10; Sonnenberg Gardens $10; Rockwell Museum $6; Rose Hill Mansion $4; wineries $10; lake cruise $30.

Staying and Dining at Moderately Priced Lodgings and Restaurants: From $160 to $320 per day for two.

Lodging: Rose Inn $110-$165; Geneva on the Lake $181–$213; Benn Conger Inn $82–165; Belhurst Castle $96–$134; Lake Keuka Manor $81–$103; Rosewood Inn $86–$110; Sherwood Inn $77–$99; Taughannock Farms Inn $82–$137; Buttermilk Falls B&B $93–$110; J. P. Morgan House $91–$112.

Dining: Breakfast: included except at Belhurst Castle ($15). Lunch: Ginny Lee Café, Wild Winds, or Bully Hill $15–$20. Dinner: Benn Conger Inn $60; Abby's $60; The Station $60; Taughannock Farms Inn $65; Sherwood Inn $50; Lincoln Hill Inn $60; Belhurst Castle $70.

Admissions: Corning Glass Center $10; Sonnenberg Garden $10; state parks $6; wineries $10; lake cruise $30.

Staying and Dining at Less Expensive Lodgings and Restaurants: From $100 to $170 per day for two.

Lodging: Red House Country Inn $51–$82; Buttermilk Falls B & B $71–$84; Sherwood Inn $66–$83.

Dining: Breakfast: included. Lunch: Doug's Fish Fry $10–$15. Dinner: Geneva on the Lake (early bird) $25; Sherwood Inn (tavern) $25; Joe's $35; Moosewood $35; Village Tavern $35.

Admissions: Corning Glass Center, $10; Sonnenberg Garden, $10; state parks, $6; wineries, $10; lake cruise, $30.

SUGGESTED READING

Slim Fingers Beckon, Arch Merrill. Empire State Books, Box 299, Interlaken NY, 14837; $8.50 postpaid. First published in 1951. The author writes about the details of history and the personalities of the lakes, towns, and villages in the region: "Owasco Lake is a sapphire gem of purest ray serene seemingly born to shimmer unseen, away from the casual tourist's gaze"; "Seneca lake is a lovely vixen"; "One notes a New England influence in the architecture of the older houses. That is because there lived in the village from 1812 to 1820 an artisan who came directly from Salem, Mass. It was he who built the 'Salem doorways' and added other touches that made the old homes of Skaneateles so distinctive."

The Grapevine's Finger Lakes Magazine. Published bi-monthly by Grapevine Press, 108 South Albany Street, Ithaca, NY 14850; (607) 272-3470 or (800) 331-1413 (New York State only). One-year subscription (six issues), $10. This is a seventy-page magazine with color photos. Articles feature people working in the region's vineyards, crafts, farms, sailing, fishing, boating, and so on. Each issue includes a detailed calendar of events.

THREE

NIAGARA-ON-THE-LAKE, ONTARIO

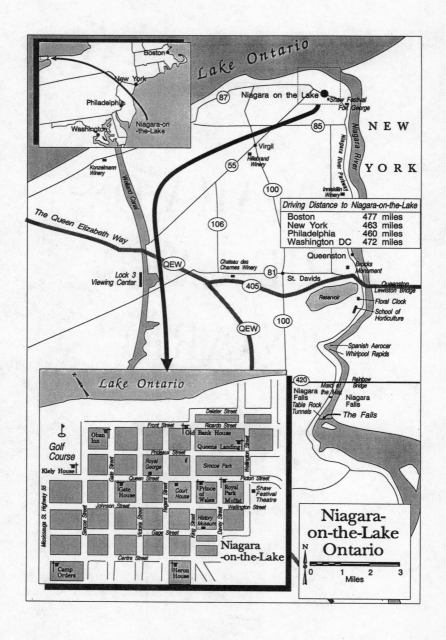

Niagara-on-the-Lake is a timeless, picturesque Victorian town that brings us back year after year for its fabulous Shaw Theater Festival. This graciously hospitable town offers just the right amount of recreational stimulation and happens to be twenty minutes north along a horticultural parkway from Niagara Falls, one of the grand natural phenomena in all the world. If you long to call at least a temporary halt to your hectic pace, catch your breath, and relax, Niagara-on-the-Lake has just what you need.

From 1792 through 1797, the town was the capital of Upper Canada. It's a natural for U.S. visitors, since it was settled by Americans—refugee loyalists leaving the United States after the Revolutionary War. But the first real wave of American "visitors" were New York militia under George McClure during the War of 1812. Frantically fleeing before the British attack in 1813, they stayed only long enough to show the residents a really "hot time in the old town"—by burning the place to the ground.

Rebuilt after the war, Niagara-on-the-Lake today boasts beautifully maintained historic homes. Spared further catastrophes over the next 150 years, this peaceful town lets you step back into the nineteenth century. There are well-kept gardens, manicured lawns, stately flowering chestnuts, maples, and firs lining the streets, and clean, litter-free parks.

Along these same tree-lined avenues, you'll find sixty-five of the

JANE STAUFFER

The Prince of Wales Hotel is at the center of picturesque Niagara-on-the-Lake.

best-organized B&Bs ever assembled in one place. We have never before found such a wonderful system for aiding travelers who appreciate special lodgings and personal treatment.

More than fifty homes are registered with the area Chamber of Commerce (so you know they're on the up-and-up), inspected by the fire marshal (so you're assured they're safe), and restricted to renting out just three rooms (so you're guaranteed personal attention). For a modest $5 fee, the Chamber of Commerce will play "matchmaker" and pair you up with the ideal lodgings for your needs, preferences, and tastes.

Niagara-on-the-Lake Chamber of Commerce. 153 King Street (corner of King and Prideaux), Niagara-on-the-Lake, Ontario LOS 1JO, Canada; (416) 468-4263. May through August: Monday through Friday, 9 A.M. to 7 P.M.; Saturday, 11 A.M. to 7 P.M.; Sunday, 10 A.M. to 6 P.M. September through October 15: Monday through Friday, 9 A.M. to 5 P.M.; Saturday, 10 A.M. to 6 P.M. October 16 through April 30: Monday through Friday, 9 A.M. to 5 P.M.

SPECIAL EVENTS THROUGHOUT THE YEAR

Late April through Early November.   Shaw Festival. Plays, musicals given nightly, matinees. Closed Mondays. Niagara-on-the-Lake; (416) 468-2172.

Late May.   Virgil Stampede. Rides, food, horse shows, crafts, fireworks. Virgil Centennial Arena, Virgil (about three miles from Niagara-on-the-Lake); (416) 468-7020.

First Saturday in June.   Niagara Foundation House Tour through Niagara-on-the-Lake's historic homes; (416) 684-1165.

Early July.   Canada Day Celebrations. Picnic in Simcoe Park, parade to Fort George, fireworks. Niagara-on-the-Lake; (416) 468-4263.

Artistry by the Lake. The work of artists and artisans is displayed in a picturesque setting. Queen's Royal Park, Niagara-on-the-Lake; (416) 468-4263.

Early December.   Christmas Shopping Showcase. Shopping displays, concerts. Shaw Festival Theater, Niagara-on-the-Lake; (416) 468-4263.

WHERE TO GO, WHAT TO DO

The Shaw Theater Festival.   All the town's a stage . . . at least that's how it seems. From late April through early November, three theaters in town present plays from 1850 to 1950. This is roughly the century bracketing the life of George Bernard Shaw (1856–1950), the famous Irish dramatist, critic, and novelist. No other theater festival in the world specializes in Victorian, Edwardian, and Georgian plays.

The festival is first-rate, as good or better than much of the theater we see in New York City. A recent production we enjoyed was *Cavalcade,* written by Noel Coward in the 1930s and the basis for the popular PBS series "Upstairs, Downstairs." The costume department made over 400 costumes, worn in twenty-one vignettes, to portray life in England from 1900 to 1930.

Other recent favorites have been Shaw's *Major Barbara*, Barrie's *Peter Pan* (the all-time classic), and Cole Porter's musical *Anything Goes* (remember the song "I Get a Kick Out of You"?).

Musicals and mysteries at the Royal George are the most popular plays, so make your reservations far in advance, especially for performances on Saturday night.

Because of the changing value of the Canadian dollar against the U.S. dollar, it is far easier to phone the box office and to pay using your credit card. Rush seats for unsold tickets of weekday plays go on sale at 10 A.M. on the day of the performance, for $10 to $12 each depending on the theater. There are also some special performances when tickets are up to $12 off the regular price, and special matinees when seniors and students pay just $10. Wheelchair access is available at the Festival Theater; tickets $17 to $39.

Write Shaw Festival Box Office, Box 774, Niagara-on-the-Lake, Ontario LOS 1JO, Canada, or call (416) 468-2172 any day, 10 A.M. to 9 P.M., to get a current listing of plays.

SHOPPING

Stroll the main street of Niagara-on-the-Lake and you'll see many interesting shops, including three ice cream parlors, two "fudgeries," and a pair of bakeries—more than enough to satisfy anyone's sweet tooth. Generally, though, our favorite "fast-food" spots tended to be of a different nature. Here are our top choices for this area.

Kurtz Orchard. Motoring around the Niagara peninsula, you'll notice an abundance of farm markets. This area is the heart of Ontario's "fruit belt." You'll be tempted to stop, but hold out for Kurtz Orchard, by far the best of the bunch.

The Kurtz family works hard, and it shows. Their stand has excellent produce, plus a juice bar, bakery, and salad bar with over two dozen items to satisfy your immediate cravings. You'll find yourself dawdling over the interesting tidbits they've posted about how many acres the family orchards have devoted to various fruit trees, or the country of origin for any produce that isn't locally grown.

We stopped here several times to get salads for a light lunch or pre-theater meal. You'll find Kurtz's on the Niagara Parkway just before entering town.

Trisha Romance Gallery. This gallery is perfectly at home in a Victorian gingerbread house. Step through the gate in the white picket fence, past the wicker chairs on the porch, and enter the world of Trisha Romance. Trisha is a respected artist in her thirties who paints delightful watercolors of her children. She has a genius for capturing those fleeting childhood moments one wishes could be captured on film. Trisha makes a limited-edition run of 950 prints of each painting, which she signs and sells for $130 to $190 apiece (the originals, which are auctioned off each year, sell for around $15,000!).

The prints go quickly; as we walked around the gallery on our last visit, we overheard a woman lamenting that she had been unable to buy one of Trisha's prints before they had all been sold. 177 King Street, just off Queen; (416) 468-4431.

Note: If you pay more than $7 in Ontario tax on any item you take out of Canada within thirty days of purchase, you can get a full refund. Ask a customs officer for the brochure "Provincial Sales Tax Refunds for Visitors to Ontario" when you cross the U.S.–Canadian border.

Greaves Jams. William Greaves established his business on this same corner fifty years ago, using his wife's recipes and produce from the family farm. Today, Greaves makes a large variety of jams, marmalades, and preserves using the same recipes. 55 Queen Street; (416) 468-2512.

Loyalist Village. You're sure to find something you like in this wonderful shop. The large selection of high quality, handmade Canadian clothing and crafts includes sheepskin hats and boots, leather jackets, feather purses, carved decoys, soapstone and ivory carvings, even designer-type matching sweaters and skirts. You'll also find some very unusual one-of-a-kind items—all at prices that we found reasonable, especially figuring in the exchange rate. 12 Queen Street; (416) 468-7331.

Cobble Stone Galleries. It's certainly worth your time to check out this gallery with its striking display of paintings and sculpture by contemporary Canadian artists. Enjoy a snack of cheese, crackers, and coffee served in china cups. 223 King Street; (416) 468-2097.

Old Niagara Bookstore.   If you like bookshops as much as we do, you're going to find this one a gem. We were particularly impressed with the large selection of travel and history books covering the region, as well as its collection of the plays being presented at the Shaw Festival. 44 Queen Street; (416) 468-2602.

HISTORIC SITES

Fort George National Historic Park.   We were quite startled the first time a staff member in period military dress turned the corner in front of us, but he was very disarming and eager to answer our questions. Then he excused himself to participate in interpreting the period from August 1811 to July 1812.

That's the way it went all day in this fort where past and present happily co-exist. Military craftsmen in the artificers' shops and the cook in the officers' kitchen provide authentic glimpses into the life of a soldier nearly two hundred years ago, just before the start of the War of 1812. British officers were housed at this outpost, where they were expected to live like gentlemen. There is even a pianist in period dress playing the pianoforte in the officers' games room.

We found the audiovisual presentations particularly worthwhile.

The park is open mid-May through October, 9 A.M. to 5 P.M. Demonstrations are held throughout the day. Adults, $2; children 5 to 16, $1; children under 5 and seniors free. You will find Fort George just as you enter Niagara-on-the-Lake from the south; (416) 468-4257.

Niagara Historical Society Museum.   In the beginning, there were Iroquois Indians. Then came the United Empire Loyalists Immigration, the War of 1812, and the Victorian and Edwardian eras. With its collection of some 20,000 artifacts, including many

documents and papers from the late eighteenth and early nineteenth centuries, this museum traces the area's colorful background.

Open daily April through October, 10 A.M. to 5 P.M.; November,
December, March, 1 to 5 P.M. Saturday, Sunday 1 to 5 P.M. the rest
of the year. Admission, $2. Inquire at the museum about the guided
walking tours of the town, which are given periodically. Castle-
reagh and Davy Streets; (416) 468-3912.

Laura Secord Homestead.   In 1813, the Americans carefully
planned a surprise attack they hoped would help bring the war that
had started the previous year to a speedy close. But a daring young
woman named Laura Secord slipped out from under their watchful
eyes, and this Canadian "Pauline Revere" traveled nineteen miles
through the underbrush to warn the British that "The Yanks are
coming, the Yanks are coming."

We think it is worth a stop to read the large outdoor display
retelling the legend. The homestead is typical of the period; guided
tours are given by women in appropriate period costume.

Open daily in spring, summer, and fall. Located ten minutes
south of Niagara-on-the-Lake in Queenston.

NIAGARA FALLS

Of course you'll go to see the falls. With 100,000 cubic feet of
water taking a 170-foot plunge each second, it's one of the largest
in the world. The falls are truly a spectacular sight, and a very
entertaining way to spend the day.

People Mover.   To avoid the hassles of parking and driving
around tourist-packed Niagara Falls, we heartily recommend taking
the people mover, which runs throughout the day from the falls up
the parkway to the floral clock (a clock with a face made of live
plants) and makes stops all along the way. During the summer, the
transit system operates 8 A.M. to 11:30 P.M.; hours are shorter during
the winter. The best place to park is the Rapids View parking lot.
An all-day pass is $4.50 for adults, $2 for children.

Drive down to the falls after dinner one evening to see them illuminated—it's an absolutely stunning sight!

Following are details on each of the major attractions near the falls.

Table Rock Scenic Tunnels.   Tunnel attendants give you yellow slickers to put on. Then you descend via elevator about 120 feet below the gorge embankment, 24 feet above the river's edge, to get a close view of the falls from an observation deck and tunnels behind the falls. You will get wet here, but you'll have fun doing it!

Open all year, 9 A.M. to 5 P.M.; to 11 P.M. during the summer. Adults, $4.25; senior citizens, $3.85; children, $2.15; under 6 free. Call (416) 358-3268 for information.

Maid of the Mist Boat Tour.   Diesel boats leave from both the Canadian side (docking at the foot of Cliften Hill Street) and the American side (docking at Prospect Point) to transport you to the Horseshoe Basin directly in front of the falls. Waterproof slickers are provided.

Boats leave at various intervals starting at 9 A.M., from mid-May until October 24. Adults, $7; children, $3.90; under 6 free. Incline railway, 75¢. (416) 358-5781.

The Maid of the Mist boats have been a popular attraction at Niagara Falls since 1846.

Great Gorge Trip and Daredevil Museum. Descent via elevator to the river's edge to view exhibits of Niagara's famous (and some not-so-famous) daredevils, and to stroll on boardwalks beside the rapids of the lower Niagara River.

Open 9 A.M. to 9 P.M. during July and August; 9:30 A.M. to 7:30 P.M. in May and September; 9:30 A.M. to 5:30 P.M. in October. Adults, $3.50; senior citizens, $3.15; children, $1.75. Located north of the Whirlpool Rapids Bridge on River Road; (416) 356-2241.

Whirlpool Aerocar, Niagara Spanish Aerocar. Suspended over the churning river and the whirlpool basin, you are in for quite an exciting ride as you travel over the Niagara Gorge in a tram. Open May to mid-October: May to Labor Day; daily, 9 A.M. to dusk, Labor Day to mid-October daily, 9 A.M. to 5 P.M. Adults, $3.50; senior citizens, $3.15; children, $1.75. Located two miles below the falls, near the Great Gorge Trip and Daredevil Museum; (416) 356-2241.

Niagara Parkway. Niagara means "Big Water" in the Iroquois language, and the falls are big on beauty. But through the years, they have caused inhabitants of the area no end of transportation trouble. Today, the canals and roads built to circumvent the falls are rewarding travel experiences in themselves.

This scenic 35-mile drive starts at Niagara-on-the-Lake and heads south along the Niagara River to Fort Erie, passing through 2,800 acres of the Niagara Parks System.

Floral Clock. Among the highlights is a 40-foot-diameter floral clock formed by 15,000 plants. The Centennial Lilac Gardens, featuring 256 varieties with over 1,500 shrubs, is in bloom from May until early June. Just writing this brings back their heady aroma.

School of Horticulture. Motor on to the School of Horticulture and enjoy a visual feast of over 100 acres of immaculate gardens. We could easily spend a full day here. An endless variety of iris and Canada's finest collection of ornamental trees and shrubs are on display at the arboretum here. Located 5 miles north of the falls on Niagara Parkway. Grounds open daily throughout the year; (416) 356-8554.

There are dozens of lovely spots to stop for picnics and view the Niagara River. Pick up the parkway driving south out of Niagara-on-the-Lake on Queen Street.

WINE TOURS

A combination of warm winters and cool summers, due to the moderating effects of Lake Ontario and the Niagara River as well as the shelter from the cliff-like Niagara escarpment, make this region ideal for growing fine European wine grapes.

Winemakers from France and Germany began making quality wines from the vinifera grapes in the 1970s. Today, the Niagara region is starting to be recognized as a top producer of award-winning wines. There are sixteen wineries located in the Niagara area that produce high-quality varietals from Riesling, Chardonnay, Gamay Beaujolais, Pinot Noir, and other fine grapes. Following are four vineyards, all of which provide tours as well as tastings.

Chateau des Charmes.   In the course of our private tour, we observed the attention given to pruning the vines, then tasted the delicious results of wines made in the French style: an excellent Pinot Noir and a fine oak-aged Chardonnay.

Tours and tastings are given Monday through Saturday at 11 A.M., 1:30 and 3 P.M. Located on Four Mile Creek Road in the town of St. Davids; (416) 262-5202.

Hillebrand.   We were proudly shown a new 10,000-liter state-of-the-art computerized wine press, so gentle that "off-flavors" do not taint the juice. This winery produces a fine Eiswein that has won prestigious medals at international competitions.

Tours and tastings are available Monday through Saturday at 11 A.M. and 1, 3, and 5 P.M., with deluxe tours by appointment. Located on Highway 55; (416) 468-7123.

Inniskillin.   In the Champagne loft here we saw how *vin mousseux* is made using the traditional *méthode champenoise.* The Inniskillin product receives a lot of publicity these days, as it is now served on Air Canada as well as at the Helmsley Palace Hotel in New York City. Tours and tastings are given Monday through Saturday at 10:30 A.M. The winery is on Line 3, just off the Niagara Parkway; (416) 468-2187.

Konzelmann Vineyards.   The German-style wines produced by Herbert Konzelmann on forty acres along Lakeshore Road are traditionally light and fruity. The 1986 Gewurztraminer put him on the wine map. Call for tour times; (416) 935-2866.

WELLAND CANAL

Have you ever seen a 1,400-ton moving oil tanker from a distance of about twenty-four feet? It is an awesome experience! On a good day at Lock 3, you can meet at least one ocean-going behemoth, and a number of smaller "lakers," up close and personal.

The canal was built to circumvent Niagara Falls, and connect Lake Erie with Lake Ontario. Eight locks raise and lower vessels 325 feet. It takes a ship twelve hours to travel the full length of the canal, but they go up and down much faster as twenty-five million gallons of water fills or empties each lock in about ten minutes.

The complex, which includes a visitors center showing audio-visual presentations on the canal's history, an information booth, a restaurant, gift shop, and the St. Catherine's museum, is open all year. Summer hours are 9 A.M. to 9 P.M.; the rest of the year, 9 A.M. to 6 P.M. Ships traverse the canal from spring, when the ice breaks on the Great Lakes, until December 25, the official closing date of Great Lakes shipping. Call beforehand for the day's schedule so you can plan your visit to coincide with a ship's transit. The Lock 3 viewing center is located at the end of Route 55 and is easy to find. Follow the blue and white signs that appear as you approach the Queen Elizabeth Way (Q.E.W.). If you are driving on the Q.E.W., exit at Glendale Avenue (Route 89) and follow the signs; (416) 685-3711 or (416) 688-6462.

WHERE TO STAY

In addition to the sixty-five fine bed-and-breakfasts we mentioned in the introduction, Niagara-on-the-Lake boasts some lovely inns and hotels. Arrangements to stay at most of the accommodations can be conveniently arranged through the helpful staff of the Niagara-on-the-Lake Chamber of Commerce, tourism section, located at 153 King Street (corner of King and Prideaux), (416) 468-4263. For a fee of $5, which you can charge to your credit card, the staff will match you with lodgings to fit your every requirement.

Request accommodations according to price range; whether you prefer twin, double, queen- or king-size beds; a private or shared bath; with or without breakfast. Inquire about the acceptability of children, pets, or smoking. Specify if you'd like air conditioning, a pool, a historic establishment, or lodgings within walking distance of the center of town.

Prices range from $45 to $110 for a double room with breakfast; most cost around $75. The homes we stayed in were clean, the breakfasts large, and the hosts eager to fill us in on historic information, places to visit, restaurant suggestions, and the like.

All B&Bs are inspected by the fire marshal, as well as the Chamber of Commerce. Ontario law states that no B&B may rent out more than three rooms, so you are assured personal attention.

The Niagara-on-the-Lake Chamber of Commerce office is open from May through August: Monday through Friday, 9 A.M. to 7 P.M.; Saturday, 11 A.M. to 7 P.M.; Sunday, 10 A.M. to 6 P.M. September through October 15: Monday through Friday, 9 A.M. to 5 P.M.; Saturday, 10 A.M. to 6 P.M. October 16 through April 30: Monday through Friday, 9 A.M. to 5 P.M. The best time to call for reservations and information is in the morning.

Please remember: all prices are quoted in Canadian dollars.

Gate House Hotel

Here in Victorian Niagara-on-the-Lake is a truly luxurious, contemporary Italian hotel. Lots of glass, brass, shades of gray and black, and stained glass windows introduce guests to the stark lobby. The owner is an Italian industrialist who has vacationed here for the last ten years and wanted to create a little part of his homeland in Niagara-on-the-Lake. Most of the interior, including the Ristorante Giardino (see *Where to Dine,* page 124), was built in Italy and shipped to the site.

The hotel does stand out on the Victorian main street. The guest rooms are sumptuous if you like the modern high-tech look. All the rooms have mini bars, Sony televisions, black leather couches and chairs, angular designer lamps, and muted gray wall-to-wall carpeting. The bathrooms have double sinks, hair-dryers, bidets, beveled-glass showers, and floor-to-ceiling tiles. Large contemporary paintings by Canadian artists provide color in the rooms.

Ten rooms; eight with two double beds, $125–$165, and two with queen-size beds, $147. Breakfast is available but not included. 142 Queen Street, Box 1364, Niagara-on-the-Lake, Ontario LOS 1JO, Canada; (416) 468-3263.

The Kiely House Inn

This large, white grande dame was built in 1832 and is owned by Heather and Ray Pettit. It is located at one end of the main street, adjoining the golf club, a block away from the water. Here we were able to enjoy the quiet surroundings and still were able to walk comfortably to all parts of the town.

Over the entranceway is an appealing Palladian window. Dominating the first floor is the unique, formally furnished double parlor with twin working fireplaces adorned with intricately carved walnut mantels.

We stayed in room 6, the original master suite. The queen-size four-poster bed with a full, rose-colored, floor-length canopy seemed small in this spacious room. Floral-patterned wallpaper, pine floors, small scatter rugs, an antique armoire, a working fireplace, and even an extra-large Victorian bath with a clawfoot tub are all found here. A wide, spacious classic porch overlooking the gardens and adjacent golf course completes the tranquil setting of this deluxe accommodation.

Another suite across the hall, room 8, has a softer feel. A large wool carpet and wallpaper of warm rose and Wedgwood blue complement the love seat, antique writing desk, and four-poster queen-size bed. A modern bath, working fireplace, and adjoining porch add the perfect finishing touches.

Another favorite is the former kitchen, room 10. The mantel over the fireplace is twelve feet wide and dominates the room. As you lie in bed, imagine what it must have been like to prepare meals over this fireplace. A screened-in private porch looking out over the back garden extends from this room.

JANE STAUFFER

The first floor of the Kiely House Inn has a double parlor with twin working fireplaces.

In addition to these three rooms, and another of similar proportions, there are nine smaller rooms, some of which are located in what formerly were the servants' quarters. We suggest that you stay in the larger, far more elegant accommodations, or stay elsewhere.

A pleasant touch is the working fireplace in the breakfast room where muffins, scones, and croissants are served along with cereal, fresh fruit, and juices.

After breakfast, wander among the extensive planting of rose bushes in the garden. Bicycles are available free to the guests for exploring the town, the Niagara Parkway, or the shores of Lake Ontario.

Thirteen rooms, all with private bath, $85–$165. Breakfast included. Children not encouraged. No pets. 209 Queen Street, P.O. Box 1642, Niagara-on-the-Lake, Ontario LOS 1J0, Canada; (416) 468-4588.

The Old Bank House

The Old Bank House is the one exception to the "three-room" rule for B&Bs in Niagara-on-the-Lake. This historic, circa 1817 structure was the first bank in Upper Canada. If you are interested, ask to see the original vault chamber.

Ownership of the inn has changed several times in the past five years, with each new owner adding his or her special touch. The current owners, Marjorie and Don Ironmonger, like the Laura Ashley look. The inn is located a short two blocks from the center of town on a half-acre lot directly across the street from Lakefront Park near the mouth of the Niagara River. On a recent visit we stayed in the Garden Room, which has a double bed, private bath, private entrance, and trellised deck. It has a small refrigerator along with coffee, tea, and supplies for brewing. Our favorite accommodation is the Gallery Suite, with a double bed in a large room overlooking the garden and the lake. It has a dressing room, a modern bathroom, and a private entrance off the front porch. This room also has a refrigerator and is stocked with coffee and tea. The Rose Suite at the back of the house has two bedrooms, one with a twin bed and one with a double, as well as a sitting room and a private bath.

Our least favorite accommodations, which we don't recommend, are the four second-floor rooms. Each has a wash basin but all share one bath.

The living room has a working fireplace with comfortable chairs and books about the region. A full English country breakfast is served at one end of the living room. For breakfast we had porridge served with honey, brown sugar, and cream; scrambled eggs; breakfast sausage; herbed tomatoes; Kedgeree, a spiced Indian rice dish; and muffins. Marjorie and Don make a special effort to do nice things for their guests, such as staying up late to create a special dish for breakfast or remembering birthdays and anniversaries.

Six rooms, two with private bath, $110, $105. Four rooms with sinks share two toilets and one shower, $88. Two suites with private bath, $125, $195. All rooms air-conditioned. A full breakfast is included. Rates 25% lower from November 1 to March 31. Children over 12, $15 additional. Pets allowed in some rooms. 10 Front Street, Box 1708, Niagara-on-the-Lake, Ontario LOS 1JO, Canada; (416) 468-7136.

The Oban Inn

Sitting over cocktails before a roaring fire in the pub at the Oban Inn one evening, we had a particularly animated and satisfying discussion about the Shaw Festival. Little wonder—looking up from our drinks, we saw on the walls above us a large oil painting of G. B. Shaw himself, and many photographs of scenes from his plays.

The pub here can help you get into the "spirit" of things, but the Oban Inn offers many other attractions as well. The house was built about 1824 for Duncan Milloy, a sea captain from Scotland. This inn is the area's most popular hostelry. Making reservations here is difficult, especially during the Shaw Festival season. Because the inn does a large restaurant business and there is a constant influx of diners (see *Where to Dine,* page 125) as well as outsiders who enjoy coming for a drink or afternoon tea on the enclosed plant-bedecked porch, the inn has the feel of a small hotel. All of the rooms are furnished differently with antique reproductions. Most have double or twin beds. There is one room with a king-size bed and three with queen-size beds. All of the rooms have baths with tubs and most also have showers. All have phones and televisions. The best rooms at the inn are those that overlook the water; of these the choicest ones are in the Oban House, the building next door to the main inn. While these probably are no larger than the rooms in the main inn, they are quieter and seem to be a touch nicer. One apartment/suite has a bedroom with two twin beds and a separate sitting room with a small refrigerator.

Twenty-two rooms, all with private bath, $110–$140; one apartment, $165. Breakfast is available but is not included. Children welcome. Small, well-trained pets permitted. Box 94, Gate Street, Niagara-on-the-Lake, Ontario, LOS 1JO, Canada; (416) 468-2165.

The Prince of Wales Hotel

With 106 rooms, the Prince of Wales does not qualify as an intimate B&B. However, it offers a combination of amenities you won't find at a private home: babysitting, a heated indoor swimming pool, sauna, whirlpool, exercise room, and platform tennis, as well as reception and meeting rooms.

But this establishment is also very different from the usual "hotel." The rooms are attractively arranged in a series of interconnected brick buildings, which are convincingly designed and landscaped to look like two-story brick, nineteenth-century homes. Manicured pocket gardens along the front of the property are overflowing with colorful displays of seasonal flowers. Some rooms offer a fireplace as well as kitchen facilities.

The location is right on the main street, next door to shopping and across the street from the town green. After an evening at the Shaw Festival, guests appreciate having rooms just one block away from the theater.

106 rooms, all with private bath. A standard room with double or twin beds $112–$128. Deluxe rooms and suites, some with fireplaces, balconies, patios, or kitchen facilities, $145–$228. No-

vember through April, $106–$220. Children welcome, $5–$12 additional. Babysitting service with advance notice, $12 extra per child over 2; cribs free. No pets. 6 Picton Street, Niagara-on-the-Lake, Ontario LOS 1JO, Canada; (416) 468-3246; (800) 263-2452..

The Moffat Inn

The four patio garden rooms, each with a private outdoor area set with chairs, are the most popular rooms at this inn just two blocks from the Shaw Festival. Two of the patio rooms also have wood-burning fireplaces, making them a top choice for the cooler seasons. The largest rooms have a queen-size bed or two double beds plus a sitting area.

Each room has a television, phone, and hair-dryer, as well as an electric tea kettle with a supply of coffee and tea.

Twenty-two rooms, all with private bath, $75–$95. Lower rates in the winter. Breakfast is available at the inn's restaurant but is not included. Children welcome; under 13, $5 additional; third adult in room, $10 additional. Box 578, 60 Picton Street, Niagara-on-the-Lake, Ontario LOS 1JO, Canada; (416) 468-4116.

Bed-and-Breakfast Homes

Sixty-five bed-and-breakfast homes in Niagara-on-the-Lake are registered with the Chamber of Commerce. These are two of the families registered with the Chamber of Commerce that take overnight guests.

Camp-Orders House. Fred and Peggy Orders have spent years furnishing and bringing back their 1818 home to near museum quality. A two-story 1830 addition features two guest rooms with private baths and separate entrances. The first-floor room has an original tin bathtub. A breakfast of fruit juice, biscuits, coffee or tea is placed outside your room in the morning. Ask for a tour of the house and have a look at the whimsical stuffed cows that Peggy makes for sale at Toronto craft fairs.

Two rooms, $75. Breakfast is included. 307 Mississauga Street, Niagara-on-the Lake, Ontario LOS 1JO Canada; (416) 468-7996.

Heron House. Katherine and Paul Heron operate this cheerful B&B out of their Victorian-inspired home in one of the residential neighborhoods of Niagara-on-the-Lake. The rooms are clean, air-conditioned, carpeted wall to wall, and decorated in Laura Ashley style with lacy white linens on the brass and white iron beds. There is a deck area for guests' use. The guest rooms are in a section of the house that was designed so that the guests' activities don't interfere with family life and vice versa. Breakfast is fruit salad, tea biscuits, homemade breads, and cereal served on fine china with antique silver. Children are welcome here in the off season if you take both rooms.

Two spacious rooms with private baths, $80. 356 Regent Street, Niagara-on-the-Lake, Ontario LOS 1JO, Canada; (416) 468-4553.

Newer Hotels in Niagara-on-the-Lake

Royal Park Hotel. This hotel, located next to the Shaw Festival theater, opened in June 1990. Standard rooms have two double beds and Colonial-style furnishings. Draperies, quilts, and bedskirts are coordinated. Rooms all have stocked mini-bars; televisions tucked into armoires; phones; and private baths with hairdryers and heat lamps. The deluxe rooms have four-poster queen-size beds, marble-lined baths, double Jacuzzis, and fireplaces.

Twenty-four standard rooms, $120. Ten deluxe rooms, $150–$160. Breakfast is available in the hotel's restaurant but is not included. Children welcome, $10 additional. No pets. 92 Picton Street, Niagara-on-the-Lake, Ontario LOS 1JO, Canada; (416) 468-5711.

Colonel Butler Inn. This hotel opened in May 1990. It is about a twenty-minute walk from the Shaw Festival. Of all the accommodations in this chapter, this one is the farthest from the center of town. Accommodations include rooms with two double beds, queen-size beds, king-size beds, and suites. Some of the rooms and suites have Jacuzzis and fireplaces.

Twenty-six rooms: standard rooms, $105; deluxe rooms, $160. Third person in room $10 additional. No pets. Meals available but not included in rate. 278 Mary Street, Niagara-on-the-Lake, Ontario LOS 1J0, Canada; (416) 468-2050.

Queens Landing Hotel. This hotel opened in January 1990. It is located near the water, within walking distance of the Shaw Festival theater and the shops in town. Standard rooms have two double beds; deluxe rooms have a fireplace and Jacuzzi.

137 rooms, $135–$195. Children under 12, no charge. Third adult in room, $15 additional. Meals available but not included in rate. P.O. Box 1180, 155 Byron Street (corner of Melville Street), Niagara-on-the-Lake, Ontario LOS 1J0, Canada; (416) 468-2195.

WHERE TO DINE

FINE DINING

Ristorante Giardino

The decor is sleek Italian modern with huge picture windows. One hundred and ten lucky diners sit on two levels looking at the hotel's garden and the main street. The stark colors accent the sharp angles of the restaurant. The floors are tile, the walls gray and white. The highly polished marble on the bar and front desk was imported from Verona. You sit on black molded chairs and dine on white Rosenthal china and crystal with angular sides. Silverplate flatware is set on white damask tablecloths. The fresh pink carnations in cut-crystal vases and the large modern paintings by Canadian artists provide color in the restaurant.

The chefs are from Northern Italy. The antipasto offerings were superb. Thin slices of aged tenderloin beef Carpaccio (raw, for the uninitiated) were served with braised vegetables. Authentic Parma ham was wrapped around slices of local melon. Smoked breast of goose was accompanied by sautéed mushrooms with a hint of garlic, and a tasty salad of radicchio, field greens, and bocconcini cheese was served with a basil vinaigrette.

We enjoyed a pasta course of ravioli filled with prosciutto and mascarpone cheese in a strong pesto sauce of basil and pine nuts. Another dish on the menu was fresh pasta seasoned with sage and rosemary and served with lamb sauce. Other selections included cannelloni with turkey and spinach stuffing and penne sautéed with eggplant, pesto, and tomato.

Fish courses included sashimi-size pieces of swordfish marinated in olive oil and herbs and quickly grilled to perfection. Prawns were sautéed and served with truffle cream sauce. Braised escargots with shallots, red wine, and Italian parsley served with grilled polenta had an intense, hearty flavor. A perfectly grilled T-bone steak served rare as requested was served with tasty Italian peppers.

Many of the wines were personally selected by the owners in Italy and imported specially for this restaurant.

If you don't make the tiramisu recipe in this chapter, try the real thing at this restaurant. The Trento chocolate torte is wonderful, as is the cold Italian soufflé with strawberry cream sauce. Finish off the meal with an espresso or cappuccino.

Open for lunch, May through October, 12 to 2 P.M.; prix fixe, $13. Dinner, 5:30 to 8:30 P.M. Entrées, $18–26. Closed Monday November through February; closed in January. 142 Queen Street, Niagara-on-the-Lake, Ontario L0S 1J0, Canada; (416) 468-3263.

The Oban Inn

A large oil painting of G. B. Shaw himself, photographs of scenes from his plays, and a properly prepared Pimm's Cup garnished with cucumber, lemon, orange, a cherry, and mixed with Store's ginger beer appeared altogether right-minded in this thoroughly English inn. We moved to the dining room and sat at a window table overlooking the Niagara River across the road. Large floral arrangements, antiques, and hanging plants enhanced the elegant rooms in the formal dining area.

The consistently well-prepared, conservative menu gives diners plenty to eat; no nouvelle cuisine here. The rack of lamb with a garlic cream sauce and the stuffed pork tenderloin are recommended. Poached salmon, prime rib, and lobster Newburg as well as filet mignon keep most diners happy. A good selection of local wines is on the list. Try a bottle of Herbert Konzelmann's Gewurtstraminer.

The desserts include the popular Grand Marnier frozen soufflé made by whipping heavy cream with Grand Marnier liqueur; the mixture is frozen and served scooped into a delectable chocolate cup. Meringue chantilly, English trifle, and apple crisp are other standard choices. A lighter supper in the $7 to $8 range is available in the pub called Shaw's Corner and in the glass-walled, plant-filled verandah.

Dinner seatings at 5:30 and 8 P.M. during the Shaw Festival season, at 6 and 8 P.M. in the winter. Entrées, $17.50 to $19.75. A lighter bar menu is available until midnight. Gate Street, Niagara-on-the-Lake, Ontario LOS 1JO, Canada; (416) 468-2165.

Prince of Wales Hotel

The main dining room is appointed with well-spaced tables facing flower beds that overflow with seasonal flowers. In the spring, when we were last here, these beds presented a panorama of giant tuberous begonias, rhododendrons, parrot tulips, and Exbury azaleas. At tableside, straw planters filled with bright pink hydrangea bring the outdoors in and contribute to your privacy.

Luncheon entrées we enjoyed were grilled breast of chicken with a light Champagne sauce, and fettucine with tomatoes, basil, and ham. Alas, the dessert menu was too tempting to pass. We recommend the crispy fluted basket filled with scoops of raspberry, blueberry, and peach ice. The colors of the ice and their arrangement of fresh fruits made for a very pretty treat.

The dinner menu includes such favorites as poached salmon served with celery root; rack of lamb with mint or thyme sauce; fricassée of rabbit with wild mushrooms; and whole guinea fowl with Burmese rice stuffing. A bargain is the pub supper, served in the bar, which includes hot sandwiches, barbecued chicken, and other dishes for $5 to $9.

Open daily for lunch, 12 to 2 P.M.; $9.50–$12. Dinner, Tuesday through Saturday, 5:30 to 10 P.M.; Sunday and Monday to 9 P.M. Entrées, $17–$23. 6 Picton Street, Niagara-on-the-Lake, Ontario LOS 1JO, Canada; (416) 468-3246 or (800) 263-2452.

INFORMAL DINING

The Louis House

Just off the main street near the Prince of Wales Hotel, this fixture in town serves up large portions of good food at reasonable prices. The decor includes Colonial-style chandeliers and café curtains with hanging plants in the windows for a clean and pleasant atmosphere.

The night we visited, the specials of the day were poached salmon or New York strip steak; we had the salmon. The price of $18.95 included not only a large portion of salmon, but also potato, carrots, and cauliflower, along with a choice of soup or juice, dessert, and coffee.

The menu featured numerous other fish and meat dishes, all reasonably priced, such as broiled seafood platter, prime rib, lamb chops, and veal scallops. If peaches are in season, be sure to try the peach pie made with a flaky crust and a filling that had many more peaches and less sugar than is customary. Other dessert choices are meringue chantilly, pineapple cheesecake, and the other homemade pies.

Open for lunch daily, 11 A.M. to 5 P.M., $5.95–$8.95. Dinner daily, 5 to 9 or 9:30 P.M. Entrées $9.95–$18.95. 245 King Street, Niagara-on-the-Lake, Ontario LOS 1JO, Canada; (416) 468-4038.

The Buttery Restaurant

The front porch of the Buttery offers a splendid view of the pedestrian traffic on Main Street. Bathed in cool summer breezes, we had the perfect vantage point to watch all of the action.

The fare here has a decidedly European flair featuring a Parisian favorite, croque-monsieur, made with smoked Canadian ham and Swiss cheese on a buttered, grilled roll. Among the other choices are Cornish pastie, a pastry filled with beef and vegetables; welsh rarebit; and steak and kidney pie. It's a great place to come for afternoon tea, served in the English manner with small sandwiches, hot buttered scones, strawberry jam, cakes, and teas.

Weekend nights feature the famous sumptuous Henry VIII feast, now in its nineteenth year. For a set price ($38.50 Saturday, $37.50 Friday), you are served a medieval banquet with four "removes" (courses)—all you can eat or drink. "Magicers musikers" are summoned to the feast for your entertainment.

Open daily, April through mid-November, 11 A.M. to midnight. Other times of the year till 8 P.M., Sunday through Thursday, serving a tavern menu, dinner menu, tea, and after-theater menu Friday and Saturday till midnight. On Mondays only the tavern menu is offered. Lunch, $6.95–$15.95. Dinner entrées, $15.95–$21. Main Street, Niagara-on-the-Lake, Ontario L0S 1J0, Canada; (416) 468-2564.

The Angel Inn

Tucked away off the main street in one of the oldest buildings in town is the Angel Inn, an authentic "Olde Worlde" pub and dining room. Plastered ceiling, exposed hand-hewn wooden beams supported by massive wooden posts, and worn, wide-planked floors create a memorable ambience. The tables are attached to old sewing machine bases. Walls are decorated with old portraits, lanterns, and earthenware jugs.

The service tends to be slow and inconsistent, so don't come if you're in a hurry. Order the roast beef or the half chicken with spicy sauce, or just stop by for chicken wings and beer and soak up the atmosphere.

Open daily. Lunch 11:30 A.M. to 5 P.M., $3.50–$7.95. Dinner from 5 P.M. Entrées $14.95–$23.95. 224 Regent Street, Niagara-on-the-Lake, Ontario L0S 1J0, Canada; (416) 468-3411.

Fan Court Chinese Restaurant

We'd walked by this restaurant for several days and assumed that this was just another standard Chinese restaurant. We stopped for lunch at the suggestion of a local resident, and are glad we did. The decor is typical Chinese, with an attractive, huge bird embroidery on one wall and scrolls and Chinese pictures on the other walls. There are two small rooms with yellow tablecloths and upholstered bamboo chairs.

The specialty was jumbo shrimp served on a sizzling iron plate accompanied by vegetables (the carrots were artfully carved into flower shapes). Filet of beef and vegetables were served in a crunchy noodle basket. Other choices include Szechuan-style scallops, Kung Pao shrimp served with cashew nuts, and vegetables with chili sauce. With a day's notice the chef will prepare traditional Peking duck in two courses: the skin served in pancakes, and the shredded meat stir-fried with vegetables and served in a noodle basket.

Open Tuesday through Sunday. Lunch, 12 to 2:30 P.M.; $5–$7.50. Dinner, 4:30 to 9 P.M.; entrées, $8–$16.80. 135 Queen Street, Niagara-on-the-Lake, Ontario L0S 1J0, Canada; (416) 468-4511.

Queenston Heights Restaurant

This is a dining room with a view. Queenston Heights is at the top of the escarpment overlooking the Niagara River and the peninsula. The panorama from the restaurant's two-story expanse of windows is not to be missed.

Popular lunch choices in the summer include banana and pine nut salad and homemade chilled plum soup. Winter soup specialties include white onion soup and apple cider and brie soup. Popular dinner choices are prime rib, poached salmon, and saddle of hare.

Open year-round. Late May through September, 11:30 A.M. to 9:30 P.M. Other times, lunch 11:30 A.M. to 3 P.M., $6.50–$8.95; dinner

5 to 9 P.M., entrées $13.95–$17. High tea served 3 to 5 P.M. daily in summer and on weekends at other times of the year. Located in Queenston Heights on the Niagara Parkway about a ten-minute drive from Niagara-on-the-Lake; (416) 262-4274.

RECIPE

Tiramisu

Many people feel that this dessert has been overdone, but the recipe is so good that we had to include it. It was brought from the Trentino region of Italy to the Ristorante Giardino by chef Remo Penesa. We have translated the recipe, as the chef speaks only Italian.

5 egg yolks
½ cup sugar
1 pound mascarpone cheese
⅛ teaspoon vanilla extract
3 egg whites

2 cups espresso coffee (the stronger the better)

2 tablespoons Amaretto liqueur
4 tablespoons Marsala wine

2 dozen ladyfingers
½ cup unsweetened cocoa

In a large mixing bowl, beat egg yolks and sugar until mixture is white. Add mascarpone cheese and stir gently. Add vanilla.

In a separate bowl, whip egg whites until peaks form. Fold into egg-yolk mixture.

Combine coffee, Amaretto, and Marsala. Dip each ladyfinger quickly in the mixture and place in bottom of a 9- by 12-inch pan. Cover with a layer of filling, using half the mixture. Repeat the process. Sprinkle cocoa over the top, using a strainer or sifter.

Refrigerate and serve cold.

YIELD: 8 servings

ITINERARY

Highlights of a visit to this area are Niagara Falls, the Shaw Theater Festival and the charm of the town of Niagara-on-the-Lake.

DAY ONE. Take a **walking tour** of Niagara-on-the-Lake. Visit the **shops and galleries**. Drive out to the **Welland Canal** in mid-afternoon. Have an early dinner at the **Oban Inn**. Attend a performance at the **Shaw Festival** in the evening.

DAY TWO. Visit **Niagara Falls**, taking the people mover to **Maid of the Mist, Table Rock Tunnels**, and **Floral Clock**. On your return to Niagara-on-the-Lake, stop and stroll the grounds at the **Horticultural Center**. Have dinner at **Ristorante Giardino**. See another play at the **Shaw Festival**.

DAY THREE. Stop by the **historical museum** in Niagara-on-the-Lake, tour **Fort George**, or head out for a **vineyard** (or two or three). Later, take your seat at a performance at the **Shaw Festival**, or drive down to **Niagara Falls** to see them illuminated. Have dinner at the **Prince of Wales Hotel**.

Getting to the Area

By car. Niagara-on-the-Lake is a twenty-minute drive from Niagara Falls. If you go to the falls first, take the Niagara Parkway north into town.

To get to Niagara Falls from one of the major northeastern cities, take the New York Thruway I-90. Exit onto I-290 (the Buffalo Beltway) heading north, ten miles to I-190. Fifteen miles north on I-190, you'll cross the Canadian border. Immediately after the toll booth, turn right onto the Niagara Parkway. At the stop sign, turn left and follow the parkway six miles north to Niagara-on-the-Lake.

By air. Buffalo Airport is served by US Air. From the airport, get onto I-290, pick up the directions above and you'll be in Niagara-on-the-Lake in about a half-hour.

BUDGETING YOUR TRIP

To help you get the most for your money, here are some travel suggestions at three budget levels (cost per day at peak season with two people sharing a room, including tax, 15% gratuity at meals, and service charges). Prices are approximate and intended for planning purposes only. Lodgings are categorized by price. Meal prices at lunch include an average entrée and beverage. Dinner prices include an appetizer, entrée, beverage, and dessert. Wine or alcoholic drinks are not included. Admission prices vary widely based on activities.

Staying and Dining at Expensive Lodgings and Restaurants: From $360 to $430 per day for two.

Lodging: Old Bank House $205; Kiely House Inn $152–$173; Oban Inn $157–$173; The Gate House Hotel $173; Prince of Wales Hotel $152–$239; Royal Park Hotel $157–$168; Queens Landing Hotel $142–$205; Colonel Butler Inn $168.

Dining: Breakfast included at the Kiely House Inn and the Old Bank House; others $15. Lunch: Ristorante Giardino or Prince of Wales Hotel $30. Dinner: Ristorante Giardino $85; Prince of Wales Hotel $80.

Admissions: Shaw Festival $80; Fort George $4; Maid of the Mist $14; Table Rock Scenic Tunnels $8.50; Aero Car $7.

Staying and Dining at Moderately Priced Lodgings and Restaurants: From $240 to $310 per day for two.

Lodging: Kiely House $110–$142; The Gate House Hotel $131; The Moffat Inn $95–$100; Prince of Wales Hotel $118–$134; Old Bank House $105–$131; Royal Park Hotel $126; Queens Landing Hotel $126; Colonel Butler Inn $110.

Dining: Breakfast: included at Old Bank House; others $15. Lunch: The Buttery, Queenston Heights Restaurant, or Fan Court $20. Dinner: Oban Inn $70; The Louis House, Queenston Heights Restaurant, or The Buttery $50–$60.

Admissions: Shaw Festival $80; Fort George $4; Table Rock Scenic Tunnels $8.50; Maid of the Mist $14.

Staying and Dining at Less Expensive Lodgings and Restaurants: From $170 to $190 per day for two.

Lodging: Old Bank House $92; Kiely House $89; Moffat Inn $79–$100; Heron House $84; Camp-Orders House $79.

Dining: Breakfast: $15; included at Old Bank House, Kiely House Inn, Heron House, and Camp-Orders House; lunch, take out at Kurtz Orchard, $10. Dinner: Angel Inn, Fan Court, $40.

Admissions: Shaw Festival rush seats, $24; Fort George, $4; Maid of the Mist, $14; Scenic Rock Tunnels, $8.50.

SUGGESTED READING

The Old Niagara Bookstore is an excellent source for books about local history as well as writings by and about George Bernard Shaw, including the current plays being presented at the Shaw Festival. 44 Queen Street, Niagara-on-the-Lake, Ontario L0S 1J0 Canada; (416) 468-2602.

Ontario's Niagara Parks, George A. Seibel. Niagara Falls, Ontario: The Niagara Parks Commission, 1987; 344 pages, $20. Many historical photographs, maps, paintings in color and black and white. Starting with the early European explorers in the sixteenth century, this history of the establishment of tourism at Niagara Falls is richly illustrated with paintings, photographs, and maps. The book includes a full chapter on the Maid of the Mist boats, which started plying the waters below the falls in 1846; the stunters who walked across the falls on tightropes, and rode over them in wooden barrels also are covered in depth. Other chapters describe the illumination of the falls, the establishment of the parks and gardens, and the generation of electric power.

Bicentennial Stories of Niagara-on-the-Lake, edited by John L. Field. Niagara-on-the-Lake Bicentennial Committee, 1981. 142 pages; $4. This is a compilation of thirty-one articles covering the history of Niagara-on-the-Lake from 1781 to the present. The book is available from the Niagara Historical Society Museum, Castle-reagh and Davy Streets, Niagara-on-the-Lake, Ontario L0S 1J0 Canada; (416) 468-3912.

Niagara-on-the-Lake Guidebook, John Field. Niagara-on-the-Lake, Ontario: self-published, 1984. 85 pages; $6.95. Seven walking tours of Niagara-on-the-Lake are accompanied with maps, photographs, history of the town and its architecture. The author describes the days of the lake steamers and the railway, and points out curiosities most visitors wouldn't find on their own.

FOUR

NEW HOPE AND THE DELAWARE RIVER VALLEY OF PENNSYLVANIA AND NEW JERSEY

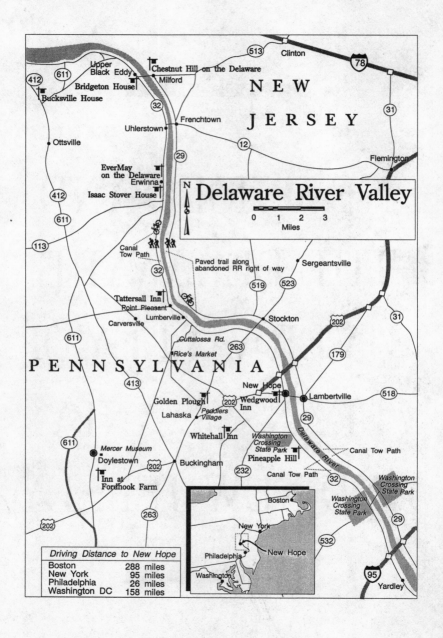

Delaware River Valley

The Delaware Canal on the Pennsylvania side and the Delaware and Raritan Canal on the New Jersey side of the Delaware River were vital links in the great network of Northeastern waterways that stretched from Lake Erie to New York City in the middle part of the nineteenth century. Many small towns prospered along its banks. New Hope, Lambertville, Upper Black Eddy, Stockton, Lumberville, and others all enjoyed high times building, servicing, and providing lodging and meals for the hardy men and their mules who operated the more than 3,000 barges and boats hauling coal from upstate Pennsylvania. But with the advent of railroad and motor travel, business along the canal dried up and these quaint towns lay nearly forgotten.

Like so many of the areas we visit, this region has had a long road back to prosperity. The historic village of New Hope led the way. At the turn of the century it was an artists' town, and some of the day's leading painters called it home. Later, after another period of neglect, it was resurrected in the 1960s by "counterculture" craftspeople, only to become a rather disagreeable bikers' haven in the 1970s. Today it is a thriving suburban arts center, with numerous galleries and unusual shops, surrounded by dozens of first-rate antique dealers, restaurants, and inns.

Your travels here will take you over ageless scenic roads, many of them paved-over Leni Lenape Indian forest trails and subsequently used by George Washington's Continental Army. For the outdoor enthusiast, there's hiking or biking the towpath on the Pennsylvania side and along the abandoned railroad right-of-way on the New Jersey side. A great summer attraction is spending a lazy day floating down the Delaware River. You can even arrange for ballooning, taking a carriage ride, or a ride on the canal in a mule-drawn barge. For the shopper there are antique stores, galleries, and clothing stores. Bargain hunters can spend days perusing the discount stores in Flemington or at Rice's, a once-a-week outdoor market. Fine dining and an evening spent at the theater or listening to jazz, rock, Dixieland, or folk music will cap your day's activities.

The New Hope Information Center. Be sure to stop in for maps, brochures, information on special events taking place in New Hope, and public restrooms. Open Monday through Friday, 9 A.M. to 5 P.M.; Saturday and Sunday, 10 A.M. to 6 P.M. At Mechanic and South Main Streets, New Hope, PA 18938; (215) 862-5880.

Bucks County Tourist Commission. 152 Swamp Road, Doylestown, PA 19801; (215) 345-4552.

SPECIAL EVENTS THROUGHOUT THE YEAR

Mid-March. William Penn Charter Day. Tours, Colonial craft demonstrations, Washington Crossing Historic Park; (215) 493-4076.

Late April–May. Bucks Fever. Events celebrating the performing and visual arts, festivals, and history at locations throughout the county; (215) 348-3913.

May. Strawberry Festival. Country events, entertainment, crafts fair and demonstrations. Peddler's Village, Lahaska; (215) 794-7438.

Sheep Shearing Days. Demonstrations of sheep shearing and herding. Washington Crossing Historic Park; (215) 493-4076.

Folk Fest. Festival of Early American crafts and entertainment. Mercer Museum, Doylestown; (215) 345-0210.

June. Antiques Show and Sale. Solebury High School, New Hope; (215) 598-7868.

Village Fair, Doylestown; (215) 345-0210.
Fine Art Festival. Garden displays, art displays, entertainment.
Peddler's Village, Lahaska; (215) 794-7438.
Fourth of July. Eighteenth-century Encampment. Coryell's
Ferry Militia. Logan Inn, New Hope; (215) 862-2050.
Fireworks over the Delaware River. Lambertville and New
Hope; (215) 862-5880.
July. Antique Auto Show. Doylestown; (215) 345-4552.
August. New Hope Auto Show; (215) 862-5880.
September. Festival of the Arts to showcase arts and artists
throughout New Hope; (215) 862-5880.
Market Fair. Annual English fair: craftspeople, musicians, Mor-
ris dancers, food. Pennsbury Manor; (215) 946-0400.
Crossing of the Liberty Bell. A celebration of the Revolutionary
War event. Coryell Militia, New Hope; (215) 862-2050.
Tyler State Craft Festival. Tyler State Park, Newtown; (215)
860-0731.
Late September–October. Juried Art Show. Phillips Mill
Community Association; (215) 862-9262.
October. Semi-annual Antiques Show. Bucks County Conserv-
ancy, Warwick; (215) 345-7020.
Historic Fallsington Day. Tours of the buildings in the village,
crafts, food. Fallsington; (215) 295-6567.
William Penn Heritage Day. Washington Crossing Historic Park;
(215) 493-4076.
November. Apple Festival. Craft fair, music, square dancing,
foods made with apples. Peddler's Village, Lahaska; (215) 794-
7438.
Handweavers of Bucks County exhibit and sale. Washington
Crossing Historic Park; (215) 493-4076.
Antiques Show and Sale. New Hope Historical Society, New
Hope; (215) 598-7868.
Tree lighting ceremony. New Hope; (215) 862-5880.
Late November–mid-December. Christmas tours of build-
ings decorated for the holidays. Pearl Buck's Home, Dublin; (215)
249-0100.
Fonthill Christmas Candlelight Tour. Doylestown; (215) 348-
9461.

Holly Night at Pennsbury Manor; (215) 946-0400.

Candlelight Tour, Washington Crossing Historic Park; (215) 493-4076.

Dress rehearsal of Washington's crossing the Delaware in 1776. Washington Crossing State Park; (215) 862-2050.

December 25. Washington's Crossing Reenactment. Washington Crossing State Park; (215) 493–6577.

WHERE TO GO, WHAT TO DO

NEW HOPE, PA

This well-known artists' community is over 300 years old, has over 180 occupied structures dating from 1787 or before, and is just a forty-five-minute drive north of Philadelphia.

On weekends or holidays, our experience fighting the crowds and traffic along the main street has overshadowed many of the town's more pleasant attributes. But walk a block off the main street, and you'll find that the mood has changed completely. Be sure to take time to walk the side streets and look for stairs leading from the street level to the towpath along the canal.

On the surface, New Hope appears to be a tourist attraction with the usual complement of "trinket and trash it" shops. But you can also uncover a host of one-of-a-kind establishments proffering a wealth of unique wares. Here are some of our favorite stores as well as museums and things to do in New Hope.

Golden Door Gallery. This renovated 1751 stone house has two floors of gallery space. Make sure to visit the Bucks County room, one of our favorites. Located next to the Bucks County Playhouse at 52 South Main Street; (215) 862-5529.

Robin Larsen Gallery. Showing her own jewelry and work of contemporary artists, mainly from Bucks County, Larsen's tiny showroom is worth a stop. 32 West Mechanic Street; (215) 862-9308.

Greene and Greene Gallery. Jeffrey Greene, master craftsman, creates contemporary furniture from rare woods. His wife,

Valerie, has an attractive and enticing display of contemporary jewelry, pottery, and handblown glass. The collection of gold and silver earrings is one-of-a-kind but affordable. 88 South Main Street; (215) 862-9620.

Three Cranes Oriental Gallery. Owner Bert Johnson lived in Japan for eight years and has cultivated trusted sources for the excellent merchandise he imports for sale in this elegant gallery: finely crafted Japanese furniture, wood-block prints, paintings, scrolls, clothing, fabrics, and more. 18–22 West Mechanic Street; (215) 862-5626. He also has a new gallery on Main Street.

Zoli. Call it new wave, au courant, or what you will, this is one of the best places outside New York City to buy trendy, progressive clothing. 112 South Main Street; (215) 862-5142.

Japan Artisans. If you have any interest in ikebana (Japanese flower-arranging) as a participant or spectator, stop here—the store has a full supply of everything except the flowers, along with Oriental writing and painting implements, lacquer ware, tea sets, toys, and abacuses. 15 West Ferry Street; (215) 862-2429.

Living Earth Plant. Next door to Japan Artisans, this charming little garden center is permeated with rich, earthy scents and sights. 7 West Ferry Street; (215) 862-5844.

Katy Kane Antique Clothing & Fine Linens. This store has been written up in *The New York Times* for its vintage wedding dresses, pillows, bed linens, and more. We spotted an ornately embroidered Victorian cape for $750, and a delicate lace wedding dress for $1,000. 34 West Ferry Street; (215) 862-5873.

Lock House #11. This store has a large stock of weaving and basket-making supplies. The novice or the expert can take a workshop, such as a three-hour course in weaving a scarf, or a two-day basket-making workshop to create a Shaker basket. 48 Ferry Street; (215) 862-5807.

Hobensack & Keller. There's no sign here, just look for the antique garden fountain, outdoor sculpture, and wrought-iron fences. Then wend your way to this shop that features Oriental rugs and assorted antique items. Owner George Hobensack is a font of information and always seems ready for a friendly chat. West Bridge Street; (215) 862-2406.

in detail. The day we stopped in this ever-changing, eclectic interior-accessory shop, it was stocked with a collection of Santa Fe furniture and high-tech lamps, flatware, plates, dishes, and glassware. 111 South Main Street; (215) 862-5558.

Farley's Bookstore. This store is truly a bibliophile's delight, overflowing with titles on every subject. It's strong on travel, cooking, and Bucks County history, and has a large children's section complete with reading area. A great place to browse after dinner, Farley's is open until midnight on Friday and Saturday, until 10 P.M. Tuesday through Thursday. 44 South Main Street; (215) 862-2452.

Ney Alley/New Hope Canal Walk. On a crisp afternoon, listen to your feet fall on the soft earth path along the calm waters of the canal. Follow your walk with a sit on one of the wooden benches set against the stone walls. Even on the busiest New Hope weekend afternoon, you can duck the hubbub of the shopping district by slipping into Ney Alley, between Mechanic and Broad streets. The brick walkway historically has been a home street for craftspeople and their shops. Then walk down a short flight of stairs and step into New Hope's distant past as a canal town, and stroll along the quiet towpath where mules once pulled barges loaded with soft coal destined for Philadelphia and New York.

Mule Barge Ride. Reminiscent of a bygone era is a ride on the open-sided mule-drawn barge. During the busier season you will be entertained with folk songs and stories about the history of the canal.

Rides in April on Wednesday, Saturday, and Sunday at 1, 2, 3, and 4:30 P.M. May through October 15 daily at 1, 2, 3, 4:30, and 6 P.M. October 15 through November 15 on Wednesday, Saturday, and Sunday at 1, 2, 3, and 4:30 P.M. Adults, $5.50; seniors, $5; students, $4.50; children under 12, $3. P.O. Box 164, New Hope, PA 18938; (215) 862-2842.

Coryell's Ferry. You probably wouldn't want to cross the Delaware River the way Washington did in the middle of the winter, but during the more clement months you can take a half-hour ride across the river on this forty-foot pontoon boat.

Monday through Friday, hourly 11 A.M. to 5 P.M.; weekends starting at 12 P.M. Adults, $5; children, $3. For tickets go to the Gerenser Ice Cream store. 22 South Main Street; (215) 862-2050.

OUTSIDE OF NEW HOPE

George Nakashima. This renowned master woodworker's altar for peace is found in the Cathedral of St. John the Divine in New York City; one of his tables, a desk, and conoid lounge chairs are in the Japanese wing of the Metropolitan Museum of Art. The Museum of Contemporary Crafts in New York City had a major exhibition of his work. George died in 1990, but his shop continues to produce fine tables, chairs, and cabinets under the direction of his daughter, Mira. If you appreciate fine contemporary furniture or like to see and feel beautifully finished wood, a visit here is a definite must—to look, to touch, and to be tempted to purchase.

Showrooms are open Saturday afternoons, 1 to 4:30 P.M. Call for an appointment if you wish to discuss a custom-designed piece, but be prepared to wait often up to eighteen months for delivery of the popular conoid chairs. From New Hope take River Road (Route 32) south about two miles. Follow Aquetong Road for about half a mile. Look for the small sign on the left. 293 Aquetong Road, New Hope, PA 18938; (215) 862-2272.

Rice's Market. This is a bargain hunter's market, similar in some respects to the markets in Lancaster County. Most of the stalls are outdoors, where new items such as sweaters, pants, sheets, watches, candles, crafts, spices, gift novelties, and so on are spread out on tables. You can spend hours walking from stall to stall. If it's antiques you want, come early while the selection is the best. The antiques and collectibles are in the back section. The Amish wares are in the main building.

Parking is in an open field. Restroom facilities are portable chemical toilets. Bargaining is acceptable at this outdoor market, especially if you're buying in quantity or shopping at the secondhand counters.

Linda Castagna, the owner and innkeeper of Chestnut Hill on the Delaware (see *Where to Stay,* page 154) has purchased hundreds of rolls of wallpaper, antiques, bed linens, candles, and assorted sundries here over the years. If you're interested in pointers about where to go for what at the market, we'd suggest spending Monday night at the inn; Linda usually leads a group of shoppers to the market on Tuesday morning.

Open Tuesday from 7 A.M. to noon. Take Route 263 south toward Peddler's Village. Turn right at Aquetong Road. Follow the road for two miles. Turn right onto Greenhill Road; (215) 297-5993.

Lentenboden. If you're a garden enthusiast visiting this area in April and May when daffodils and tulips are in bloom, you will want to stop to see this collection. It specializes in all the unusual varieties of daffodils, as well as tulips, other spring-flowering bulbs, and bulbs good for indoor forcing. You wander the grounds with a clipboard and a price list. The bulbs you order are shipped in the fall at the proper time for planting. If you don't know much about daffodils, you might arrive thinking that all daffodils are the standard yellow variety. However, once you start looking and comparing the intricacies, you will be amazed at the subtle differences in color of the cup, size of the cup, trumpets with ruffled edges, florets rather than a single flower, and varying scents.

Open daily during April and May, 10 A.M. to 6 P.M. Open the rest of the year Monday through Friday, 9 A.M. to 5 P.M. Located just outside of New Hope on Route 32. River Road, Star Route Box 21, New Hope, PA 18938; (215) 862-2033.

Peddler's Village. Lahaska is a ten-minute drive west of New Hope. This landscaped village has about sixty shops and was constructed using eighteenth-century homes which were moved to this site. Stroll along the miles of herringboned brick paths that connect the shops for hours of browsing in this "Disney World"-perfect fairyland. You'll find clothing stores, handcrafts, gift items, and six restaurants. Because of the concentration of shops and restaurants, this is a favorite stopping point for bus groups. It is a fun place to visit for a few hours of shopping and poking; but for the highest quality crafts, art, or antiques, this would not be our choice destination. At junction of Route 202 and Route 263. Lahaska, PA; (215) 794-7055.

Antiquing

Driving between the town of New Hope and the shopping village of Lahaska on Route 202 South, you'll easily see some thirty antique shops of all types, most of good quality. For antiques aficionados, pick up a brochure at the Information Center and spend a day or two exploring. If you have a limited amount of time, here are a few suggestions.

Ingham Springs Antiques. The feeling here is more like a museum than an antiques shop. This renowned dealer, known at a former location as H. and R. Sandor, specializes in eighteenth- and nineteenth-century American, French, and English antiques of the highest quality. On Route 202 between Lahaska and New Hope; (215) 862-0818.

Olde Hope Antiques. This shop specializes in prized "primitive" painted furniture and folk art. The shop and adjacent home were featured in the October 1987 issue of *Country Living* magazine. On Route 202 between Lahaska and New Hope; (215) 862-5055.

Two other very nice shops, also located along the Route 202 strip, carry more reasonably priced selections: **American Pie** on the left heading south, and **David Mancuso** (215-794-5009) on the right, in a picturesque, renovated white church at the top of a small hill.

LAMBERTVILLE, NJ

The Lambertville-New Hope ferry crossing was a primary link on a popular route from New York to Philadelphia in the 1700s. We enjoy taking a stroll across the Delaware River bridge from New Hope to Lambertville. Here are a few local galleries and shops.

The Artful Eye Gallery. Edward W. Redfield (1869–1965), one of America's leading landscape painters of the early twentieth century, was a native of this area. He won more awards in his lifetime than any other American painter, save John Singer Sargent. His paintings sell today for more than $100,000. His grandson, who paints in a similar style and whose work is far less expensive, owns this gallery. 12 North Union Street; (609) 397-8115.

The Genest Gallery. Behind the façade of this lovingly restored Victorian manor with mansard roof, sweeping gables, and spired turrets are two full floors and an outdoor sculpture gallery devoted to museum-quality contemporary art. Joseph Crilley, a local artist whose paintings you may have admired one evening at the Swan Hotel, has his paintings in this gallery. Friday through Sunday, 12:30 to 5 P.M. 121 North Union Street; (609) 397-4022.

The Lambertville Trading Co.   This coffee shop reminds us of Italy. The cappuccino, mochacchino, and assorted pastries are great for a mid-afternoon snack.

Open Tuesday through Saturday, 9:30 A.M. to 5 P.M.; and Sunday, 10 A.M. to 4:30 P.M. 43 Bridge Street; (609) 397-2232.

FLEMINGTON, NJ

Factory Outlets.   You can buy Villeroy and Boch china; wares from Mikasa, Corning, Dansk, Pfaltzgraff, Revere; designer clothing with such labels as Anne Klein, Harvé Bernard, and Calvin Klein; luggage, lingerie, linens, and a whole lot more—all at outlet prices. Shopping at these high-quality shops is an art in itself. But be aware: it's always a good idea to do some comparative shopping to know if you've found a great bargain.

The stores are scattered throughout Flemington, so stop in one of the outlets for free tabloid shopping papers that list clear, concise directions to each outlet. Most stores are open daily, 10 A.M. to 5:30 P.M., with extended holiday hours. From New Hope take Route 202 north over the Delaware.

DOYLESTOWN, PA

We recommend a walking tour of this lovely town—note especially the Federal town houses on the section of East Court Street called "Lawyers Row." But what makes a side trip to Doylestown definitely worthwhile is a visit to the Mercer Museum, the lifelong passion of the late Henry Chapman Mercer.

The Mercer Museum.   Blessed with a wealthy aunt from Boston who took young Henry on grand European tours at an early age, financed his Harvard education, and ultimately left him a sizable inheritance, Mercer was free to pursue his lifelong love: archaeology. Never believing something had to be buried in the earth to make it a treasure, he foraged the area junkyards during the early twentieth century and built a living archaeological collection of America. Within this unusual structure, formed of reinforced concrete, is an amazing hodgepodge of items: the tools and crafts from over sixty trades from before 1850; and, suspended from the six-story atrium ceiling, a conglomeration of items highlighted by a Conestoga wagon and a whaling boat.

We suggest you take the elevator to the top floor and work your way down. The upper floors reflect Law (with a gallows and prisoners block); Death (a hearse); and Learning (a schoolroom). Winding downward, you arrive at the second floor with its displays of objects from everyday life: redware pottery, bathtubs, butter- and cheese-making tools. We even inspected a couple of Shaker stoves. The museum is a unique experience—a little overwhelming, even a bit weird, but absolutely wonderful.

Open Monday through Saturday, 10 A.M. to 5 P.M., Sunday, 12 to 5 P.M. Closed January and February. Adults, $4; seniors, $3.50; students, $1.50. The adjoining Spruance Library has an extensive collection of Bucks County genealogy and history as well as a

Within the Mercer Museum are thousands of American tools and handcrafted objects from before 1850.

resource center for early American crafts; open Tuesday, 1 to 9 P.M., and Wednesday through Saturday, 10 A.M. to 5 P.M. Pine Street, Doylestown, PA 18901; (215) 345-0210.

Fonthill.   Henry Mercer was fascinated by a newly developed construction material called "reinforced concrete." Its unique characteristics seemed so ideal, he decided to build his home of it— from the footings to the mullions in the windows.

Fonthill was one of the first large-scale uses of reinforced concrete in the area, and it is as amazing today as it was when completed in 1912. Idiosyncratic in his interior design as in everything else, Mercer built his home with no formal dining room; as a bachelor, he preferred to eat wherever and whenever the mood arose. Couches were cut down to fit existing spaces, and bureaus are cemented to the walls to eliminate cleaning behind them, or the temptation to rearrange the furniture. This was clearly a man's house, and is clearly worth a visit.

Open Monday through Saturday, 10 A.M. to 5 P.M.; Sunday, 12 to 5 P.M. Tours given approximately every half-hour. Adults, $4; seniors, $3.50; students, $1.50. East Court Street, Doylestown, PA 18901; (215) 348-9461.

The Moravian Tile Works.   Wooden molds, slip paints, and wood-fired kilns have been part of making clay tiles since man's earliest days. Mercer discovered tiles everywhere in his world travels as an archaeologist, collected them, and started his own tile works. Moravian redware tiles run the gamut from simple 2½-inch-square specimens to dramatic 2-foot-square designs of Boston harbor, with a bit of everything in between.

Start your self-guided tour of this operating museum with a slide show. Then follow the arrows to see the timeless hand-process, chat with the craftspeople, and finish up in the gift shop, where you can purchase their work. The tiles are durable, practical, and very attractive, suitable for floors and wall decorations. If you're smitten, stop by the Bucksville House (see *Where to Stay,* page 164) to see how the original Mercer tile floor in the dining room has held up.

Open daily, 10 A.M. to 5 P.M. Closed January and February. Adults, $2. seniors $1.50, students $1. 130 Swamp Road (Route 313), Doylestown, PA 18901; (215) 345-6722.

James Michener Arts Center.   This arts center has changing fine and contemporary art exhibitions and a sculpture garden. Past exhibits have included the collected paintings of Michener and an exhibit of George Nakashima's furniture. What makes the center particularly interesting is its location at the historic site of the 1800s Bucks County jail.

Open weekdays, 10 A.M. to 4 P.M.; weekends, 11:30 to 4:30 P.M. Adults, $3; seniors, $2.50; students, $1.50. Located adjacent to the Mercer Museum. 138 South Pine Street, Doylestown, PA 18901; (215) 340-9800.

PERKASIE, PA

Pearl Buck's Home.   Pearl Buck's home is furnished with Oriental and American art including the desk she used when writing *The Good Earth.* The house is preserved to look exactly as it did during her lifetime. The foundation she established to help Amerasian children abroad has its headquarters here.

Tours are given March through December; Tuesday through Friday, 10:30 A.M. and 2 P.M.; Saturday, 10:30 A.M., and Sunday, 1:30 and 2:30 P.M. Adults, $5; seniors and students, $4. Located 6 miles northwest of Doylestown. Green Hill Farm, 520 Dublin Road, Hilltown Township, Perkasie, PA 18944; (215) 249-0100.

WASHINGTON CROSSING, PA

Washington Crossing State Park.   General Washington strides down to join his men along the ice-encrusted banks of the Delaware River. Standing in the bow of a small boat, he points the way as the brave patriots row through the frozen waters to battle the hated Hessian mercenaries in Trenton.

That's how we all picture the scene, calling to mind Leutze's heroic 1851 painting, "Washington Crossing the Delaware." But here the panorama, complete with fife and drum corps, comes to life on Christmas Day as the militia reenact that historic day. (We recommend you go to the dress rehearsal in mid-December, as the crowds are much smaller.)

If the weather is clear, climb the stairs or take the elevator in Bowman's Tower. From its 110-foot height, you can enjoy the same view over the river valley as Washington's sentries. You can also explore a wildflower preserve and nature trails.

The park is open dawn to dusk. Visitors center hours are Monday through Saturday, 9 A.M. to 5 P.M., and Sunday, 12 to 5 P.M. Located at the intersection of Routes 32 and 532, Washington Crossing, PA 18977; (215) 493-4076.

MILFORD, NJ

About 3½ miles north of Frenchtown is a quiet town with an outstanding B&B. The best restaurant in town is the Mill Ford Oyster House. For a burger and the atmosphere of an English pub, stop at the Ship Inn. Maria's Café is the local "undiscovered" casual Italian restaurant serving large portions at low prices. The Little Shop by the Bridge will pack you a box lunch for a day hike along the towpath. The Baker at 60 Bridge Street (201) 995-4040 is a great source for all-natural, whole-grain bread and rolls. When they have a large quantity of day-old bread, they sell it at half off their discounted price. The quality is fine, particularly if you use the bread immediately or freeze it.

NIGHTLIFE

The New Hope area hosts some lively gatherings until the wee hours of the morning. The clubs here are small, more like cafés by metropolitan standards: quiet, a bit more laid back, and intimate. Perhaps that's why we like them so much. The area also has musicals, plays, and dinner theater.

Bucks County Playhouse.   Crowds come to New Hope to see the musicals here. Shows have included *La Cage aux Folles, Fiddler on the Roof, Oklahoma!, Me and My Girl,* and *The King and I.*

The season runs from mid-April through late November. Box 313, 70 South Main Street, New Hope, PA 18938; (215) 862-2041.

Havana.   There's live entertainment nightly, such as a piano bar or jazz bands. Open for lunch and dinner daily from 11 A.M. 105 South Main Street, New Hope, PA; (215) 862-2069.

Odette's. A long-time favorite of the local crowd, Odette's features a piano bar nightly except on Tuesday. Open for lunch and dinner daily. South of New Hope on River Road; (215) 862-2432.

The Swan Hotel. Not a hotel at all, but a great spot for a drink. The work of well-known local painters, such as Joe Crilley and Ranulph Bye, are displayed on the wood walls. Secluded nooks with easy chairs and couches make this one of our favorite finds. This old building has a risqué history, as it once was a bordello. Few tourists find their way here. Open Tuesday through Saturday, 4 P.M. through 2 A.M.; Sunday, 2 P.M. to 11 P.M. Anton's at the Swan Hotel occupies part of the building and serves creative American cuisine. While we haven't been to the restaurant, it comes highly recommended by area innkeepers. Open for dinner Wednesday through Saturday, 6 to 10 P.M.; Sunday 3 to 8 P.M. Entrées $19–$22. Swan and South Main Street, Lambertville, NJ; (609) 397–3552.

The Boat House. Have a drink here any night or come on Tuesday for Irish folk songs. The intimate interior is modeled after a comfortable club of yesteryear. Nautical prints cover the walls. Open Monday through Friday, 4 to 12 P.M.; Saturday, 4 P.M. to 2 A.M.; Sunday, 2 P.M. to 12 A.M. 8½ Coryell Street, The Pork Yard, Lambertville, NJ; (609) 397-2244.

Towpath House. Here you'll find theater entertainment along with dinner. "Murder on the Menu" is the dinner theater, and at Christmas time there's a madrigal feast (mull soup, wassail bowl, plum pudding, yule log) with a lord and lady of the court, jugglers, and musicians. Dinner theater on Friday and Saturday evenings. 20 West Mechanic Street, New Hope, PA; (215) 862-5216.

John & Peter's Place. This is the longest-running rock-and-roll club in the Delaware Valley. It's popular with the younger crowd. Open 365 days a year. 96 South Main Street, New Hope, PA; (215) 862-9951.

Karla's. There's no music here, but after a late night of music or theater it's a popular spot to come for omelets and crêpes. Open for lunch, dinner, and till 4 A.M. on Saturday and Sunday. 5 West Mechanic Street, New Hope, PA; (215) 862-2612.

Bristol Riverside Theatre. This state-of-the-art theater is in lower Bucks County, less than a thirty-minute drive from New Hope. The regional theater company uses local and top Equity actors to produce five shows a year. You'll find a repertoire that includes musicals, a murder mystery play, Pulitzer Prize-winning plays, and world premiers.

The season runs from late September through early May. Box 1250, Bristol, PA 19007; (215) 788-7827.

ROADS, HIKING TRAILS, TUBING, AND CANOEING

In the lovely hills along the Delaware River, particularly on the Pennsylvania side, routes lead through beautiful woodland and by rushing streams. Head north along Route 32. We've found that beyond Center Bridge there are attractive roads, such as Cuttalossa Road, Fleecy Dale, Dark Hollow Road, Headquarters Road. You're bound to make a wrong turn at some point, but that's all part of the adventure. A Bucks County map is a good investment. You can purchase one at Farley's Bookstore in New Hope (see page 142).

Stockton, NJ.   Before you begin your trip along the towpath, stop at Meil's Bakery (see *Where to Dine,* page 171) to fortify yourself with coffee and croissant. Then strike out across the bridge over the Delaware River, taking the stairs down to the towpath (located just before you reach Center Bridge on the Pennsylvania side). As you stroll along toward Lumberville, you'll see many gorgeous homes that pass unnoticed from the road. You'll also pass the studio where Redfield, the famous New Hope artist, painted. The studio has no sign but is located on the towpath between the canal and the river. At Lumberville, leave the towpath and backtrack along the road to the General Store (open daily, 8 A.M. to 6 P.M.). This is the real thing—store, post office, and soup-and-sandwich counter all rolled into one. Cross the footbridge back into New Jersey and continue your walk through Bulls Island State Park, following the path, constructed on an abandoned railway line, back into Stockton. Back in town, stop in Phillip's Wine Shop (on Bridge Street) to look over the surprisingly vast selection of wines.

Cuttalossa Road, Lumberville, PA.   You wanted to get away, so how about a touch of Europe? Just below Lumberville, on River Road, turn onto Cuttalossa Road. Cross the one-lane bridge, and drive into a scene straight from the Jura region of Switzerland.

On the right are several alpine-style stone and frame houses. On the left, in a verdant glen where the Cuttalossa Creek flows into a small pond, sheep graze under a canopy of grand old sycamores. On most days bags of corn are placed by the roadside for folks to feed the sheep. A cup is provided to leave a donation which the owners of the property give to the homeless. If you do feed the sheep, notice their antique bells from Saignelegier, a lovely Swiss town in the Jura region.

Covered Bridge Tour. Contrary to popular belief, covered bridges were not built to provide shelter to travelers or animals. Actually, the roof was designed to protect the supporting beams from the deteriorating effects of weather. A driving tour in search of covered bridges will take you through some of the area's nicest scenery. Stop at the Information Center in New Hope (at Mechanic and South Main streets) for the covered bridges brochure, which shows the specific location of the thirteen bridges still standing in Bucks County. Be sure to purchase a county map, as the roads are confusing.

Tubing. A pleasant way to see and appreciate the countryside on a hot day is to sit in the middle of an inner tube lazily floating down the Delaware River. You pick up an inner tube (size is determined by your weight) and a life jacket. A school bus provides the transportation up the river—leaving you to float lazily back to the starting point. A map, printed on the tube, alerts you to the location of the mini rapids and the location of islands where you can stop to explore. At the height of the season there's even a hot dog stand on one of the islands. (Inquire in advance so you don't go hungry.) Canoes, kayaks, and rafts are also available for rental.

There are three base camps on the Delaware River for tubing and canoe rentals. The Point Pleasant base is open May through October. Upper Black Eddy and Martins Creek are generally open Memorial Day through Labor Day.

Tubing, weekends: adults, $12; children under 12, $10. Midweek: adults and children, $10. The main base is Bucks County River Tubing and Point Pleasant Canoe, Box 6, Point Pleasant, PA 18950; (215) 297-8181. Point Pleasant Canoe—Upper Black Eddy Base, Box 143, Upper Black Eddy, PA 18972; (215) 982-9282. Point Pleasant Canoe—Martins Creek Base, Box 154B, R.D. #1, Easton, PA 18042; (215) 258-2606.

Tubing down the Delaware River on a hot summer day.

Biking.   Bicycles can be rented at the Lumberville Store Bicycle Rental Company. The store has five- and ten-speed, mountain, and tandem bikes. Open daily April through mid-October, 8 A.M. to 6 P.M. Route 32, Lumberville, PA, 18933. (215) 297-5388.

WHERE TO STAY

Chestnut Hill on the Delaware, Milford, NJ

The brochure for this 1860s treasure says, "You are welcomed as guests and leave as friends." We'd be crazy to disagree. Owners/innkeepers Linda and Rob Castagna have made this one of the truly great B&Bs, a destination by itself.

Walking through the front door, you are greeted by a properly dressed Victorian mannequin. A couple of their equally carefully attired compatriots add an air of charming informality to both the dining room and high-ceilinged living room. We have a wonderful mental collage of the three second-floor rooms: pictures, books, baskets of apples, chocolates on the pillow, and English toiletries— even monogrammed toothbrushes! The Pineapple Room, the former servants' quarters, is now a spacious room with private bath, color television, and reading area. Peaches and Cream has both a double and a twin bed, and shares the hall bath with the Bayberry Room. In Teddy's Place, a third-floor secluded two-bedroom suite that can be rented for one or two couples, more than one hundred forty bears are in residence. For total privacy, stay in the Country Cottage, located next to the inn. Lying in the queen-size bed you have a clear view through the glass doors and the living room to the river beyond. The cottage has a full kitchen and a private Victorian porch which also overlooks the river.

For an artistic treat at breakfast, sit at the head of the table in the formal dining room and enjoy the view of the Delaware River, nature's impression of a Monet canvas. Then focus your attention on the fruit juice mixture served in crystal Champagne glasses, fresh fruit salad in stemmed fruit dishes, German apple pancakes, and Linda's prized muffins.

Stay on a Monday night, and Linda will be happy to give you a tour of Rice's Market in the morning (see *What to Do,* page 143). You would never know from looking at the antiques and always fresh-looking upholstered chairs and couches that much of the inn's furniture, Victorian wallpaper, and fine linens were purchased at Rice's Market.

Five rooms, two with shared bath, $70–$95. Full breakfast included. The Country Cottage is $125 a night, breakfast food provided. Two-night minimum stay on the weekends. No smoking. Not appropriate for children. No pets. Box N, 63 Church Street, Milford, NJ 08848; (201) 995-9761.

The Whitehall Inn, New Hope, PA

Prepare to be pampered as you arrive for the weekend at this circa 1794 B&B outside the village of historic Pineville. It's the little touches that all add up: pressed velour robes, fine hand-pressed lacy linens, chocolate truffles, a bottle of wine from a local Bucks County vineyard in your room, plus a working fireplace to ward off the chill on a blustery winter eve. Sitting by the fireplace in the living room, which is decorated with antiques, Oriental rugs, and comfortable sofas—we couldn't imagine a more delightful spot to enjoy the afternoon tea and cookies or cakes beautifully served on fine china.

Our favorite room is Albert Hibbs, which has a wood-burning fireplace and a queen-size bed made with the finest cotton sheets. Next to this room is the Gerald Gimsey, equally spacious, but which shares a bath with another room. Phineas Kelly, a small first-floor room with a private bath, is located next to the living room.

Mike and Suella Wass awaken their guests' morning palates with four-course candlelit gourmet breakfasts served on heirloom china. It is one of the finest breakfasts we've ever eaten; it's one of the highlights of the inn; and it does take about an hour and a half to enjoy it at a leisurely pace.

Six rooms, four with private bath, $120–$160. Four of the rooms have working fireplaces. Afternoon tea, full breakfast, and a bottle of wine included. Children over 12 welcome. No pets. No smoking. Pineville Road, New Hope, PA 18938; (215) 598-7945.

The Inn at Fordhook Farm, Doylestown, PA

Having pored over the Burpee catalog for years, we eagerly anticipated our stay at the Burpee family home. This eighteenth-century mansion situated on sixty acres is an ideal place to satisfy anyone's craving for life on a sprawling country estate. While the inn has Burpee memorabilia in the common rooms, do not come here expecting to talk to family members.

The expansive living room has a high ceiling and fireplace; it is furnished with Burpee antiques and mementoes. Adjacent to this room is the formal dining room, where breakfast is served. French doors lead to a terrace shaded by a 200-year-old linden tree.

Our favorite room is Mr. Burpee's master bedroom, which has a queen-size antique bed and a fireplace. To get to the bedroom, you go through what was once his private wood-paneled office and climb his private staircase. Our second choice is the large Atlee room, which has a king-size bed and a fireplace. Both the Atlee room and Mr. Burpee's room have private balconies. The Simmons room, one of the rooms with a shared bath, is a bright airy peach-colored room with a queen-size four-poster. The Curtis room, on the third floor, has a queen-size bed and a small private bath (with only a shower). The carriage house has two bedrooms, one with a king-size bed and one with a queen-size bed.

Five rooms in the main house, three with private bath, $93–$126. A carriage house is $163 for one couple, $227 for four people. Afternoon tea and full breakfast included. Children over 12 welcome; $20 additional. No pets. Located 1⁶⁄₁₀ miles west of Doylestown, just off Route 202. 105 New Britain Road, Doylestown, PA 18901; (215) 345-1766.

Wedgwood Collection of Historic Inns, New Hope

Carl Glassman and Dinie Silnutzer own three historic buildings along West Bridge Street, about two blocks from the center of New Hope. Guests stay in the Wedgwood House, Umpleby House, or the Aaron Burr House. Carl and Dinie, whose own home is adjacent to the property, greet each guest at some time during their stay. Assistant apprentice innkeepers live in each of the homes.

One of the main advantages of a stay here is that you are close to the shops and restaurants of New Hope. You can leave your car at the inn and easily walk anywhere in New Hope or in Lambertville. The inn is on one of the main streets, so it is easy to find. However, light sleepers should be aware that street traffic is audible in the front rooms. For this reason, on summer nights you will probably want to use the air-conditioner rather than open the windows. There is plenty of room for relaxing in the two gazebos, on the porches set with wicker chairs, on the lounge chairs under the trees, or in one of the three common rooms, each with a fireplace or stove.

There are six rooms in each of the three houses. Our favorites are the suites and those in the quieter back sections of each house. In the Wedgwood House we like the suite with a sitting room, a white iron daybed, wicker chair, and a wood stove. The bedroom has a double bed, and the bath has an oversize old-fashioned tub. In the Umpleby House our favorite is the spacious room with a queen-size antique sleigh bed, wood-burning fireplace, and large bath.

Behind the Umpleby House is a small carriage house, our choice for complete privacy. On the first floor is a living room with a wood stove. The second floor has a four-poster double bed and a private porch set with wicker chairs. The house includes a television, phone, and cooking facilities.

The most recently acquired building in the collection is the Aaron Burr House. The best room here is a back corner second-floor room with nine windows, a king-size bed, gas fireplace, and a large bath. On the third floor there is a three-room suite with a king-size bed, day bed, dressing room, and a large bath. The floors throughout this house are made of black walnut. The doctor who built this house traded his fee for a grove of black walnut trees, which he cut down and had made into the planks found in this house.

A small carafe of a smooth almond liqueur that Carl learned to make from his Austrian grandfather is a before-bedtime treat. An expanded continental breakfast of juice, fresh fruit, granola, and muffins is served in one of the three houses during the week and in each house on the weekends.

Eighteen rooms and suites. Weekends: private-bath rooms, $85–$120; shared-bath rooms, $80; suites, $145; carriage house, $155; about $10–15% less on weekdays. Contintental breakfast included. Children welcome, $20 additional. Pets allowed in selected rooms. No smoking. 111 West Bridge Street, New Hope, PA, 18938; (215) 862-2570.

Isaac Stover House, Erwinna, PA

Sally Jessy Raphael, a successful television talk-show host, spared no expense in decorating this historic French Second Empire brick house in nineteenth-century High Victorian elegance. Innkeeper Sue Tettemer, not Sally, operates the inn.

In the double parlor, small breakfast tables are arranged in one half of the room. The other half is a sitting room furnished in Renaissance Revival furnishings with a maroon Victorian couch, easy chairs, crystal table lamps, Oriental rugs, and puppets and baskets from Bali and Nepal that Sally and her husband Carl brought back from their travels. Features of the room that caught our eye were the lacy curtains, a pair of crystal chandeliers, and the two working fireplaces.

A greenhouse room, complete with a parrot in residence, is a more informal lounge. Wine, juice, a filled cookie jar, and a bowl of fresh fruit are left out for afternoon and evening snacks.

The exquisitely restored nineteenth-century Isaac Stover House overlooks the Delaware River.

The six guest rooms are filled with decorative and often whimsical objects. The two-room bridal suite faces the Delaware River. It has a white iron double bed, covered with lots of pillows, and a working fireplace. In the sitting room, there is a television, bamboo chairs, and a convertible sofa. Just outside this room is a small television-viewing area for the use of all the guests.

The Emerald City Room, which has a working fireplace, looks out over the back of the house and the fields. Wizard of Oz memorabilia, a cradle filled with stuffed animals, a life-size panda, and a stumpf fiddle are the decorations. This room has a large private hall bath. The Loyalist Royal, a room for history buffs, faces the river and has a double bed and fireplace.

The full breakfast features muffins and a rich egg dish such as a potato-cheese frittata served the day we were there.

Four rooms with private bath, $175, two rooms with shared bath, $150, bridal suite, $250. Full breakfast and afternoon refreshments included. Children over 12 permitted, $15 additional. No pets. Located on Route 32. Box 68, Erwinna, PA 18920; (215) 294-8044.

EverMay on the Delaware, Erwinna, PA

This inn, sitting on twenty-five acres of prime Bucks County land, borders the Delaware Canal and Route 32, the River Road, and the Delaware River beyond. Ron Strouse and Fred Cresson split the duties as innkeepers and the chefs. They have created an inn with a quiet, formal, elegant atmosphere.

The double parlor, which has two working fireplaces, is furnished with tapestry-patterned Victorian couches and chairs, an antique grandfather clock, a baby grand piano, and a carved armoire. The conservatory is used for breakfast and as one of two dining rooms for the formal dinners that make this inn justifiably famous.

All of the rooms, furnished in Eastlake-style Victorian, have telephones that include a modem for use with a laptop computer. A basket of fresh fruit with a little box of candy is put in each room. Rooms are priced according to size rather than location; you can decide whether to have the view of the river with a small amount of traffic noise, or the quieter back view looking out over the grounds and the woods beyond.

The Colonel William Erwin Room, a second-floor river-view room, is a favorite. This spacious room has a matching Eastlake carved headboard and bureau, Victorian sofa, rocking and easy chair, and an Oriental rug. This room, like most of the other rooms, has a bath with a tiled stall shower. If you prefer a tub, say so when you make reservations since there are only three in the inn. The Pearl Buck Room, which also faces the river, is the only room with a king-size bed.

A favorite on the third floor is the David Burpee Room, which looks out over the back of the property. It has a double bed with an Eastlake headboard and matching marble-topped dresser, as well as a chaise longue. The Edward Hicks Room, one of the lower-priced rooms, has a double bed attractively decorated with a half canopy. Two couples traveling together would enjoy the privacy of the two-bedroom and living room suite, which is the second floor of the carriage house.

A formal tea is served at four. A glass of Amaretto, Kahlùa, or hazelnut liqueur is placed in the room at night along with a card indicating the probable weather conditions for the following day. Continental breakfast includes juice, fresh fruit, and a basket filled with croissants, Danish, and homemade flaky palmiers.

Splendid seven-course dinners are served to the inn guests as well as to the public each Friday, Saturday, and Sunday (see *Where to Dine,* page 166).

Sixteen rooms, all with private bath, $75–$135. Two-bedroom suite, $175 (per night for four people). Continental breakfast and afternoon tea included. Children over 12 welcome, $15 additional. No pets. The inn is located on Route 32. River Road, Erwinna, PA 18920; (215) 294-9100.

Pineapple Hill, New Hope, PA

This inn is filled with Linda and Hal Chaize's collection of Early American furniture. We felt a calm as we walked into the attractively furnished Colonial common room used for both breakfast and for relaxing. Windsor chairs are arranged around the long oak table; shelves display pewter plates and jugs; and at the end of the room there is a fireplace, couch, and easy chairs.

Pineapple Hill feels like home because guests are told to help themselves to the lemonade or iced tea and cookies whenever they want. Out back a swimming pool is built into the ruins of a stone barn. From the inn, you can walk four and a half miles along the Delaware Canal towpath to New Hope.

The second-floor master suite has a four-poster queen-size bed with a blue and white quilt, an Oriental rug, and a sitting area with two wingback chairs. The third-floor suite has a double bed and a sitting room. All four rooms have a Colonial feel with antique queen-size or double beds, old quilts, plank floors, armoires, and walls decorated with old samplers.

The full breakfast often includes pancakes, Linda's specialty, which she tops with strawberry, blueberry, or lemon sauce. She also makes eggs strata, quiches, and French toast.

Two suites and two rooms, all with private bath, $85–$115 (weekends), $75–$100 (midweek). Full breakfast included. Children welcome, preferably during the midweek, $20 additional. No pets. Located four and a half miles south of New Hope on Route 32. 1324 River Road, New Hope, PA 18938; (215) 862-9608.

Tattersall Inn, Point Pleasant, PA

The aroma of freshly baked apple muffins on a cold damp day welcomes us to this inn. The large stone walk-in fireplace in the common room is a natural gathering spot in late afternoon where hot or cold cider, cheese, and crackers are served at 5 P.M. This is the original part of the house that dates from 1740. Gerry Moss has decorated the inn with her paintings and husband Herb's working collection of vintage phonographs, including a 1903 Edison cylinder machine. Express an interest and Herb will give a musical demonstration. If you have old 78 RPM records you haven't been able to play at home, bring them along.

The Squire's Room on the first floor has a four-poster queen-size bed, convertible couch, and a full bath with a tub. This is the only room that is used for families. The Royal Lavender Room has a queen-size four-poster bed with a lacy canopy and the largest bath in the house. Because the rooms of the inn tend to be on the dark side, we favor the rooms which are the brightest. The Laura Ashley Room is the brightest of all the rooms. The little table set in front of the bay window makes a perfect private breakfast nook. The Wintergreen Suite has a bedroom with a queen-size bed and a small sitting room, which is particularly useful if one person likes to stay up late and read.

While all of the rooms have full baths, the ones made from closets are quite small and only have showers. A breakfast of juice, croissants, muffins, and breads can be eaten in the dining room or can be delivered to your room. If the weather is appropriate we suggest having breakfast alfresco on one of the porches.

Six rooms, all with private bath, $85–$99 Friday through Sunday; $10 less on weekdays. Continental breakfast and afternoon refreshment included. Children welcome in selected rooms, $15 additional. No pets. Box 569, Cafferty and River Roads, Point Pleasant, PA 18950; (215) 297-8233.

The Bridgeton House, Upper Black Eddy, PA

Across the bridge from Milford, New Jersey, on the banks of the Delaware, stands this 1836 structure owned and restored by Bea and Charles Briggs. Barbara Paul is the resident innkeeper. The decor and design of the rooms and common spaces vary from the country classic look to stark modern.

Of all the rooms that we've seen in inns on both sides of the river, the newly completed penthouse room, which reminds us of the Post-Modern architecture school, takes the prize for the largest room with the most dramatic view of the river. The high, angular ceiling is accented with recessed lighting. A king-size bed and two black-leather reclining chairs face a wall of sliding glass doors. There is a gas fireplace and a bath with a deep soaking tub and a separate shower.

We also like the three second-floor country-style river-view rooms. The rooms are fairly small, but each has a private, screened verandah. The ground-floor suite has a king-size bed, gas fireplace, and a private, screened verandah. The only drawback to this room and the other river-view rooms on the ground floor is that the view of the river is partially blocked by the cars in the inn's parking lot.

Amenities in each room include terrycloth robes, a couple of pieces of fruit, some candies, and fresh flowers. Barbara prepares a different breakfast daily. There's always juice and fruit, such as a fruit salad or baked pears and cream. The entrée might be eggs Roxanne (scrambled eggs with herbs and cream cheese served with salsa), vegetable frittata, pancakes and bacon, or wholewheat and pecan waffles.

The inn is right at the corner of the bridge that crosses the Delaware River. The traffic noise on the bridge and the sound of cars and trucks turning the corner make the rooms on the village side of the inn the least desirable.

Nine rooms, all with private bath. Penthouse suite, $175; river-view rooms and suite, $105–$140; village-side rooms and suite, $75–$125. Monday through Thursday, $65–$140. Full breakfast and afternoon tea included. No pets. Children under 8 permitted during midweek only. No smoking. Box 167, River Road, Upper Black Eddy, PA 18972; (215) 982-5856.

The Bucksville House, Kintnersville, PA

Sitting in the dining room here one night, watching the coals glow in the walk-in fireplace, we couldn't help thinking of the folks who pulled up to this hostelry in the late 1700s on the stagecoach route between Philadelphia and Allentown. As the flames cast shadows on the original Mercer tile floor, we hoped those weary travelers enjoyed even a fraction of the excellent hospitality we were experiencing.

Owners/innkeepers Barbara McLaughlin and Joe Szollosi just can't do enough to make you feel welcome here. Barbara tells how guests often spend a pleasant evening exploring their extensive collections which include, but are not limited to, quilts, jugs, boxes, and napkin rings—and it's all immaculate. Guests are not made to feel as if they are in a museum. The casual, cozy den has a coal stove, television, and board games, there's a more formal den, and our favorite room, the dining room.

Two of the guest rooms have working fireplaces and one which is handicapped-accessible, has a gas fireplace. All of the rooms are decorated with antiques and country reproductions that Joe has made. The double beds are covered with quilts and more quilts, baskets, and Americana decorate the walls.

One suite, $125. Four rooms with private bath, $95. Full breakfast included. Children over 12 welcome; $25 additional. No pets. No smoking. Open weekends and holidays during the school year, daily during the summer. RD 2, Box 146, Route 412, Buck Drive, Kintnersville, PA 18930; (215) 847-8948.

Golden Plough Inn, Lahaska, PA

Earl Jamison built Peddler's Village, a collection of about sixty shops and restaurants. Wanting to provide overnight accommodations, he built luxurious rooms on top of the shops. He recently expanded the village to provide additional overnight accommodations, which mainly cater to conference business during the week. If you are traveling with children, if you are looking for a small hotel, or if you want to "shop till you drop," this would be a good choice.

In the main building there are twenty-two rooms, most with queen-size four-poster canopy beds and a few with king-size beds. There are thirteen rooms scattered throughout the village on the second floors above the retail shops. There are four deluxe two-level suites that have gas jet fireplaces and double Jacuzzis.

All of the rooms have a television (some have videotape recorders), a phone, a small refrigerator stocked with a split of Champagne, sodas, and snacks. The executive guest rooms have gas jet fireplaces. Guests are given a voucher for continental breakfast at the Spotted Hog restaurant in Peddler's Village.

Thirty-eight rooms, all with private bath, $85–$145. Seven

suites, $145–$200. Continental breakfast included. Children welcome, $15 additional. No pets. Peddler's Village, Route 202 and Street Road, Lahaska, PA 18931; (215) 794-4004.

WHERE TO DINE

FINE DINING

EverMay on the Delaware, Erwinna, PA

Owners Ron Strouse and Fred Cresson split the chef and maître d' duties on Friday, Saturday, and Sunday nights when their inn becomes one of the finest restaurants in this area. As the dinner hour of 7:30 approaches, guests congregate in the inn's double parlor. Larger parties usually are seated in the formal dining room, which is decorated with oil paintings, an enormous antique armoire, and newly upholstered pink chairs. We sat in the more informal conservatory room, which is extremely popular in the summer months. The glass wall of windows overlooks the terrace, landscaped with mass plantings of brightly colored impatiens and an expansive lawn that leads back to the Delaware Canal.

Dinner includes a set seven-course dinner with a choice of two entrées and two desserts, along with a Champagne aperitif and a few hors d'oeuvres. The menu changes based on Ron's whim and market availability. Changes that have occurred over the years include more grilled dishes, and eclectic combinations of regional American cuisine and Provincial French cooking.

Dinner began with an aperitif of Freixenet with Cognac, accompanied by hors d'oeuvres that included a smoked trout salad, sundried tomato crostini, and a country pâté. The fish course was cioppino with saffron croutons, followed by a slice of Mediterranean vegetable tart, and a salad of Boston and mache lettuce with violets and toasted walnuts. The choice of entrées included grilled yellowfin tuna with a lime-caper hollandaise, or roast loin of veal with lentils served with a wild mushroom sauce. Both entrées came with asparagus and gingered baby carrots. A selection of cheeses followed. Desserts included chocolate chestnut torte or Kahlùa honey-almond ice cream. A large wine list includes a wide selection of California Chardonnays.

When we finished our dessert, we were amazed that we did not feel overly full—quite a compliment to the chef. EverMay earns high marks from *The Discerning Traveler* based on the owners' thorough understanding of what it takes to orchestrate a truly fine dining experience.

Dinner served Friday, Saturday, and Sunday at 7:30 P.M. Holiday dinners at different times. The prix fixe is $42 per person, not including wine, tax, or tip. River Road, Erwinna, PA 18920; (215) 294-9100.

The Frenchtown Inn, Frenchtown, NJ

When it comes to tracking down fine restaurants, we often find that the seemingly minor details tip you off to the major successes. The Frenchtown Inn is an example. Yellow roses on the table and even in the ladies' room coordinated with the green and yellow decor; a plate of miniature hors d'oeuvres arrived when we were seated; chocolate truffles and cookies accompanied the check. These small but important touches are unmistakable clues to an outstanding kitchen.

We've dined here on several occasions, and while the menu changes seasonally, we have never been disappointed. We prefer to sit in the dining room with the old brick walls. We can still recall the taste of such appetizers as the excellent feuilleté of snails, asparagus, and prosciutto; linguine tossed with duck sausage; cabbage purses stuffed with shrimp, lobster, and crab served with two sauces; and panache of shrimp and scallops with arugula and tropical fruits.

The entrées are imaginatively prepared and garnished. The slices of duck breast and the leg of duck served with potato purée came with rhubarb pancakes. Sirloin steak had a bell pepper and horseradish paste and was served with spinach soufflé. Grilled tuna au poivre was surrounded by leeks and onions.

Our table of four shared three desserts: a flourless chocolate torte served with raspberry sauce, chocolate hazelnut Bavarian with a Grand Marnier sauce, and an apple and blueberry tart with cinnamon sauce.

As you enter the restaurant you walk through an old-fashioned bar that spans the length of the room. The bar serves drinks and a lighter menu, so you take advantage of the kitchen's expertise even if you don't want a full dinner.

Lunch served Tuesday through Saturday, 12 to 2:30 P.M.; $6.50–$9. Dinner Tuesday through Friday, 6 to 8:30 P.M.; Saturday and Sunday, 5:30 to 9:15 P.M. Sunday brunch, 12 to 2:30 P.M. Dinner entrées, $17.75–$24.75; brunch, $15.95. Frenchtown, NJ; (201) 996-3300.

La Bonne Auberge, New Hope, PA

This is the place to come for a fine classical French meal. The prices are high, but for a special occasion we feel it is worth the money. The front part of the restaurant dates from 1762. About ten years ago, Rozanne and Gerard Caronella built an addition that incorporated the two-story 1762 stone wall with dramatic effect. The result is an open, airy room with a soaring two-story slanted ceiling.

Rozanne orchestrates the smooth working of the dining room while chef Gerard makes sure your dinner lives up to the atmosphere. The Andalouse soup, a light tomato preparation, was excellent. An order for sautéed shrimp in a tomato-garlic sauce brought six large shrimp to our table, bathed in a delicious sauce we couldn't resist sopping up with excellent, crusty French bread.

Lobster tail, often available as a special, contained chunks of lobster meat combined with mushrooms, pimiento, cheeses, and a Champagne sauce. It was utterly divine. The veal is served with a tarragon sauce. The night we were there, the veal scallops were served with a morel sauce. Vegetable accompaniments included creamed celery root and tomato Provençal. The plate of chilled seedless grapes served to us after our entrée was a nice touch. At other times of the year you may be served cherries instead of grapes. The desserts are expensive, but the portions are large. We decided to order only one slice of coconut mousse cake with white chocolate shavings and an extra fork. We were impressed that they divided the dessert for us in the kitchen, put a small scoop of homemade ice cream on top of each plate, and garnished it with a ripe New Zealand strawberry. The wine list is extensive and very expensive.

Open for dinner, Wednesday through Saturday, 6 to 10 P.M. (Saturday seatings at 6 and 9 P.M.); Sunday, 5:30 to 9 P.M. Entrées, $30–$35, desserts, $9. American Express is the only credit card accepted. Located in Village 2, entrance off Mechanic Street, New Hope, PA 18938; (215) 862-2462.

Sergeantsville Inn, Sergeantsville, NJ

The glow from the wood-burning fireplaces in these intimate dining rooms, plus the candlelight, flowers, and shadows that dance on the thick exposed stone walls create a romantic atmosphere: just what you need to warm body and soul on a winter night. Our preference is for a table near the fireplace in the smaller of the two dining rooms. On a lower level there is a small quiet room with six tables and a wood stove; this room is used on weekends and for private parties.

We dined here with another couple and were able to sample a wider range of items from the menu. An appetizer of fresh mushroom strudel was light and flaky. Other good appetizer choices are escargot served in puff pastry, and sliced duck breast.

Entrées that are always on the menu include the ever-popular crabmeat strudel in phyllo, filet mignon, pork chops with a garlic and sausage stuffing, roast pork, and a pasta dish (often linguine with smoked salmon). Two fish dishes are always on the menu, rotating among swordfish, salmon, tuna, or mahi mahi, based on market availability.

We had a boneless duck attractively arranged in a fan shape (our request for both the green peppercorn and the currant and cassis sauces served separately caused no problem). A unique, and unusually tasty, entrée was a Norwegian venison chop served with a rich game sauce.

Open Tuesday through Sunday. Lunch, 12 to 2:30 P.M.; $5–$8. Dinner from 5:30 P.M. Dinner entrées $16.50–$26. Route 523, Sergeantsville, NJ 08557; (609) 397-3700.

The Inn at Phillip's Mill, New Hope, PA

You see the bend in the road, slow down, and spot the flag fluttering in the breeze before an ivy-covered stone building: The Inn at Phillip's Mill.

Inside, the stone walls reflect the fireplace's glow, and the tiled floor gives the restaurant an old world mood. This inn is unquestionably high on our list of the most romantic restaurant settings not only in the Bucks County area, but throughout the East. Our party of six was seated in the private library alcove. If you like to sit outside, a few attractive tables are set on a stone patio. Tables by the fireplace, a porch room, and a second-floor room are used on busy weekends.

We started with a Caesar salad and a bowl of chilled cucumber soup. Our serving of lamb chops was four single rib chops. The duck had a crisped skin but still had a slight layer of fat. Baked salmon served with hollandaise sauce was a generous portion cooked to perfection. The boneless duck breast was served medium rare and attractively presented.

The frozen lemon meringue pie, one of the specialties, had a refreshingly mild lemon taste. Should you care to spend the night, there are four attractive country-style rooms located above the main floor of the restaurant and off one of the second-floor dining rooms. There is also a small cottage on the property that offers a great deal more privacy.

Open nightly, 5:30 to 9 P.M. Entrées $14–$19.50. No credit cards. Bring your own wine. Located on North River Road, New Hope, PA 18938; (215) 862-9919.

Old Mill Ford Oyster House, Milford, NJ

A favorite of area innkeepers, this is the kind of unpretentious place you probably wouldn't walk into without a recommendation. The portions are large, the service is friendly, and owners Jim and Edna are there nightly to do the cooking and greet the guests.

Having dined here numerous times, we can vouch for many of the entrées. Superb things are done with the fish. The red snapper was a full half filet. Shellfish stew is served in a large bowl brimming with mussels, clams, scallops, shrimp, and a small lobster tail. The coconut shrimp tempura with curry rice and honey mustard, and crab Norfolk were also top rate. For the non-seafood lover, they make a good duck and also have boneless chicken and strip steak on the menu. Edna makes her own coleslaw and chunky applesauce, in season.

The dessert worth having, and big enough for two, is the crêpe filled with ice cream and served with hot chocolate-rum sauce. Everyone speaks highly of Edna, so try to go when she's in the kitchen (Monday is her night off).

Open Wednesday through Monday, 5 to 9 P.M.; to 10 P.M. Friday and Saturday. Entrées $10.95–$17.95. No credit cards. Bring your own wine. 17 Bridge Street, Milford, NJ 08848; (201) 995-9411.

Meil's Bakery and Restaurant, Stockton, NJ

This casual café restaurant has only about a dozen tables, but the menu is huge. You can come for breakfast, lunch, or dinner, or just stop in for a piece of sour cream coffeecake or a cinnamon bun and coffee. Even if you come for dinner, you can choose from a dozen salads and light entrées as well as pasta and main courses.

Specialties include hearty regional American fare such as the Thanksgiving dinner (served nightly), which includes turkey, stuffing, cranberry sauce, mashed potatoes, gravy, and vegetable.

The meat loaf platter included two enormous slices along with potatoes and vegetable. Other choices are Pennsylvania Dutch–style chicken pot pie, chili, crabcakes, roast chicken, and grilled salmon.

Salads include delicious-sounding combinations such as grilled shrimp with roasted pepper, artichokes, green beans, mushrooms, tomato, egg, and onions; warm sesame duck salad; or prosciutto and goat cheese salad.

Open Wednesday through Monday, 9 A.M. to 9 P.M.; to 10 P.M. Friday and Saturday. Lunch, $4.50–$10.25; dinner $4.75–$16.95. At Main and Bridge Streets, Stockton, NJ 08559; (609) 397-8033.

Hamilton's Grill, Lambertville, NJ

Tucked at the end of an alley called The Pork Yard, across from an upscale bar called The Boathouse, Hamilton's Grill is one of our favorite moderately priced restaurants and has the feel of an Italian trattoria. Chef and owner Melissa Hamilton works in the front room and talks with patrons who are sitting at the raw bar. This is a fun place to sit since you can watch Melissa prepare the individual-size pizzas and cook them in the beehive-shaped oven, which is in full view in the dining room. Pizza combinations such as pesto with shellfish, white pizza with gorgonzola and garlic, or three-cheese pizza are refreshingly different. Other appetizers include baked mussels with garlic butter, carpaccio, and sautéed goat cheese.

You can graze your way through appetizers, soup, and salad or go on to the entrées, which lean heavily in favor of fish dishes. We've had grilled tuna with rosemary and sautéed soft-shell crabs; both were excellent. Other choices include seafood stew with aioli, salmon, swordfish, grilled ribeye steak, roasted chicken, or a two-pound Maine lobster.

We felt the desserts definitely were worth the calories. Top choices that we've sampled include the lime tart and the Malicious Delicious chocolate cake.

Open for dinner Wednesday and Thursday, 6 to 10 P.M.; Friday and Saturday, 6 to 11 P.M.; and Sunday, 5 to 10 P.M. Entrées $9.50–$24. 8½ Coryell Street, Lambertville, NJ 08530; (609) 397-4343.

Siam, Lambertville, NJ

Although Siam is the only Thai restaurant in the area, it is the equal of many good ones we've frequented over the years. Siam is a delightful choice when you crave the unusual and spicy. To start, try a serving of satays (barbecued pork or beef served with a peanut sauce). The majority of dishes are stir-fry combinations of chicken, beef, pork, seafood, or vegetables. Our favorite, pad Thai—a combination of noodles, bean sprouts, shrimp, peanuts, and Thai spices—presented no special challenge for the chef even though it wasn't on the menu.

Open Tuesday through Thursday, 6 to 9 P.M.; Friday and Saturday, 6 to 10 P.M.; Sunday, 4 to 9 P.M. Entrées, $3.25–$11. No credit cards. Bring your own wine. 61 North Main Street, Lambertville, NJ 08530; (609) 397-8128.

OTHER PLACES

Other suggestions, particularly for informal lunches, include the following:

Karla's.   5 West Mechanic Street, New Hope, PA; (215) 862-2612. Try Karla's for sandwiches, dinner, or early morning breakfast. The large portion of mussels and linguine is a good value.

Mother's Restaurant.   34 North Main Street, New Hope, PA; (215) 862-9354. Mother's is New Hope tradition that hasn't lost its appeal. Burgers, homemade soups, or complete meals are available. With more than thirty desserts to choose from, this is a good spot for dessert and coffee.

Martine's.   7 East Ferry Street, New Hope, PA; (215) 862-2996. Enjoy good burgers by the fire in this historic stone building.

RECIPE

Whitehall Inn Coffeecake

Innkeeper Suella Wass serves this frequently requested treat at breakfast, but we find it equally appropriate for dessert.

2 cups flour	5 eggs
1½ cups sugar	8 ounces cream cheese
1 tablespoon baking powder	1 box powdered sugar
1 teaspoon salt	(1-pound size)
3 tablespoons shortening	1½ tablespoons vanilla
1 stick butter, melted	

Preheat oven to 350° F. In a large bowl, combine flour, sugar, baking powder, and salt. Cut in shortening. Blend in 3 of the eggs and the melted butter; mix well. Spread batter in a greased 9- by 13-inch pan.

Combine cream cheese, 2 eggs, powdered sugar (less 2 tablespoons), and vanilla. Pour cream cheese mixture over batter in pan. Bake 15 minutes at 350° F. Remove cake from oven and sprinkle reserved 2 tablespoons powdered sugar on top. Return cake to oven and bake another 25 minutes.

Note: The cake should be slightly soft in the center. Don't over-bake.

YIELD: One 9- by 13-inch cake.

ITINERARY

This beautiful area around the Delaware River is as diverse as it is scenic, and has much that will appeal to every taste.

DAY ONE. Drive along River Road to **New Hope**. Stop at the **information center** for a map of the town, list of galleries, map of the area showing the location of antique shops, map of the covered bridges in Bucks County, and to use the rest rooms. Visit the **galleries** (the **Golden Door Gallery** is the largest) and wander the streets, making sure you walk down to the canal. Have lunch in New Hope at **Karla's, Martine's**, or **Mother's**. In the afternoon you could take the **mule barge** for a ride on the canal, take **Coryell's Ferry** for a tour of the river, or walk over the bridge to **Lambertville** to visit more galleries. Be sure not to miss the **Genest Gallery**. For an afternoon pick-me-up, stop at the **Lambertville Trading Co.** for an excellent cup of cappuccino. Have an elegant dinner at **La Bonne Auberge** or a more informal dinner at **Hamilton's Grill**. For a pre-dinner or after-dinner drink, stop at **The Boathouse** or **The Swan Hotel**, both in Lambertville.

DAY TWO. Drive south along Route 202 to sample some of the dozens of **antique shops** between New Hope and Lahaska—make sure to visit **Ingham Springs**. If you like to walk through dozens of little shops, stop at **Peddler's Village** and have lunch there. Drive to **Washington Crossing State Park**. The two sections of the park, both along River Road, are four miles apart. See the copy of the painting *Washington Crossing the Delaware,* Bowman's Tower, and the Thompson-Neely House. Take time to walk through the wildflower preserve. Have dinner at **The Frenchtown Inn** or at the **Old Mill Ford Oyster House**.

DAY THREE. Take Route 202 south again, past Lahaska and on to **Doylestown** for a visit to the **Mercer Museum, Fonthill**, the **Moravian Tile Works**, and the **James Michener Arts Center**. Have dinner at **EverMay on the Delaware** (must be on a Friday, Saturday, or Sunday.)

DAY FOUR. Take the eight-mile **Stockton-Lumberville walking** or **bike tour**, stopping for lunch at the **Lumberville General Store** or at **Meil's**. An alternative in summer months is to go **tubing** down the Delaware River, leaving from Point Pleasant or farther up the river at Upper Black Eddy. Shoppers could easily spend the entire day in **Flemington** visiting the upscale discount stores. Or, get a map of Bucks County and spend a few hours searching out some of the thirteen of the original thirty-six **covered bridges** in Bucks County. Be sure to stop on **Cuttalossa Road** to feed the sheep and to admire the idyllic setting. The

Cuttaloosa Inn is a beautiful spot for a late afternoon drink. Have dinner at the **Sergeantsville Inn, The Inn at Phillip's Mill**, or at **Siam**.

Getting to the Area

To get to New Hope from New York, take the New Jersey Turnpike to exit 10. Take Route 287 north to Route 22 west, to Route 202 south (pick up Route 202 south in Somerville, New Jersey). Follow Route 202 over the Delaware River Bridge. Exit immediately to Route 32 south into New Hope.

From Philadelphia, take I-95 to Route 32 north.

BUDGETING YOUR TRIP

To help you get the most for your money, here are some travel suggestions at three budget levels (cost per day at peak season with two people sharing a room, including tax, 15% gratuity at meals, and service charges). Prices are approximate and intended for planning purposes only. Lodgings are categorized by price. Meal prices at lunch include an average entrée and beverage. Dinner prices include an appetizer, entrée, beverage, and dessert. Wine or alcoholic drinks are not included. Admission prices vary widely based on activities.

Staying and Dining at Expensive Lodgings and Restaurants: From $270 to $450 per day for two.

Lodging: Fordhook Farm (carriage house) $173; Wedgwood Collection (suites and cottage) $154–$164; Bridgeton House (penthouse) $186; Isaac Stover House $159–$265; Whitehall Inn $127–$170; EverMay on the Delaware (suite) $186.

Dining: Breakfast: included. Lunch: Sergeantsville Inn $30. Dinner: EverMay on the Delaware $110; Frenchtown Inn $100; Sergeantsville Inn $100; La Bonne Auberge $140.

Admissions: Mercer Museum $8; Fonthill $8; Moravian Tile Works $4; tubing $24.

Staying and Dining at Moderately Priced Lodgings and Restaurants: From $170 to $260 per day for two.

Lodging: Wedgwood Collection (private bath rates) $85–$127; Chestnut Hill on the Delaware (suite and cottage) $102–$134; Bridgeton House $80–$148; Tattersall Inn $90–$105; EverMay on the Delaware $79–$143; Pineapple Hill $90–$122; Bucksville House $100–$133; Fordhook Farm $98–$134; Golden Plough $90–$154.

Dining: Breakfast included except at Phillip's Mill. Lunch: $20 at Mother's, Karla's, or Martine's. Dinner: Phillip's Mill $85; Hamilton's Grill, Old Mill Ford Oyster House, or Karla's $60–$75.

Admissions: Mercer Museum $8; Fonthill $8; Moravian Tile Works $4.

Staying and Dining at Less Expensive Lodgings and Restaurants: From $130 to $150 per day for two.

Lodging: Chestnut Hill on the Delaware $75–$91; selected rooms at the Wedgwood Collection, Bridgeton House, and Ever-May on the Delaware $80.

Dining: Breakfast: included. Lunch: Meil's, Little Shop by the Bridge (Milford), or Lumberville General Store $10. Dinner: Siam, Old Mill Ford Oyster House, Meil's, Mother's, or Martine's $40–$50.

Admissions: Mercer Museum $8; Fonthill $8; Moravian Tile Works $4.

SUGGESTED READING

The books about Henry Chapman Mercer listed below are available from The Mercer Museum, Pine Street, Doylestown, PA 18901; (215) 345-0210. The books about the Delaware Canal and New Hope are available from New Hope Information Center, Mechanic and South Main Streets, New Hope, PA; (215) 862-5880.

Henry Chapman Mercer and the Moravian Pottery and Tile Works, Cleota Reed. Philadelphia: University of Pennsylvania Press, 1987; $55. Includes drawings and photographs of the tiles. This is the definitive work on Mercer, a ceramic artist and architect, and his contributions to the fields of archaeology, folklore, and museum design. The book describes the construction of Mercer's home, tile works, and museum. A detailed description of his tile-making process includes a complete list of the 431 stock designs offered by the Moravian Pottery and Tile Works between 1901 and 1930; these tiles were one of the most distinctive products of the American Arts and Crafts movement.

The Mercer Mile, Helen Hartman Gemmill. Doylestown, Pennsylvania: The Bucks County Historical Society, 1987; $3.95. Illustrated with new and old photographs. Short history of Henry Chapman Mercer, how the tiles were made, history of the building of Fonthill, the Moravian Pottery and tile works, and the Mercer Museum.

Bucks County: Photographs of Early Architecture, Aaron Siskind, text by William Morgan. Doylestown, Pennsylvania: The Bucks County Historical Society, 1974; $12.95. Ninety-six superb black-and-white photographs taken in the 1940s capture typical Bucks County scenery: eighteenth-century stone farmhouses, massive barns, simple meeting houses, picturesque bridges. A short text accompanies the photographs. Available at the Mercer Museum in Doylestown.

A Guide to the Delaware Canal, Willis M. Rivinus. New Hope, Pennsylvania: self-published, fifth edition, 1984; 40 pages, $2.50. Includes photographs and maps. This well-written, thoroughly researched booklet can provide days of interesting walks along the sixty-mile canal that goes from Easton to Bristol, Pennsylvania, dropping 165 feet through twenty-three locks. The canal saw its peak in 1855 when more than one million tons of coal were towed by mules down the canal in 3,000 barges eighty-seven feet long and ten feet wide. Historic photographs, up-to-date maps, and detailed descriptions show how to explore the canal on foot, bicycle, even horseback along some stretches.

The Walking Tour of Historic New Hope. New Hope, Pennsylvania: New Hope Historical Society, 1985; 32 pages, $3. A two-page history of New Hope is followed by six separate tours of the most significant historical structures and sites. Photographs of the structures accompanied by a minimal description of each, along with a map, provide a good start to this fascinating village. The route along South Sugan Road, West Mechanic Street, and Old Mill Road will lead you away from the tourist traffic.

FIVE

LANCASTER COUNTY, PENNSYLVANIA

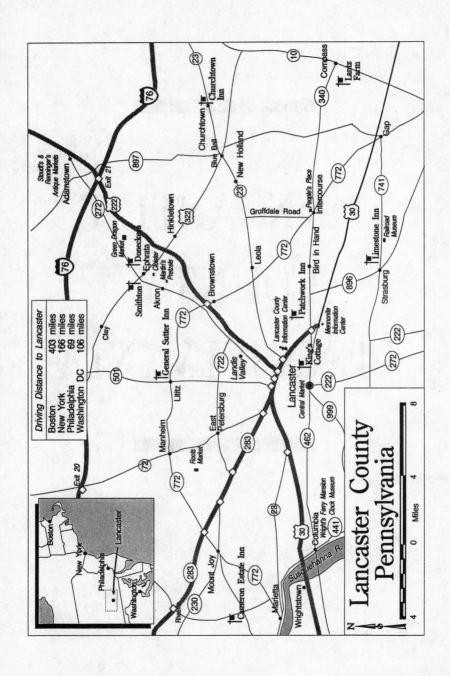

Lancaster County Pennsylvania

Driving Distance to Lancaster

Boston	403 miles
New York	166 miles
Philadelphia	69 miles
Washington DC	106 miles

It hadn't been your average evening. Our bounteous meal of honest Pennsylvania Dutch foods included chicken corn soup, cornbread, mashed potatoes with sausage and gravy, a garden salad, bean salad, chow-chow, and pickled beets. Now we were enjoying strawberry pie, banana-oatmeal cake, and chocolate cookies. And as we relaxed in Jack and Dee Dee Meyer's house, we reflected on just how different their lifestyle is from our own.

Often dismissed as a quaint curiosity because of their somber, old-fashioned clothing, the Plain People and their way of life offer the discerning traveler a fascinating and thought-provoking experience.

Lancaster County's Plain People are composed of three basic groups: Amish, Brethren, and Mennonite. They are non-resistant, intensely devout people who seek to preserve traditional family values and serve God as their ancestors did. (Non-resistance is a stand against participation in war or violence, but shouldn't be confused with pacifism, which is politically oriented. Non-resistant people will not go to court, sue the government or participate in demonstrations, while pacifists will.) They are peaceful, happy people who want the modern world to leave them alone.

You may have caught a glimpse of their lifestyle if you saw the movie *Witness*—which, although it was not made with Amish "extras," was largely filmed in Lancaster County and gives a reasonable impression of the Amish way of life.

We've visited this area many times over the years, following the Amish buggies at their fifteen-mile-per-hour gait. We've reveled in the pastoral vistas of rolling hills, immaculately kept farms, and the stark serenity of the bonneted women hanging their darkly colored quilts out to dry on the line. We've watched the men with their distinctive beards, straw hats, black trousers, and suspenders plowing their fields.

The Old Order Mennonites and Amish trace their roots to the Protestant Reformation. They live, with some variation from sect to sect, as their ancestors did more than 200 years ago. In our stay here, we came to realize that to observe these people is to gain a living understanding of the richness and interdependency of rural American society, circa 1800.

In this community, close-knit families work together on a farm, or in small businesses directly adjacent to the fields: a blacksmith, harness maker, or fruit and vegetable stand. Visiting these same businesses in operation today, we saw the pace of life the community fosters—steady and earnest; not harried, never hassled. There always seems to be time to share a story, to be friendly and caring.

We found that if a Plain Person works for you, he may stay late on the job because "it just wasn't going right." He'd be surprised if you offered him overtime pay; he is simply proud of his workmanship, and wants it done right.

Quality of life is not measured in material wealth here—many families live quite comfortably on incomes the rest of American society considers poverty level. And while some other religious communities have failed to prosper, the Plain People flourish: today they number over 46,000, with 15,000 in Lancaster County alone. Their present success is deeply rooted in the traditions and values of their past.

The Anabaptists were a strict Swiss Reformation group, formed in the early 1500s. Nicknamed Mennonites and Amish after their leaders Menno Simons and Jacob Amman, they believed that to be pure, true Christians must separate themselves from the world. They also advocated adult baptism. Their unusual theology was met with severe persecution. Driven from the cities, they moved to the countryside and became farmers.

Centuries later, William Penn's sons met the outcast Mennonites and Amish as they searched for potential settlers for their extensive tracts of land in the New World. In exchange for the purchase of land, the Penns offered the Plain People religious freedom and a home in what later became the state of Pennsylvania. Historically, the Amish are a part of the Anabaptist family (preachers of adult baptism). Anabaptists trace their origins to sixteenth-century Switzerland; they were later called Mennonites for Menno Simons, an influencial leader and writer who joined the Anabaptists in 1536. In the late 1600s a group led by Jakob Amman, who felt the Mennonites were not conservative enough, began to worship separately from the rest of the Mennonites and thereafter became known as Amish. Old order Amish are forbidden to have cars, electricity, or telephones. Conservative Mennonites also adhere to these restrictions but have a meeting house for Sunday services; the Amish hold services in members' homes, rotating each Sunday. Old-order Amish do not believe in proselytizing. Their children attend one-room schools until the eighth grade. By contrast, liberal Mennonites wear ordinary clothing, drive cars, and generally live in the modern world. They have established colleges and missions throughout the world.

The "Pennsylvania Dutch," as they were called, began arriving in the late 1600s. They initially settled in the Germantown section of Philadelphia, but quickly moved out to the fertile land of Lancaster.

But Lancaster was not destined to be theirs alone. Lying as it did along the main road to the early American frontier, Lancaster was at the hub of the Western migration. By 1750, the city of Lancaster was America's largest inland city.

For more than a hundred years (1750–1850), the famed Conestoga wagon (or prairie schooner, as it came to be known) was built in Lancaster County. The long rifle was also developed here and shipped south and west, where it gained fame as the Kentucky Rifle. The area's fortuitous combination of the legendary Swiss skill with timepieces and English furniture-makers formed a famous clock and watchmaking industry. The German tradition also made Lancaster County a brewing center—at one time it had over seventy breweries.

Lancaster County attracts more than four million visitors a year. Many of these visitors are lured by the appeal of "Pennsylvania Dutch Country"—traditional home cooking at down-home prices, the chance to spot the Amish in their buggies, a long-distance view of their glorious farms.

But it's easy to miss the subtleties. You could stay for weeks here and not meet an Amish person face to face. By following the back roads, going to the markets, and stopping at their small shops, you can gain a heartfelt appreciation for a stalwart people living their own way. We guarantee you a rewarding experience.

Pennsylvania Dutch Convention and Visitors Bureau. The bureau has brochures, maps, an introductory film, and restrooms. Open daily, 9 A.M. to 5 P.M., with later hours during the summer. Take the Greenfield Road exit off Route 30. 501 Greenfield Road, Lancaster, PA 17601; (717) 299-8901.

SPECIAL EVENTS THROUGHOUT THE YEAR

Tuesdays. Roots Country Market: Produce, meats, bakery items, small animal auction. 9 A.M. to 9 P.M. Conestoga Auctions start at 6 P.M. On Graystone Road near the intersection of Route 72, near Manheim.

Tuesday, Friday, Saturday morning. Central Market, (farmers Market). 6 A.M. to 4:30 P.M.; Saturday, 6 A.M. to 2 P.M. Queen and King Streets, Lancaster.

Fridays. Green Dragon Farmers Market and Auction: Produce, meats, clothing. Auctions for livestock, hay and straw, other items. 10 A.M. to 10 P.M. Green Spot Road, north of Ephrata, off Route 272; (717) 738-1117.

Sundays. Adamstown Antique Market: Hundreds of dealers at Reininger's, Stout's, Shupp's Grove. 8 A.M. to 5 P.M. Adamstown; (215) 267-2177.

Early March. Gordonville Fire Co. Auction. One of the biggest in the area: quilts, food, farm equipment, animals; (717) 768-3869.

Mid-May. Cloister Chorus Spring Concert. Sacred music. Trinity Lutheran Church, Ephrata; (717) 733-6600.

Mid-May. Carriage and Sleigh Auction. Intercourse; (717) 768-8108.

Late May. Spring Craft Show. Central Park, Lancaster; (717) 295-1500.

First weekend of June. Craft days at Pennsylvania Farm Museum of Landis Valley. Lancaster; (717) 569-0401.

Third week of June. Rural Life and Cultural Exhibits. Pennsylvania Farm Museum of Landis Valley. Lancaster; (717) 569-0401.

Late June through October. Weekends, Renaissance Fair. Mt. Hope Winery, north of Manheim; (717) 665-7021.

Early July. All-American Ragtime Festival and Contest. Strasburg; (717) 687–6521.

Second week of July to Labor Day, Saturday evenings. Vorspiel performances at Ephrata Cloister: Musical drama about life at the cloister. Ephrata; (717) 733–6600.

Third week of August. Annual Threshermen's Reunion. Features steam-powered engines, tractors, trains, exhibits. Rough and Tumble Museum. Kinzer; (717) 442-4249.

Second Saturday of August. Herr House Heritage Day. Craft demonstrations. Willow Street; (717) 464-4438.

First Weekend in October. Harvest Days at Pennsylvania Farm Museum of Landis Valley. Lancaster; (717) 569-0401.

Early December. Tour of Bed and Breakfast Inns in Lancaster County. Decorations, holiday foods; (717) 397-1017.

Second week of December. Christmas at the Cloister. Bell choir, chorus. Ephrata; (717) 733-6600.

Third Tuesday of December. Christmas at Pennsylvania Farm Museum of Landis Valley. Lancaster; (717) 569-0401.

Late December. Christmas Candlelight Tours, Ephrata Cloister; (717) 733–6600.

WHERE TO GO, WHAT TO DO

There are dozens of attractions throughout Lancaster County—the Dutch Wonderland Theme Park, the Choo Choo Barn, Abe's Buggy Rides, factory outlets, and more—and you can locate all of them quickly and easily by picking up a guidebook or stopping at the visitors center.

MUSEUMS

The People's Place. "Who are the Amish?" That question, asked by nearly every visitor to this region, is well answered by a three-screen documentary film of the same name, on view here daily.

After this introduction to the workings of the Old Order Amish community, head upstairs to Amish World, a hands-on collection of Amish objects and memorabilia. Climb aboard a buggy and work the turn signals. Look over the extensive collection of buggy models from the different Amish and Mennonite communities. Flip through a series of photographs showing a barn-raising. Let the kids dress up in Amish clothes and sit at the schoolroom desks. The displays are designed for students of all ages.

Spend a little time in the room that displays the folk art of Aaron Zook. These sculpted three- by five-foot, framed diorama three-dimensional scenes depict many stages of Amish life: barn-raising, a funeral, harvest time. Our favorite was the Central Market. If you'd like to purchase some of Mr. Zook's work, you'll find a gallery at the Talbott Factory Outlet (note the difference in spelling from the well-known women's clothier), located in the Plain and Fancy Mall on Route 340, or you can contact him at his studio, (717) 768-3370.

Open Monday through Saturday, April through October, 9:30 A.M. to 9:30 P.M.; November through April, 9:30 A.M. to 5 P.M. Adults, $2.50; children, $1.25. *Who Are the Amish* is shown continuously from 9:30 A.M. to 4:30 P.M. Adults, $4; children, $2. *Hazel's People,* a feature-length movie made by Merle and Phyllis Good, directors

of The People's Place, is shown nightly except Sunday at 6 and 8
P.M. from April through October. An extensive selection of books
is available for purchase. Combination tickets for the museum and
films are available. The People's Place, Main Street, Intercourse,
PA 17534; (717) 768-7171.

Pennsylvania Farm Museum of Landis Valley. The morning of our visit to the harness shop on the grounds of this forty-acre
museum, we had just come from a harness shop owned by an
Amish man that used tools virtually the same as those displayed
here. The farm wagons on exhibit are almost identical to those
spreading manure in nearby Amish fields, and the one-room schoolhouse here has any number of twins sitting along rural lanes in the
surrounding countryside.

So while this museum holds relics of America's agricultural *past,*
it also houses a nice collection of the Plain People's *present.*

The museum was started by Henry and George Landis, two
farmers who began collecting the implements of daily agricultural
life about the same time as Henry Mercer was building his fabulous collection in Doylestown, PA (see Chapter 4). This museum
is now owned by the Commonwealth of Pennsylvania. The extensive collection includes everything from wagons and farm vehicles to pots, pans, corn scrapers, and flat irons—and the
collection keeps growing.

No matter what time of the year you visit, numerous special
events and constant demonstrations explain the phases of the agricultural calendar.

Open Tuesday through Saturday, 9 A.M. to 5 P.M.; Sunday, 12 to
5 P.M. Adults, $3; seniors, $2; children 6 to 17, $1.50. Off Route 272,
north of Lancaster. 2451 Kissel Road, Lancaster, PA 17601; (717)
569-0401.

Ephrata Cloister. As we wound our way through damp,
dreary dwellings, ducked underneath the five-foot-high doorways,
and viewed the small, spartan cells where the members of this
monastic order lived, we got a clear sense of the self-imposed
deprivations this communal order endured. We also gained an in-
sight into the reality of religious freedom in America.

After 200 years, it's often very easy to take our basic freedoms
for granted. But in the late seventeenth and eighteenth centuries,

religious persecution was a part of life for many people. Founded in 1732 by a German priest, this order came to America for the same reason the Amish and Puritans immigrated: religious tolerance.

While touring the buildings on the compound, we couldn't help comparing this community to that of the Shakers. The contrast between these and the Shakers' well-lighted, airy dwellings was sharp, as was the size of the groups themselves. At the height of their popularity, the Shakers had about 6,000 members, living in several communities; the Ephrata Cloister attracted a scant seventy to eighty celibate members and 225 married believers. The Shakers' inventiveness has had a lasting impact on our society; this group's extinction in the early 1880s went largely unnoticed, and its history is virtually unknown today.

Yet, in their time, the members of the Ephrata Cloister were renowned. After the Battle of Brandywine, many wounded Continental soldiers were nursed here. The order was famous throughout Colonial America both for its printing press and for the magnificent illuminated books it produced in the Fraktur calligraphic style. Examples of the order's work are on display, along with the largest book published in Colonial America, *Martyrs Mirror* (1,200 pages), produced for the Mennonites.

Open April through November, Monday through Saturday, 9 A.M. to 5 P.M.; Sunday, 12 to 5 P.M. December through March, Tuesday through Saturday, 9 A.M. to 5 P.M.; Sunday, 12 to 5 P.M. Adults, $3; seniors, $2; children 6 to 17, $1.50. 632 West Main Street, Ephrata, PA 17522; (717) 733-6600.

National Clock and Watch Museum.   Opening the door to this museum is like walking into the model Walt Disney used for Geppetto's workshop in the film *Pinocchio*. Your eyes and ears meet an endless and endlessly amusing array of wall clocks, case clocks, mantel clocks, pocket watches, pendant watches—ticking and tocking, clicking and whirring, dinging and donging.

Look for the 1892 matrimonial clock: the face shows a different advertisement for bridal items every five minutes. Read the story of how a similar timepiece helped a man successfully marry off his seven daughters. We enjoyed watching the novelty clocks with moving eyes, and the tower clock with exposed works.

We're not collectors, but as mere sightseers we were fascinated. Open Tuesday through Saturday, 9 A.M. to 4 P.M. Adults, $3; seniors, $2.50; children 6 to 17, $1. 514 Poplar Street, Columbia, PA 17512; (717) 684-8261.

Strasburg Railroad Museum.   This state museum has more than fifteen train cars, twelve engines, a re-created railroad station, railroad memorabilia, and an enthusiastic corps of volunteers that maintain the equipment and give tours. Children and railroad enthusiasts will delight in the large number of cars open for close inspection.

Open July and August, Tuesday through Friday, 9 A.M. to 5 P.M.; Saturday, 9 A.M. to 7 P.M.; Sunday, 11 A.M. to 7 P.M. May, June, September, Monday through Saturday, 9 A.M. to 5 P.M.; Sunday, 11 A.M. to 5 P.M. Closed Mondays the rest of the year. Adults, $3; seniors, $2; children 6 to 17, $1.50. Route 741, Strasburg, PA 17579; (717) 687-8628.

Toy Train Museum.   Children will be particularly interested in seeing the three operating scale train displays. Included are both antique and twentieth-century model trains.

Open May through October daily, 10 A.M. to 5 P.M. Weekends in April, November, the first two weekends in December, and December 26–31, 10 A.M. to 5 P.M. Adults, $2.50; seniors, $2; children 6 to 12, $1. Paradise Lane, east of Strasburg, PA 17579; (717) 687-8976.

Demuth Place.   Art lovers can visit the restored home, flower garden, and studio of modern painter Charles Demuth, and tour a gallery that displays the work of Demuth and some of his contemporaries.

Open Monday through Saturday, 10 A.M. to 2 P.M.; Sunday, noon to 2 P.M. 114 East King Street Lancaster, PA 17602; (717) 397-6613.

Hans Herr House.   This 1719 stone building, depicted in a number of paintings by Andrew Wyeth, is Lancaster County's oldest home. (Andrew Wyeth is a descendant of Hans Herr.) A tour includes visits to the blacksmith's shop, sheds filled with farm tools, and the two-story restored and furnished house. There is also an orchard and a visitors center with an exhibit on Mennonite farm life.

Open April through December, Monday through Saturday, 9 A.M. to 4 P.M. Adults, $2.50; children 7 to 12, $1. 1849 Hans Herr Drive, Willow Street, Lancaster, PA 17584; (717) 464-4438.

Walking Tour of Lancaster City. Costumed guides lead you along streets lined with restored eighteenth- and nineteenth-century homes.

Ninety-minute tours are given April through October, Monday through Saturday, 10 A.M. and 1:30 P.M.; Sunday, 1:30 P.M. Adults, $3; seniors, $2.50; students, $1.50. 15 West King Street, Lancaster, PA 17603; (717) 392-1776.

Heritage Center of Lancaster County. This museum has artifacts from folk to fine art crafted by generations of local artisans.

Open May through Thanksgiving. Tuesday through Saturday, 10 A.M. to 4 P.M. Donations accepted. On Penn Square, King and Queen Streets, Lancaster, PA 17603; (717) 299-6440.

Wheatland. Costumed guides lead tours through this restored mansion of the fifteenth U.S. president, James Buchanan. The house has many of the original furnishings.

Open daily, April through November, 10 A.M. to 4:15 P.M. Adults, $4; seniors and students, $3; children under 12, $1.75. 1120 Marietta Avenue, Lancaster, PA 17603; (717) 392-8721.

Wright's Ferry Mansion. This 1738 stone house features an outstanding collection of eighteenth-century Philadelphia furniture in the William and Mary and Queen Anne styles.

Open May through October, Tuesday, Wednesday, Friday, and Saturday, 10 A.M. to 3 P.M. Adults, $3; children 6 to 18, $1.50. Second and Cherry Streets, Columbia, PA 17512; (717) 684-4325.

MARKETS

Farm markets, especially those whose stalls have been used by the same families for generations, have timeless appeal. A visit to the markets should be high on your list, even if you have no interest in purchasing anything. We suggest bringing a cooler, since the bargains may be hard to resist.

The Central Market. This is almost exclusively a food market. In the late fall and early winter, look for locally grown celery. While it's a bit unusual to rhapsodize over celery, these stalks are something special—raised with soil carefully mounded around the plants as they grow, they are virtually all white, with very few strings. Hodecker's Celery Farm from East Petersburg sells the Penn Crisp variety, the best we've ever eaten. Kreider's was a close second.

Long's Horseradish sells only the very freshest stuff. It's ground right before your eyes, which will smart if you step in too close.

After checking out some of the healthy food, we went in search of a newly discovered passion: homemade potato chips. Thick and crunchy, fried in lard, they are in a class by themselves.

Open Tuesday and Friday, 6 A.M. to 4:30 P.M.; Saturday, 6 A.M. to 2 P.M. Get parking stickers good for one hour each from the merchants when you make a purchase. Located at the intersection of Queen and King streets in the middle of downtown Lancaster.

The Green Dragon Market. Throughout the long buildings, barns, and outdoor tables sprawled in the fields outside Ephrata, you'll find everything a self-sufficient agricultural society needs being sold and traded. Anyone interested in rural American culture cannot afford to miss a jaunt to The Green Dragon.

You'll find no yuppies here. But if you have two doves or several pet rabbits for sale, you're likely to find a buyer. The goods are a bit jumbled, but if you know quality you can find just about anything.

The auctioneer, John Harvey Frye, has worked at The Green Dragon for over thirty years. He starts at 6:30 P.M. and goes nonstop until everything for sale has been sold. Chickens, rabbits, ducks, guinea pigs, and more are sold in the barn starting at 7 P.M. Outside is a hay and straw auction. Restaurants and stands inside the several buildings serve low-cost lunches and dinners.

Open every Friday, 10 A.M. to 10 P.M. Located on Green Spot Road. Follow the signs off Route 272, north of Ephrata; (717) 738-1117.

Roots Market and Conestoga Auction. This market is a smaller version of the Green Dragon. There is a barn where chickens, rabbits, and pigeons are auctioned, and stands of local farm produce. You'll also find handicrafts, pies, potato chips, meats, sandwiches, and fried food for sale.

Down the road a few hundred feet is the Conestoga auction. Every Tuesday evening there is an auction; antiques are auctioned on the last Tuesday of the month.

Open Tuesday, 9 A.M. to 9 P.M. The auction starts at 6 P.M. Take

Route 72 south from Nanheim, bear left onto Graystone Road to the market.

New Holland Sales Stables. This is one market where the stock really moves. Horse traders, bull swappers, sheepish farmers—you can rub elbows with them all as you watch the fascinating process of buying and selling livestock.

In the Beef Barn, we tread the plank walkways above the animal pens for a good look at the stock and the goings-on. We watched and listened as buyers and sellers poked and prodded the livestock, while debating the animals' merits in both English and Pennsylvania Dutch.

After the inspection period, the animals are paraded to the auction block. Keep your hands still, or you could wind up with an unplanned addition to the family.

Auctions are held on Monday starting at 9 A.M., Wednesday starting at 12:30 P.M., and Thursday starting at 11 A.M. Animals include hogs, horses, mules, ponies, bulls, steer, sheep, dairy cows, and heifers.

Located off Route 23 in New Holland, PA. Going east on Route 23, turn right on Railroad Avenue (opposite Kauffman's Hardware). Cross the railroad tracks, turn right onto Fulton; (717) 354-4341.

STORES

What attracts us to this area is the opportunity to sample an authentic Early American way of life as practiced by the Plain People. The listings below will help you experience something of their daily routine, and absorb a bit of the serenity offered by a lifestyle that has changed little since the founding of the nation.

Good's Store. Wander through the men's clothing department, for example. You'll instantly get a feel for cultural differences as you browse the racks of somber, dark-colored Amish suits. Note the lack of lapels on the jackets, and the stand-up collars. You'll also find the felt and straw hats worn by Amish men.

In the fabric department, note the stiff white fabric the Amish and Mennonite women use to make their prayer caps.

Located on Route 23 at the intersection of Route 897, next to the Shady Maple Smorgasbord.

The Shady Maple Grocery. Walk down the snack aisle here and see if you don't agree that the display is enough to make your arteries constrict. If you've always dreamed of having a chip- and pretzel-tasting party, this is the place—we spotted 120 feet of potato chips and pretzels, from sixteen manufacturers! If you are an afficionado of shoo fly pie, that peculiarly sweet Pennsylvania Dutch molasses confection with the crumbly crust, the pies here are excellent.

Open Monday through Saturday; closed Sundays. On Route 23 at the intersection of Route 897.

Hinkletown Store. We could see no sign as we pulled up to this green and yellow building, but were thrilled to find a warm, coal-burning potbellied stove straight out of the 1800s waiting inside to warm our hands on a January afternoon. Of course, some things change even here: the price of the pretzels in Hinkletown's traditional metal bin has skyrocketed from two for a nickel to two for fifteen cents. The store is frequented by the Wenger Mennonite sect, an old-order congregation named for the bishop who founded it in 1927.

Closed Sunday. Located east of Ephrata on Route 322, beyond Martindale Road, on the left before Hinkletown.

Kauffman's Hardware. When your Old Order clientele arrive in buggies and regularly have such items as lamp wicks and a pump handle on their shopping list, your stock takes on a peculiar look. In this rambling hardware and general merchandise store you'll see corn cutters, scrapple pans, gall powder, and dozens of other items no longer found on the shelves of your hometown market.

Open Monday through Saturday. On Route 23, in New Holland; (717) 354-4606.

Zimmerman's Store. This is the grocery store filmed in the movie *Witness.* Plain People purchase various dry goods and bulk foods here, such as cereals, oatmeal, rice, beans, and sugar. Look for the generous hunks of Wilbur chocolate made in nearby Lititz.

Open Monday through Saturday, 9 A.M. to 5 P.M. On Main Street in Intercourse.

A.L. Kauffman's Fruit Market. This small market specializes in fresh seasonal fruit, and deals in bulk goods year round. We spotted many good values here. Oatmeal, for example, is about 45 cents a pound. Similar low prices can be found on rice, spices, beans, even chocolate bits.

Some Old Order Amish rent freezer space here for their meats and home-frozen vegetables, as they do not have electric freezers in their homes. They'll usually stop in once or twice a week and take home a supply of foodstuffs to store in their propane gas refrigerators.

Open Monday through Saturday until 5 P.M. Located on the corner of Route 340 and Harvest Road, just east of Bird-in-Hand.

AMISH "SMALL SHOPS"

Do you need a book bound, a piece of metal forged, or a picture framed? Might you be interested in a piece of custom cabinetry? As you drive the back roads of Lancaster County, you'll see numerous small, hand-lettered signs modestly advertising Amish workmanship. Don't be afraid to stop and inquire; you can probably get the job done for less than you'd pay elsewhere, and at better quality. Shopping in these stores is also a wonderful way to meet the Amish or the Old Order Mennonite on their own ground and have a mutually rewarding conversation.

Family Farm Quilts. Quilts are a cottage industry in this part of the country; most are hand-pieced and quilted by Amish and Mennonite women in their homes. What a pleasure to peruse the wide selection here in the basement showroom of the Lapp family farmhouse instead of a touristy highway shop. Not only is the atmosphere less commercial, but the prices are lower than many we've seen elsewhere. You'll also find handmade dolls, wall hangings, and pillows. If the shop is not busy, you can ask to see the room arranged in the style of the Old Order Amish off the kitchen upstairs.

Open Monday through Saturday. 115 South Groffdale Road, Leola, PA 17540; (717) 656-6348. Take Route 23 east, turn right on Groffdale (2½ miles beyond Leola).

Wash day at an Amish farmhouse.

Lapp Valley Farm. All the cooking in Pennsylvania Dutch Country is done with real cream. Many potato chips and most pie crusts are made with lard. So it's no surprise that while most commercial ice cream is made with around 10% butterfat, Lapp Valley ice cream is 16 to 19% butterfat, and is also very good. You can buy the family product here and at The Green Dragon Market only.

There is virtually no tourist trade here, as there is no parking for tour buses. Speaking of cows and cream, ask for a tour of the barn. There are fifty Holsteins here, some weighing in at over a ton, that are milked three times a day. If you're interested, it's worth asking the Lapps if they will show you the mechanized conveyors that bring alfalfa, soybeans, and corn in from the silos for feed.

Open Monday through Saturday until 5 P.M. Ice cream cones are 75 cents for a single scoop, $1.25 for a double. Lapp Valley Farm, 244 Mentzler Road, New Holland, PA 17557; (717) 354-7988. From Route 340 east, beyond Intercourse, turn left on New Holland Road, left on Peter's Road, right on Mentzler Road to their farm.

Martin's Fabrics. It's easy to tell that most of the fabrics in Emma Martin's store are purchased by Mennonites, since there are so many bolts of small prints. You'll also find homemade windbreakers with snaps for $10. But what interested us most were the quilts. If you enjoy quilting you can purchase a pieced or appliquéed top; better yet, you can pick the fabrics and the pattern that you want and order a custom-made quilt. A queen-size quilt costs about $400–$500. Pieced tops are about $165, and appliquéed ones about $200.

Open Tuesday through Friday, 9 A.M. to 8 P.M.; Saturday, 9 A.M. to 4 P.M. Starting in Akron, take Diamond Street past Martin's Pretzels, right at Tobacco Road, left at Pool Road, right at stop sign onto Metzler Road, and left onto Snyder Road. Turtle Hill Road, Leola, PA 17540; (717) 656-7486.

Nolt's China Shop.   Look for the little sign that says "Nolt's China Shop and Hardwares." This store is located at the end of a driveway behind a farmhouse. In one corner of the one-room store are neatly wrapped surprise packages labeled for the teacher, baby, or secret pal and priced at about $3. We've purchased jams, jellies, tomato juice, chow chow, and pickles here. All are made locally and cost far less than they would anywhere else we've been. All kinds of items, from gift selections to housewares, fill the shelves. This store is heated by a kerosene stove. You won't see any electric lights or telephones here.

Open Monday, Wednesday through Saturday, 7 A.M. to 6 P.M. Heading south on Route 772, turn left on Locust Avenue (after Brownstown), right onto Maple Avenue. 339 North Maple Avenue, Leola, PA 17540.

Smuckers Dry Goods.   You can tell that this store caters mainly to the Amish from the selection of dark-colored plain fabrics and the Amish blue and black bonnets. Notice also the organdy that the Mennonite women use to make their caps, and the homemade wooden toys.

Open Monday through Saturday, 7 A.M. to 6 P.M. After you leave Nolt's continue south on Maple Avenue. Take the second right, Peace Road. The store is at the corner of Peace Road and Glen Brook Road (Route 772). 102 Glen Brook Road, Leola, PA 17540.

Windsor Chairs.   These Windsor chairs with poplar seats, hickory frames, and maple legs are left unfinished so customers can decide if they want them stained or painted. The chairs come in styles with and without arms, and most are held together with wooden pegs instead of nails. The prices range from about $100 to $150. Add about another $50 for staining or painting.

From Hinkletown on Route 322, head west toward Ephrata. Turn right at Martindale Road, left at Glenwood Drive, right onto Hahnstown Road. Paul and Lena Martin's house is the yellow house, the fifth one on the left past the Glendale intersection. Open Monday through Saturday, 7 A.M. to 5 P.M.; (717) 738-0477.

Oak Tables.   Floyd Weaver makes small oval solid-oak tables with three legs in a size perfect for an end table, at a price that's hard to beat: under $30. The tabletop is about 19 by 14 inches, small enough to fit into the back seat of a car. In addition to the tables, Floyd makes good-looking clothes hampers and clothes trees in his basement workshop.

The Weaver family belongs to a conservative Mennonite group, so has no phone. To find Floyd's home, turn right on Martindale Road off Route 322, just after Hinkletown. Turn left on Glenwood Road. Just before the underpass of Route 222, turn right onto Woodcrest Road. His house is on the right at the cul-de-sac. Open Monday through Saturday, 9 A.M. to 5 P.M.

The Stone Mill.   Built in 1760, this Amish mill may turn a bit slowly, but it grinds exceedingly fine. In use for over 200 years, the mill is still operated by the Amish to grind their corn.

Open for tours May through October, Monday through Saturday, 9 A.M. to 4 P.M. On Stumptown Road, at the corner of Newport Road (Route 772), north of Route 340.

Zimmerman's Butcher Shop.   The product is local, the butchering done on the premises, and the prices low. People come to Zimmerman's from as far as Philadelphia to stock up their freezers.

If you have a strong stomach, ask the staff if they have recently butchered an animal, or are about to. We saw a whole steer cut in half. This is a great place to learn about the location of various cuts of meat.

Open Monday through Saturday, 8 A.M. to 4 P.M. The shop doesn't have a large selection, so it's best to come early. West Farmersville Road, Farmersville, PA. From Brownstown (Route 772) take Main Street east to Farmersville Road.

Pretzels and Chocolate

Almost anyone who has grown up in the Lancaster County area has developed a fondness for pretzels. Supermarkets carry "Pennsylvania Dutch-style" pretzels. Here you can visit the source, taste the difference between mass-produced and handmade, and even try your hand at making them yourself.

Martin's Pretzel Factory. We give Martin's our vote for favorite pretzels. This is a small one-room factory where you'll be able to see the entire operation and sample a pretzel directly as it comes from the dryer. The factory is so small that one of the girls who usually rolls out the pretzels or puts them in bags will stop what she is doing to help you. You may be lucky enough to come in while the girls are singing a hauntingly beautiful hymn as they work.

Martin's is an absolute must-see. Hunks of dough are put into hand-cranked machines and cut into uniform pieces. The pieces are deftly hand-rolled into snake shapes, then hand-twisted into pretzels. From here they are dipped into caustic soda water, placed on long boards, sprinkled with salt, and cooked.

Our favorite pretzels are the specials cooked in caustic soda but with just a small amount of salt on the outside. Other varieties include whole wheat, light pretzels cooked in baking soda water, and pretzels with sesame seeds.

Here are some sample prices: 8-ounce bags, $1; 22-ounce bucket, $3; 3-pound box, $4.25; 8-pound box, $9.50. Broken pretzels cost $8 for 8 pounds. For pretzels to be shipped, 3 pounds, $9; 8 pounds, $17. Open Monday, 6 A.M. to 9 P.M.; Tuesday through Friday, 6 A.M. to 4 P.M.; and Saturday morning. 1229 Diamond Street, Akron, PA 17501; (717) 859-1272.

Anderson Bakery Co. The scale of the pretzel-making operation here is many, many times larger than at Martin's. Visitors walk along the catwalk above the automated pretzel machines. Looking down on this fully automated operation, you can marvel at the pace that produces sixty-five tons of pretzels daily. Count as eighteen machines twist pretzels at the rate of forty-eight per minute. See the 200-foot-long pretzel oven, the longest in the world. This tour is a lot of fun, and especially fascinating as a contrast to Martin's. When it comes to taste, however, the handmade pretzel gets our vote.

Open Monday through Friday, 8:30 A.M. to 3 P.M. 2060 Old Philadelphia Pike (Route 340), Lancaster, PA 17602; (717) 299-2321.

Sturgis Pretzel House. Established in 1861, this pretzel bakery is the oldest in the country. It is a regular stop on the tour bus route. If you are traveling with children you may want to visit, since the formal tour includes twisting your own soft pretzel. We suggest phoning in advance to find out when the factory is in production and what the wait will be for a tour. A gift shop has a full selection of pretzels, including chocolate-covered ones.

Open Monday through Saturday, 9 A.M. to 5 P.M. Admission, $1. 219 East Main Street, Lititz, PA 17543; (717) 626-4354.

Wilbur Chocolates. You will smell this sweet factory the moment you enter Lititz. The factory is not open for tours, but there is an excellent chocolate museum with old-time equipment, molds, and a display of the chocolate-making process on the first floor of the factory. There are chocolate buds to sample and a full array of their products to purchase. It's fun to purchase locally made foods, but we felt that the quality of these chocolates was no better than Hershey's.

Open Monday through Saturday, 10 A.M. to 5 P.M. 48 North Broad Street, Lititz, PA 17543; (717) 626-0967.

ANTIQUE MARKETS AND DEALERS

Like all areas of the Northeast that date to the pre-Colonial period, Lancaster County is rich in antiques. Fortunately, it is also rich in antique markets. Adamstown bills itself as the "Sunday Antiques Capital of the United States," and offers a number of indoor/outdoor antique malls that are closer in flavor to farmers' markets than suburban shopping centers. The following malls generally are regarded as the best.

All the antique malls are open 8 A.M. to 5 P.M. on Sundays. Dealers do come, so if you are a serious collector it's a good idea to come early. Take exit 21 off the Pennsylvania turnpike and head north on Route 272 for a few miles. You'll pass numerous other markets in addition to the few we mention.

Stoudt's.   During the winter, we suggest you head first to this mall, which operates indoors year round and carries fine-quality merchandise. Stoudt's Brewing Company, a small pub brewery, produces a nice German-style lager beer made with no preservatives. The brewery is on the premises, and we recommend stopping for a glass when you tire of browsing among the dealers. Tours can also be arranged in advance by calling Carol Stoudt at (215) 484-4387.

Renninger's.   Closer to the Adamstown exit off the Pennsylvania Turnpike, Renninger's is the largest of the antique malls, with some 500 dealers. Goods here are somewhat lower in price than Stoudt's and sometimes in quality. We must admit we found the mall a bit claustrophobic and were overwhelmed by the quantity of merchandise in each stall; (215) 267-2177.

GUIDED TOURS

There is a lot of ground to cover while exploring the daily life of the Plain People. The only way to meet them and see what their world is really like is to meander along the back roads to meet and talk with them. We found four ways to approach this, each with its own advantages.

JANE STAUFFER

Touring the countryside at a slower pace, in an Amish buggy.

Taped tour. Renting a "Pennsylvania Dutch Country" tape, we headed down a number of back roads, following its running commentary of the sights as we absorbed its explanations of Amish life. We felt the tape was informative, provided a basic familiarity with the roads, and was well worth the time and money as a basic introduction to the area. By following the tape, you'll be directed to many places set up specifically for tourists: the Anderson Baking Co., Weavertown School (not an operating school), the stone mill, a chair shop, the Strasburg Railroad Museum, and so on. The basic tour takes between two and five hours, depending on the number of stops you make.

The tape and a portable player can be rented for $10.50 from the Holiday Inn next to the visitor's center off Greenfield Road, or at Dutch Wonderland or the Wax Museum, both on Route 30. To purchase the tape in advance, send $12.95 to CC Inc. Auto Tape Tours, P.O. Box 631, Goldens Bridge, NY 10526.

Private guides. You can arrange for a guide from the Mennonite Information Center to accompany you in your car. This approach is a good idea for a first-time visitor, since it lets you see the most in the shortest amount of time. It has the advantage of allowing you to move from place to place when you're ready, not when the tour group is ready. You can also ask questions about the Amish or Mennonite way of life.

For a $4 fee, the center will arrange for a guide who will go with you in your car for a $7.50 hourly charge (two-hour minimum). Open Monday through Saturday, 8 A.M. to 5 P.M. Mennonite Information Center, 2209 Millstream Road (off Route 30, just west of Dutch Wonderland), Lancaster, PA 17602; (717) 299-0954.

Self-directed tours. Of course, no one knows where you'd prefer to go better than you, once you have a good idea of what's available. Purchase a detailed Lancaster County map from the visitors center on Greenfield Road or at a local bookstore and take off. A few pointers:

• Shop where the Amish and Mennonites shop: you'll have a reason for poking around, you won't be as obvious as a casual tourist, and you'll find excellent buys.

• Be on the lookout for auctions, firehouse suppers, and quilt sales. These are the telltale focal points of this area's indigenous traditions and offer wonderful opportunities to experience the special charm and personality of this region from the inside out. See what the locals are willing to pay for items, what they eat, how established auctioneers deal with their "regulars." Check with your innkeeper for local goings-on and the best times to go—you'll be in for a real treat.

• Refer to the Do's and Don'ts box below for helpful hints on your dealings with the Plain People.

Buggy rides. Sitting in an Amish carriage and seeing the countryside at a slower pace gives an appreciation for the land in a way that's not possible when you drive in an air-conditioned or heated car at a speed three or four times faster. You can learn a great deal about the Amish in the course of the ride.

Jack Meyer (the same person we refer to in the introduction and in the *Where to Dine* section) drives buggies at Abe's Buggy Rides. We suggest you ask for him. Recently he has worked out of the stables next to the Plain and Fancy restaurant on Route 340, a few miles west of Intercourse. Abe's main stables are a few miles farther along Route 340, west of Bird-in-Hand. 2596 Philadelphia Pike, Lancaster, PA 17505; (717) 392-1794. Open all year, Monday through Saturday. Adults, about $10 per person. Children under 12, $5.

DO'S AND DON'TS OF LANCASTER COUNTY.

Respect the Plain People, their customs and traditions. *Don't gawk* and *don't take pictures of the Old-Order Amish.* It is against their religious beliefs to have their pictures taken. There are some beautiful books available in gift shops with far better pictures than you'd probably end up with, anyway.

By all means, *do* lodge on an Amish farm. *Do* spend time with an Amish guide. *Do* feel free to stop along the road at Amish homes that advertise crafts for sale, but never on a Sunday. *Do* purchase a detailed map of Lancaster County for backroading.

WHERE TO STAY

The Smithton Inn, Ephrata

The fire burned low, candlelight danced on the walls of our room, and as we snuggled down beneath the collector-quality quilt on our bed, we discussed the reasons why our stay here was so very special.

First, there is the minute attention to detail that owners Dorothy Graybill and Allan Smith have lavished on every room in this 1763 stone house. Our room had an authentic feather bed, for example, and an angel night light. Couches and chairs were upholstered in high-grade leather. Triple-pane windows preserved the peace and quiet by blocking the noise from the street.

Then, there are the historic details throughout the inn. It seems only appropriate that the inn reflect numerous decorative influences from the Ephrata Cloister, as this was once a home for the married worshippers. The wooden door hinges are duplicates of

The Gold Room at the Smithton Inn.

some of those at the Cloister next door. The motif of our room's quilt matched the painted birds, found outside on the inn's sign, inspired by Cloister drawings. There is a Cloister bench in the south wing. Dorothy's handmade cut lampshades in the inn also were inspired by Cloister drawings. Alan planed 200-year-old floorboards, made clay tiles for bathrooms, and crafted a Cloister-inspired buffet for the dining room, all by hand.

Six rooms, all with private baths and fireplaces, one offering a Jacuzzi. Weekends and holidays, $95–$115; midweek, $65–$95. A two-floor suite, with fireplace, Jacuzzi, cupboard bed for a third person, stocked kitchen, and enclosed porch is $170 on weekends, $140 during the week. Two-night minimum required on weekends. Breakfast included. Well-behaved children and pets permitted. No additional charge for infants; children under 12, $20 additional; third adult in room, $35 additional. 900 West Main Street, Ephrata, PA 17522; (717) 733-6094.

The King's Cottage, Lancaster

This restored 1912 Spanish-style home is tastefully decorated in colors taken from the living room's Oriental rug. The entire first floor, which includes a formal living room with a fireplace, a more casual library with a television and a fireplace, and a dining room, is common space for the use of the guests.

On the second floor there are five rooms, and on the third there are two. We stayed in the King Room, which has a king-size brass bed, a large walnut wardrobe, and a stained-glass window. The bath is private, but is a few steps down the hall. It has a six-foot-long soaking tub, a separate shower, and an other original stained-glass window. Another favorite is the Queen's Room, with a king-size brass bed and stained-glass window and a private, but not adjoining, bath. The Princess Room is more secluded than the other rooms. It has a queen-size bed and windows on three sides. A private balcony off this room overlooks the courtyard. The bath, which adjoins the room, has an antique marble double sink and a claw-foot tub.

In the morning, a candlelit breakfast includes fresh-squeezed orange juice, fresh fruit, and a hot dish such as French toast and sausage fresh from the Central Market, strawberry-topped waffles, blueberry sour-dough pancakes, or plum torte.

Seven rooms, all with private bath, $75–$105. Full breakfast, afternoon tea, liqueurs, and chocolates at night are included. Children over 12 welcome. Third person in room $25 additional. No pets. 1049 East King Street, Lancaster, PA 17602; (717) 397-1017.

Donecker's, Ephrata

The original section of this inn, called The Guesthouse, is situated next to an outstanding men's and women's clothing store also owned by the Donecker family. A few blocks away is the inn's second building, called The 1777 House. The feeling here is more like an upscale hotel than an inn. Many of the rooms in both buildings have Jacuzzis.

Hooked rugs decorate the walls in all the rooms. In The Guesthouse we'd pick room 4, which has a spectacular oval double Jacuzzi surrounded by a raised tile platform. The spacious bedroom has a queen-size bed at one end and a sitting area with inlaid wood floors, as well as a separate bath with a shower. Two rooms in each building have both a fireplace and a Jacuzzi. In The Guesthouse, these rooms are numbers 14 and 15; both are suites.

The 1777 House is used primarily on the weekends. Room 1 has an original green marble fireplace, a double Jacuzzi, a queen-size bed, and a stone floor. Room 2 has a more masculine feel, but also has a corner fireplace and a Jacuzzi. Each building has a parlor with a television.

The ultimate accommodations are two Carriage House suites located at the 1777 House. Each multi-level suite includes a queen-size bed, fireplace, double Jacuzzi, cable television, and small refrigerator. An expanded continental breakfast includes fresh-squeezed juice, hot baked apples, cheese, sausage, croissants or muffins, and cereal.

Nineteen rooms and suites at The Guesthouse, two with shared bath, $59–$145. Ten rooms and suites in The 1777 House, all with private bath, $69–$145. Two Carriage House suites, $175. Continental breakfast included. Children welcome. Rollaway bed, $10 additional. No pets. The Guesthouse, 318–324 North State Street, and The 1777 House, 301 West Main Street, Ephrata, PA 17522; (717) 733-8696.

Cameron Estate Inn, Mount Joy

Secluded and quiet, this majestic 1805 country estate sits on fifteen wooded acres in the less touristy part of Lancaster County.

Spend your time relaxing before the working fireplace in the living room, or on the porch overlooking the grounds. Fish for trout in the stocked stream, or hike the trails. If you're looking for a special weekend requiring minimal planning, you need never leave the grounds; both lunch and dinner are served in the inn's dining room.

Owners Betty and Abe Groff, well-known local restaurateurs (see *Where to Dine,* page 214) and entrepreneurs, have masterfully restored the elegance to this magnificent property. The inn reflects the care taken to preserve it. But if chatting with the innkeepers is part of the travel experience you look for, this is not the place; the Groffs do not live here, and the Cameron is run more like a small hotel. The rooms range in size from generous rooms with working fireplaces to cozy little rooms tucked beneath the third-floor dormers. The Simon Cameron Room is the largest, with a king-size bed and a fireplace. Other rooms with fireplaces and king-size beds are the Honeymoon Room, Mary Cameron Room, and Harvest Room.

Eighteen rooms, sixteen with private bath, seven with working fireplaces, $70–$105 March through November; $60–$90 the rest of the year. Continental breakfast included. Children over 12 permitted. Rollaway bed $10 additional. No pets. Two-night minimum required on weekends in season. Located on Donegal Springs Road. R.D. #1, Box 305, Mount Joy, PA 17552; (717) 653-1773.

Churchtown Inn, Churchtown

There is more camaraderie and interaction between the guests and the innkeeper here than at almost any other inn we've visited. Innkeeper Stuart Smith, a former choral director, believes that most people who come to his inn want to be with others.

The series of planned activities that Hermine and Stuart Smith and Jim Kent orchestrate, mainly from mid-November through May, makes this inn unique. Special events include a musical holiday weekend, candlelight dinner, Thanksgiving dinner, Valentine's party, mystery weekend, barbecues, Amish wedding feast weekend, and dinner with a Mennonite or a River Brethren family. While you are not required to participate, the majority of the guests get involved.

The largest room in the inn, favored by honeymooners, is the Carriage House. To give an idea of the size, this room is used for the annual Victorian ball and is used for square dancing (obviously with the furniture removed). Another favorite room is Edward Davies, which has a queen-size bed with a lavender half-canopy.

For those on a budget, especially if two couples are traveling together, we'd ask for the two dormer-style rooms on the third floor, which share a bath. All of the rooms except for those on the third floor have televisions. The inn is situated at the edge of Route 23, so if the sound of traffic disturbs you, ask for a quieter back room.

A full five-course breakfast is served at 9 A.M. It includes juice, fresh fruit, cereal, and an entrée such as eggs, soufflé, granola oatmeal pancakes, Grand Marnier French toast, or fresh fruit parfait with granola, followed by homemade coffee cake.

Eight rooms, 3 with private bath, $49–$95. Carriage House $125. Breakfast included. Children over 12 welcome. No pets. Route 23, Churchtown, PA; (215) 445-7794. Mailing address 2100 Main Street, Narvon, PA 17555.

Patchwork Inn, Lancaster

This small bed-and-breakfast inn is run by Lee Martin. Racks of quilts decorate the living room, more adorn the dining area, and the beds upstairs are covered with (you guessed it) even more quilts. If you are a quilt collector, this is a good place to stay: you can spread them out and discuss their history with Lee in the casual living room. If you are interested in purchasing a quilt, Lee can direct you to out-of-the-way shops. The inn, a nineteenth-century farmhouse, overlooks an Amish farm. This is an ideal place to stay during planting or harvest season, as it offers a nice view of the fields and horse-drawn equipment.

The choice accommodation is the suite, which has a bedroom with a queen-size bed and a sitting room with a kitchenette and a private entrance. The other rooms all have queen-size beds and are decorated in traditional country decor.

One room with private bath, $65; two rooms with shared bath, $55. Two-room apartment, $75. Full breakfast included. Not appropriate for children except in the suite. No pets. Located on Route 340 just before Smoketown. 2319 Old Philadelphia Pike, Lancaster, PA 17602; (717) 293-9078.

General Sutter Inn, Lititz

If you enjoy staying at an inn where you can walk around town in the evening, we recommend staying at "The General" and exploring the town of Lititz.

A historic Moravian town filled with a sweet aroma from Wilbur's Chocolate and Sturgis Pretzel factories, (see page 201), Lititz also boasts a 1787 Moravian church, a street of pleasant shops, many restored homes, and an attractive city park.

The General Sutter Inn is the center of activity in the town. The Rotary Club meets here. Locals come in for the reasonably priced dinners, and the even less expensive early-bird specials. The inn has a comfortable, eccentric, Victorian character. It has been operating as an inn continuously since 1764. In the lobby, there are exotic birds to entertain the guests, plus a church organ and easy chairs. Downstairs, there's an interesting addition to the men's room that we'll leave for you to discover for yourself. Dining room guests share the lobby, so it's not the quiet, relaxing place that you'd find at an establishment without an attached restaurant.

Upstairs, the rooms are decorated with heavy Victorian furniture. The rooms have one or two ornately carved, antique Victorian double beds, bureaus (covered with knickknacks and accessories such as old-fashioned brush and comb sets), white wicker furniture, and ruffled curtains. The largest rooms are numbers 210 and 310, the honeymoon suite. Each room has a television and an air-conditioner.

Twelve rooms, all with private bath, $70–$90. Children welcome, $4 additional. No pets. Meals are available but are not included. 14 East Main Street, Lititz, PA 17543; (717) 626-2115.

Limestone Inn, Strasburg

Conestoga wagons once rolled by this renovated 1786 stone house on the main street in Strasburg. Today, the hefty front door with its original hardware welcomes you to a gorgeous, small bed-and-breakfast inn, lovingly restored by Jan and Dick Kennell. Jan, a former tour guide in historic Annapolis, has furnished the interior with a trained eye for authentic Colonial detail.

On the second floor there are two rooms, one with twin beds and one a double. On the third floor there are four additional rooms decorated in the Federal style, each with double beds. There are two baths on this floor. Guests who prefer to have a private bath can pay a premium to make sure that the other bedroom that would normally share the bath is not rented for the night.

A full breakfast is served, which includes juice, fruit and a hot entrée such as sourdough pancakes, French toast, or sausage casserole.

Six rooms, shared bath $65. Private bath $80. Full breakfast included. Children over 12 welcome; rollaway bed $20 additional. No pets. 33 East Main Street, Strasburg, PA 17579; (717) 687-8392.

STAYING ON A FARM

As most discerning travelers' main interest in this area will be the Plain People, we feel that a night spent on an Amish or Mennonite farm with these warm, hospitable folk is very likely the finest experience Lancaster County can offer.

There are more than thirty families listed with the Mennonite Information Center, as well as others registered with the visitor's center, who take in guests. If you don't mind sharing a bath, or staying in immaculately clean but sparsely decorated rooms in return for a chance to get personally acquainted with these remarkable people, this is a wonderful and inexpensive option (usually $25–$50 per night for two, including breakfast).

Jonathan and Lydia Lantz

We stayed with the Lantzes just one night, yet left with a heartfelt understanding of Amish daily life and the feeling that we'd made some new friends, not merely found an "authentic" spot to spend the night.

We were welcome to wander about the farm and volunteer our help with the dairy cattle, chickens, steers, and goats. After dinner or breakfast, Jonathan and Lydia were happy to chat a bit about their religion and way of life. Our conversations also revealed how wrong we can be in assuming that these rural folk have little relevant to say about current American society: for the past twenty years they, like many Lancaster County families, have hosted inner-city children through the Fresh Air program. They know more about today's urban plight than many of us would care to think about.

For the past few years, the Lantzes have welcomed guests into their home, as well as into Lydia's father's attached home (or *grosdaddihaus*). Their home is immaculate, plain (as you'd expect), and welcoming.

We appreciated spending time away from other tourists while learning about farm life with this warm and inviting family.

Six rooms with double beds share two baths. $25 for two includes a country breakfast of eggs, potatoes, toast, and juice. You may also have dinner with the family if you make prior arrangements. Children welcome; there is an additional charge for a cot. Route 10, Gap, PA 17527; (717) 442-8229. Turn right off Route 340 onto Route 10. They are the second farm.

WHERE TO DINE

Now and then we take a bit of ribbing for the types of meals we tend to favor—fish, chicken, salads, whole-grain breads, with a preference for lower calories, fat, sodium, and cholesterol. Still, there's a case for good American cooking and the comforting flavor of chicken pot pie or mashed potatoes and gravy made the old-fashioned way. And Lancaster County is the place to find it! The Pennsylvania Dutch enjoy traditional foods and old-time values, so the prices are reasonable and portions enormous just about everywhere.

The Where to Dine section is divided into two parts: First, a sampling of the Pennsylvania Dutch–style eating, then a selection of good restaurants that take advantage of the wonderful, locally grown fresh ingredients.

PENNSYLVANIA DUTCH STYLE

Dining at a home with Plain People, Manheim

The food is authentic, tasty, and bounteous in quantity when you join Jack Meyer, his wife, Dee Dee, and their six children (Rachel, Sarah, Joshua, Jessica, Miriam, and Caleb) for dinner.

You'll dine in a River Brethren home at a long table with Jack and Dee Dee and often some of the children. Dinner will be a bounteous Pennsylvania Dutch meal served family style. Many of the vegetables have been either picked fresh from the garden that day or canned the previous season. After dinner the children leave the table to wash the dishes and get ready for bed, leaving the adults to discuss the values, beliefs, and lifestyle of the Plain People.

This is not a restaurant. Please dress respectfully. Do not use alcohol prior to your arrival, or smoke on the property. Leave your camera in the car.

Fifteen dollars per person (children half-price) discreetly left on the table is an appropriate contribution for the evening. Mrs. Meyer accepts guests, including your children, Monday, Tuesday, Thursday, and Saturday. Plan to arrive by 6:30 P.M. Call for more information or reservations. 869 Sunhill Road, Manheim, PA; (717) 664-4888.

Groff's Farm Restaurant, Mount Joy

Betty Groff is a bit of a celebrity, "discovered" some years back by Craig Claiborne and James Beard, who talked her into preparing a cookbook of her delicious family-style recipes. This led to a few television appearances and book reviews in major magazines and newspapers—and today, the restaurant has gone "upscale country," redecorated with wall coverings and fabrics sold under the Groff's Farm Collection label.

A family institution in these parts for over thirty years now, Groff's is especially recommended for dinner. Betty and husband Abe are usually here in the evenings, greeting guests throughout the various dining rooms in what was once the family residence (built circa 1756). Though Betty doesn't spend much time in the kitchen any longer, son Charlie (a graduate of the Culinary Institute of America) presides over the kitchen.

Have everyone at your table order from the "all you can eat" dinner menu and you can feast in the traditional family style. Starting with chocolate cake and cracker pudding, your meal arrives on platters and includes relishes, appetizer, vegetables, and dessert. Or, order à la carte and sample Charlie's culinary techniques. Family-style entrées include smoked ham, prime rib, chicken, and a seafood combination; the à la carte menu includes your choice of the above, plus broiled lobster tail, baked stuffed flounder, steaks, and daily specials.

Open Tuesday through Saturday. Lunch, 11:30 A.M. to 1:30 P.M. Entrées, $5–$7.50. Dinner, seatings at 5 P.M. and 7:30 P.M. by reservation only; all-you-can-eat prices, $12.50 to $21.50. 650 Pinkerton Road, Mount Joy PA 17552; (717) 653-2048.

Shady Maple Smorgasbord, East Earl

"Take all the food you want, but please do not take more than you can eat." "No doggie bags allowed." "Anyone taking food from building will be charged for another meal."

Signs like these only hint at Shady Maple's reputation as a true all-you-can-eat heaven. Of all the area smorgasbords at which we fattened ourselves, we vote this one tops. You can choose from forty-six salads, fourteen vegetables, eight meats, eight breads (try the blueberry, peach, or pepper), four cheeses, three soups, ten cold desserts, three hot desserts, eight pies, six cakes, plus make-your-own sundaes with every conceivable trimming and topping.

Breakfast starts at 5 A.M. A cook prepares eggs and omelets to order, plus all you can eat of sausage, ham, scrapple, bacon, pancakes, French toast, waffles, pudding, mush, oatmeal, biscuits, cereal, fruit, doughnuts, sweet rolls, muffins, shoofly pie, juice, coffee, tea, and hot chocolate. Breakfast is crowded every day during the summer months, and on Saturdays the rest of the year.

The place is spotlessly clean, and with 1,000 seats it's designed for crowds. The tourist buses have their own entrance. Don't come on a holiday weekend unless you enjoy queuing up for a couple of hours. The line to get in generally moves quickly, however, and a second buffet line keeps the wait to a minimum.

On the lower level there is a gift shop full of knickknacks that seemed to us very touristy.

Open Monday through Saturday for breakfast, 5 A.M. (we mean it!) to 10 A.M.; lunch, 10:45 A.M. to 4 P.M.; dinner, 4 P.M. to 8 P.M. Breakfast, $4.29; lunch, $6.49; dinner, $7.99. Tuesday night is seafood night, all you can eat for $9.99 (we ate about $14 worth of shrimp alone). Saturday lunch and dinner, $8.99. Seniors over 60 get a 10% discount. Children 10 and under, half-price. Reservations for breakfast or lunch can be made Monday through Friday. During some winter months, dinner reservations can also be made. Located on Route 23 at the intersection of Route 897, next to Good's. East Earl, PA 17519; (717) 354-8222; in PA, (800) 238-7363; out-of-state, (800) 238-7365.

Yoder's Steakhouse & Restaurant, New Holland

If you can make do with only forty items in the salad and dessert line and want to spend even less money for a hearty meal, continue west on Route 23 and try Yoder's hot buffet—broasted chicken plus three other hot entrées, potato filling, homemade soups, and so on. You won't find tourists here, or atmosphere, either—just a lot of local folks enjoying a lot of food at low prices. For local products, check out Yoder's Market adjoining the restaurant.

Open Monday through Saturday, 11 A.M. to 8:30 P.M. All you can eat, $5.99. Seniors 62 and over get a 10% discount. Children pay 60¢ per year of age. Route 23, New Holland, PA 17557; (717) 354-4748.

Akron Restaurant, Akron

Whenever we see an eatery with its parking lot three-quarters full, weekday or weekend, we know it's time to stop and investigate. Our waitress told us the "old Akron" was in the center of town, and on Sundays after church the line of people waiting for a table wound around the block. When the owners moved out to the edge of town and built a big, new restaurant, business continued to boom. From an extensive menu, we selected a hearty, baked chicken pie, and real, down-home hot chicken with gravy, mashed potatoes, and peas. Vegetables included pepper cabbage, rhubarb sauce, red beet eggs, and chow-chow.

Open Monday through Saturday, 6 A.M. to 8 P.M.; Sunday, 11 A.M. to 7 P.M. Lunches cost less than $5; most dinners platters cost $6.95 and include three vegetables; desserts an additional $1–$2. Wheelchair accessible. Located on Route 272 in Akron, PA 17501; (717) 859-1181.

Brownstown Restaurant, Brownstown

This venerable bastion of Pennsylvania Dutch cuisine has a loyal local clientele. The decor is not fancy—we sat in a big room with oilcloth-covered tables. The baked beans, corn chowder, and raisin pie are excellent, and a cup of coffee includes free refills. The best bargains are the daily blackboard specials.

Open daily, 6 A.M. to 8 P.M.; Tuesday, 6 A.M. to 2 P.M.; and Sunday, 11 A.M. to 7 P.M. Lunch, under $5. Dinner platters with three vegetables, $5.50–$8.55. On Route 772 just off Route 222, Brownstown, PA 17508; (717) 656-9077.

THE BEST OF THE REST

Accomac Inn, Wrightsville

If you enjoy exceptional cuisine, fair prices, and a historic eighteenth-century building, you'll want to drive the extra distance to reach this wonderful restaurant.

Situated on the western side of the Susquehanna River about thirty minutes from downtown Lancaster, the Accomac Inn offers a wealth of epicurean delights in a simply splendid atmosphere. Sixteen-inch tapers grace every table and niche of the dining rooms in this rebuilt 1775 stone building, which features reproduction Queen Anne furniture, Armetale service plates from the nearby Wilton factory, and lovely oil paintings adorning the walls. We had dinner in the main dining room, replete with a blazing fire, and what a fine meal it was!

We began with two excellent appetizers: baby American snails baked with garlic-herb cheese in phyllo pastry, and lobster sausage with tangy whole-grain mustard sauce. Entrées use some of the popular ingredients in contemporary cuisine, such as chicken breast sautéed with sun-dried tomatoes and Parmesan cream sauce with chives, and boneless duck with shiitake mushrooms and brandied green-peppercorn sauce. We felt that all the items on the menu, regardless of price, were prepared with equal care and attention—which is, after all, as it should be. An extensive wine list, with bottles ranging in price from the teens to three figures, is sure to satisfy the oenophile in any party. The desserts change nightly. We shared an excellent banana chocolate cake.

Open Monday through Saturday. Lunch, 11:30 A.M. to 2:30 P.M.;

$6.75–$9.95. Sunday brunch, 11:00 A.M. to 2:30 P.M., $15.95. Dinner daily, 5:30 to 9:30 P.M. Entrées, $13.95–$26.50. Take the first exit off Route 30, after you cross the Susquehanna. Turn right and follow the signs. Wrightsville, PA 17368; (717) 252-1521.

Haydn Zug's, East Petersburg

While you'll find nothing truly exotic on the menu here, the sixteen-inch tapers, Armetale serving platters, and oil paintings are unmistakable clues that the present owner of the Accomac Inn once controlled operations here, since these items are the same in both restaurants. (There really was a Haydn Zug, however, who operated this site as a hardware store, bar, and boarding house for many years.)

The food is designed for the business crowd and tourists. Items on the menu include broiled tenderloin of beef, jumbo shrimp, seasoned crabmeat baked with cheese over wild rice (a choice we recommend), and roast young pheasant. All were nicely prepared, but not extraordinary.

The old brick walls and floors, beamed ceilings, and fresh flower arrangements add a lot to the atmosphere.

Open Monday through Saturday. Lunch, 11:30 A.M. to 2 P.M.; $4.95–$7.95. Sunday brunch, 11:30 A.M. to 2:30 P.M., $5.95–$10.25. Dinner Monday through Saturday, 5 to 10 P.M.; Sunday, 4 to 9 P.M. Entrées, $9.95–$22.95. Located at the intersection of Route 722 and Route 72, about four miles north of Lancaster, at 1987 East State Street, East Petersburg, PA 17520; (717) 569-5746.

Windows on Steinman Park, Lancaster

For a leisurely evening of fine dining in a spectacular setting, Windows on Steinman Park is one of our top choices. Each of the three floors is only wide enough for two well-spaced tables. Tables on the first and third floors are next to the three-story wall of windows; those on the second floor are set back from the windows.

All overlook a brick courtyard dramatically illuminated in winter with tiny white lights on the branches of the honey locust trees, and in summer by floodlights shining through the leaves. A sixteen-bottle cruvinet stretches along the back of the bar; huge bouquets of flowers are changed weekly; windows sparkle; the china is Ceralene Limoges; and a jazz pianist provides background music nightly.

The skilled captain took the time to explain the dishes clearly; he deftly prepared the popular Caesar salad from scratch at tableside. The fruits de mer included puff pastry with pieces of shrimp, scallops, and lobster in a cream sauce. Veal chops, stuffed with a mixture of duxelles, Gorgonzola, and spinach, were sliced and served in a robust madeira sauce garnished with shiitake mushrooms—a superb dish. The Dover sole, a popular entrée served with raspberry Champagne sauce or with lemon and butter, is filleted tableside. Other entrées include sweetbreads, grilled venison, beef tenderloin, pheasant, and chateaubriand.

If you choose banana Foster, cherries jubilee, or baked Alaska for dessert, you will enjoy more tableside service. We had a tasting selection of three cakes from the cart: an eight-layer chocolate ganache, a raspberry genoise with layers of hazelnut meringue, and praline cheesecake, served with a spoonful of rich sabayon cream sauce. The wine list is extensive and reasonably priced. The restaurant is owned by the Steinman family, who also owns the Lancaster newspapers.

Lunch, Monday through Friday, 11:30 A.M. to 2 P.M., $6.75–$9.75. Dinner, Sunday through Thursday, 5:30 to 10 P.M.; Friday, 5:30 to 11 P.M.; Saturday, 5 to 11 P.M. Entrées $19.75–$26.75. Sunday brunch, 11:30 A.M. to 3 P.M., $16.75. 16–18 West King Street, Lancaster, PA 17603; (717) 295-1316. Complimentary parking is provided in the adjacent garage.

The Restaurant at Donecker's, Ephrata

The same family that owns the Guesthouse at Donecker's and the 1777 House (both on page 207) also owns a fine department store known for its high level of personal service; Artworks, a former shoe factory that now houses artists, craftspeople, antique and art galleries; and one of the better restaurants in the area.

Chef Jean-Maurice Jugé has been executive chef since the restaurant opened in 1984. There are two restaurants here, one serving fine French cuisine and the other offering a lower-priced café menu. We had dinner in the fine dining section of eight tables, a few steps up from the café. The décor features stenciled walls and high-quality oil paintings. Because this section overlooks the activity of the cafe, the noise level is higher than in comparable top-quality restaurants. This was our only reservation about an otherwise outstanding dinner.

The creamy seafood bisque, with an abundance of scallops, shrimp, and mussels and a puff pastry lid, was more expensive than the other soups but well worth the extra cost. Selected appetizers and entrées are prepared without butter or heavy cream. Heart-healthy appetizers include grilled quail on a bed of greens, shrimp salad, or a mosaic of vegetables with a bell pepper sauce. Thin slices of salmon served between layers of puff pastry and lobster tail with a cilantro sauce sounded most promising.

The tenderloin of veal served with a rosemary sauce and little pockets of duxelles at only 350 calories fooled us—the rich sauce tasted as if it were made with butter. Boneless duck had a dry fruit stuffing, served with a garnish of slivered lime and a lime-ginger sauce. Other choices included salmon, rack of lamb, pheasant, Dover sole, and chateaubriand. All entrées came with a choice of spinach salad and warm prosciutto and goat cheese dressing, or a green salad. An intermezzo of peach and thyme sorbet surrounded by wine granité was attractive and refreshing.

Desserts in the fine dining section are presented on a cart. The portions are large, and a single serving garnished with fresh fruit and a raspberry sauce more than sufficed for two.

Open Monday through Saturday, closed on Wednesday. Lunch, 11 A.M. to 2:30 P.M., $6.25–$12.75; Sunday brunch, 11:30 A.M. to 3 P.M., $12.95. Dinner: Café, 4 to 10 P.M., $6.25–$13.75; Fine dining, 5:30 (Saturday 5 P.M.) to 10 P.M., entrées $17.95–$24.75. 333 North State Street, Ephrata, PA 17522; (717) 738-2421.

RECIPE

Easy Corn Pudding

As Dee Dee Meyer explained to us one evening, "This recipe is handy because you can keep the ingredients in the pantry and mix it up quickly before company comes or even after they arrive. I always get compliments on this and it always turns out well." If you have dinner at the Meyers' this dish is frequently on the menu.

½ *cup sugar*	*16-ounce can evaporated milk*
3 *tablespoons cornstarch*	*16-ounce can cream-style corn*
2 *eggs*	3 *teaspoons butter*

In a mixing bowl, stir together the sugar and cornstarch. Add eggs, evaporated milk, and corn. Slice the butter and add. Bake in a buttered baking dish at 350°F for about an hour, or until a knife inserted in the center of the pudding comes out clean.

ITINERARY

All of the places we've included are close enough to each other that you can use one inn as your base. Because Lancaster County offers such a diversity of lodging experiences, however, we suggest that you stay at least two places for a richer appreciation of the area.

Note: Day one or two of this itinerary can take place on any day except Sunday. If you can arrange to visit during the week, you'll avoid many of the tourists, and also avoid having to be concerned with missing many of the family-owned shops and tour services that are closed Sunday.

DAY ONE. Head to the **People's Place** in Intercourse, PA, for an introduction to the Amish, then go to the **Mennonite Information Center** on Route 30 to arrange for a tour of the area. If you are coming during the busier times (summer and fall), call ahead.

Or, poke around on your own with a county map and **tape tour** which will take you many of the same places you'd go with a guide. As evening falls, drive to the **Accomac Inn** for a gourmet meal.

DAY TWO. Using your map of Lancaster County, a real necessity for backroading, spend the day visiting and perhaps purchasing items at the little stores and shops throughout the area. Take time to look and talk instead of rushing from place to place. If you're here on a market day, be sure to visit and graze your way from stall to stall. The **Ephrata Cloister** is worth a visit. Have dinner with **the Meyers**. We found that a day of backroading and an evening with Jack Meyer and his family greatly increased our understanding of the Plain People.

DAY THREE. **Stay with an Amish farm family** for the day and night. You'll leave with a personal understanding of the people, their beliefs, and way of life that very few Americans will ever gain. Or, visit some of the museums such as the **Clock and Watch Museum** and the **Strasburg Railroad Museum**, and take the **walking tour of Lancaster**.

DAY FOUR. Head to the **Pennsylvania Farm Museum of Landis Valley** just north of Lancaster on Route 272. From there, take a ride to **Shady Maple Smorgasbord**. Then do some poking around to wear off the calories. Depending on the day of the week (much is closed on Sunday, and the markets are open on various days), you might visit **Lapp Valley Farm Quilts**; compare the various methods of pretzel-making at **Martin's Pretzels** and/or **Anderson's Baking Co.**; or stroll through the **Central Market** or **The Green Dragon**, where you can sample ice cream from the **Lapp Valley Farm** if the munchies hit.

Getting to the Area

Allow about one and a half hours from Philadelphia, two and a half from the Washington, D.C., area and three hours from New York City.

From either Philadelphia or New York, take the Pennsylvania Turnpike to Route 222 south (exit 21). Take Route 30 east to the Greenfield Road exit (tourist information center).

From Washington and Baltimore, take I-83 to Route 30 east to the Greenfield Road exit (tourist information center).

BUDGETING YOUR TRIP

To help you get the most for your money, here are some travel suggestions at three budget levels (cost per day at peak season with two people sharing a room, including tax, 15% gratuity at meals, and service charges). Prices are approximate and intended for planning purposes only. Lodgings are categorized by price. Meal prices at lunch include an average entrée and beverage. Dinner prices include an appetizer, entrée, beverage, and dessert. Wine or alcoholic drinks are not included. Admission prices vary widely based on activities.

Staying and Dining at Expensive Lodgings and Restaurants: From $240 to $300 per day for two.

Lodging: Smithton Inn (South Wing) $180; Donecker's $133, $186.

Dining: Breakfast: included. Lunch: Accomac Inn, Windows on Steinman Park, $20. Dinner: Accomac Inn, Windows on Steinman Park, Donecker's, $80.

Admissions: Mennonite Guide (four hours) $35; Farm Museum $6; People's Place $8; Ephrata Cloisters $6; Wheatland $8.

Staying and Dining at Moderately Priced Lodgings and Restaurants: From $140 to $220 per day for two.

Lodging: General Sutter $74–$95; Patchwork Inn $80; Churchtown Inn $73–$132; Smithton Inn $101–$122; King's Cottage $80–$111; Donecker's or Cameron Estate Inn $69–$117; Limestone Inn $85.

Dining: Breakfast: included except at General Sutter ($10). Lunch: Akron Restaurant, Shady Maple, $15; Dinner: Donecker's, $15–$20; Groff's $40–$60; Meyers' home $30; Swan Hotel $45.

Admissions: Mennonite Guide (three hours) $29; Farm Museum $6; People's Place $8.

Staying and Dining at Less Expensive Lodgings and Restaurants: From $75 to $110 per day for two.

Lodging: Patchwork Inn $58–$69; Limestone Inn $69; Farm stay $27; Churchtown Inn $52.

Dining: Breakfast: included. Lunch: snacks at farm markets $8. Dinner: Shady Maple Smorgasbord $20; Yoder's $14; Akron or Brownstown $25. Admissions: Tape tour $11; Farm Museum $6; People's Place $8.

SUGGESTED READING

We've reviewed many books and feel that this selection will provide a good introduction to the Amish and Mennonite people, their quilts, and their recipes. All of these books are available at The People's Place, Main St., Intercourse, PA; (717) 768-7171.

Who Are the Amish? Merle Good. Intercourse, PA: Good Books, 1985; softcover $19.95. A basic, readable book written by one of the leading authorities, unofficial spokesman and interpreter for the Amish, and director of The People's Place.

The Amish—The Enduring Spirit. Leslie Ann Hauslein. New York: Crescent Books, 1990; $10.95. Beautiful color photographs and text make this a fine remembrance of your trip to Lancaster County.

The Mennonite Community Cookbook. Emma Showalter. Scottsdale, Pennsylvania, PA: Herald Press, 1978; hardcover $17.95. More than 1,000 recipes from old Mennonite cookbooks contributed by folks from communities throughout the country, including Pork Cake, Rhubarb Conserves, Oyster Pie, and Wiggle Glacé.

The Amish Quilt, Eve Wheatcroft Granick. Intercourse, Pennsylvania: Good Books, 1989; $45. Everything you want to know about Amish quilts is detailed in this large format hardcover edition. The history, patterns, museums, shops, quilting techniques, along with beautiful full color photographs of Amish quilts, make this a great book for the quilt collector.

The Budget. Sugarcreek Budget Publishers, Inc., 134 North Factory Street, Sugarcreek, Ohio 44681-0249. Single-copy price, 45¢. Available at the Mennonite Information Center and The People's Place. This weekly newspaper serves the Amish-Mennonite communities throughout the Americas, and includes gossipy news and advertisements of items of interest to the Plain People.

Why Do They Dress That Way? Stephen Scott. Intercourse, PA: Good Books, 1986; softcover $5.95. Black-and-white photographs, line drawings. This comprehensive book about the reasons for plain dress by the Old Order Amish, Mennonite, and Brethen includes details on men's and women's clothing, where the plain patterns of dress came from, and common objections to plain dress. Many illustrations compare bonnets, hats, capes, suspenders, shirts, and beards of the different plain groups.

SIX

THE BRANDYWINE RIVER VALLEY, PENNSYLVANIA AND DELAWARE

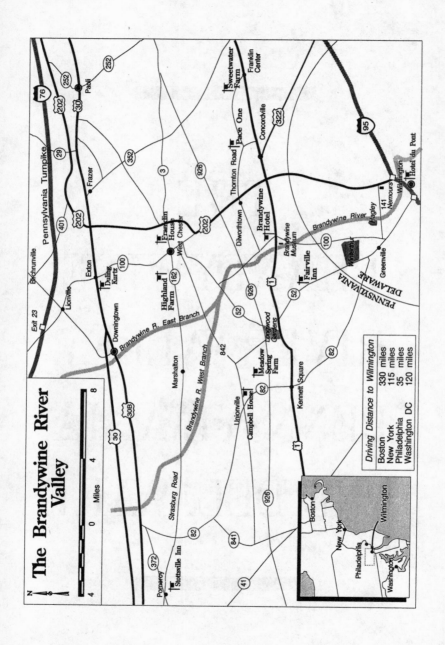

The Brandywine River Valley

N

Miles
0   4   8

Pennsylvania Turnpike

Pomeroy
372
Scottsville Inn

30
30B

Strasburg Road

Exit 23

Birchrunville

401
202

Lionville

Exton

Downingtown

Brandywine R. East Branch

Brandywine R. West Branch

Marshalton

Unionville

Campbell House

82

841

41

82

842

Meadow
Spring
Farm

Kennett Square

1

926

82

Longwood
Gardens

52

926

Fairville
Inn

52

1

100

Greenville

Winterthur

DELAWARE
PENNSYLVANIA

Brandywine
Museum

Brandywine
Hotel

Dilworthtown

202

West Chester

Franklin
House

Highland
Farm

Duling
Kurz

100

162

3

352

926

Frazer

29

202
401

252

252

Paoli

76

30

Thornton Road

Pace One

Sweetwater
Farm

Concordville

Franklin
Center

322

95

Brandywine River

Hagley

Nemours

141

Wilmington

Hotel du Pont

Driving Distance to Wilmington

Boston	330 miles
New York	115 miles
Philadelphia	35 miles
Washington DC	120 miles

Boston

New York

Philadelphia

Washington

Wilmington

Will your first destination be the world-class formal gardens of Longwood, the incredible display of hand-crafted early American furniture of Winterthur, or the exquisite museum along the banks of the Brandywine that holds a grand collection of Wyeth family paintings? During the past ten years this area has seen a good deal of development. However, there are still pristine pockets of the valley where the traveler can experience the lovely landscape. Original eighteenth-century Quaker-built fieldstone farm houses still dot the countryside, and many have been converted to restaurants and lodgings. The fabulous estates of the Du Pont family and the many horse farms still stand as elegant reminders of the gentry's gracious past.

These mansions are a far cry from the huts of animal skin and bark that housed the area's earliest residents, the Leni Lenape Indians. In 1623, the Dutch arrived in the area that is now Wilmington, Delaware. In 1631, they were massacred by the Lenapes.

The Swedes came in 1638 and tried to coexist with the natives peacefully, only to be ousted by the Dutch in 1651. The English seized the area thirteen years later, and finally stabilized the region when William Penn arrived in 1682.

Through the early 1700s, Quakers moved into the Brandywine area and, as millers and farmers, began to supply the rapidly expanding Colonial city of Philadelphia. The stone houses that we have the good fortune to visit, stay, and dine in today were built at this time.

The industry of the early settlers made the Brandywine Valley vital to the American cause during the Revolutionary War. Powder mills supplied munitions for Washington's army. The Battle of the Brandywine was one of the largest engagements of the war, with more than 30,000 soldiers involved. It was a resounding defeat for the Colonists, and many Tories proclaimed the "end of the War." But Washington's crippled army wintered at nearby Valley Forge, crossed the Delaware at Trenton at Christmas, and, as they say, the rest is history.

Before the Civil War, the area was an important link in the Underground Railroad. In the mid-1800s, the Du Pont company became the prominent employer in the valley. By the turn of the century, Howard Pyle and the artists of the Brandywine School were building the artistic style that carried on through three generations of the Wyeth family.

Today, the area around Kennett Square is still the mushroom-growing capital of the world. With the nation's growing interest in exotic foods, and with new techniques allowing such "wild mushrooms" as the shiitake, oyster, portabella, and cremini to be grown in controlled conditions, fresh life has come to an almost-forgotten industry.

Brandywine Valley Tourist Information Center. Located at the entrance to Longwood Gardens, Route 1, Kennett Square, PA 19348; (215) 388-2900 or (800) 228-9933. The complete listing of all local events is available here. Open daily 10 A.M. to 6 P.M.; January to mid-March, 10 A.M. to 5 P.M.

SPECIAL EVENTS THROUGHOUT THE YEAR

March. The week before and after Easter, Longwood Gardens Easter Conservatory Display; (215) 388-6741.

Early May. Winterthur Point-to-Point Races; (302) 888-4600.

Late May. Brandywine Battlefield Revolutionary War Encampment; (215) 459-3342.

Mid-June through August. Longwood Gardens Festival of Fountains. Tuesday, Thursday, Saturday evenings; (215) 388-6741.

Third week of September. Chester County Mushroom Festival, Kennett Square; (215) 344-6365.

Mushroom Symposium and Mushroom Banquet, Thursday night. Longwood Inn, Kennett Square; (215) 444-3515.

First Saturday in October. Chester County Day. Historic house, driving, garden, and walking tours. Advance purchase tickets required. Box 1, West Chester, PA 19381; (215) 431-6353.

Early November through Thanksgiving. Chrysanthemum Festival, Longwood Gardens; (215) 388-6741.

Friday after Thanksgiving through first week of January. A Brandywine Christmas. Model trains exhibit. Brandywine River Museum, Chadds Ford; (215) 388-7601.

Late November through December. Yuletide at Winterthur; (302) 888-4600.

December. Christmas Conservatory Display and Outdoor Lighting, Longwood Gardens; (215) 388-6741.

WHERE TO GO, WHAT TO DO

MUSEUMS AND GARDENS

Winterthur. Henry Francis Du Pont had an enormous family fortune and an insatiable passion for collecting the finest examples of handmade American furniture and decorative arts. He not only amassed a collection of more than 89,000 objects, but he also collected entire rooms from historic homes destined for the wrecker's ball and moved them intact—including the moldings, staircases, and wallpaper—into his family's mansion, which he continued to enlarge until it encompassed a total of 196 rooms. His collection of objects is displayed in these room settings that represent periods of American history from 1640 through 1840.

The best way to appreciate this collection is to take one of the reserved tours, usually of no more than four persons, led by a knowledgeable, highly trained guide. As you walk through the rooms you'll see an apparently endless number of priceless high-style antiques, wall upon wall of porcelain displays, rare textiles, mirrors, clocks, lamps, silver, and rugs.

Reserved Tours of the Mansion. The structure of the tours was revamped in 1988. Each tour has a different theme and appeals to visitors with different interests. Each is offered with a one-hour and a two-hour option. "American Interiors" introduces basic furniture styles, regional differences, and Henry Francis Du Pont's collecting philosophy. This tour usually is most appropriate for the first-time visitor. "A Diverse Nation" celebrates early America's ethnic and regional diversity and is designed for those interested in the history of the young nation. This tour includes room settings and artifacts representative of the Pennsylvania Germans, the New York Dutch, the English, and the Shakers.

"American Craftsmanship" traces the design of American deco-

At Winterthur there are 196 rooms filled with the finest examples of handmade American furniture and decorative arts.

rative arts with a special emphasis on furniture. The tour covers regional differences in the furniture-making styles of Boston, Newport, and Philadelphia, along with the influences of English, French, and Chinese designs. Most of the finest pieces in the collection are visited on this tour, including the Montmorenci Stair Hall, the Chinese Parlor, the Port Royal Parlor, and the Blackwell Parlor. For the connoisseur of fine furniture, this is our choice.

These tours are by reservation only. They run from the second week in January through early April and from June through mid-November; $12.50 for the two-hour tours and $8 for the one-hour tours. Children under 12 not admitted to these tours.

"Yuletide at Winterthur." During the holiday period, the focus of the museum shifts away from the decorative arts and highlights the holiday-entertaining customs of early America. This seventy-five-minute tour goes through twenty-one rooms decorated with platters of holiday foods (sorry, no samples). This is the only tour in the main house that accepts young children.

The Yuletide tour is offered from mid-November through December. Adults, $9; children under 17, $4.50. This tour is popular, so make reservations early.

Special Interest Tours. A tour of the museum with a more directed focus can also be arranged. Some of the topics include needlework, English ceramics, Oriental rugs, American silver, Queen Anne or Chippendale furniture, American glass, American clocks, or German folk art.

Reservations a week or more in advance usually are required; $50 includes admission for up to four adults. These same specialized tours also are open to the general public on a rotating schedule. The topics and times change each year.

Nonreserved Tours. "Port Royal Tour." During the spring when the bulbs and flowering trees are at their peak, a modified tour of the main building is offered. This forty-five-minute tour goes to sixteen of the rooms in the main house, which are normally included on the reserved tours.

"Two Centuries Tour." This tour is open to children of all ages. The setting is more like a conventional museum with exhibit areas that show the development of American interiors from 1640 to 1840.

From mid-April through May a ticket includes the Port Royal tour, Two Centuries tour, and garden tram tour. Adults, $9; children over 12 and seniors, $7.50; children under 12, free.

A new two-story building scheduled to be completed in 1992 will have three self-guided galleries. The American Experience gallery will replace the Two Centuries tour. The Furniture Exhibition gallery will be a changing exhibit of highlights from the museum's collection, and a third gallery will have changing exhibits.

Winterthur Gallery Shop. More than 800 items are for sale in the shop. They range from fine furniture pieces to ceramics, jewelry, garden plants, and garden furniture.

Gardens. The 200-acre garden is at its peak during the spring when the bulbs, azaleas, and rhododendron are in bloom. Miles of trails and paths crisscross the 1,000-acre, landscaped estate.

Visitor Pavilion. The collection of books for sale here on the decorative arts is among the best available anywhere. The garden cafeteria serves breakfast, lunch, and snacks Tuesday through Sunday, 8 A.M. to 4 P.M.

Library. Admission is free to the comprehensive decorative arts library of American arts (Colonial times to 1920) and to the rare book library. We've used the facilities as we researched original Shaker recipes and door styles found in the Lower Connecticut River Valley. Open Monday through Friday, 8:30 A.M. to 4:30 P.M.

The museum is open Tuesday through Saturday, 9 A.M. to 5 P.M., and Sunday, 12 to 5 P.M. The last tour is at 4 P.M. General admission to the gardens includes admission to the Two Centuries tour. Adults, $8; children over 12 and seniors, $6.50; children under 12, free. Specialized tour prices as indicated above. Located on Route 52, six miles northwest of Wilmington. Winterthur, DE 19735; (302) 888-4600 or (800) 448-3883.

Longwood Gardens. The 350 acres of this magnificent, perfectly manicured paradise include an Italian water garden; rock garden; vegetable, perennial, wildflower, and other gardens. There are also sculptured topiary, fountains, a bell tower, and four acres of stunning, landscaped conservatories.

This is a place to visit in any season, as the flowers and plants in the great open areas of the conservatory are changed frequently.

The main conservatory at Longwood Gardens.

In January and February, even when snow is on the ground, massive displays of tulips, azaleas, camellias, daffodils, and pansies greet you at every turn. At Easter there are fragrant lilies, daffodils, freesias, and tulips. From late October to Thanksgiving there is a display of giant chrysanthemums. From Thanksgiving through New Year's Day, large crowds come to see the Christmas display of 2,000 poinsettias and towering, illuminated outdoor Christmas trees. Permanent display areas of the conservatory include the orchid, rose, fern, tropical plant, desert, and rain forest rooms.

From mid-June through August there are illuminated fountain displays with coordinated music on Tuesday, Thursday, and Saturday evenings. For a few nights during the summer, fireworks accompany the fountain displays; reservations are a must on these nights. In addition, visitors can enjoy an outdoor theater, pipe organ concerts in the conservatory, and a variety of special events.

In the middle of the gardens is a restaurant serving cafeteria-style food, with seating outside in warm weather, and a formal, full-service restaurant.

Open daily, 9 A.M. to 5 P.M. The conservatories are open 10 A.M. to 5 P.M. The Terrace Restaurant is open daily, 11 A.M. to 3 P.M. and on evenings when the gardens are open late. There are also evening hours during the summer and winter holiday season. Adults, $8; children, 6 to 14, $2; children under 6, free. For a detailed listing of special events, send a stamped, self-addressed business envelope. Located on Route 1, three miles northeast of Kennett Square. Box 501, Kennett Square, PA 19348-0501; (215) 388-6741.

Nemours Mansion and Gardens.   Visitors to this 102-room, Louis XVI-style chateau built by Alfred Du Pont in 1909–1910 view the home as it was when the Du Ponts lived here. Upon arrival, visitors are given a flower grown in the chateau's greenhouse; on our visit it was a long-stemmed rose. A complimentary glass of orange juice is often served at the start or conclusion of the tour, on the terrace if the weather is nice.

The tour takes you through the formal living rooms, bedrooms, and kitchen, and then down to the billiard room and two bowling alleys. The home is furnished with antique furniture, Oriental rugs, tapestries, and paintings dating back to the fifteenth century. There is a bottling room where spring water was bottled for use on the estate. A glimpse at the backup heating and electrical system installed throughout the mansion shows visitors the practical side of Alfred Du Pont.

The bus then takes you through the landscaped 300 acres, stopping at various points in the formal garden and at the building that houses a collection of vintage automobiles. We suggest that you stroll through the formal gardens, which stretch for more than a third of a mile along the main vista from the mansion. They are among the finest examples of French gardens in the United States.

Open May through November. Tours are given Tuesday through Saturday at 9 and 11 A.M., 1 and 3 P.M. On Sunday, tours are given at 11 A.M., 1 and 3 P.M. Reservations are required. Visitors must be over 16. Admission, $8. Box 109, Rockland Road, Wilmington, DE 19899; (302) 651-6912.

Hagley Museum.   Learn about industry in early America while exploring this 230-acre site of the Du Ponts' first black-powder works, the foundation upon which the family fortune was built. Start in the visitor center, where a video presentation and dioramas introduce you to the process of making gun powder.

A bus takes you to the top of the property to visit Eleutherian Mills, the house built by E. I. Du Pont in 1803 and occupied by five generations of the family. Displays include a 1911 electric car and a custom-designed, 1928 Du Pont motor car, a cooper's workshop where the art of making wooden barrels is demonstrated, the Du Pont's first office, and a French Renaissance garden that specializes in espaliered trees and herbs, vegetables, flowers, and fruits from the early nineteenth century. We suggest taking the Powderman's tour, which begins at the machine shop where the turbine is started. You then watch the operation of the roll mill and, after a charge of gun powder is exploded, you will see how they test its purity.

You can also visit Blacksmith Hill, a workers' community. Restored buildings include a one-room school and a typical worker's home. In one of the nineteenth-century buildings a local caterer operates a small café. Sit on the porch in summer or by the fire in winter to enjoy homemade soups, salads, sandwiches, and desserts.

Open daily, April through December, 9:30 A.M. to 4:30 P.M. Open weekends January through March, 9:30 A.M. to 4:30 P.M. On weekdays during the winter a guided tour begins at 1:30 P.M. Adults, $8; seniors and students, $6.50; children 6 to 14, $3; children under 6, free. Located on Route 141 in Wilmington. Box 3630, Wilmington, DE 19807; (302) 658-2400.

Brandywine River Museum. This restored nineteenth-century gristmill on the banks of the Brandywine River is now home to three generations of Wyeth paintings, which are always on permanent display. The third-floor Andrew Wyeth gallery exhibits approximately forty watercolors, dry brush, and tempera paintings that represent Andrew Wyeth's career from 1938 to the present. The Brandywine Heritage galleries include works by Howard Pyle, N. C. Wyeth, and other members of the Wyeth family, along with Jasper Cropsey, Maxfield Parrish, and others.

The museum itself, a notable architectural restoration, includes two glass towers that offer dramatic views of the Brandywine. The view from the benches in front of the full-length glass windows overlooking the Brandywine is a perfect complement to viewing the Wyeth paintings, as many were painted in the local area and along the banks of this river.

A yearly tradition for train fanciers of all ages is the holiday display of working O-gauge model trains. On the first floor is a bookstore and a cafeteria that overlooks the river. A nature trail outside winds along the river, sculptures, and a wildflower garden.

Open daily, 9:30 A.M. to 4:30 P.M. Adults, $4; seniors over 65, $2.50; children 6 to 12 and students, $2; children under 6, free. Restaurant open 11 A.M. to 3 P.M. Located on Route 1 at the intersection of Route 100. Box 141, Chadds Ford, PA 19317; (215) 459-1900.

The Christian C. Sanderson Museum.   Imagine an old-fashioned schoolteacher who taught nine grades in a one-room schoolhouse; a personal friend of the Wyeth family who appears in many of Andrew's paintings; a historian who attended every presidential inauguration from Teddy Roosevelt to Lyndon Johnson; and, most important, an incurable pack rat who lived eighty-five years and saved every important scrap of paper he came across throughout his long life. This incredible storehouse of "stuff" includes a wealth of Wyeth family memorabilia and some of Andrew Wyeth's early paintings. Other items in the collection include artifacts from the Revolutionary and Civil wars, World Wars I and II. This small museum is staffed by volunteers who enthusiastically tell stories about the items on display.

Open Saturday and Sunday, 1 to 4:30 P.M. A donation is requested. Located 100 yards north of Route 1 on Route 100. Chadds Ford, PA 19317; (215) 388-6545.

Delaware Museum of Natural History.   At this museum, you can walk on a sheet of Plexiglas and look down on an array of shells for a sense of what it's like to walk on an Australian barrier reef. All that's missing are the sharp pieces of coral and the sea cucumbers we encountered when we walked on the real thing. In the showcases are unusual shells and carvings done on shells, such as a detailed cameo on a helmet shell and scrimshaw done by political prisoners in New Caledonia in the 1860s. This shell collection is one of the finest in this hemisphere.

Other sections of the museum include the Hall of Mammals, the Hall of Birds, and an undersea world. Nature films are shown daily. Open Monday through Saturday, 9:30 A.M. to 4:30 P.M.; Sunday, 12 to 5 P.M. Adults, $3.50; seniors over 65, $2.50; students and children, $2; children under 3, free. Located on Route 52 in Greenville, DE. Box 3937, Wilmington, DE 19807; (302) 658-9111.

Delaware Art Museum. This museum houses 250 works of Howard Pyle (1853–1911), the noted American illustrator acknowledged to be the father of the Brandywine School of painting. His students included, among others, N. C. Wyeth and Maxfield Parrish.

A new wing, completed in 1987, houses an outdoor sculpture terrace, children's participatory gallery, and a museum store. Highlights of the permanent collection include an important pre-Raphaelite English collection and works of prominent American painters from 1840 to the present.

Open Tuesday, 10 A.M. to 9 P.M.; Wednesday through Saturday, 10 A.M. to 5 P.M.; Sunday, 12 to 5 P.M. Admission is free. 2301 Kentmere Parkway, Wilmington, DE 19806; (302) 571-9590.

The Franklin Mint Museum. At one time or another, we've all seen promotions from the Franklin Mint: collectible plates, porcelain, bells, dolls, ingots, and thimbles. Where does it all come from? This museum is on the property of the world's largest private mint, which produces all these collectibles. Many days, you can watch artists at their craft. The museum theater shows a film that describes the art of minting. Many of the items currently being produced are for sale in the shop.

Open Tuesday through Saturday, 9:30 A.M. to 4:30 P.M.; Sunday 1 to 4 P.M. Free admission. Located on Route 1, south of Media at Franklin Center, PA 19091; (215) 459-6168.

The Wharton Esherick Museum. "Art is a reflection of nature," stated the famous woodworker Wharton Esherick. The house he built, which blends into the hillside near Valley Forge, PA, is a physical testament to his philosophy. The roof curves down toward the earth. The walls slope upward, the way a tree trunk grows. A magnificent, red-oak spiral stair twists its way skyward through the interior. The house is filled with furniture and sculpture crafted by the artist.

Open March through December. Saturday, 10 A.M. to 5 P.M.; Sunday, 1 to 5 P.M. Reservations required. Adults, $3; children under 12, $2; children under 2, free. Ask for directions. Located near Valley Forge Park. Box 595, Paoli, PA 19301; (215) 644-5822.

Brandywine Battlefield State Park. The Marquis de Lafayette, a wealthy French teenager, joined the American revolutionary forces in the fall of 1777. He was immediately given the rank of Major General by a Continental Congress starved for Europeans knowledgeable in the art of warfare, and was put to the test just three weeks later in the Battle of the Brandywine. Watch the story unfold in an excellent slide show at the museum here. Pick up a map and a detailed 23-mile driving tour at the museum which shows the geography, terrain, and actual positions of each army on the day of the battle September 11, 1777. Much of the terrain is little changed from Revolutionary days. You can also tour the farmhouses that served as Washington's and Lafayette's headquarters.

Open Tuesday through Saturday, 9 A.M. to 5 P.M.; Sunday, 12 to 5 P.M. Free admission. Located on Route 1 just south of Route 202; (215) 459-3342.

Phillips Mushroom Place. Kennett Square is known as the mushroom-growing capital of the world. Not only do they grow the common button mushroom but, with the growing interest in edible wild mushrooms, they have expanded to include more exotic varieties: shiitake, portabella, cremini, and oyster mushrooms. The taste of these is far more flavorful than the button mushroom and the prices are reasonable.

The farm buildings where the mushrooms are grown are not open for visitors, so this museum, which has dioramas, a movie, slides, and exhibits showing real mushrooms in all their stages of development, is the best way to learn about mushrooms.

The store is packed with hundreds of gift items that have a mushroom motif. You can purchase button mushrooms ranging from the small type good for marinating and pickling, to large ones good for stuffing, as well as the exotic varieties described above. Jars of pickled and marinated button mushrooms are also for sale.

The store is open daily, 10 A.M. to 6 P.M. Museum admission: adults, $1.25; seniors, 75¢; children, 7 to 12, 50¢; children under 6 and educational groups, free. Located on Route 1 south of Longwood Gardens, Kennett Square, PA 19348; (215) 388-6082. If the store doesn't have the size or variety of the mushroom you want, ask for directions to the farm, located a few miles outside of Kennett Square.

WINERY

Chaddsford Winery. If you are interested in tasting the wine that is made today from Pennsylvania-grown grapes, then stop by Chaddsford for a taste. Since 1982 Eric Miller's production at this small boutique winery has grown from 7,000 to approximately 50,000 gallons. Visitors can take a self-guided tour of the winery. On weekends, the better quality wines are available for sampling; there is a $5 charge for a glass.

Open Tuesday through Saturday, 10 A.M. to 5:30 P.M.; Sunday, 12 to 5 P.M. Located on Route 1, five miles south of Route 202. Box 229, Chadds Ford, PA 19317; (215) 388-6221.

SHOPPING

Dilworthtown Country Store. The homey atmosphere of this converted old general store, at the intersection of two back roads, is a great place to browse and buy. Folk art, baskets, quilts, antiques, pottery, and furniture—everything for the country look— is attractively displayed.

Open from Monday through Saturday, 9:30 A.M. to 5:30 P.M.; October to Christmas, Sunday, 12 to 4 P.M. Take the first right-hand turn off Route 100 north of Route 1. 275 Brinton's Bridge Road, West Chester, PA 19382; (215) 399-0560.

Northbrook Orchards. The strawberries from these fields are worth a special trip. We go every year. You can pick your own berries or buy them at the farm stand. Cider doughnuts are made fresh at the store. When the strawberry season is over at the end of June, the picking continues with peaches, apples, pumpkins, and squash.

Open daily, June through October, 9 A.M. to 5 P.M. Call ahead to check what's available for picking. Located at the corner of Route 842 and Northbrook Road, West Chester, PA 19382; (215) 793-1210.

Baldwin Book Barn. Housed on five floors in an old barn are vast quantities of old books, neatly organized by subject matter. This is the kind of place where you could spend hours browsing. To offset the cost of your purchases, you may want to bring a stack of hardcover books (no textbooks) to sell.

Open Monday through Saturday, 9 A.M. to 5:30 P.M.; Sunday, 10 A.M. to 5:30 P.M. Located on Route 100 just south of West Chester, 865 Lenape Road, West Chester, PA 19382; (215) 696-0816.

CANOEING AND TUBING

Northbrook Canoe Company. A leisurely way to enjoy the river valley is to rent either a canoe or a tube for a paddle or float down the river. Canoe trips can range from an hour up to six hours. Tube trips are either two or three hours long. Transportation is provided back to the starting point.

The staff will help you plan a trip. The more isolated section of the river is the stretch from Mortonville to Northbrook instead of the section going toward Chadds Ford.

Open daily, April through October, 9 A.M. to 5 P.M. Reservations are essential. Approximate costs: tubes, two-hour trip, $7 per person; three-hour trip, $9 per person. Canoe rentals range from a one-hour trip for $16 to a six-hour trip for $35. From Kennett Square take Route 82 to Unionville. Take Route 842 three miles to Northbrook Road. From West Chester take Route 162 to Marshalton. Turn left on Northbrook Road; (215) 793-2279 or (215) 793-1553.

DRIVING TOURS

The Brandywine Hunt Country. An area of Chester County rarely visited is the miles and miles of open land stretching on both sides of Route 82, starting beyond Unionville and ending before Coatesville.

The preservation of this area started at the depths of the Depression when F. Plunkett Stewart, an avid fox hunter, and William Du Pont purchased vast tracts of land. Much of this land then became part of the huge King Ranch, and was used to fatten cattle for eastern markets. As you drive on the back roads, pay attention to the panels in the fences put there to make it easier for the fox hunters to cross from one field to the next. A few miles beyond Unionville on Route 82 are the kennels built for Mr. Stewart's Cheshire Fox hounds and now used by the Unionville hunt. Also along the road you'll see the home, rinks, and jumps used by Bruce Davidson, three-time winner of the Olympic three-day equestrian event.

With the hounds barking and the riders in their red jackets, the beginning of a hunt is an impressive sight. To find out when and where a hunt is leaving, we suggest calling the Unionville Saddle Shop, (215) 347-2320. Hunts are held from November through March, generally leaving at 11 A.M. on Tuesday, Thursday, and Saturday. Whether you see a hunt off or drive or bicycle on the back roads, we feel that you will be amazed by the unobstructed vistas. Follow these detailed instructions and have a county map available as a back-up (purchase one at the visitor's center next to Longwood Gardens) in case you make a wrong turn or want to continue backroading.

A Driving Tour East of Route 82. Start at Unionville with a stop at Sestrich's Country Market (closed on Sunday) for coffee, soup, or sandwiches. Drive two miles north on Route 82. Turn right on Green Valley Road. At the crossroad, turn right onto Apple Grove Road. Just before the corner is Thompson's custom butcher shop. At the corner is a tiny self-service vegetable stand. Immediately after turning the corner, notice the beautiful stone barn on your left. Bear left at the white barn with red doors. Follow along the Mortonville Creek (on your right) to Mortonville. Just before the bridge, turn left onto Strasburg Road. Take an immediate left turn onto Fair View Road. (*Note:* The road goes from pavement to dirt to gravel and back to pavement.) At the T intersection, turn right onto Du Pont Road. Follow this road, whose name changes to Doe Run Church Road. Turn left on Strasburg Road. At the gas station and deli, turn left onto Hep-

zibah Hill Road. After crossing the covered bridge, take an immediate right onto Covered Bridge Road (there is no sign). Follow
this road to Route 82. Turn left to get back to Unionville. This
tour is twelve miles.

A Driving Tour on the West Side of Route 82. To continue
from the preceding tour, turn left on Route 82 north and go two
miles to Route 841 south where you will turn right. (From Unionville, turn left—south—onto Route 841 five miles beyond the
town.) Take the second right turn at the Country Place store. Turn
left onto Runnymede Road, the first road on the left. Turn right on
Rosenvick Creek Road. At the T turn left on Gum Tree Road.
Beyond the Gum Tree Store Press, turn left on Wilson Road. At
the bottom of the hill, bear right onto Creek Road. Bear left at the
fork in the road (Friends Meeting Road goes to the right). Turn left
onto Greenlawn Road. At the fork, bear to the right. Go across
Route 841 and follow Sharitz Road (a dirt road) to a T. (*Note:* For
the next few miles the road is hard-packed dirt.) Turn left on
Thouron Road. Turn right onto Hicks Road, the first road on the
right. At the T under the power lines, turn left. Follow this road
to Route 842 and turn left. Take the second left onto Newark Road.
Turn right on Route 82. You will pass the kennels of the Unionville
hunt on the left. Follow Route 82 back into Unionville. This tour
is fifteen miles.

Driving along the Brandywine. From Longwood Gardens,
take Route 52 south to Winterthur. To see some of the large
estates, turn left on the roads that go between Route 52 and
Route 100. Continue along Route 52 to Route 100. Take this
twisting road north along the banks of the Brandywine River.
At the intersection of Route 1 and Route 100 is Hank's
Place, a local diner. The Christian Sanderson Museum, where
you'll find a collection of Wyeth memorabilia, is on Route 100
on the right-hand side. Brinton's Bridge Road, which will take
you to Dilworthtown Country Store, is the first road to the
right. Return to Route 100. Beyond Lenape is the Baldwin
Book Barn, a great place for old-book lovers. To avoid West
Chester, backtrack on Route 100 to Route 52. Follow this
road back to Longwood Gardens.

THEATER

The Playhouse Theatre. This 1,200-seat theater, located in the Hotel du Pont, presents plays and musicals before and after their Broadway runs. Reservations are essential. Du Pont Building, Wilmington, DE 19801; (302) 656-4401.

People's Light & Theatre Company. Comedies and drama are presented on two stages by a resident professional company. 39 Conestoga Road, Malvern, PA 19355; (215) 647-1900.

WHERE TO STAY

Hotel du Pont, Wilmington, DE

The Hotel Du Pont is one of the preeminent, grand old hotels in America. First-time visitors may find it hard to believe that such magnificence exists behind the nondescript exterior. The hotel was built in 1913 by the Du Pont Company. It was constructed in the grand European style by European craftsmen using the finest of materials. The lobby is a copy of a Venetian palace with walls of Italian travertine marble and a coffered ceiling with gold, pink, and red sculpted rosettes. Massive, intricately carved walnut doors lead into a foyer where a grand stairway of Italian marble sweeps down into the ninety-foot-long and thirty-foot-high, ornate and perfectly maintained ballroom.

Eight hundred original paintings by Brandywine artists are displayed throughout the hotel. The highlight of this collection is the three generations of Wyeth paintings that hang in the Brandywine–Christina dining room.

A major restoration and upgrading of the rooms is in process. To increase the size of the rooms, the hotel is reducing the total number of rooms. Renovations on floors six and seven are complete, and the results are wonderful. All the rooms have original art from the hotel's collection, high-quality Queen Anne- and Chippendale-style furniture, televisions hidden in armoires, direct-dial telephones, individually controlled air-conditioning and heating, and fully stocked mini-refrigerators that operate on the honor system. Each room has wall-to-wall carpeting and is decorated in quiet good taste. Walls are painted in subdued, restful hues interspersed with wood paneling. There is a king-size bed, couch, easy chairs, desk, double sink, thick terrycloth robes, glass-enclosed shower, a suit press, and shoeshine service. At present there are eight Executive Deluxe King rooms with Jacuzzis and forty Deluxe King rooms that have been renovated. Be sure to ask for one of the renovated rooms. Starting in July 1991 and continuing until March 1993, major renovations are scheduled for all of the rooms that have not yet been renovated. During this period there will be no rooms rented. However, the restaurants and the banquet and conference facilities will not be affected.

295 rooms, all with private bath. Sunday through Thursday, $100–$200. Friday and Saturday, $80–$150. Breakfast is not included. Children are welcome, no additional charge. No pets. Should you want to eat dinner and brunch at the hotel, be sure to inquire about the weekend packages: The Brandywine Overnighter, $79–$129 per person, and The Connoisseur's Weekend, $140–$185 per person. 11th and Market Streets, Wilmington, DE 19899; (302) 594-3125 or (800) 441-9019.

Sweetwater Farm, Glen Mills, PA

Turning in the circular drive, off a narrow country road dotted with private estates, we arrived at this eighteenth-century fieldstone manor house. A flag fluttered above the front door; the brick walkway was lined with bright flowers; graceful, majestic trees told us that skilled arborists had been at work. Sweetwater is far more than an elegant inn. Its special features include cottages and a swimming pool, and it is surrounded by fields where you may see horses or sheep grazing and rows of corn and alfalfa. This idyllic retreat is the epitome of genteel farm living.

The library, with an overstuffed couch, easy chairs, dish of candy

Sweetwater Farm is an eighteenth-century fieldstone manor house on a narrow country road.

or crackers, wood-burning fireplace, and a wall of books, is the favored gathering-spot during the winter. A more formal parlor, the dining room, and a conference room are also on the first floor. In warm weather the terrace, set with tables and chairs and overlooking the fields and swimming pool, is a favorite spot.

All of the rooms and cottages have telephones and are air-conditioned; most have televisions. For the ultimate in privacy we'd choose the Hideaway Cottage. On the first floor, there is a cozy living room with a wood-burning fireplace and a full kitchen. Upstairs, the bedroom has a four-poster double bed with a fishnet canopy, a glass-topped dressing table, and a private bath. Outside is a private sitting area that overlooks a horse rink and the pastures.

In the main house, the Fan-window Suite on the third floor is a favorite with honeymooners. The room is white with pink roses, white plaster walls, white wicker couches, white chairs, and a white headboard for the queen-size bed. The small bathroom has a charming white clawfoot tub.

Across the hall is the Loft Room with both a queen-size and a double bed. This room has a more masculine feel; it reminds us of Andrew Wyeth, with dark woods, a large spinning wheel, a basket of yarn skeins, and a staircase that once led to the attic. In contrast to the bath next door, this one is large and modern.

For those on a budget who want the romance of a fireplace room and don't mind sharing a bath, we suggest the Georgian Room, which has a high four-poster queen-size bed with a fishnet canopy. Across the hall is the master bedroom, which also has a fireplace and shares the hall bath.

Breakfast, served in the country kitchen or in the formal dining room, includes fresh eggs, country sausage, fresh fruit, juice, and homemade bran muffins.

Note: Guests spending daytime midweek summer hours outside by the swimming pool may hear some sounds from a nearby quarry.

Six rooms with private bath, $130–$140. Three rooms with shared bath, $120. Four cottages, $120–$165. A country breakfast is included. Swimming pool. Children under 18, no charge; third adult in room, $25 extra. Pets are permitted in the cottages. From the junction of Route 202 and Route 1 go north on Route 1 for five miles to Valley Road (Franklin Mint intersection). Turn left. At the T (1½ miles), turn left and then take an immediate right for ¾ mile to Sweetwater Road. 50 Sweetwater Road, Glen Mills, PA 19342; (215) 459-4711.

Fairville Inn, Mendenhall, PA

This inn has an ideal location on a main road halfway between Winterthur and Longwood Gardens. Two new buildings in the back allow guests to enjoy the convenient location yet have the feeling that they are in a country setting. Innkeepers Ole and Patricia Retlev run their inn like a small European hotel. "We like to be sure that our guests are comfortable when they arrive, and then we leave them alone. If they have questions, someone is always available," Ole explained to us.

In the main house, built in the 1820s, there is a staffed front desk, a comfortable breakfast and afternoon tea room, and a parlor.

Patricia Retlev has decorated the large rooms with quilted bed-spreads, matching draperies, and color-coordinated carpeting and bath towels. All of the rooms have cable televisions hidden in armoires, direct-dial phones, and individually controlled heating and air-conditioning. Five of the rooms have fireplaces. Most of the rooms have queen- or king-size beds and a sink that's separate from the bathroom. Of the five rooms in the original 1820s building, our favorite is the yellow room with a king-size bed: it is very bright and located in a quiet back corner of the inn.

The best rooms are in the newly constructed carriage house at the rear of the property overlooking fields. A top choice is the second-floor suite with a king-size bed, quilted bedspread, and a love seat upholstered in a matching fabric. It has two easy chairs set in front of the fireplace and a private balcony. The television and telephone are in the attached sitting room. Another favorite in the carriage house is the cathedral-ceilinged green room with a queen-size canopy bed, private deck, oversized bathtub in its own room, and a separate room with a shower.

After a walk or a jog on the route that begins at the back of the property and winds through miles of country roads, return for tea and homemade cookies served between 4 and 5 P.M.

Breakfast is freshly squeezed orange or grapefruit juice or homemade tomato juice (made from Pat's grandmother's recipe), homemade scones, breads, and muffins served with home-canned jams and jellies.

Thirteen rooms, all with private bath, $95–$145. Two suites, $150. Tea and continental breakfast is included. Children over 10 welcome, $10 additional. No pets. Route 52, Box 219, Mendenhall, PA 19357; (215) 388-5900.

Highland Farm Bed and Breakfast, West Chester, PA

Located on the top of a hill overlooking farmland is this large, four-story, 1850 Georgian Revival house. Wide Southern-style col-umned porches are filled with wicker furniture during the summer. Grand old trees surround the property. A large swimming pool in the back is surrounded by fieldstone walls, one of innkeeper John

O'Brien's ongoing projects. Congenial, gracious hostess Diane O'Brien is an accomplished interior decorator who has created what she refers to as a European-style country B&B. You probably will also meet Alex, their son, and Corny, their sheepdog. As Diane told us, "My two men (husband John and son Alex) keep me from making this into a full-time business. I'm doing this because I love meeting people."

Upon entering we felt as though we had discovered the ideal country home. To the left is an informal sitting area with wingback chairs and a wood-burning fireplace; to the right, a baby grand piano and pastel-colored Victorian couches; and beyond, a dining room and another sitting room with a wood-burning fireplace. The oak floors are covered with fine Oriental rugs. The ceilings are twelve feet high. Windows are draped with flowered-chintz designer fabric, and throughout is an abundance of fresh flowers, books, and decorative objects.

All of the beds have a feather bed as well as a down comforter on top of the mattress. Terrycloth robes are in all of the rooms. The two spacious rooms on the second floor share the hall bath. The Morning Glory Room has a double Portuguese (hand-painted) bed and a splendid view of the countryside, including perhaps the largest weeping beech tree on the East Coast. A wicker couch and two easy chairs are at one end of the room. The Duchess Rose Room has a queen-size bed covered by a half canopy. The draperies, sheets, pillows, and upholstered down-filled chaise longue are all coordinated with rose patterns. Both of these rooms get good morning sun.

On the third floor are two suites, each with a private bath as well as a separate sitting room. The Sunrise Room has a four-poster queen-size bed with Ralph Lauren white-on-white patterned cotton sheets and a chaise longue upholstered with white damask. The private bath has a six-foot soaking tub with dolphin feet. When we asked about the large collection of books in the adjoining sitting room, Diane happily said, "It's not a room without a pile of books." The Sunset Room has a double bed with both Laura Ashley and Ralph Lauren pink- and rose-colored bedding. The sitting room has a leather chair and a convertible couch.

Diane serves a full breakfast, but instead of a set routine she likes to accommodate her guests' preferences. Irish oatmeal, a gourmet house specialty served with buttermilk, is always available, as is homemade granola and fresh fruit. As a Southerner, Diane cooks a Southern breakfast upon request. She makes muffins daily and always has bacon and eggs for traditionalists.

Two rooms on the second floor share one bath, $105. Two suites on the third floor with private bath, $135. Swimming pool. Children permitted with prior approval only, $10 additional. No pets. Room air-conditioners in summer when needed. Highland Farm Road, West Chester, PA 19382. (215) 431-7026.

Campbell House Bed and Breakfast, Kennett Square, PA

Your hosts, Judy and Bill Campbell, are antique dealers specializing in fine eighteenth- and early nineteenth-century American furniture and accessories. The Keeping Room in this restored eighteenth-century stone farmhouse is where guests tend to congregate in the late afternoon over a glass of wine. Facing the massive stone walk-in fireplace that stretches the length of the room are sofas and an easy chair. Baskets hang from the 200-year-old beams. This room and two living rooms, all of which are for the use of the guests, are furnished with pieces from the owners inventory. Examples of exquisite and expensive pieces you'll find are a 1760 Connecticut Queen Anne highboy, a 1790 New London dining room table and chairs, and a collection of English Moka ware. Except for a few family pieces, everything is for sale and the prices are discreetly marked.

The three upstairs bedrooms are furnished with antique double beds, old quilts, and rag rugs. Two of the bedrooms share a bath. The smaller one is popular during the winter, as it has a wood-burning fireplace. The larger shared-bath room has two double beds and a collection of old quilts. There are small cracks between the floorboards in this room, so the sound of people talking in the Keeping Room filters in; if this room is occupied, guests are asked to leave the Keeping Room by 10 P.M. The third bedroom has an 1800s fishnet canopy bed and a large, modern, private bath.

Bill's special breakfast dish is shirred eggs made with eggs from their hen house. Judy's special dish is rum raisin French toast or a ham and cheese soufflé. In the summer, breakfast is served on the screened porch; in winter, at an antique table in the dining room. Antiquers should be sure to visit the shop next to the house. The large swimming pool gets a lot of use during the summer months.

Open all year except for times when the owners are away at antique shows. One room with private bath, $70. Two rooms with shared bath, $60. Full breakfast included. Swimming pool. Children over 12 welcome. Third person in room $15 additional. No pets. 160 East Doe Run Road, Kennett Square, PA 19348; (215) 347-6756.

Meadow Spring Farm, Kennett Square, PA

This 200-acre farm is one of the oldest working farms in the area. One of the buildings was constructed before 1710. At one time this was a dairy farm; now beef cattle and pigs are raised here, and hay, sweet corn, soy beans, barley, and clover are some of the crops farmed by the Hicks family. The large pond out front is a stopover for thousands of Canadian geese on their fall and spring migrations.

Owner Ann Hicks, who raised her family in this farmhouse, has decorated the living and dining room with a gallery of stuffed animals, dolls, and old family antiques. Ask to see the third-floor doll room where Ann's lifetime collection is attractively arranged. In the front part of the country kitchen next to the wood stove is a hot tub. Downstairs there's a game room with a pool table and a Ping-Pong table. Outdoors there's a large swimming pool. Guests are welcome to look around and explore the farm.

All of the bedrooms are air-conditioned and each has a television. In the farmhouse our favorite bedroom is the Canopy Room, with a fishnet-canopy queen-size bed, wallpaper that matches the dust ruffle, shelves of books, and an enormous private bath. The Fireplace Room, one of those that share a bath, includes a queen-size bed with a high wood headboard, chaise longue, and a working fireplace.

Two large rooms, each with a private bath, have recently been constructed above the garage. They each have wall-to-wall carpeting. One has a queen-size bed, desk, and chaise longue. The other has twin beds and is furnished with wicker chairs, sofa, and headboard.

A full farm breakfast is served in the dining room or, in warm weather, on the screened porch. A favorite of guests is the mushroom omelet served with sausage, scrapple, or bacon. Oatmeal or cold cereal, fruit, and juice are always available. From here, Longwood Gardens is only a mile away.

Three rooms with private bath, $75. Three rooms with a shared bath, $55. Children welcome, $10 additional. No pets. Full farm breakfast included. 201 East Street Road (Route 926), Kennett Square, PA 19348; (215) 444-3903.

Franklin House, West Chester, PA

Located across the street from one of the five public parks in the lovely historic town of West Chester, among many early eighteenth-century Greek Revival buildings, is this Federal-style three-story in-town guesthouse. "My family grew up here," Mary Ann Morgan-Porter told us, "so I can tell you a story about every piece in this house." George Porter, an accomplished painter in the American Impressionist style, has his studio in the Carriage House and currently is working on a series of alleyways of West Chester. His work is carried by a prominent Philadelphia gallery. His work, both oil paintings and metal sculptures, is displayed in the living room and dining room. Interested guests are welcome to visit him in his studio.

Mary Ann believes in giving her guests choices: a feather bed or an electric blanket, down or synthetic pillows, regular or decaffeinated coffee, and a room with or without a phone. When you get to your bath you'll find large bars of glycerine and Dial soap and a basket with both a loofah and a sponge which you're welcome to take with you. The house is centrally air-conditioned and all of the rooms have televisions.

Our two favorite bedrooms are those on the second floor, as they are large and airy. The spacious light-filled north bedroom has twin beds with colorful bedspreads that match the curtains. An adjoining bedroom shares the bath but is only used when both rooms are rented by the same family. The master bedroom, a corner room with four large windows, has a high queen-size pencil-post bed and a red gingham–upholstered easy chair. The private bath is down a single step. On the third floor is Poor Richard's Room, a garret-type room with new wall-to-wall beige carpeting, a double bed, and a child-size rocking chair. Mary Ann decorated the bathroom with sayings from Poor Richard's Almanac. What better way to contemplate the hidden meaning of Benjamin Franklin's words of wisdom than by soaking in an old-fashioned clawfoot tub?

For special occasions you can arrange to have a private dinner party for two to six in your own dining room. The tables are set with candles, china, crystal, and sterling flatware. Dinners are catered, so guests make their selections about three weeks in advance. The dinner and lodging package includes lodging (use of the room for 24 hours), dinner, breakfast, and a limited-edition print by George Porter ($200 per couple).

A continental buffet breakfast of fresh fruit, juice, Danish or muffins, and cold cereal is served in the dining room.

Three rooms, all with private bath, $75; $65 per night for two nights. There is a reduced rate if one family rents all three rooms. No children. No pets. No smoking. Continental breakfast and late-afternoon wine and cheese included. Franklin Street, West Chester, PA 19380. Call for directions; (215) 696-1665 or (215) 696-7727.

Brandywine River Hotel, Chadds Ford, PA

Set back from busy Route 1 in the center of Chadds Ford, practically across the street from the Brandywine River Museum, is this recently built, forty-room brick and cedar-shingle hotel. The standard rooms, all with two double beds, have individually controlled air-conditioning, remote-control televisions hidden in armoires, desks, and two telephones. The rooms are large and decorated with Queen Anne–style reproduction furniture, quilted bedspreads, and matching draperies. The larger rooms, here called suites, have a queen-size bed, a convertible couch, a desk, a fireplace that uses Duraflame logs, a double Jacuzzi, a stall shower, and a small refrigerator (not stocked).

Complimentary tea and cookies are set out in the lobby by the fireplace from 4 to 7 P.M. A continental buffet breakfast is served in an attractively decorated dining room. It includes granola, fresh fruit, croissants, bagels, sweet breads, and Danish. During the week breakfast is served from 6:30 to 9:30, and on the weekends from 8 to 11:30.

Twenty-nine rooms, all with private bath, $109. One room is wheelchair accessible, $109. Ten fireplace rooms with Jacuzzi, $125. Continental buffet breakfast and afternoon tea included. Children welcome, $10 extra; cribs available. No pets. Box 1058. Route 1 and Route 100, Chadds Ford, PA 19137-1058; (215) 388-1200.

Duling Kurtz House & Country Inn, Exton, PA

This 150-year-old stone house and barn complex, converted into a country inn and restaurant, was once in a rural setting. While the inn complex has remained the same size, the surrounding land has been developed into industrial parks. The rooms are individually decorated, giving it the feel of a country inn. However, the only common area for guests is the lobby area and a small second-floor porch room.

During the week, all of the rooms are rented for the same extremely low price. Some of the slight imperfections that would bother us at higher prices, such as the sound of cars (in some of the rooms) from a nearby busy road, the lack of views from some of the windows (one side of the inn faces a home improvement store), and the minimum amount of common space for a lounge or for a breakfast room are less significant because the midweek prices are so reasonable.

The rooms vary greatly in size and quality. All of them have reproduction Colonial furniture, a television, air-conditioning, and telephone. A basket with an apple and an orange and a fortune cookie greets each guest. Most of the windows have attractive fabric shutters that match the wallpaper.

The favorite room for many is the spacious George Washington Room on the first floor, which has a king-size, high-post cherry-wood canopy bed, and a step-down bath with a clawfoot tub (no shower) and a bidet. Also on the first floor is the Lincoln Suite with twin beds, a small sitting room, and a private courtyard. The Thomas Jefferson Room on the second floor has a queen-size bed, a desk, and a working fireplace. The James Buchanan Suite is perfect for three people. The bedroom has a double bed and the living room has a convertible couch as well as a second full bath. On the third floor our favorites are the Anthony Wayne, which has a queen-size bed and a nice view of the fields, and the Susan B. Anthony, a third-floor garret-type room with a slanted ceiling and a king-size bed.

A new addition to the inn is a second-floor brick-floored sitting room with windows on three sides and furnished with pillow-covered iron furniture. When you return to your room at night, you'll find chocolates and port wine. As there is no breakfast room, a continental breakfast tray with fruit, muffins, croissants, and jams is delivered to your room at the hour you specify.

Fourteen rooms, all with private bath, $80–$120. Sunday through Thursday, all rooms are $49.95–$69.95. Continental breakfast included. Children welcome, $15 additional. No pets. 146 South Whitford Road, Exton, PA 19341; (215) 524-1830.

Stottsville Inn, Pomeroy, PA

This is a classic pre-Civil War inn that once served as a stopover for travelers; Stottsville was the halfway point on the old Philadelphia-Lancaster Road. As was typical of inns along routes connecting the cities and towns of the day, meals and drinks were served on the first floor (see *Where to Dine,* page 265) and rooms for weary travelers were on the upper floors.

Throughout the inn are reminders of the past such as highback walnut and oak beds, dressers, brass chandeliers, and a Victorian pump organ, all original to the inn. In a glass showcase at the top of the stairs, one of the inn's ledgers displays the signatures of prominent people who stopped here in the late 1800s on their way to and from Philadelphia.

The rooms are spacious and are a good value both during the week and on the weekends. The innkeepers are working on upgrading the furnishings and adding their own individual touches. All of the rooms have direct-dial telephones, a television, and two easy chairs. Our favorite is room 4, which has a high double bed and a sunken tub and bidet. The innkeeper told us that they want their guests to have fun, so they put bubble pipes and rubber ducks in this bathroom.

We also like corner room 7 with a high carved antique double bed, and corner room 8 with a queen-size carved Victorian bed. Room 9 has a cherrywood king-size bed, and room 12 has a queen-size bed with a wicker headboard.

The bedtime turndown service here may bring back childhood memories: You'll find a small bottle of milk in a bowl of crushed ice, and a plate of homemade cookies.

A self-serve buffet breakfast is available in the green dining room on the second floor. It includes fresh fruit, juice, granola, and muffins. If you like spring water, bring your jugs; down the road is a 8,600 gallon-per-day natural spring where the local people come to fill their jugs free of charge.

Ten rooms, all with private bath. Sunday through Thursday, $55.95; Friday and Saturday, $75.95. Continental breakfast included. Children over 12 welcome, no additional charge. No pets. Route 372 at Strasburg Road, Pomeroy, PA 19367; (215) 857-1133.

Pace One Restaurant and Country Inn, Thornton, PA

The building that houses this restaurant and inn is on a steep hill so we suggest parking in front to save carrying your bags up the equivalent of an extra flight of stairs. The restaurant (see *Where to Dine,* page 263) is on the first floor, meeting rooms are on the second and third floors, and guest rooms are on the fourth floor. The rooms, many with sloping ceilings and garret-type windows, have a casual country feel. Each room has a hardwood floor and is furnished simply: a double bed covered with a quilt, a couch, wooden chairs, and end tables. The wreaths of dried flowers and the prints by a local artist give the rooms a country look. All of the rooms are air-conditioned and have private telephones.

Six rooms, all with private bath, $65–$85. Continental breakfast included. Children welcome—no extra charge. No pets. Concord-Thornton and Glen Mills Road, Thornton, PA 19373; (215) 459-3702.

Should all of these accommodations be filled, the visitor center at the entrance to Longwood Gardens has a listing of additional accommodations including motels, hotels, and inns as well as bed-and-breakfast homes. Be aware that the visitor center can help direct you to the type of accommodation you want, but will probably not give you an opinion rating one place over another; (215) 388-2900 or (800) 228-9933.

WHERE TO DINE

FINE DINING

Hotel du Pont, Wilmington, DE

The luxurious Green Room, recently refurbished to its original 1913 elegance, is on par with the world's great hotel dining rooms. You dine in the warm glow of handcrafted gold chandeliers, which hang from a twenty-five-foot vaulted ceiling with gold leaf accents. Guests are serenaded by a harpist in the musician's gallery during the evening meal. The service is properly attentive, but not obtrusive.

Dinner features elaborate preparations done in the French continental style. At a recent meal, we enjoyed a delicate seafood sausage with a white wine sauce and chunks of Maine lobster and truffles with a walnut oil dressing. A seafood medley of lobster, scallops, scampi, and jumbo lump crabmeat with just a touch of tarragon and Pernod and flamed with brandy was an utter luxury. The chateaubriand is superb here, as is the veal sautéed with apples and Calvados sauce. Desserts include such specialties as phyllo layers filled with lemon cream served with fresh raspberry sauce, or layers of chocolate and orange ice cream with fresh julienne of orange and a Grand Marnier sauce.

Lunch is served in both the Green Room and in the Brandywine Room. Both the calories and cholesterol are listed next to each item on the menu. The grilled swordfish, which was cut too thin for our taste, came in at 671 calories and 81 milligrams of cholesterol; the single crabcake was surprisingly favorable at 283 calories and 179 milligrams of cholesterol. The turkey club sandwich, at 965 calories and 139 milligrams of cholesterol, was prepared in the traditional way. The most healthful item on the menu turned out to be a favorite of ours, Caesar salad, at 173 calories and just 16 milligrams of cholesterol—which seemed low given the egg yolk and Parmesan cheese in the salad. A plate of properly chewy almond macaroons and chocolate candies was presented with the bill.

The decor and menu in the Brandywine-Christina room is altogether different. Paintings from the Brandywine School are displayed on walnut-paneled walls. If you wish to sit amid the painting of three generations of the Wyeth family, ask to be seated in the large middle room with a high ceiling. The cooking is American/International, and highlights seafood preparations. Start with a salad of lobster, scallops, and shrimp; sautéed shrimp with garlic and fresh herbs; or local Kennett Square mushrooms with crabmeat and hollandaise sauce. Entrées include grilled swordfish with an herb crust and white wine sauce, large tender poached sea scallops served with a saffron sauce, and a succulent two-pound broiled Maine lobster that is almost always available. Rack of lamb, prime New York sirloin, and chateaubriand for two are specialties for meat lovers.

Sunday brunch is the bargain for those who want to sample the haute cuisine and ambience of the Green Room. No sooner are you seated than your waitress brings a continuously refilled glass of fresh-squeezed orange or grapefruit juice. A beautiful buffet table awaits. Perfectly arranged plates of cold meats, pâtés, seafood salad, fruits, cheese, bread, and croissants will get you started. An entrée of traditional eggs Benedict, grilled salmon filet, a fluffy three-egg lobster and wild mushroom omelete, or the famous Hotel du Pont crab and cheese sandwich is available. Leave room to visit the dessert table, which includes Linzer tortes, napoleons, Black Forest cakes, and more. *Bon appétit!*

Green Room is open for breakfast, 7 to 11 A.M.; lunch, Monday through Saturday, 11:30 A.M. to 2 P.M.; $11.00–$17.00. Sunday brunch, 9:30 A.M. to 2:30 P.M.; $24.95. Dinner, Friday and Saturday, 6 to 9:30 P.M. Entrées, $25–$45. (302) 594-3154.

Brandywine Room is open for lunch, Monday through Friday, 11:30 A.M. to 2 P.M.; $10–$17. Dinner, Monday through Saturday, 6 to 11 P.M. Entrées, $19.75–$30. (302) 594-3156. 11th and Market Streets, Wilmington, DE 19899.

Silk Purse—Sow's Ear, Wilmington, DE

On an obscure side street just outside the center of Wilmington, Ezio Reynaud has for more than ten years pampered his guests with elegant dining in an intimate atmosphere. Classic cuisine is prepared by a highly competent kitchen staff and served to you by a well-trained, discreet staff at fourteen well-spaced tables. The prices are high, but so is the quality. On a recent evening, appetizers included an intriguing Stilton and celery soup, wild mushrooms and fontina fondue in a puff pastry, lobster ragout with saffron, and shad roe with a sorrel and bacon sauce. Several game dishes were featured the night we dined: a loin of rabbit with basil and mustard sauce, and venison with green-peppercorn sauce. Other entrées included sweetbreads with a wild mushroom ragout, a perfectly prepared piece of salmon with a red wine sauce, and a tenderloin of beef with parsley and wild mushrooms. On Friday and Saturday nights reservations are a must.

The new trend for restaurateurs is to open a less expensive bistro on the same premises. Judging from the crowd at the Sow's Ear, which opened in November 1989, Ezio Reynaud appears to have a winner. Here the tables are closer together and neither the lighting or conversation is subdued. The banquettes are covered with Oriental carpeting, as are the folding chairs. The white walls are stenciled to look like trees; the floor is painted bright red; tables are covered with yellow-and-white checkered oil cloth.

This is a menu good for grazing: you can order a couple of

appetizers and soup if you don't want an entrée. The house drink
is the sow's ear, made with Champagne and passion fruit liqueur.
Appetizers included oysters wrapped in bacon, grilled goat cheese
in grape leaves, grilled squid with lemon garlic butter, and an
outstanding portion of country bread with pesto and smoked trout.
Main courses included a strongly flavored pork chop with cracked
fennel and beans, lamb with white bean ragout, and rabbit with red
wine sauce served on buttered noodles.

Desserts include a hot fudge banana sundae, apple brown Betty
with whipped cream, or aged Stilton and pears. The eclectic background music ranged from Louis Armstrong, to The Anvil Chorus
from *Il Trovatore,* country and western to '60s rock.

Silk Purse is open for dinner Monday through Saturday, 6 to 9
P.M. Dinner entrées $22.50–$31.50. The Sow's Ear serves lunch
Monday through Saturday, 11:30 A.M. to 2 P.M.; $9.25–$13.75. Dinner, Monday through Saturday, 5:30 to 10 P.M.. Dinner entrées,
$9.25–$13.75. 1307 North Scott Street, Wilmington, DE; (302)
654-7666. Parking for both restaurants is on the street and in
nearby lots.

Vickers, Lionville, PA

Table-side service for classic preparations such as steak Diane,
Caesar salad, cherries jubilee, crêpes Suzette, and bananas Foster
is presented with panache by skilled European waiters. Owner
Arturo Burigatto, originally from Venice, is always on site to over-
see the dining experience at this moderate-size restaurant, which
seats about 100 in three dining rooms.

On a cold day, our favorite spot is the table for two facing the
open walk-in fireplace in the New Room. From the appetizer cart,
choose from a selection of smoked fish, meats, and fresh pâtés.
Have a Caesar salad prepared table-side, or a puff pastry shell filled
with seafood in a lobster sauce, lobster ravioli, or shrimp and wild
mushrooms in garlic butter. An unusual entrée is the medallion of
bison, which is not as gamy as venison. The rack of lamb for two
is a popular choice, done here with rosemary, thyme, mustard, and
port wine. Fish entrées include Dover sole sautéed with lime,

orange, and grapefruit sauce; salmon with radicchio and walnut and watercress sauce; and red snapper with artichokes and a red wine sauce. A spinach salad and vegetables accompany all of the entrées. We ordered sautéed quail with rosemary and a sherry wine vinegar sauce, the classically prepared beef Wellington, and finished with a wonderfully flaky napoleon selected from a tray of pastries baked on the premises. Consistency is the key here; over the years we have never had a bad meal.

A nice tradition commemorates the beginning of this restaurant in 1980. Once a year, from mid- to late February and continuing for five weeks on Monday, Tuesday, and Wednesday nights, all entrées have 1980 prices (approximately half-price in the '90s).

The name "Vickers" is taken from the three generations of the Vickers family that made pottery at this early 1800s farmhouse for some fifty years. Pottery is still made here three nights a week (Wednesday, Saturday, and usually Friday) by a potter you'll encounter at the entrance to the restaurant. The ware is for sale to the patrons.

Open for lunch, Monday through Friday, 11:30 A.M. to 2 P.M.; $7.95–$11.50. Dinner, Monday through Saturday, 5:30 to 10 P.M. Entrées, $17.50–$25.95. Located just off Route 100, three miles north of Exton. Gordon Drive, Lionville, PA; (215) 363-6336 or (215) 363-7998.

Dilworthtown Inn, Dilworthtown, PA

Take a beautiful stone building dating back to 1758. Add an elegant continental menu, an outstanding wine cellar (winner of a *Wine Spectator* award of excellence for the past five years), and the remarkable ambience of an entire restaurant lit only by candles and oil lamps—and you have the recipe for an unforgettable dining experience.

The Dilworthtown Inn seats 220 on three floors in thirteen rooms, many of which have about five tables. It enjoys a fine reputation, so Saturday night reservations need to be made a week or two in advance. Three of the eleven fireplaces are used, one in the bar and two in the larger dining rooms. The wood floors are covered with Oriental rugs. Redware plates, decoys, lanterns, and a fine collection of original paintings and limited-edition prints, produced by local artists including Andrew Wyeth, decorate the walls throughout the inn.

Two exceptional appetizer specials we recommend you ask for, even if they don't show up on the menu, are a medley of wild mushrooms sautéed with Chartreuse and sherry, and the wild mushroom pasta in a vodka cream sauce. From an extensive list of main courses (veal, steaks, seafood, capon, salmon, and so on), we chose an entrée for two, a two-pound Australian lobster tail, and ordered it stuffed with lump crabmeat. Other favorites are the elegant rack of lamb marinated in brandy and rosemary, then roasted and topped with Dijon mustard and herbs. The loin of venison is from New Zealand and is frequently on the menu, as is the quail, which is listed as a special when locally obtainable.

This is a restaurant for wine lovers, as the extensive regular list comprehensively covers the wines of the world. For wine connoisseurs there is a special list with bottles in the three- and four-figure price range. Diners who do not enjoy dimly lit restaurants should consider going elsewhere.

Open for dinner, Monday through Saturday, 5:30 to 10 P.M., and Sunday, 3 to 9 P.M. Entrées, $12.25–$25. Located ¼ mile off Route 202 on Old Wilmington Pike, West Chester, PA 19382; (215) 399-1390.

Pace One Restaurant and Country Inn, Thornton, PA

Situated on a quiet side road in a restored 1740s stone barn, Pace One presents imaginative menu combinations in an intimate setting. Dine in the porch room, the new bar with its potbelly stove, or the inside room with its low ceiling and hand-hewn poplar beams. The window recesses in the two-foot-thick stone walls are filled with plants.

For lunch we had salmon, whitefish, and bay scallop pâté and marinated, charcoal-grilled tuna. Sandwiches at lunch are made to order. Have your club with ham, turkey, or roast beef, or order a hamburger with your choice of béarnaise sauce, bacon, mushrooms, or cheese. Shrimp are wrapped with bacon and stuffed with horseradish.

At dinner you can order sea scallops baked in mayonnaise, mustard, horseradish, and bacon sauce; veal tenderloin; a creamy crabmeat mixture baked and served with hollandaise sauce; or the mixed grill, which includes baby lamb chops, venison sausage, and quail accompanied by apple chutney. The half pineapple, filled with fresh fruit and glazed with honey and walnuts, is always available and can be ordered as an appetizer or for dessert. On Thursday nights the chef creates unique seafood preparations.

Open for lunch, Monday through Friday, 11:30 A.M. to 2 P.M.; $5.25–$9.50. Dinner, Monday through Saturday 5:30 to 10 P.M.; Sunday, 10:30 A.M. to 2:30 P.M. Sunday dinner 5 to 9 P.M. Dinner entrées, $12.95–$22.95. Thornton and Glen Mills Road, Thornton, PA 19373; (215) 459-3702.

Birchrunville Café, Birchrunville, PA

This simply charming café in northern Chester County is so out of the way that even local residents have trouble finding their way here. "The inspiration for my cooking and my restaurant is modeled after what you find in the small provincial villages in the south of France," chef and owner Wynne Milner told us as she flamed our dessert on a foggy, wet February evening.

The building, originally a general store built in 1898, is located in a pristine, tiny crossroad village beside a stream. The café is in the same building as the local post office; in fact, to use the restroom you need to go across the porch into the post office.

Brown gingham tablecloths, pine country cupboards with dried flowers, pine arrow-back chairs, pottery oil lamps, lace café curtains, and copper pots evoke the atmosphere of Provence. Each week a different set meal is served. When you call for reservations, ask for John Milner's suggestion before you select a wine to bring along. Plan to spend the evening and enjoy yourself, as the meal is served in a very leisurely manner.

Our meal started with eggplant purée and black olive tapenade dips served with raw vegetables. The main course was an excellent bourride, a hearty fish stew made with firm white fish and court bouillon, served with toasted French bread, aïoli and rouille sauces. At John's suggestion we brought along a French Muscadet, a soft but very dry white wine whose pale golden color and taste blended perfectly with the fish stew. A salad of fresh greens and an assortment of soft cheeses was served. At another table we overheard the waitress suggesting that the diners might like to take home the unfinished pieces of cheese. The dessert was a flaming sweet pear omelet and coffee.

The quality of the food is excellent; the portions moderate in size; the taste refreshingly different. Other recent dinners have included lamb's liver in a wild mushroom-grape sauce, a roast leg of lamb with herbs, duck with olives, and a squab casserole. Desserts have included profiterolles, wine-poached pears, Alsatian farm cheesecake, and prune and Armagnac flan.

Call ahead for the evening's menu, and be sure to get exact directions. Food substitutions for diners with special dietary requirements are available with prior notice.

Open for dinner Wednesday through Saturday evenings. Complete dinner, $28. Bring your own wine. Corking and serving fee, $2.50 per bottle of wine. Hollow and Flowing Springs Roads, Birchrunville, PA 19421; (215) 827-7366.

Stottsville Inn, Pomeroy, PA

Since the Stottsville Inn is at the edge of fox hunting country, you may see riders stopping here after the day's hunt. If you're out driving the back roads on our driving tour (see *Where to Go,* page 242), this inn is the ideal stop for lunch. If it's not busy at lunch you may be able to have the Caesar salad prepared table-side. A special of the day was a well-prepared, tender shrimp dish served over fresh pasta. Other items at lunch included a tall turkey club sandwich and a crab sandwich. Excellent sticky buns made at the inn are served to all the diners.

The evening menu includes such appetizers as lightly sautéed chunks of salmon served over angel hair pasta with a Champagne, shallot, and heavy cream sauce, and crabmeat-filled ravioli with an herbed cream sauce. Entrées include sautéed lobster medallions with a garlic butter sauce, rainbow trout stuffed with crab imperial, and the always-popular beef Wellington. Twice-baked potatoes and a julienne of carrots and zucchini accompanied the entrées the night we dined. Off the main dining room is a private dining room, Josephine's Parlor, with windows on three sides, which seats up to four. It is available at no extra charge, upon advance reservation.

A lower-priced dinner menu is served in the pub room. It includes fajitas, big burgers, Cajun dishes, and sizzling salads in tortilla shells. Alcoholic ice cream drinks are a specialty: One tastes like an Almond Joy candy bar, and another is called raspberry à la mode. There's piano music in the pub room on Friday and Saturday. On Friday it's jazz and blues; on Saturday it's classical music.

Open for lunch Tuesday through Friday, 11:30 A.M. to 2 P.M.; $5.95–$8.95. Dinner, Tuesday through Saturday, 5:30 P.M. to 9:30, Friday and Saturday till 10 P.M. $13.95–$22.95. The pub is open for meals Tuesday through Friday, 4 to 9:30 P.M. Friday till 10 P.M., Sunday 4 to 8 P.M. For drinks and music it is open on Friday and Saturday until 1:30 A.M. Pub meals $5.95–$8.95. Route 372 at Strasburg Road, Pomeroy, PA 19367; (215) 857-1133.

Duling-Kurtz House, Exton, PA

On a sunny spring day we sat in the glass-enclosed porch dining room which overlooks the formal garden, a favorite spot often used for wedding pictures. There's also a small curtained dining area with just one table which overlooks the garden; there's a $25 surcharge for this special romantic nook. The Hunt Room, one of the smaller of the seven dining rooms, is a favorite of many for its gas fireplace, dark green walls, classic hunt prints, and lamps in the shape of hunting horns.

Lunch choices range from sandwiches such as pork barbecue, grilled Reuben, and burgers, to tostada, Greek, or chicken and cashew salads, to such entrées as crabcakes, omelets, and fettuccine.

At dinner the Caesar salad is made and the trout deboned at your table. The trout is served with cashews and capers. The lobster, shrimp, and scallops are sautéed in a basil cream sauce and served over fettuccine. The veal, stuffed with ricotta cheese and mushroom duxelles, was a tasty combination of flavors. Other entrées include grilled rack of lamb and boneless chicken stuffed with feta cheese, prosciutto, and spinach and topped with shiitake mushrooms.

Open for lunch, Monday through Friday, 11:30 A.M. to 2 P.M.; entreés, $6.95–$9.50. Monday through Saturday, dinner, 5:30 to 10 P.M. Entrées, $19.95–$24.95. 146 South Whitford Road, Exton, PA 19341; (215) 524-1830.

Marshalton Inn, Marshalton, PA

The light from the candles and the wood-burning fireplace played softly against the white plaster walls of the dining room. Old wrought-iron chandeliers, old prints in old frames, well-worn scuffed wooden floors, and wooden tables with drips of candle wax created the ambience in this 1793 stone Federal tavern, which has been on the National Register of Historic Places since 1977. The cooking here is good but not outstanding; the atmosphere makes up for the deficiencies in the kitchen. About the only thing that lets you know the 1990s are here is the large satellite dish on the back roof for the television in the bar.

We started with the seafood bisque, actually more of a broth with many pieces of shrimp. Our waiter told us that the seafood used in the soup changes depending on what the chef has on hand. Escargot sautéed with slices of large, locally grown portabella mushrooms in a garlic, white wine, and butter sauce was bread-sopping good. The tasty grilled wild mushrooms served with fresh, lightly cooked asparagus came with a small cup of Gorgonzola dressing.

A range of entrées included broiled salmon filet served with citrus butter; calf's liver with bacon and onions; and filet mignon with shiitake hollandaise. On Friday and Saturday evenings, prime rib with Yorkshire pudding is served; hearty English fare seems appropriate for this restaurant. The rack of lamb with a honey-mustard-ginger sauce is a good value.

Next door is a casual, popular bar with a lower-priced menu called The Oyster Bar. The menu, written on a blackboard, includes burgers, ribs, London broil jambalaya, a stirfry or two, and a couple of pasta dishes such as seafood Alfredo and stuffed shells. During the summer months a jazz band performs in the parking lot on Thursday night and draws the crowds. As schedules change from one year to the next, we suggest calling to confirm which night jazz is played.

Open for lunch, Tuesday through Friday, 11:30 A.M. to 2 P.M.; $6.95–$8.95. Dinner, Tuesday through Saturday, 5:30 to 10 P.M., Sunday 4 to 9 P.M. Dinner entrées, $14.95–$19.75; (215) 692-4367. The Oyster Bar is not open for lunch but serves dinner Tuesday through Saturday, 6 to 11:30 P.M., and Sunday brunch, 11 A.M. to 3 P.M. Route 162, Strasburg Road, Marshalton, PA; (215) 692-5702.

INFORMAL DINING

Buckley's Tavern, Centreville, DE

Centreville is a picturesque, gentrified village that straddles Route 52. This wonderful old tavern building oozes atmosphere. Its location is convenient for lunch, as it is just north of Winterthur. We particularly enjoy dining in the wood-paneled old tavern room, whether for lunch or for lighter fare late at night. There are two larger dining rooms, one with parquet floors and Orientals and the other a light-filled large room with a high ceiling and expansive windows. In the summer the outdoor terrace tables are popular.

For lunch we had scallop cakes served with a rich buttery sauce. Omelets are made with herbed Montrachet cheese and walnuts. Individual pizzas are made with wild and domestic mushrooms and sun-dried tomatoes. At dinner most of the sandwich and burger items are offered along with such entrées as grilled salmon, Thai roast duck, Flemish beef stew, chicken with figs, and seafood mixed grill.

Open for lunch daily, 11:30 A.M. to 2:30 P.M.; $5.50–$8.50. Dinner,

Monday through Saturday, 5:30 to 9 P.M. $5.50–$17.95. The tavern menu is served 4 to 11 P.M. Bar menu, $2.75–$6.75. 5812 Kennett Pike (Route 52), Centreville, DE 19807; (302) 656-9776.

Longwood Inn, Kennett Square, PA

After a visit to Phillips Mushroom Place, a meal at a restaurant specializing in mushrooms seems most appropriate. We had heard rave reviews about the mushroom strudel served here, a tasty combination of domestic and shiitake mushrooms, ham, dried beef, spinach, Parmesan cheese, and a rich cream sauce. We enthusiastically recommend this dish as well as stuffed mushrooms à la Grecque (see *Recipe*, page 270). Other mushroom dishes include mushrooms stuffed with crab imperial, sautéed domestic and shiitake mushrooms, sautéed shiitakes and tenderloin, French-fried mushroom caps, and cream of mushroom soup.

In addition there is a lobster tank and a full dinner menu that emphasizes seafood dishes, but also includes beef, veal, lamb, and chicken dishes. On Thursday nights there is a buffet with Oriental, Greek, and mushroom specialties. For mycolophagists, a seven-course mushroom banquet and symposium is held here annually on a Thursday during the third week of September.

Open for lunch, Monday through Saturday, 11 A.M. to 3 P.M.; $3.95–$6.95. Dinner, Monday through Thursday, 4 to 9 P.M.; to 10 P.M. on Friday and Saturday. Open Sunday, 11 A.M. to 8:30 P.M. Dinner entrées, $13.95–$22.95. Located one-half mile south of Longwood Gardens on Route 1. 815 East Baltimore Pike, Kennett Square, PA 19348; (215) 444-3515.

Hanks Place, Chadds Ford, PA

If you have gone across the street to the Brandywine River Museum and marveled at Andrew Wyeth's paintings that include local residents, you'll notice a resemblance to the regular patrons who frequent this local hangout. Sit at the counter or at a table; look at the paintings on the wall; be sure to check the blackboard for homemade soups and the day's specials. The food is typical diner fare: bacon and eggs, pancakes, soup, cheese dogs, hamburgers, and steak, meatball, tuna fish, and BLT sandwiches.

Open Monday through Saturday, 5:30 A.M. to 7 P.M.; Sunday, 8 A.M. to 3 P.M. Typical diner food at low prices. Located at the junction of Route 100 and Route 1, Chadds Ford, PA.

RECIPE

Stuffed Mushrooms à la Grécque

Peter and Voula Skiadas, owners of The Longwood Inn in Kennett Square (the mushroom-growing capital of the world), serve this mushroom dish at both lunch and dinner. Voula combined feta cheese, which reflects the couple's Greek heritage, and locally grown mushrooms to create a delicious and easy-to-prepare dish. *Note:* It's best to cook this in a convection oven, as the feta cheese tends to drip in a regular oven.

2 to 3 dozen silver-dollar-size (large) mushrooms
1 pound lean bacon, finely chopped and partially cooked
½ pound ham, finely chopped
4 cups seasoned croutons, ground

1 pound feta cheese, half grated and half sliced thinly
1½ cups imported Romano cheese, grated
1 pound ripe tomatoes, peeled, seeded, and chopped

Steam or blanch the mushrooms until tender, approximately 1½ minutes. Cool the mushrooms. In a mixing bowl, combine the chopped bacon, chopped ham, ground croutons, and grated feta and Romano cheeses. Add the chopped tomatoes to the other ingredients and mix thoroughly. Stuff each mushroom with about 2 heaping tablespoons of the filling. Top with a small slice of feta cheese. Bake in a convection oven at 350°F for 12 to 15 minutes.

Note: If stuffing seems to fall apart, add a little more ground, seasoned croutons.

ITINERARY

DAY ONE. Drive to the **visitor center** at **Longwood Gardens** to purchase a detailed map of Chester County and to get a copy of *The Brandywine,* which has a complete listing of special events and often includes discount coupons for area attractions and restaurants. Visit the gardens and conservatory at Longwood Gardens. Have lunch at the Terrace restaurant inside Longwood Gardens or nearby at **Longwood Inn**. Take a reserved tour at **Winterthur**. Stroll through the gardens and visit the Gallery shop. If you're interested, **The Playhouse** in the **Hotel du Pont** presents top Broadway plays and musicals. Dine in Wilmington at **The Silk Purse** (the casual bistro here is The Sow's Ear) or at the **Green Room** or **Brandywine Room** at the **Hotel du Pont**.

DAY TWO. Visit the **Brandywine River Museum** in Chadds Ford. Have lunch at the museum, across the street at **Hank's Place,** or at **Pace One** in Thornton. Head south on scenic Route 100 to Wilmington for a tour of **Nemours Mansion and Gardens**. Dine elegantly at **Dilworthtown Inn** or **Vickers**, or casualty in the country at **Birchrunville Café**.

DAY THREE. Take Route 82 to **Unionville**. Check to see if a hunt is being held that day, as you may want to see the riders and hounds leave. Take the **driving tours**. Have lunch at the **Stottsville Inn** or pick up sandwiches at Sestrich's Country Market in Unionville. If the weather is warm you may want to go canoeing or tubing on the Brandywine River. Pack your picnic and head to the **Northbrook Canoe Company**. Or, head for the **Hagley Museum** in Wilmington to learn how gun powder was made. Dine in the Colonial atmosphere at **Marshalton Inn** (the **Oyster Bar** is next door), or at **Duling-Kurtz House**.

DAY FOUR. As **Winterthur** is one of the finest museums in this country, we suggest reserving a place on a second tour. Have lunch at the museum or at **Buckley's Tavern**. Sample wines at **Chaddsford Winery**, tour the **Brandywine Battlefield**, or head to one of the smaller museums. **Wharton Esherick** and **Christian Sanderson** museums are open only on the weekends. Other museums are **Delaware Museum of Natural History**, **Franklin Mint**, and **Delaware Museum of Art**. The **Dilworthtown Country Store** is a fun place to browse even if you don't want to make a purchase. Buy some fresh or marinated mushrooms at **Phillips Mushroom Place** to take home.

Getting to the Area

From New York, Philadelphia, or Washington, D.C., take I-95 to Wilmington. Take Route 52 north to Route 1. You will pass the entrance to Winterthur on your right as you drive along Route 52. Go south on Route 1 to Longwood Gardens.

BUDGETING YOUR TRIP

To help you get the most for your money, here are some travel suggestions at three budget levels (cost per day at peak season with two people sharing a room, including tax, 15% gratuity at meals, and service charges). Prices are approximate and intended for planning purposes only. Lodgings are categorized by price. Meal prices at lunch include an average entrée and beverage. Dinner prices include an appetizer, entrée, beverage, and dessert. Wine or alcoholic drinks are not included. Admission prices vary widely based on activities.

Staying and Dining at Expensive Lodgings and Restaurants: From $290 to $360 per day for two.

Lodging: Hotel du Pont (deluxe) $133-$159; Sweetwater Farm (suites and top cottages) $154-$175; Highland Farm (suites) $143; Fairville Inn (suites) $149; Brandywine River Hotel (suites) $133.

Dining: Breakfast: included except at Hotel du Pont ($20). Lunch: Hotel du Pont $35. Dinner: Silk Purse $100; Hotel du Pont– Green Room or Vickers $90.

Admissions: Longwood Gardens $16; Winterthur Museum (two tours) $50; Hagley Museum $16; Nemours Mansion $16; Brandywine River Museum $8.

Staying and Dining at Moderately Priced Lodgings and Restaurants: From $200 to $270 per day for two.

Lodging: Hotel du Pont $85–$133; Sweetwater Farm $127–$137; Fairville Inn $101–$155.

Dining: Breakfast: included except at Hotel du Pont ($20). Lunch: Marshalton Inn, Stottsville Inn, Duling-Kurtz, Sow's Ear, Pace One, Buckley's Tavern, or Longwood Inn $20. Dinner: Dilworthtown Inn, Stottsville Inn, Duling-Kurtz, Hotel du Pont– Brandywine Room, Birchrunville Café, Marshalton Inn, Longwood Inn, or Pace One $70–$80.

Admissions: Longwood Gardens $16; Winterthur Museum $25; Brandywine River Museum $8; Hagley Museum $16.

Staying and Dining at Less Expensive Lodgings and Restaurants: From $110 to $170 per day for two.

Lodging: Campbell House $64–$74; Meadow Spring Farm $58–$80; Franklin House $80; Stottsville Inn $80; Pace One $69.

Dining: Breakfast: included. Lunch: Hank's Place, cafeterias at Longwood Gardens, Winterthur, Brandywine River Museum, or Hagley Museum, $10-$15.

Dinner: Buckley's Tavern $60; Sow's Ear $50; Oyster Bar, Stottsville Pub, or Buckley's Bar $30.

Admissions: Longwood Garden $16; Winterthur Museum $16; Brandywine River Museum $8; Hagley Museum $8.

SUGGESTED READING

Books about the history of the area, the Du Pont family, the collections at Winterthur Museum, the Wyeths, and Longwood Gardens are best purchased at these museums:

Longwood Gardens.　The garden shop sells a variety of books on horticultural topics.

Brandywine River Museum.　Look for books about the Wyeths, other painters, and about Chester County.

Winterthur Museum.　Books about American decorative arts are for sale here, along with detailed books on the museum's own collection.

SEVEN

CAPE MAY, NEW JERSEY

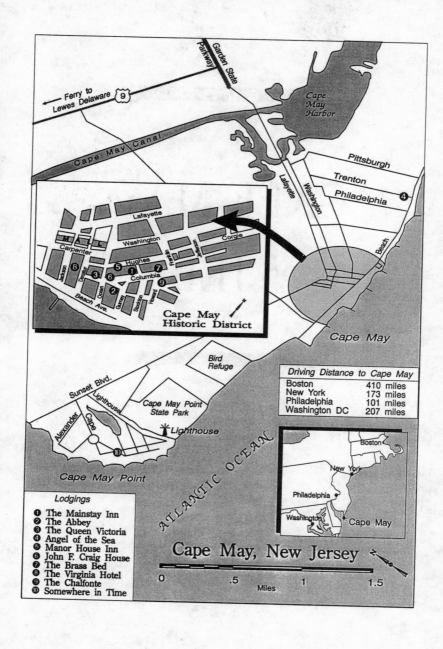

Ferry to
Lewes Delaware ⑨

Garden State Parkway

Cape May Harbor

Cape May Canal

Pittsburgh
Trenton
Philadelphia ❹

Lafayette
Washington
Beach

Cape May
Historic District

Lafayette
Washington
Carpenter
Hughes
Columbia
Decatur
Ocean
Gurney
Stockton
Howard
Franklin
Jefferson
Corgie
Jackson
Beach Ave.

❽ ⑤ ③ ❻ ① ⑦ ❾ ②

Cape May

Bird
Refuge

Sunset Blvd.
Lighthouse
Alexander
Cape
Cape May Point
State Park

★ Lighthouse

❿

Cape May Point

ATLANTIC OCEAN

Driving Distance to Cape May	
Boston	410 miles
New York	173 miles
Philadelphia	101 miles
Washington DC	207 miles

Boston
New York
Philadelphia
Washington
Cape May

Lodgings

❶ The Mainstay Inn
❷ The Abbey
❸ The Queen Victoria
❹ Angel of the Sea
❺ Manor House Inn
❻ John F. Craig House
❼ The Brass Bed
❽ The Virginia Hotel
❾ The Chalfonte
❿ Somewhere in Time

Cape May, New Jersey

0   .5   1   1.5
Miles

In the summer months, life in Cape May revolves around the Victorian porch. What better way to spend the late afternoon than lazily rocking away with a glass of iced tea and a plate of tea cakes and cookies at your side? This is the time to escape into the pages of a romantic novel, without feeling guilty about all of the things you "should" be doing. The breezes waft in from the ocean and provide natural air-conditioning. The only sound you hear is the clip-clop of the horse-drawn carriages. The cadence of the hoof-beats slackens as the carriages approach the inn. Every now and then a bicycle-powered surrey passes by, driven by a family pedaling together as the young children laugh and joke in seats attached to the handlebars. Bathers with their umbrellas and sand chairs wander slowly back home.

It is on these same porches that the properly attired ladies and gentlemen of the Victorian era would pass the time. Women's skirts were floor-length and corsets were snug. Men wore three-piece suits and top hats and carried a cane. When outdoors, the women would carry a parasol to protect their complexion from the sun.

Seeing and being seen was of utmost importance in Victorian times. As you sit today on many of the porches of Cape May you can look down the street from porch to porch and visit with your neighbors, just as you could in the late nineteenth century.

In Colonial times, residents of Philadelphia, New York, and Baltimore as well as southern plantation owners started to summer in breezy Cape May. By the beginning of the nineteenth century, the first of the large wooden hotels that would eventually hold thousands of visitors were built. Sporadically, fires would sweep across the windy peninsula. Most of Cape May's original buildings were destroyed at one time or another because the town lacked effective fire-fighting equipment. An unprecedented building boom followed the largest of these fires in 1878. Wealthy Philadelphia coal barons, bankers, and railroad owners hired the best architects and skilled craftsmen, who worked for decades building hundreds of colorful, architecturally significant structures. One was more lavish than the next; Cape May was the place to be. President Benjamin Harrison had his summer White House here. John Philip Sousa played before thousands.

Then, as so often happens, the beautiful people left. The automobile made its appearance at the beginning of the twentieth century, and Atlantic City and the shore towns closer to Philadelphia siphoned away the summer pleasure seekers. Cape May went into decline for fifty years. The grand summer homes became inexpensive summer boarding houses. The wooden gingerbread decayed. The paint peeled. The roofs leaked.

Starting in the 1970s, idealistic young couples, fascinated with Victoriana and tired of corporate America, purchased many of these "white elephants." With more "sweat equity" than cash equity, they restored these fine old houses room by room, ceiling by ceiling, shingle by shingle. Reborn, one by one the buildings became elegant bed-and-breakfast inns, faithfully restored and furnished with exquisite period antiques. Excellent shops and restaurants followed. The town became a certified historic landmark. The street lamps were converted to the warm glow of gas lighting. The grand old trees were cared for and lovely gardens began to sprout everywhere. A new era for Cape May had begun.

The Welcome and Information Center. 405 Lafayette Street (across from the bandstand), Cape May, NJ 08204; (609) 884-9562.

Chamber of Commerce of Greater Cape May. 609 Lafayette Street (opposite the Acme), P.O. Box 109, Cape May, NJ 08204; (609) 884-5508.

Mid-Atlantic Center for the Arts (MAC). 1048 Washington Street, P.O. Box 340, Cape May, NJ 08204; (609) 884-5404.

SPECIAL EVENTS THROUGHOUT THE YEAR

Late February. Cape May Cooks: Demonstration cooking school conducted by Cape May's top chefs; (609) 884-4710.

Early April. Shakespeare in Cape May. Lectures, performances, Renaissance music; (609) 884-5404.

Late April. Tulip Festival. Dutch folkdancing in native costume, tulips in bloom throughout the town, craft show; (609) 884-9562.

Third weekend in May. New Jersey Audubon Spring Birding Weekend at peak of the spring migration. Workshops, field trips, evening programs; (609) 884-2736.

Early July. Independence Day parade, picnic, sand sculpture contest.

Early September. Clam Pitching Tournament, Windsor Beach.

Late September or early October. New Jersey Audubon Autumn Birding Weekend, peak of the fall migration. Workshops, field trips, evening programs; (609) 884-2736.

Early October. Victorian Week. The top event in the town last ten days. Tours of Victorian homes, Victorian fashion and vaudeville shows, evening stained-glass tours, lectures on Victorian architecture, Victorian dinner and ball, and Victorian mystery theater; (609) 884-5404.

Weekends in December. Christmas Grand Tour of restored Victorian bed-and-breakfast inns. Victorian Christmas presentations at each; (609) 884-8075.

Early December. Dickens Extravaganza. Lectures, readings, Dickensian feast; (609) 884-8702.

Late December. Christmas Candlelight House Tour. Self-guided tour of homes, guesthouses, and churches specially decorated for the holidays; (609) 884-5404.

WHERE TO GO, WHAT TO DO

Unlike many beach towns along the coast, Cape May is not a one-season town. There is much to do in Cape May whether you are a beach person, a birder, or a Victoriana buff. For many, a summer vacation in Cape May means spending days at the beach and evenings at a fine restaurant. Flocks of birders are attracted to the area, especially during the peak fall and spring migration periods. With more than 600 Victorian structures, many of which are restored, Cape May has the greatest concentration of buildings from this era in the country.

Cape May Welcome Center. Stop in for a schedule of the week's special events. The professional-quality videotape is a fitting introduction to the town. If you've arrived without reservations, there are direct phone lines to inns in Cape May available for your use. You can park in the adjacent lot free for thirty minutes while you get information and use the restrooms. The Welcome Center is located across from the bandstand in a converted 1853 church with an onion dome over the cupola. 405 Lafayette Street; (609) 884-9562.

VICTORIAN CAPE MAY

Mid-Atlantic Center for the Arts. This organization is one of the driving forces of the town. Its purpose is to preserve Cape May's Victorian heritage and to promote the performing arts year round. The Center sponsors the house tours, trolley tours, walking tours, and special events. If you are interested in taking a number of the tours, it is worthwhile to take out a membership—not only will you help the organization, but you'll save a few dollars as well.

Membership (Individual, $20; Joint, $25; and Family, $30) includes free unlimited admission to the Physick Estate, lighthouse, walking and trolley tours. Membership privileges also include reduced admission to the vintage films at the Chalfonte, invitations to special events throughout the year, and a newsletter. You can register for membership by mail or in person at the office, located at the Physick Estate, weekdays during business hours. MAC, Box 340, Cape May, NJ 08204; (609) 884-5404.

Emlen Physick Estate. The eighteen-room Victorian Stick-style mansion was designed in 1879 by noted architect Frank Furness, who is best known as the architect of the Pennsylvania Academy of Fine Arts in Philadelphia. The house was built for Dr. Emlen Physick, Jr., whose grandfather is considered "the father of American surgery." In order for Dr. Physick to obtain his sizable inheritance, he had to attend medical school and become a doctor. The day after he received his degree in Philadelphia, Dr. Physick retired to Cape May to assume the life of a country gentleman.

The house, with its oversize porch brackets, "jerkinhead" dormers, and huge "upside-down" chimneys, was saved from demolition in 1970 and is now authentically restored and furnished with many of the original Eastlake-style pieces. We felt that the guide made the tour lively by interjecting stories about Dr. Physick with the description of the rooms. Four times a year a formal Victorian dinner for twenty-four is held in the dining room. These popular events provide an excuse to wear and view the "latest" in Victorian fashions and to taste dishes that were popular during the period.

The Cape May Art League has its offices and holds exhibits in what was once the estate's carriage house. The outdoor summer theater is on the same property. Other buildings on the estate house the administrative offices for the Mid-Atlantic Center for the Arts.

During July and August, 1¾-hour tours are given daily except Friday, 10 A.M. to 3:30 P.M. During the rest of the year, tours are given on weekends and on a reduced midweek schedule. Adults, $4; children 6 to 12, $1. 1048 Washington Avenue, Cape May, NJ 08204; (609) 884-5404.

Walking Tours. A walking tour is the best way to view the various styles of Victorian architecture (Queen Anne, Carpenter

Gothic, Mansard, Italianate, Colonial Revival, and Exotic Revival). You will soon be able to spot straight, convex, and concave mansard roofs, finials and pendants, shark-tooth and fin-scale shingles, and more. The little second-floor porches on stilts that you see (particularly on Hughes Street) were built when indoor plumbing came to the town—the porches enclose the added toilets and baths. The guides on these tours spice their descriptions of the architecture with information about the customs and traditions of the times. This tour should not be missed.

The tours last 1½ hours. During the summer they are given daily either at 10 A.M. or 7 P.M. Consult the calendar of events for other times of the year. Adults, $4; children 6 to 12, $1. The tour begins at the Washington Street Mall Information Booth.

Mansions by Gaslight.   Included in this tour is the Emlen Physick Estate and three Victorian mansions that are now inns: The Mainstay, The Abbey, and the Humphrey Hughes House. At each of the inns, the innkeepers describe the history of the house and the furnishings in detail. This tour is a good way to see the first floor of each inn, and to determine if this is an inn you'd like to return to as a guest.

The tour lasts about two hours. It is held every Wednesday evening 7:30 to 10 P.M., during the summer months and on holiday weekends. The tour starts at the Emlen Physick Estate. Adults, $12; children 6 to 12, $6. 1048 Washington Street, Cape May, NJ; (609) 884-5404.

Victorian Sampler Tours.   If you are curious about the interiors of more of the authentically restored mansions, or if you want to preview possible accommodations, then this is the tour to take. More than fifty bed-and-breakfast inns, guest houses, and private homes participate; each time the tour is given, about five places are open for tours.

The tour is held Saturday and Monday afternoon 4 to 6 P.M. during the summer, and Saturday afternoon only during the other times of the year. Adults, $10; children 6 to 12, $5. A trolley shuttle is included and begins at the Physick Estate, 1048 Washington Street. You may also purchase your tickets at the first house on the tour; (609) 884-5404.

Trolley Tours.   If you're not up for walking, the weather is stormy, or if you want to get a broader view of Cape May, this is a good choice. We had a grand time riding the trolley bus and hearing the stories of Cape May's heyday as told by an experienced guide. You can ride in an open-air trolley in the summer and in a heated and enclosed one in the winter.

Historic East End Tour. Features Columbia Avenue, Hughes Street, Ocean Street, and the Physick Estate.

Historic West End Tour. Features Congress Hall, Perry Street, and Decatur Street. *Note:* The walking tour covers parts of both the East End and West End trolley tours.

Historic Beach Drive Tour. This tour features a century of beach-front housing from Victorian cottages and turn-of-the-century mansions to those of contemporary design.

Tours take about half an hour each. During the summer they leave 10 A.M. to 7:45 P.M. Adults, $4; children 6–12, $1. The trolley leaves from Beach Drive at Gurney Street. During the winter, the East End and the West End tours are combined into a single tour, offered either by itself or in combination with a tour of the Physick Estate.

Carriage Rides. Sitting on the porches of the bed-and-breakfast inns, you hear the clip-clop of the horses as they pull the carriages. The properly attired drivers will tell you about the buildings as you ride through the historic district at a leisurely pace. We particularly enjoyed the evening ride through the gaslit streets.

Mid-June to mid-September, half-hour tours leave 10 A.M. to 2 P.M. and 6:30 to 10:30 P.M. daily except Sunday. Tickets for the evening tour go on sale at 6 P.M. Spring and Fall tours (weather permitting), 12 to 4 P.M. daily except Sunday. Adults, $6; children 2–11, $3. Carriages leave from Ocean Street and Washington Street Mall, next to the Catholic Church; (609) 884-4466.

BEACHES

You need to wear a Cape May beach tag during the summer between the hours of 10 A.M. and 5 P.M. Most of the bed-and-breakfast inns provide the tags free of charge for their guests. Tags can also be purchased from the beach attendants for $2 per day or $5 per week. Some inns also provide beach towels, beach chairs, and umbrellas. Ask what the inn provides when you make your reservation.

Steger's Beach Service.   The blue tents and blue boxes that you see along the beaches are all owned by Steger's. You can rent a tent or a box to hold beach paraphernalia, or you can rent umbrellas and chairs by the day. The advantage of renting at Steger's is that you don't have to carry the stuff to and from the beach.

Poverty Beach.   This is the most northerly beach in Cape May. The "big deal" surfers come here for the large waves; because there is a very steep drop-off, it's not recommended for amateurs. At high tide or after a storm the spray is impressive.

This beach is the best place to look for clam shells suitable for clam pitching. Look for the large unbroken ones with thick heavy shells. These shells are properly weighted and can be controlled far more easily than the thinner shells. One of the yearly events at Cape May is a clam pitching contest. The winners all find their shells at this beach.

The Surfing Beach.   To the right of Convention Hall is the surfing beach, where those with surf boards or boogie boards congregate.

Broadway Beach.   The advantage of this beach is its proximity to the restrooms and snack bar.

Steger's blue tents and beach boxes are a Cape May tradition.

Windsor Beach. Everyone has a favorite and this is ours. It is one of the wider beaches, is used by many families, and offers good views of the ocean even if you sit a fair distance from the water.

Second Avenue Beach and the Fishing Jetty. This beach is next to the best fishing jetty. It's a good choice if part of your group wants to fish and part wants to swim.

Walking to the Lighthouse. Road access to the beach ends at Second Avenue. A great walk is the mile or so stretch along the beach starting at the jetty and ending at the lighthouse. As you walk along the water, you can observe a variety of birds—the fields to your rights are part of the Cape May Migratory Bird Refuge, owned by The Nature Conservancy. Beyond this is Cape May Point State Park and the lighthouse. You may want to bring a snack, as there is no food service at the lighthouse or at the state park.

BIRDING

Roger Tory Peterson calls Cape May "one of the country's outstanding bird-watching areas." Warblers to wading birds, falcons to finches can be found in Cape May, and every fall an average of nearly 80,000 birds of prey pass through on their way south along the Atlantic Flyway. If you're not already hooked on birding, we suggest that you take a walk with one of the knowledgeable birders at the observatory.

Cape May Bird Observatory. The New Jersey Audubon Society has an office here. Walks and workshops are held regularly on the weekends. Stop in to get directions to Higbee Beach (a great birding area), advice on the best viewing spots, a listing of activities, or to register a sighting.

Each year the Audubon Society sponsors two major weekend events held during the peak of the spring and fall migration periods. These usually take place on the third weekend in May and the last weekend in September or the first in October. Throughout these weekends visitors can enjoy a full schedule of workshops, field trips, and evening programs. Contact the Cape May Bird Observatory, Box 3, Cape May Point, NJ 08212; (609) 884-2736. The office

is located at 707 East Lake Drive (off Lighthouse Avenue) in Cape
May Point. Open Tuesday through Saturday, 9 A.M. to 3 P.M.

Birding Hotline. Every Thursday throughout the year this
phone recording is updated with details of sightings and information
on the best places and times of day for birding. You can call at any
time; (609) 884-2626.

Cape May Migratory Bird Refuge. This refuge used to be
called the cow pasture when cows grazed here. To preserve the
land, The Nature Conservancy purchased the 188 acres, hired
rangers to patrol and protect, and opened it to visitors. It is open
from dawn to dusk. Located one mile south of Cape May off Sunset
Boulevard.

Cape May State Park. One of the best places for birding, this
park offers three miles of trails and boardwalk that meander by
ponds and through the wooded and marshy area. A half-mile trail
for the disabled is wheelchair-accessible. We particularly like the
raised platforms overlooking the larger ponds and the photography
blinds.

Kids love to run along the wooden platforms. We don't blame
them; now that the boardwalk has been improved, many visitors
are eager to find out what is beyond the next bend in the path.
However, the birds don't stay around when they hear the tromp
of little feet. We suggest getting here around 7 or 8 A.M. to see the
birds in the pools before too many kids arrive.

Rangers stationed at the small museum can help with wildlife
identification.

Open daily year round. No admission. Restrooms available.
From Cape May take Sunset Boulevard West. Turn left on Lighthouse Avenue. The road ends at the state park; (609) 884-2159.

Higbee Beach. Because of its location along the southern-
most tip of New Jersey, this area has long been touted as one of
the best bird-watching spots in the East. Migrating birds gather
here before or after crossing the Delaware Bay. What makes this
area unique is the variety of habitats, which include fields, meadows, wooded areas, freshwater ponds, sand dunes, a jetty, and a
1½ mile beach that supports a wide variety of wildlife. Sightings of
over 200 species of birds (including eleven that are listed as endan-
gered in New Jersey) have been recorded at Higbee. To get to

Higbee Beach from Cape May, go south on Sunset Boulevard. Turn right on Route 607. At the intersection of Route 607 and Route 641, turn left and follow this road to Higbee. Once at Higbee, the dirt road on the right takes you to the beach. The wide path on the left (beyond the chain that prevents vehicles from entering) goes through a wooded area and through fields.

CAPE MAY POINT

Lighthouse.   For the best view of Cape May Point and beyond, wear your sneakers and be prepared to climb 218 steps to the outside Watch Gallery of this 1859 structure. Unlike many towers that we have climbed, we felt secure here; the edge of each step is lighted and there is a handrail on both sides of each step. On the way up, there are side platforms where you can rest and take in the views. The beacon at the top of the 157-foot brick structure flashes every ten seconds and is visible up to twenty-four miles out to sea.

Open daily in the summer, 9 A.M. to 8 P.M. Shorter hours during the rest of the year. No admission to see the exhibits on the ground floor. To climb to the top: adults, $3; children, $1.50. Lighthouse Avenue, Cape May Point, NJ; (609) 884-5404.

Cape May diamonds.   The Cape May "diamonds" that you see in the storefronts along the boardwalk near Convention Hall can be found along the beaches near the sunken ship at Cape May Point. These colorless quartz stones somewhat resemble diamonds when they are wet. When they are dry, they become dull. The shiny ones that you see in the stores have been tumbled for months. Bring a pail and you can spend hours sifting through the pebbles to find perfectly formed ones. Their colors range from colorless to yellow, amber, green, blue, or pink. They're great for the bottom of an aquarium, as they will keep their luster underwater.

Sunset Viewing.   Cape May Point is the best place to see the sunset. If you go to the sunken ship, you will be asked to stand while the national anthem is played over the loudspeaker and the flag is lowered. If you want more privacy (and the same great view), take Sunset Boulevard to Cape May Point, and turn left on

Cape Avenue (you'll know it by the white stucco and brick pillars on each side of the street). Go 1/10 mile, turn right on Alexander Road and take it to the end. This is also a great place to find Cape May diamonds.

GETTING OUT ON THE WATER

Cape May Sightseeing Cruise.   Captain Schumann conducts two-hour sightseeing cruises around Cape May aboard a 200-passenger cruiser. You will learn about the wetlands, ecology, and local marine life. Taking the cruise on a warm summer evening, watching the sun set, and seeing dolphins is a great way to start the weekend.

The Big Blue Sightseer Cruiser casts off from Ottens Harbor, 4500 Park Boulevard, Wildwood, Friday evening at 7 P.M. and Sunday at 10:30 A.M. Tickets must be purchased at the Physick Estate or at the Trolley Station at Beach and Gurney. Adults, $5.50; children 3 to 12, $3; (609) 884-5404.

Sailing on a Catamaran.   If you want to feel the breezes and move over the water at a faster speed, go for a cruise with Captain Wilsey in his twenty-seven-foot catamaran. He takes up to six passengers at a time. The trips leave from Sunset Beach at the end of Sunset Boulevard. Adults, $10; (609) 884-8347 or (609) 884-6333.

Cape May–Lewes Ferry.   This seventy-minute ferry goes from Cape May to Lewes, Delaware. The ferry holds about 100 cars. In the winter, when the bay can be rough, there are four round trips daily; during the summer there are about fifteen daily departures. Sample fares: car, $16; passengers, $4; bicycle and passenger, $7. Reservations are not accepted. Box 827, North Cape May, NJ 08204. Cape May terminal, (609) 886-2718. Lewes terminal, (302) 645-6313.

ENTERTAINMENT

Coast Guard Graduation.   Every Friday morning at 11 A.M. (be there by 10:45), the public is invited to see the Coast Guard recruit graduation held at the culmination of eight weeks of training. Coast Guard Base, Training Center, Pittsburgh Avenue, Cape May.

Vintage Film Festival. Films that were popular during the 1930s, 1940s, and 1950s, are shown at the Chalfonte Hotel Monday evenings during July and August. Shows are at 7 and 9:30 P.M. Adults, $3; MAC members, $2.50; children under 12, $1. 301 Howard Street, Cape May; (609) 884-8409.

Theatre by the Sea. The East Lynn Company, a professional summer stock theater, performs outdoors during the summer on a stage located behind the Christian Admiral (Beach and Pittsburgh avenues). Contact the Center for the Arts for their schedule; (609) 884-ARTS.

Jazz at the Virginia Hotel. Come for a drink and listen to Steve Lamanna, a jazz pianist who entertains in the lobby of the hotel on Monday and Thursday from about 5 to 9 P.M. We suggest contacting the hotel to check his schedule. 25 Jackson Street, Cape May; (609) 884-5700.

The Shire. You may just hear a good jazz group at this club. Different groups perform throughout the year. 305 Washington Street Mall, Cape May; (609) 884-4700.

Nightlife. If you want the best in top-name entertainment, you're in the wrong place; head north forty miles to the casinos at Atlantic City. For a listing of show information, consult the Friday Weekend section of *The Philadelphia Inquirer.*

Bike and Surrey Rentals. As the distances are short, one of the best ways to get around is by bicycle. The single or double surreys are fun for taking a self-guided tour around the historic district.

Bicycles: $3 per hour, $8 per day. Regular surrey, $10 per hour; double surrey, $20 per hour. The Village Bicycle Shop is located at Ocean Street, at the beginning of the Washington Street Mall. Open 7 A.M. to 8 P.M.; (609) 884–8500.

Miniature Golf. There are four miniature golf courses in Cape May. The best course is at the corner of Pittsburgh and New Jersey avenues behind the Water's Edge Restaurant. It is attractively landscaped with real trees and shrubs.

Fishing. The best place to go fishing is at the Second Avenue jetty. Another good spot is the World War II bunker by the lighthouse at Cape May Point. Go to Jim's Bait and Tackle, located just beyond the bridge as you come into Cape May, to buy bait, tackle, or a tide table.

Tennis. There are three clay and twelve Har-Tru courts at the William Moore Tennis Center on Washington Street, just before the entrance to the Physick Estate. Tournaments as well as clinics are held during the summer. Lessons are available; (609) 884-8986.

SHOPPING

Petroff's. What is the beach without salt water taffy? The Petroff family has been making taffy here for over seventy years. Be sure to come when the taffy-puller machine in the window is operating. 425 Beach Avenue, Cape May; 08204.

Mother Grimm's Bears. Bring in any kind of old fur piece (mink, beaver, Persian lamb) and Ellen Grimm will transform it into a custom-designed teddy bear complete with a birth certificate. She also makes less expensive handmade bears, but these specialty bears (about $130) are unique. 727 Beach Avenue, P.O. Box 2226, Cape May 08204; (609) 886-3004.

Cape Maynia. Promoting architecture is the concept behind this new store with puzzles, buildings to construct, Victorian design books, rubber stamps of the Chalfonte, Abbey, and Mainstay hotels, and Physick Estate. Emlen Physick Estate Carriage House, 1048 Washington Avenue, Cape May, NJ; (609) 884–6650.

Fudge Kitchen. Wander by each evening to watch the strong-armed fudge makers whip the mixture into mesmerizing ribbons of fudge and to sample some of the fifteen varieties. This is the best we tasted. Two stores, on the Washington Street Mall and at 728 Boardwalk, Cape May, NJ 08204; (609) 884-4287 or 1-800-23-FUDGE.

For the Birds. Stop in for all the necessities needed for birding and exploring: birding guides, tapes, binoculars, butterfly nets, and clothing. 324 Carpenters Lane, Cape May; (609) 884-7152.

Colliers. This shop has a good selection of wines to bring to the BYOB restaurants. Jackson Street, Cape May, NJ 08204; (609) 884-8488.

The Pink House.   Here's a great gift shop for Victoriana such as jewelry, wrapping paper, picture frames, and cards. If your feet get tired, sit on the wicker couch on the porch. 33 Perry Street, Cape May; (609) 884-2253.

Elaine's Victorian Winchester Restaurant and Bridal Shop. Victorian wedding dresses are sold on the second floor. On the first floor is a dinner theater. 513 Lafayette Street, Cape May; (609) 884-1199.

Keltie News.   If you need light beach or porch reading or a detailed book about the Victorian structures, you'll find a complete selection here. 518 Washington Street Mall, Cape May; (609) 884-7797.

The Baileywicke.   Boots and made-to-measure sandals with arches to fit your foot are a specialty. Free oiling and repairs. 656 Washington Square, Cape May; (609) 884-2761.

Victorian Sampler.   A great souvenir of Cape May is a sampler that depicts one of the Victorian buildings. This store has cross-stitch charts or kits of most of the B&B inns featured in this chapter along with one sampler of the roof tops, a street scene, and the Physick Estate. 680 Washington Square, Cape May; (609) 884-3138.

WHERE TO STAY

Porches or verandas and gingerbread trim are the signature of all the Victorian inns we've featured. Victorian architecture of every describable type is found at the inns of Cape May: mansard roofs (straight, convex, or concave), hipped and gambrel roofs, cupolas, bargeboards, balustrades, gazebos, turrets, and towers. For the most part we searched for inns or hotels located near the beach and in the historic district. While these are the accommodations we favor for a short stay, Cape May has a full range of modern motels, big old hotels, and houses or efficiency apartments to rent by the week, month or season.

INNS

The Mainstay Inn

Sitting on the grandest Victorian veranda in Cape May, with iced tea and a plate of assorted sweets in hand, the sea breezes rustling through sycamores and the clop-clop of horse-drawn carriages passing by the front of the inn, we couldn't imagine a more ideal spot to soak up the Victorian era. "We've created an environment that accurately reflects the Renaissance Revival style, but we want it to be livable for our guests," innkeepers Tom and Sue Carroll told us as we looked around in amazement at the spacious rooms filled with extraordinary, large Victorian pieces.

This two-story Italianate villa was built in 1872 as an elegant men's gambling and entertainment club. The interior is furnished with fine antiques, many of which are original to the house, such as the massive twelve-foot mirror in the entrance hall. Looking at

The Mainstay Inn has the grandest Victorian veranda in Cape May.

the fourteen-foot ceiling with its intricate design made with eighteen different Bradbury wallpapers, Tom smiled as he quipped, "I make a lot of friends lending out my scaffolding." On this floor there are two formal parlors with floor-length windows framed by heavy swag draperies, and a dining room where elegant breakfasts are served in the cooler months. The belvedere, more commonly known as a cupola, is an intimate hideaway; a pair of binoculars sits at the ready.

Next door is an equally elegant cottage with another wide veranda. The more casual wicker-filled parlor has scenes of old Cape May on the walls; it is the only room where smoking is permitted.

You may have a hard time deciding on a favorite room, as each one is totally unique. The Henry Clay Room has a wardrobe so high that the hangers are made with wooden extension handles. It has an elegant queen-size walnut bed with a massive carved headboard, a marble-topped dresser, and lighting that is adjustable (as it is in all of the rooms) from bright to softly romantic. In the Windsor room, originally the dining room, there is an ornate bird's-eye maple bed and a pair of matching men's and women's dressers. If you like to soak in a full-length tub set in a wood-paneled room, ask for President Harrison's room. The Bret Harte is a corner room with a matching dresser and bed and a private veranda.

During the spring and fall, a full breakfast of a hot or cold fruit dish, an egg dish, and homemade coffeecakes is served in the formal dining room. In the summer, cereals, yogurt, fresh fruit, juices, and coffeecakes are set out on the veranda. Each afternoon, tea and assorted pastries are served. As you leave you may want to add Sue's cookbook, *Breakfast at Nine, Tea at Four* to your collection.

Note: A stay during peak summer months must be planned well in advance. Many guests reserve their favorite rooms in early January.

Open April through mid-December. Ten rooms and two suites, all with private bath, summer and holidays $115–$140. Other seasons, $85–$125. A full breakfast (except during the summer, when there's a continental breakfast buffet) and afternoon tea are included. Three-night minimum on weekends and during the summer. Children over 12 are welcome. Third person in room, $20 additional. No pets. 635 Columbia Avenue, Cape May, NJ 08204; (609) 884-8690.

The Abbey

While you are focusing your camera on this Gothic Revival structure, with its sixty-foot central tower with cresting, you may notice a fellow wandering about the property in a pith helmet, a fez, or possibly a Mexican sombrero, don't worry—it's only innkeeper Jay Schatz airing out specimens from the hundreds of hats in his collection. As Jay and his wife, innkeeper Marianne, commented, "You have got to have a sense of humor to stay with us."

The interior of this inn, especially the public rooms, is even more ornate than the exterior. Massive, heavy pieces of carved and upholstered furniture grace the public rooms. Bradbury and Bradbury paper embellishes the walls and ceilings. "My weakness is furniture," said Marianne as we eyed a wall of books snuggled inside two 11½-foot-high bookcases that almost touch the twelve-foot ceilings of the library. "They were a perfect fit for the house, so we had to buy them both," Marianne said.

The decor of the antique-filled bedrooms is not as heavy as in the public rooms. An unusual Victorian lamp is beside each bed; ours had fringe all around the shade. The room of choice in the main building is the Newport Room, which has a sumptuous tower bath.

Another favorite is the San Francisco Room, which was the original master bedroom. The bargain is the tiny, corner Natchez Room with a private bath and a headboard made from a piece of the iron rooftop balustrade.

We stayed in the adjacent cottage. It doesn't have the ornate common rooms of the Villa, as the main house is called, but it has two parlors filled chock-a-block with Victoriana. Our room, the Baton Rouge, was one of the least expensive; it had a double bed, a Victorian couch, a dressing table, and a private bath.

Jay announces breakfast by walking through the houses, playing a set of chimes. In the warm weather a breakfast of juice, cereal, fruit, and muffins is served buffet style on the porch. During the cool seasons a formal sit-down breakfast is served in the dining room.

Another fun time (when Jay gets to continue his humorous anecdotes) is the late afternoon wine and cheese get-together. Guests and innkeepers freely offer their opinions on local restaurants. We also learned that the builder of this house was John McCreary, one of the nineteenth-century Pennsylvania coal barons whose claim to fame was his battles with the Molly Maguires.

Open late March through November. Twelve rooms and two suites, all with private bath, $80–$160. Midweek discounts spring and fall. A full breakfast (except during the summer, when a continental breakfast buffet is served) and afternoon refreshments are included. Children over 12 are welcome. No pets. Three- or four-night minimum during the summer and on most weekends. Columbia Avenue and Gurney Street, Cape May, NJ 08204; (609) 884-4506.

The Queen Victoria

Almost every morning you will see innkeeper Joan Wells meticulously tending the alyssum and heather along the iron fence that borders this distinctive 1811 corner property.

The complex called the Queen Victoria now includes four buildings. We stayed in the latest addition appropriately named Prince Albert Hall. The interior of this former rooming house has undergone an extensive adaptive restoration that includes central air-conditioning. The large rooms are decorated with Bradbury and Schumacher wallcoverings and have queen-size brass or iron canopy beds, reproduction period chairs, and ceiling fans. The larger rooms and the suites all have Jacuzzis. The suites are great for families, as they have a television, telephone, small refrigerator, and a convertible couch.

The common rooms in the original part of the inn are furnished with the clean lines of Mission-style furniture including a number of pieces by Gustav Stickley. There is a case of Roycroft ceramic pieces in the living room. At night and in the winter, the working player piano, a fireplace, a decanter of sherry waiting to

JANE STAUFFER

The Queen Victoria Inn is a distinctive 1881 corner property two blocks from the beach.

be sampled, and even a popcorn popper make the living room a jovial spot.

Rooms in this building range from cozy, economical third-floor rooms (one has a distant ocean view) with shared baths to spacious corner rooms with quilts and easy chairs. Make sure to read the excellent handbook of activities and information about the inn that's placed in each room.

If you stay across the street in the cottage, you have the advantage of viewing the marvelous Victorian garden planted just outside your door.

Personal touches include twice-daily maid service, a specially made chocolate on your pillow, little bottles of shampoo and conditioner, sewing kits, and a choice of foam or feather pillows.

Guests can choose to have their breakfast in the Queen Victoria, the Prince Albert, or can even have it brought to their room. Joan hosts one of the breakfasts and her husband, Dane, is at the other. A full breakfast of the Queen's oats (granola) and other cereals, fresh fruit, and egg dish, juice, muffins, breads, and Wolferman's English muffins is served buffet style. We liked not having to sign up for breakfast at a specific time.

Joan used to be the executive director of the Victorian Society in Philadelphia, so she has a wealth of knowledge about this period. Guests who come the first weekend in December help decorate the inn's authentic Victorian Christmas trees that each are planned around a different Victorian period. At Christmas and Thanksgiving, Joan said, "We become an extended family as we plan special weekends to include our guests."

Open all year. Twenty-four rooms, suites, and cottages. June through September, 10 suites $150–$225, 13 rooms with private bath, $105–$140, 4-room cottage with shared bath $80. Lower rates other times of the year. A full breakfast and afternoon refreshments included. Children welcome; third person in room $20 additional; babysitters can be arranged. No pets. Minimum stay of three nights during the season and two nights on weekends the rest of the year. 102 Ocean Street, Cape May, NJ 08204; (609) 884-8702.

Angel of the Sea

From a distance, this mauve and two-tone gray inn with its ornate gingerbread, porches, turrets, and manicured lawn looks like a castle from Disney World. The inn is set about a mile from the historic district and has great ocean views from the porches and from many of the rooms. It's the perfect spot for someone who wants to feel close to the ocean yet somewhat removed from the activity of the town. The prices are higher than at any of the other inns reviewed, but amenities such as a chauffeured drive back and forth to dinner in a mint 1939 black Cadillac or 1960 Rolls Royce are included.

Innkeepers John and Barbara Girton have worked magic as they and a large construction crew ripped out walls and removed layers of paint from the woodwork, scraped off layers of wallpaper, and refinished floors. "It felt a little like Christmas," John said. "You never knew what you would find each day." One of the treasures they unearthed was the carved wooden fireplace, the focal point of the living room.

The furnishings include new Victorian reproduction pieces as well as brass or four-poster beds and white wicker chairs and couches. The four front rooms, our favorites, share the two balconies. The cozier third-floor rooms also offer fine water views but don't have balconies. The price of each room is based primarily on its views.

Breakfast can be served to you in bed, on your porch, or in the dining room. Coffee, cereal, and juice are available about 7:30 A.M. and a full breakfast is served from 8 A.M. on. Bicycles, beach umbrellas, beach tags, sand chairs, towels, and soft drinks are included in the room price.

Originally this inn and the building behind it was one large building. The second building also has been renovated; the two are connected by a covered walkway. This building has thirteen rooms.

Open all year. Twenty-seven rooms, all with private bath, July and August $125–$230. Other times except holidays, $85–$175. Third person in room $20 additional. Full breakfast and afternoon refreshments are included. Children over 8 welcome. No pets. 5–7 Trenton Avenue, Cape May, NJ 08204; (609) 884-3369.

Manor House Inn

Manor House is a traditional turn-of-the-century seaside shingle house with a good-size porch, but it doesn't stand out as a dramatic architectural wonder. It is located on the oldest and one of the quietest streets in the historic district. We feel its popularity is due in part to the warmth and caring attitude of the innkeepers, Tom and Mary Snyder, who have quietly built a strong following of "alumni" (as they like to call their return guests).

There is plenty of common space for the guests. The living room has an intriguing platform rocker, Victorian couches, and a ragtime player piano.

In the back room, a large jigsaw puzzle is always in process. You can take off your shoes, sink into one of the contemporary sofas facing the woodburning fireplace, and pore through the assortment of magazines and books. Or, sit in one of the original barber chairs from the old Penn State barber shop, close your eyes, and remember the days when a hot towel and a shave cost fifty cents.

All of the rooms have ceiling fans, robes, hair-dryers, and glycerine soaps. Fine quilts made by Mary or by other members of her family are in most of the rooms. Rooms 9 and 10 have ocean glimpses through the Victorian rooftops. Room 8 is the romantic room, with lots of lace, frills, a chaise longue, and an intricate all-white Pennsylvania Dutch quilt. The suite, room 6, has a Jacuzzi and a separate shower, a queen-size brass bed, and a dressing room. Returning from dinner we found cookies on our pillows.

Mary creates superb breakfasts. Each day she offers a choice of breakfast entrées; the day we were there the choice was peach crêpes or a tomato tart, both of which we highly recommend. Apple fritters, potato latkas, Welsh rarebit, and corn pie are other entrées that she often prepares. Breakfast also includes a "freshly hugged" juice, fresh fruit, as well as muffins such as banana chocolate-chip oatmeal or Mary's famous sticky buns (see *Recipe,* page 315).

Tom is in high gear at breakfast. Come down and have a cup of coffee beforehand so that you are fully awake for his "readings." We started our day off smiling as Tom dished up puns, spoonerisms, and his version of "Saturday Night Live" along with information about what to do. You will need a sense of humor to stay here, as "the puns and jokes are a part of our innkeeping style," he said. "They seem to creep up and snap at you to keep you from being too serious."

Closed January. Eight rooms and one suite, seven with private bath. July and August and holidays, rooms $90–$130, suite, $145. Other times $60–$100. A full breakfast and afternoon refreshments included. Children over 12 welcome. No pets. 612 Hughes Street, Cape May, NJ 08204; (609) 884-4710.

The John F. Craig House

This Carpenter Gothic tucked in the row of B&B inns along Columbia Avenue has the advantage of on-site parking. On the first floor there are two porches with wicker chairs. The front door opens onto the formal living room, furnished with Victorian sofas, chairs, and a working fireplace. The woman who showed us to our room made us feel right at home when she said, "You can touch anything you want here."

Our third-floor room had an iron bed, the original gasolier light (ornamental only), and dormer windows on three sides of the room that offered a great angle for observing the architectural details of the town: colorful bargeboards, protruding gables, finials, and different types of mansard roofs. One end of this large room had a comfortable grouping of a wicker couch and chair. The bath was for our use only, but was just outside of our room.

On the second floor there are three rooms. The two large front rooms share a bath and are furnished with high-quality Victorian pieces. On the first floor in the back part of the house are three quiet rooms that share a bath.

Breakfast is served with style. Light enters the dining room through the French doors and picks up the gold tones in the Bradbury shell wallpaper. The table was set with great care: lacy linen napkins, a vase of gladioli, and a Victorian silver coffee pot. The fresh eucalyptus leaves from the innkeepers' property added a pleasant scent. The French toast, made with homemade cinnamon bread, was served with warm maple syrup and sausages and garnished with pieces of fruit.

The inn is owned by Chris and David Clemans, who live nearby in Cape May. David comes in each morning to cook the delicious breakfasts. We have nothing but praise for the staff of cordial women who efficiently and graciously manage the inn, but if meeting the innkeeper is a priority for you, this isn't the place to stay.

Open mid-March through November. Eight rooms, six with private bath. One suite. Mid-June to mid-September, suite $160; rooms with private bath, $130; rooms with shared bath $115. Other times of the year rates 15 percent lower. Full breakfast and afternoon tea included. Children over 12 welcome. No pets. Three-night minimum in season and on weekends. 609 Columbia Avenue, Cape May, NJ; (609) 884-0100.

The Brass Bed

If you express an interest in listening to the 1916 Grafonola that sits in the music room, innkeeper John Dunwoody will gladly drop whatever he is doing and delve into his extensive record collection. "That's what we're about," John and Donna said. "We came here to share our home with our guests, not to rent rooms."

Since opening more than ten years ago, the building has been spruced up from top to bottom both inside and out. The Dunwoody's son, a carpenter, designed insulated glass windows for the front and side porches that can be removed in the summer. The tiny side porch off the dining room is filled with games which, on a winter or rainy afternoon, can usually be found spread out on the dining room table in front of the working fireplace.

As fits the name of the inn, the beds are all old brass ones. On our last visit we stayed in room 7 on the third floor. A larger dormer window has been added to significantly increase the amount of headroom. "This was the room we always rented last," Donna said, "and now it's one of our favorites." Room 5 has an exceptionally heavy brass bed, emerald-green fainting couch, armoire, and rocking chair. Another favorite is room 8 with wall-to-wall emerald-green carpeting, two twin beds (which can be converted into a king), a classic Eastlake platform rocker, flowered wallpaper, and a private bath with a clawfoot tub.

John and Donna join their guests at breakfast every morning. In the summer, breakfast includes fruit, cereal, homemade muffins, and bagels. In cool weather, a hot entrée is substituted for the cereal. Popular entrées from Donna's repertoire include asparagus strata, banana pancakes (one of our favorites), deep-dish French toast, and the Brass Bed breakfast log made with flavored croutons, eggs, cheese, and chopped sausage.

Open year-round. Eight rooms, four with private bath. Mid-June through mid-September, rooms with private bath $95–$115; rooms with shared bath $80–$90. Other times of the year $55–$95. Breakfast and afternoon refreshments included. Two- or three-night minimum stay during the summer and on most weekends. Children over 12 welcome. No pets. 719 Columbia Avenue, Cape May, NJ 08204; (609) 884-8075.

HOTELS

The Virginia Hotel

The outstanding restoration of this nineteenth-century hotel was completed in 1989. The exterior has been faithfully restored; the lobby shines with fresh paint, new period wallpaper, and polished wood. There is an intimate cocktail lounge, a lobby reading room with an assortment of upscale magazines, a full-service restaurant and a full-time desk clerk. In the rooms, 1990s luxury intrudes: all have thick wall-to-wall carpeting, large bathrooms, bathrobes, king-size beds with comfortably firm mattresses, telephones, televisions with video playback units, and a selection of movies. The hotel has all the services expected of a first-class establishment, including *The New York Times* outside your door, and valet parking.

This is the ideal hideaway for someone who likes the feel of a modern full-service hotel. If you are traveling with children and want to stay in the historic district where you can get a sense of the Victorian charm of the town, yet have the convenience of a room phone and television, this would be a good choice.

Open all year but closed mid-week January through mid-February. Twenty-four rooms, all with private bath. Weekend rates during summer, $155–$220. Mid-week summer rates $135–$200. Other times of the year, $85–$185. There are two rooms with private porches overlooking Jackson Street; in season, $220. Continental breakfast included. (There is also a restaurant in the hotel.) Children welcome; over 5 years of age, $15 additional. No pets. 25 Jackson Street, Cape May, NJ 08204; (609) 884-5700.

The Chalfonte

It takes a special kind of person to love the Chalfonte. It's not a hotel in the usual sense: There are no televisions, no room phones, and the majority of rooms do not have private baths. It has a breezy summery feeling. Owners Anne LeDuc and Judy Bartella have infused a lot of love into the hotel and have sponsored yearly work weekends to help with the renovation of this breezy Victorian.

Upstairs off the long corridors are rooms filled with just the essential pieces of furniture—bed, bureau, and chair. There is no air-conditioning and the bath is down the hall. The best rooms at the Chalfonte are private-bath rooms 40, 62, and 63, as they each open onto the front porch.

In the dining room, guests at the hotel who previously didn't know each other can sit together at the common table. At other tables, groups of friends or families are gathered, partaking in their yearly summer tradition. At dinner, men are asked to wear jackets. The cuisine (see *Where to Dine,* page 313) traces its roots to the days when cholesterol wasn't known. Children under seven eat in their own dining room.

This is a people place, a place that's run with love, a place out of the past. But it's not for everyone. If you aren't sure if you'd be happy with sparse accommodations and a price structure that includes breakfast and dinner, we'd suggest that you stay elsewhere but come by for a meal. You may want to return.

Open weekends in late May and early June, daily early June through September, and weekends in October. Eleven rooms with private bath, $145. Third person in room $25 additional. Seventy rooms with shared hall baths, $73–$123. Breakfast and dinner for two included in all rates. Service charge of $6 per day per person is additional. The charge for children is for meals only, $3–$15 depending on age. 301 Howard Street, Cape May, NJ 08204; (609) 884-8409.

RENTALS

Somewhere in Time, Cape May Point

If you want a quiet, secluded spot where you can do your own housekeeping, these nine fully equipped contemporary apartments in Cape May Point are ideal. The apartments are located one block from the beach and two miles from Cape May. Owner Martha Marcus is an avid gardener of flowers and herbs; the raised beds and a grape arbor are a symphony of color. With outside gas grills and access to local produce and fresh fish, you won't need to leave this paradise for long.

Open Memorial Day through mid-October. Weekly rates: studio, $650–$775; one-bedroom, $600–$875; two-bedroom, $850–$1,100. Box 134, 202 Ocean Avenue, Cape May Point, NJ 08212; (609) 884-8554 or (215) 566-2934.

Realtors

Apartments or houses can be rented by the week, the month, or the season. A word to the wise: look at the property before you sign a contract. Tolz is the largest realtor in Cape May. Box 489, 1001 Lafayette Street, Cape May, NJ 08204; (609) 884-7001 or (800) 444–7001.

WHERE TO DINE

410 Bank Street

This restaurant has found the recipe for success: an attractively landscaped outdoor dining patio, first-rate service, and exceptional cuisine.

The knowledgeable waiters dress in the latest "mod" style: green-and-white striped shirts with black bow ties and black pants.

The semi-boned, mesquite-grilled fresh quail was served with warmed salad greens and a black walnut vinaigrette. The asparagus almondine in a puff-pastry cornet was covered with slivered blackened almonds and lemon butter. The pastry was flaky and the asparagus cooked to perfection. The Cajun spice did not overpower the tender blackened sea scallops. The Louisiana seafood sausage made of shrimp and scallops was served on a savory Creole mustard cream sauce.

A real winner of an entrée is the Cajun shellfish gumbo of lobster, sea scallops, shrimp, and smoked sausage; we mopped up the sauce with the crusty bread. The catfish filet in a coconut batter served with a lime-jalapeño sauce, bananas, and fresh tomatoes was not a favorite; the sauce had such a large amount of lime that it caused puckered lips. The sautéed soft-shell crabs served with capers, hazelnut butter, and lemon sauce were at their peak.

Mesquite-grilled salmon, swordfish, tuna, shark, and mahi-mahi steaks are served each day as available, with different sauce combinations. Other entrées included blackened prime rib, chicken breast with cranberry fruit-compote, and mesquite-grilled veal chops or lobster tail.

Desserts included a heavy bread pudding soaked in bourbon, creamy key lime pie, hazelnut cheesecake, chocolate pecan Amaretto rum pie, and, our top choice, a triple chocolate ganache made with three different, sinfully rich chocolate icings.

When the weather cooperates we prefer to dine in the outdoor garden, but be sure to bring along insect repellent. We feel that the indoor tables are uncomfortably close to each other, particularly when the restaurant is crowded.

Open April through October. Dinner daily, 5:30 to 10 P.M. Entrées, $17.95–$24.95. Bring your own bottle. 410 Bank Street, Cape May, NJ 08204; (609) 884-2127.

Restaurant Maureen

The glass-enclosed second-floor porch overlooking the beach is one of the most sought after dining spots in Cape May. It's not just the location and the food but also the fact that Maureen Horn greets her guests personally. "Good night, and thank you for coming" conveyed the feeling that she really meant what she said.

Three appetizers we especially liked were the escargot in garlic butter; the lobster ravioli, a special treat made with a pepper vodka cream sauce; and the creamy crab bisque.

Every year a special lobster entrée is featured, such as cold-water lobster tail lightly stuffed with seasoned crabmeat and baked in a rich puff pastry. A special low-cholesterol item is swordfish baked in parchment with tomatoes, leeks, carrots, basil, olives, lemon, and butter. A signature dish is medallions of veal served over lobster, shrimp, and crab and accompanied by a complex St. Milo sauce.

The purée of raspberries surrounding the dense Belgian chocolate pâté made with hazelnuts is a magical combination. Other favorite desserts include pound cake served with a praline crunch butter-cream icing, and a three-layer loaf of white chocolate, mocha, and dark chocolate mousse.

No reservations are taken at this popular restaurant. Beach attire of shorts and tank tops is not welcome here, but should you arrive "just off your boat," they have pull-on black pants and shirts for their dining guests to borrow.

Open mid-April through October. Dinner daily, 5 to 10 P.M. Entrées, $17.50–$27.50. Beach Avenue and Decatur Street, Cape May, NJ 08204; (609) 884-3774.

Water's Edge

Located across the street from the beach and a comfortable fifteen-minute walk from Convention Hall is one of Cape May's best restaurants. It features American cuisine that emphasizes fresh local seafood and vegetables combined in creative new interpretations. Because there is a sea wall across the street, the best ocean views are available from the booths on the raised platform at the back of the restaurant. Try to reserve corner booth 3 for the best view. The restaurant has a light, contemporary, open feel with picture windows and large abstract paintings on the wall.

The superb pan-fried oysters are breaded with chopped pecans and cornmeal and served with a hot spicy jalapeño mayonnaise. Grilled thin-sliced potatoes with slices of Brie and spicy andouille sausage is a tasty combination, and one that would be easy to duplicate at home.

We were impressed by our experienced waitress who recited the details of preparations for six specials of the evening, including all their sauces and accompaniments, without using any notes. The entrées arrived on fourteen-inch round plates that allowed for visually attractive presentations.

The local sea scallops smothered with julienned red and yellow peppers, carrots, and leeks were a delicious, light entrée. Two loin lamb chops in a wine sauce were accompanied by tasty sweet-and-sour red cabbage and roasted potatoes. The steamed filet of salmon was an exceptionally large portion prepared in a Chinese style with a topping of leeks, black beans, ginger, soy sauce, and sesame seeds. The sautéed breast of chicken with lemons, limes, cucumbers, and scallions topped by a dollop of crème fraîche was the least successful of the entrées we tasted.

Desserts included an intense chocolate cherry truffle torte, bourbon pecan pie, and a moist, dense chocolate brandy walnut cake. For a refreshing change, order a plate of orange pound cake and fresh fruit slices served with a dish of chocolate sauce.

Should you want a beer, you can choose from nineteen on the list, including Pinkus Weizen, Samuel Smith's Nut Brown Ale, and raspberry beer, an unusual treat that goes well with dessert. The wine list includes eighteen wines that are available by the glass.

Note: A congenial bar has tables where a lighter pub menu is offered.

Open daily, mid-May to mid-October. Breakfast, 8 to 11:30 A.M.. Lunch, 11:30 A.M. to 3 P.M.; $5.25–$7.50. Dinner from 5 P.M. Dinner entrées, $18–$25; specials even higher. Beach and Pittsburgh Avenues, Cape May, NJ 08204; (609) 884-1717.

Louisa's

The stories about this tiny twenty-seat restaurant are legendary. By 4:45 P.M. the bench is filled, and the line starts to form in front of the simple wooden window boxes that overflow with impatiens and blue lobelia. The "Louisa addicts" are arriving: the president of a liberal arts college, two innkeepers, the dean of a prominent medical school, a fisherman, a family on their two-week vacation, and even a couple of travel writers.

Inexpensive Ikea yellow, blue, and white folding chairs are arranged around card tables painted in bright colors reminiscent of elementary-school seashore scenes.

The menu changes nightly, depending on what fish is available at the Cape May docks or what fresh produce the folks at the Broadway market picked that morning. No red meat is served here.

The appetizers here are called "treats." The ginger sesame noodles served in a spicy peanut sauce was our favorite of the three variations we had in Cape May. The eggplant salad had plenty of herbs and onions. For an entrée we had steamed topneck clams with vine-ripened tomatoes and liberal amounts of chopped basil. The sweet and tender sautéed scallops were served with a dish of tamari-flavored dipping sauce. A large filet of snapper bluefish (small bluefish) was basted with lemon, garlic, and olive oil. For the vegetarian, there was fettuccine with grilled vegetables.

Large portions of desserts are served. As only a limited amount of each is made, ask to have a piece reserved if you have a particular favorite. We enthusiastically sampled the blackberry tart, the chocolate mousse pie, and the coconut brandy pie with hot fudge sauce. The excellent quality of the coffee was a nice surprise.

Unlike most restaurants that expand when they become successful, Louisa's has vowed to keep the size small and the prices reasonable.

Open May through mid-October. Dinner, Tuesday through Saturday, 5 to 9 P.M. Weekends only in March, April, and mid-October through December. Entrées, $9.50–$14. Bring your own bottle. No reservations, no credit cards. Located one half block west of the Washington Street Mall. 104 Jackson Street, Cape May, NJ 08204 (609) 884-5882.

Washington Inn

This restaurant, a long-standing tradition in Cape May, keeps getting better at what it does—serving consistently well-prepared meals. The ingredients are fresh; the flowers are beautiful; and the service is attentive.

Have a drink before dinner in the glass-enclosed porch decorated with lots of Boston ferns, or visit the Victorian bar.

Dine in the greenhouse room on glass-covered tables, on the enclosed porch where the ceiling is covered with the same chintz fabric as the tablecloths, or in the dining room.

Start with fresh baked scallops wrapped in bacon, Gorgonzola cheese tortellini, or local fresh clams on the half shell. The miniature crabcake, a favorite, is sautéed with a roasted red-pepper sauce.

Hearty eaters can get a fifteen-ounce steak served with bleu cheese butter, twin filets, or a filet mignon with béarnaise sauce. The shore seafood selections are attractively presented: broiled shrimp stuffed with lump crabmeat, broiled lobster tail, flounder topped with sautéed crabmeat, and the ever-popular surf and turf, called filet and lobster tail here.

House specialties include boneless lamb chops with a minted pear and demi-glaze, veal cutlet covered with cheese and a rich sherry sauce, and sautéed crabmeat flamed with brandy. Take note of such specials as the seasonal game dishes; the chef is given free rein to be creative.

Open year-round. Dinner daily, 5 to 10 P.M. Sunday jazz brunch. Entrées, $15.95–$21.95. No shorts or T-shirts. 801 Washington Street, Cape May, NJ 08204; (609) 884–5697.

Es-Ta-Ti

This new, upscale Northern Italian restaurant is on its way to taking its place among the better dining experiences in Cape May.

Es-ta-ti, the phonetic pronunciation for summer in Italian, is owned and operated by Maureen and Stephen Horn of the highly regarded Restaurant Maureen, which happens to be located right upstairs.

The tables are well spaced, a pleasant surprise in Cape May. The black chairs, white tablecloths, dark green Art Deco wallpaper, and cone-shaped wall lamps give the main dining room a contemporary look.

Sweet frying peppers marinated in an herb vinaigrette were served along with the bread. They were so good that we asked for seconds. For an appetizer, we started with the chilled seafood salad of mussels, scallops, shrimp, and calamari served on a bed of red pepper fettuccine, a portion that could be shared easily. Whole anchovies served with toast and seasoned with olive oil and tomato are recommended for the palates that savor this salty taste. A fresh, crisp salad of radicchio and romaine lettuce, included with the dinner, was served next.

A spicy, thick version of fra diavalo sauce was served over a large filet of red snapper. We'd vote to add this dish, or at least the sauce, to the regular menu. The cannelloni stuffed with lump crabmeat had just enough ricotta and mascarpone to bind the filling together. A pungent red shrimp sauce spread over the top made this a special treat. You can order this as an appetizer or an entrée. The fork-tender poached salmon was accompanied by spinach fettuccine and a delicate cream sauce.

Saltimbocca traditionally is served with Parma ham and sage. Here the veal is stuffed with lobster, three Italian cheeses, and spinach before it is breaded and fried. Beef lovers will not feel left out, as the filet is marinated in olive oil and black peppercorns and served with a robust barolo wine sauce.

After many attempts at making tiramisu on the premises and not being satisfied with any, Stephen now brings it in from New York City. Unfortunately, it didn't seem to surrender any of the calories on the ride down the Garden State Parkway. Having tasted many versions of tiramisu, we would splurge on this one without hesitation.

Open early March through October. Dinner daily, 5:30 to 10 P.M. Entrées, $17–$25. Beach Avenue and Decatur Street, Cape May, NJ 08204; (609) 884-3504.

Peaches

There are seven closely spaced tables inside this small, popular café. Patrons sitting at the six tables in the outdoor dining area have a pizza parlor on one side and a view of cars looking for a parking space on the other. The staff is casual; the feeling is friendly; the food is good but not superb; the prices are a bit lower than at most other restaurants; and the clientele is loyal.

The award-winning creamy clam chowder includes large pieces

of fresh clams without the usual mess of potatoes. The chilled pasta with peanut, ginger, and sesame sauce was good, but it wasn't spicy, as the menu described.

The most unusual item on the menu, and the dish that Peaches is best known for, is avocado crabcakes. Although the combination might seem odd to traditional crabcake lovers, it does work if you like avocado. This is the first curry that we've seen on any menu in Cape May, and it was good (the chef has traveled extensively in Thailand). Shrimp Siam is marinated in Thai spices, then skewered and grilled. All of the entrées are accompanied by Thai rice, a combination of four different varieties of rice cooked with carrots to give a hint of sweetness.

Desserts on the night we were there included deep-dish bourbon pecan pie, a very limey key lime pie (here we were happy to have our lips pucker), and a Viennese raspberry almond torte with chocolate that was similar in taste to the more familiar Linzer torte.

Open Easter through November. Dinner daily, 5:30 to 9 or 10 P.M. Bring your own wine. Entrées, $11.95–$21.95. 322 Carpenter's Lane at Washington Street Mall and Sawyer Walk, Cape May, NJ 08204; (609) 884-0202.

Frescos, Cape May

This moderately priced Northern Italian restaurant and 410 Bank Street, located next door, are under the same ownership. You can choose to dine outside on the porch, or inside where the overhead fans, green faux-marble pillars and wainscotting, and popular Italian opera selections create a trattoria-like atmosphere.

If you are a fan of osso buco, a house specialty, reserve an order when you make your reservation; the chef prepares only a limited amount of this time-consuming delicacy each day. It's made the traditional way: the veal shank is braised with tomatoes and fresh herbs and cooked for several hours until the meat is tender.

If you aren't overly hungry, order a few appetizers or split a portion of pasta. Don't let the seemingly high price of $3.95 stop you from ordering the marvelous, grilled garlic and Parmesan cheese bread.

High on our list of Cape May greats is the pan-fried calamari in corn-meal batter served with a delicate anchovy-tomato dip. The layered torte of baked eggplant, spinach, roasted red peppers, and Gruyère cheese looked elegant, but its taste wasn't as remarkable.

Without the recommendation of a local innkeeper we might not have ordered the fusilli puttanesca (screw-shaped pasta with an unusual, tasty sauce of ground anchovies, black olives, and capers).

Being fans of pesto (our garden produces an abundance of basil), we found the red and gold fettuccine with pesto and sun-dried tomatoes bland. We couldn't taste the basil, and a couple of whole sun-dried tomatoes were just plopped on top.

The evening we dined, the desserts were not up to the standards of the rest of the meal. The cannoli had a soft ricotta and apricot filling that leaked out of the shell. Don't waste the calories on the tiramisu, as it tasted like nothing more than sponge cake with whipped cream, rum, and raisins. For the price, we suggest having another portion of the grilled bread.

Open April through New Year's. Dinner daily, 5:30 to 10 P.M. Entrées, $8.95–$20.95. Bring your own wine. Bank Street, Cape May, NJ 08204; (609) 884-0366.

McGlade's

We became completely intoxicated by the sights and sounds of the waves rolling and breaking under this small canvas-covered outdoor restaurant. On the end of the old wooden pier next to the Convention Hall is one of the best-kept dining secrets in Cape May.

Breakfast here is for the seriously hungry. We tried two over-size omelets: the Cioci Norma is loaded with sausage, onion, and cream cheese, and TJ's special is filled with shrimp, crab, and cheese flavored with garlic. Following breakfast we had to walk two miles.

You won't dine on gourmet fare or pay high prices here, but you can find the high spots and good values on the menu. A recent evening meal included the veggie salad with iceberg, romaine, sprouts, raisins, tomatoes, and a piece of hard-boiled egg on top. We didn't taste much lump crabmeat in the highly touted crabcakes.

The chowder was filled with clams and vegetables. Our favorite entrée was the shrimp butter Rosa, a full plate of *al dente* linguine topped with plenty of shrimp and mushrooms sautéed with garlic. At $4 desserts are overpriced. Save your calories for another day, enjoy another cup of coffee, and relax to the music of the Atlantic Ocean.

If you like to feel as though you are dining at sea, plan to have your meal two hours before or after high tide. At low tide you can watch the tiny shore birds, reminiscent of a disciplined, choreographed ballet corps, dancing back and forth with the waves.

Open Memorial Day through mid-September. Breakfast from 7 A.M., lunch, 11:30 A.M. to 3 P.M. daily; $3–$8.25. Dinner, Wednesday through Sunday, 5 to 9 P.M. Entrées, $8.50–$11.25. Bring your own wine. On the boardwalk behind Morrow's Nut House, Cape May, NJ 08204; (609) 884-2614.

The Chalfonte

After a Virginia country breakfast of spoonbread, fresh fruit, biscuits, fried fish, and scrambled eggs, we stepped into the kitchen to pay our respects to Helen Dickerson, who has been a part of the Chalfonte for well over sixty years. She and her daughters Lucille Thompson and Dorothy Burton control the inner workings of the kitchen.

At dinner, men are requested to wear jackets. All guests are served a four-course dinner with relishes, soup, vegetables served family style, fish, a choice of entrée, dessert, and fruit compote. Entrées change daily: Monday, herbed roast leg of lamb or chicken; Tuesday, roast pork with apple dressing or deviled crab; Wednesday, Southern-fried or broiled chicken; Thursday, turkey or scallops; Friday, deviled crab or roast lamb; Saturday, prime rib or sea scallops; Sunday, a buffet of fried chicken, Virginia ham, seafood, salads, and desserts. At this old-fashioned restaurant you'll never, even for a moment, need to consider if the fish is undercooked or if the lamb will be served rare.

Children under the age of seven are not allowed to eat in the dining room with the adults. They eat in the children's dining room and are entertained following dinner so that their parents can enjoy a leisurely meal.

Open Memorial Day through early October. Breakfast, 8:30 to 10:30 A.M.; prix fixe, $7. Dinner, 6:30 to 8 P.M.; prix fixe, $21. Jackets required. Howard and Sewell Streets, Cape May, NJ 08204; (609) 884-8409.

OTHER PLACES

The Ebbitt Room, Virginia Hotel

This is one of the best places for a late-night meal. Menu suggestions include crabcakes, grilled tuna, grilled smoked chicken, maple Virginia ham, and meatloaf.

Open year round except midweek January to mid-February. Breakfast, dinner, 5:30 to 10 P.M. and late-night menu (10 P.M. to 12 A.M. summer only). Dinner, $12.50–$25. Late-night menu, $3.75–$12.50. 25 Jackson Street, Cape May, NJ 08204; (609) 884-5700.

Lobster House Take-Out

This complex along the water includes a large, popular restaurant that serves the usual shore dinners; a fresh fish market; a take-out section; a raw bar; and the schooner *American* that's tied to the dock and is a good place for a cocktail. We stay away during the summer season, when the complex is exceedingly crowded. The tables along the dock are a good place to have a casual take-out meal of crabs, fried clams, shrimp, and other seafood.

The restaurant, take-out, and fish market are open year round. Fisherman's Wharf, Cape May, NJ 08204; (609) 884-3064.

Famous Louie's Pizza

This is our favorite pizza in Cape May, especially the broccoli-ricotta. The seating is outside under a tent covering. Call ahead for take-out.

Open Memorial Day to mid-October. Lunch and dinner. Pizza available by the slice, $1.50–$2.50, or the pie. 7 Gurney Street and Beach Avenue, Cape May, NJ 08204; (609) 884-0305.

RECIPE

Manor House Sticky Buns

Tom and Mary Snyder grew up in Reading, Pennsylvania, where potatoes are a staple of the local diet. Tom managed the family's business, making old-fashioned potato chips until he became an innkeeper. If you stay at the Manor House, you may be treated to Mary's homemade baked potato chips or her sticky buns, which (naturally) are made with potatoes. These are some of the best we've ever had. Some day you'll see this recipe in their cookbook, which they plan on calling *Tom's Puns and Mary's Buns.*

Dough

1 pack (¼ ounce) dry yeast
½ cup warm water
⅔ cup butter
¾ cup granulated sugar
½ tablespoon salt
2 medium potatoes
1 cup potato water
2 eggs
5 cups all-purpose flour

Filling (for half the dough)

2 tablespoons light brown
   sugar
½ teaspoon cinnamon
1 tablespoon butter

Topping (for half the dough)

1 cup brown sugar
⅓ cup butter
1 tablespoon corn syrup
   nuts or raisins (optional)

Dissolve yeast in warm water. Cook potatoes (save the potato water) and mash. Add butter, sugar, salt, and mashed potatoes to hot potato water. When cooled, stir in yeast and eggs. Add flour to make a stiff dough. Turn out on a floured board and knead well. Put the dough in a buttered bowl; cover with a towel and place in the refrigerator for at least 12 hours.

Divide the dough in half. Roll out to a 12-inch circle. Sprinkle the light brown sugar and cinnamon on top. Dot with tiny pieces of butter. Roll up jelly roll style and slice into pieces ½ inch thick.

In a small saucepan, melt the butter and add the brown sugar and corn syrup. Cook until well blended. Divide in three 9-inch square glass cake pans. If you like, you can cover syrup with nuts or raisins. Place slices of dough over syrup. Cover and refrigerate at least 1 hour, until ready to bake.

Bake at 375°F for 20 minutes. Turn buns out of the pan as soon as they are baked.

If you don't want to bake all the buns at once, you can store half the dough in the refrigerator for up to a week. Punch the dough down once a day to keep it from going sour. The dough can also be used for dinner rolls or other sweet rolls.

YIELD: 2 dozen buns.

ITINERARY

You may be going to Cape May in summer to take advantage of the beach, in spring or fall for birding, or at any time of the year to see the Victorian architecture. This itinerary includes a sampling of all the attractions the town has to offer.

DAY ONE. Drive or walk to the **Emlen Physick Estate** to purchase a membership in the **Mid-Atlantic Center for the Arts**. Then take a tour of the **Physick Estate**. Have lunch overlooking the water at **McGlade's**. This is a particularly great spot if it's high tide. Spend the afternoon on the beach or, if the weather is inclement, take a **trolley tour**. Dine at **410 Bank Street** or at the **Washington Inn**.

DAY TWO. Take the **walking tour** of the historic district. (Check the weekly schedule; some days the tour is given in the morning and other days in the early evening.) Get a slice of pizza at **Louie's**. Take a **trolley tour**, the **Victorian Sampler tour**, or spend the afternoon enjoying a good book on your inn's porch. If you feel like taking a walk or a bike ride, go up to the Christian Admiral Hotel to look at the Tiffany glass dome and the stained-glass windows. Continue to the **Lobster House** and have a drink aboard the schooner *American*. Have dinner at the **Water's Edge**. Other top choices for dinner on Beach Avenue are **Maureen's** or **Es-Ta-Ti**.

DAY THREE. Head to **Cape May Point State Park** to walk on the boardwalk and view the birds. Then climb the 218 steps to the top of the **lighthouse** for great views of the point. The only place in Cape May Point for lunch is the General Store and Restaurant (500 Cape Avenue, open seasonally). Spend the afternoon sitting on the beach at Cape May Point, searching for **Cape May diamonds**, or take a ride on the **catamaran**. Higbee Beach is great if you are a birder. Dine at **Louisa's** (get there early in the summer) or **Peaches**.

DAY FOUR. If you are up early, take a **stroll along the board-walk**. Following breakfast, visit some of the **stores** in the mall area and near the beach (see our suggestions). Take a picnic with you for a **walk along the beach** (start at the Second Avenue jetty), on land preserved by the Nature Conservancy. Take the **Mansions by Gaslight tour** or, if this tour isn't offered on the days you're visiting, have tea at **The Mainstay** (Renaissance Revival Victorian) or at **The Abbey** (Gothic Revival Victorian) to see the furnishings. For a casual dinner go to **Frescos** or **McGlade's**, or for more elegant dining go to **The Chalfonte**.

Getting to the Area

From New York City or Philadelphia, take the Garden State Parkway south to the end. Take Lafayette Street to the mall. The inns are in the historic district, most a block or two east of the mall.

BUDGETING YOUR TRIP

To help you get the most for your money, here are some travel suggestions at three budget levels (cost per day at peak season with two people sharing a room, including tax, 15% gratuity at meals, and service charges). Prices are approximate and intended for planning purposes only. Lodgings are categorized by price. Meal prices at lunch include an average entrée and beverage. Dinner prices include an appetizer, entrée, beverage, and dessert. Wine or alcoholic drinks are not included.

Staying and Dining at Expensive Lodgings and Restaurants: From $270 to $360 per day for two.

Lodging: The Mainstay $150; Angel of the Sea $177–$246; Queen Victoria $160–$240; John Craig House $171; Manor House $155; Virginia Hotel $165–$235; The Abbey $128–$171.

Dining: Breakfast: included. Lunch: Water's Edge $20. Dinner: 410 Bank Street, Water's Edge, Virginia Hotel, or Maureen's $80.

Admissions: Mid-Atlantic Center for the Arts membership $25; Mansions by Gaslight $24; Cape May by Boat $11.

Staying and Dining at Moderately Priced Lodgings and Restaurants: From $190 to $240 per day for two.

Lodging: The Mainstay $123–$134; Angel of the Sea $134–$150; Queen Victoria $112–$150; Manor House $128–$139; John Craig House $123–$139; The Brass Bed $102–$123; The Chalfonte $167 (includes dinner).

Dining: Breakfast: included except at the Virginia Hotel ($20). Lunch: McGlade's $16; Lobster House take-out $12. Dinner: Es-Ta-Ti, Washington Inn, Frescos, or Peaches $70–$75.

Admissions: Physick Estate $8; Walking Tour $8; Mansions by Gaslight $24.

Staying and Dining at Less Expensive Lodgings and Restaurants: From $110 to $170 per day for two.

Lodging: The Abbey $86–$102; Queen Victoria $86; Manor House $96; The Brass Bed $86–$96; The Chalfonte $90–$144 (includes dinner).

Dining: Breakfast: included. Lunch: Louie's Pizza $8. Dinner: Louisa's or McGlade's $45; Lobster House take-out $18.

Admissions: Walking tour $8; Mansions by Gaslight $24.

Not included: Bike or surrey rentals, tennis, fishing, or birding walks.

SUGGESTED READING

Self-Guided Architectural Tours, Cape May, NJ. Marsha Cudworth. New York: Lady Raspberry Press, 1987. 82 pages. $7.95. Available at Keltie News and Cape Maynia. Whether you're walking, riding or biking, this is a good companion. Photographs and illustrations accompany descriptions of many of the Victorian buildings, and maps pinpoint their locations. The book includes a glossary of architectural terms as well as drawings of major structural details.

The Jersey Shore: A Travel and Pleasure Guide. Robert Santelli. Charlotte, North Carolina: The East Woods Press, 1986. $8.95. This is a guide to coastal Jersey towns from Sandy Hook to Cape May. Each chapter includes the history of the area and a good section of things to do. The restaurant and inns section contains listings with only a sentence or so of description.

EIGHT

THE EASTERN SHORE OF MARYLAND AND VIRGINIA

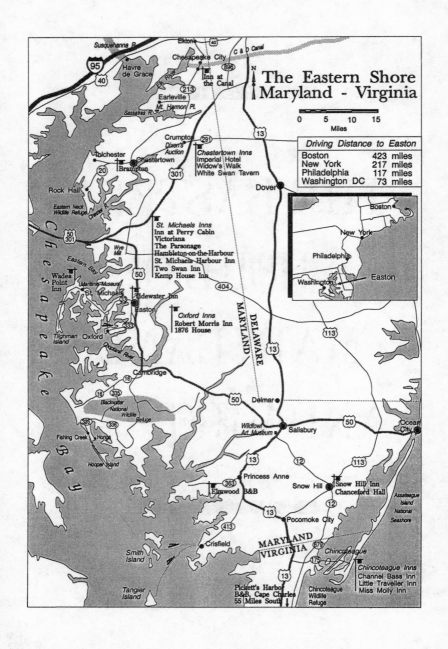

The Eastern Shore
Maryland - Virginia

0   5   10   15
Miles

Driving Distance to Easton

Boston	423 miles
New York	217 miles
Philadelphia	117 miles
Washington DC	73 miles

Boston
New York
Philadelphia
Washington   Easton

Susquehanna R.
Elkton
C & D Canal
Chesapeake City
Havre de Grace
Inn at the Canal
Elk River
Earleville
Mt. Harmon Pl.
Sassafras R.
Crumpton
Dixon's Auction
Chestertown Inns
Imperial Hotel
Widow's Walk
White Swan Tavern
Tolchester
Chestertown
Brampton
Rock Hall
Eastern Neck Wildlife Refuge
Dover
St. Michaels Inns
Inn at Perry Cabin
Victoriana
The Parsonage
Hambleton-on-the-Harbour
St. Michaels Harbour Inn
Two Swan Inn
Kemp House Inn
Eastern Bay
Wades Point Inn
Maritime Museum
St. Michaels
Tidewater Inn
Easton
Oxford Inns
Robert Morris Inn
1876 House
Wye Mill
Tilghman Island
Oxford
Choptank River
Cambridge
Blackwater National Wildlife Refuge
Fishing Creek
Honga
Hooper Island
Wildfowl Art Museum
Salisbury
Delmar
Ocean City
Princess Anne
Elmwood B&B
Snow Hill
Snow Hill Inn
Chanceford Hall
Pocomoke City
Assateague Island National Seashore
Smith Island
Crisfield
MARYLAND
VIRGINIA
Chincoteague
Chincoteague Inns
Channel Bass Inn
Little Traveller Inn
Miss Molly Inn
Tangier Island
Pickett's Harbor B&B, Cape Charles
55 Miles South
Chincoteague Wildlife Refuge
DELAWARE
MARYLAND
Chesapeake Bay

Twenty years ago, two innocent hungry adventurers stopped at an ordinary-looking roadside restaurant along a two-lane road in Maryland. When we entered, our senses were filled with the sounds of pounding hammers and the sight of trays carrying bright red crabs and piles of empty shells. Was this a crab-picking factory or a restaurant? Fun-loving people were pulling the backs off cooked crabs, breaking them in half, ripping off the legs and claws and using wooden mallets to pound the big claws with a missionary zeal. The eating utensils were knives and fingers.

We were at the one and only Maryland Eastern Shore. The dinner went on and on. Pitchers of beer and soda were quaffed to counteract the spicy crab seasoning. This messy but fun dinner is not one to be eaten abruptly or in your Sunday best. As diners consumed more crab, they pulled pieces of paper toweling off rolls placed on each table, wiped their hands, and crumpled the towels on top of the ever-expanding mound of shells. Underneath this mess of shells, towels, beer, and drippings from the crabs were long pieces of brown paper covering the tables.

This was our first experience eating hard-shell blue crabs, and we continue the ritual with enthusiasm. A crab dinner on the Eastern Shore is unlike any dining experience you've ever had. Talk to anyone who has grown up in this area and their eyes develop a wistful longing, their manner relaxes, and the stories begin. It is here on the Eastern Shore that *Callinectes Sapidus* or the Chesapeake Bay blue crab is king.

While the waters of the Chesapeake Bay give up 23 million

pounds of crabs each year to the enterprising watermen, the original settlers of this region did not come here 300 years ago to feast on this crustacean. Arriving in the seventeenth century, the settlers cleared the land and built plantations to grow tobacco. Because ships from England could sail directly up the bay into the natural deepwater harbors of Oxford, St. Michaels, Snow Hill, and Chestertown, this area flourished. As you drive the roads, impressive manor houses are visible in fields surrounded by acres and acres of farmland. Today the fields are planted not with tobacco but with corn and soybeans that is turned into feed for the millions of chickens (Purdue, Holly Farms) that are bred in the long, low, white buildings that look like motels with all the lights on.

As crops are harvested and fields are left dormant for the winter months, the farmers turn their attention to the hunters. The sound and sight of geese filling the sky in V-formation on a crisp, clear November day is exhilarating. This area is the winter home for tens of thousands of waterfowl that migrate yearly from the Canadian tundra along the Atlantic flyway. This natural phenomenon has become a big business, and attracts hunters from all over the United States.

As the weather turns colder, the pleasure boats that ply the waters dock in marinas and the crabs burrow into the mud for the winter. The watermen adapt their boats to oystering. While most oysters are harvested using hand-held tongs, a few watermen cling to the tradition of gathering them from the decks of a sailing vessel. The skipjack, the last commercial sailing vessel in the United States, plies the waters of the Chesapeake dredging for oysters. The fleet, now numbering nineteen, is based on Tilghman Island.

This is an area close to, but very different from, major cities. Visit to slow down, to eat the local shellfish, to meander down country roads, and to sit and watch the sunsets over the water.

Talbot County Chamber of Commerce.   7 Federal Street, Easton, MD 21601; (301) 822-4606. Covering Easton, Oxford, and St. Michaels.

Kent County Chamber of Commerce.   118 North Cross Street, Chestertown, MD 21620; (301) 778-0416. Of particular note is the driving-tour map of Kent County and the walking-tour guide to Chestertown.

Somerset County Tourism. Box 243, Princess Anne, MD 21853; (301) 651-2968 or (800) 521-9189.

Eastern Shore of Virginia Tourism Commission. P.O. Drawer R, Melfa, VA 23410; (804) 787-2460.

SPECIAL EVENTS THROUGHOUT THE YEAR

May. May Day Window Box Walk. Carriage rides, maypole. Chesapeake City, MD; (301) 885-5995.

Chestertown Tea Party Festival. Historic reenactment of the 1774 Tea Party, parade. Chestertown, MD; (301) 778-0416.

Springfest. Family fun at Chesapeake Bay Maritime Museum. Frog and turtle races, scavenger hunt, model skipjack races. St. Michaels, MD; (301) 745-2916.

July. Tuckahoe Steam and Gas Association Show. Antique steam and gas engines, wheat threshing, sawmills, horse pulls. Easton, MD; (301) 758-0462.

Pony Penning and Carnival Days. The carnival runs from July 15 through August 1, with the exact date of the pony swim determined each year by the tides. Chincoteague, VA; (804) 336-6161

J. Millard Taws Crab and Clam Bake. One of the best all-you-can-eat festivals in Maryland. Steamed crabs, steamed clams, raw clams, fried fresh fish, corn on the cob, onion rings, fried clam strips, fried sweet potatoes, watermelon, and beverages. Usually held around the middle of the month on a Wednesday afternoon. Crisfield, MD; (301) 968-2500.

August. Crab Day. Get to know all about the crab at the Chesapeake Bay Maritime Museum, St. Michaels, MD; (301) 745-2916.

National Hard Crab Derby and Fair. Crab cooking, crab picking, crab races, concerts, food, and fireworks. Last weekend in August or first weekend in September. Crisfield, MD; (301) 968-2682.

September. Labor Day Skipjack Race. Watermen compete for prize money on the Chesapeake Bay in these historic ships at Deal Island Harbor; (301) 784-2428.

Candlelight Walking Tour. Tour the interiors of Chestertown's nineteenth- and twentieth-century homes; (301) 778-3499.

Hunting & Fishing Day at Remington Farm. Shooting, archery, and fishing instruction. Wildlife exhibits, artists. Chestertown, MD; (301) 778-1565.

Small Craft Festival. Experience the romance and lore of wooden sailing crafts at races, workshops, and a crab feast. St. Michaels, MD; (301) 745-2916.

October.   Kent County Historical Trust House Tour. Tour of historical county houses and churches. Chestertown, MD; (301) 778-4449.

November.   Waterfowl Festival. Sale and display of waterfowl art, carving, antique decoys, duck stamps, duck- and goose-calling contests. This festival draws large crowds. Easton, MD; (301) 822-4567.

Holiday Happenings. House tours in Chesapeake City, MD; (301) 885-5995.

December.   Christmas in Historic Chestertown House Tour. Tour of the interiors of Chestertown's private and public dwellings decorated for Christmas; (301) 778-0866.

Christmas in St. Michaels. Tour the interiors of homes in St. Michaels and a nearby village; (301) 822-4606.

WHERE TO GO, WHAT TO DO

The Delmarva Peninsula, some 200 miles long, stretches from the Chesapeake and Delaware Canal to Cape Charles and the Chesapeake Bay Bridge Tunnel, bordered by Chesapeake Bay on the west and Delaware Bay and the Atlantic Ocean on the east. It is easily accessible from New York (four hours), Philadelphia (two hours), and Washington (one and a half hours), yet the pace of life here is slower and saner than in any of the surrounding urban centers. If you have bikes, take them; the land is flat and there are many back country roads perfect for exploring. This chapter concentrates on the area of the Delmarva Peninsula known as the Eastern Shore of Maryland, from Chesapeake City at the Chesapeake and Delaware Canal, south to Crisfield and the Chesapeake Bay islands of Smith and Tangier, and the stretch of barrier islands that face the Atlantic Ocean, principally Assasteague Island National seashore and Chincoteague, VA.

THE EASTERN SHORE OF MARYLAND, FROM CHESAPEAKE CITY TO OXFORD

Museums

Chesapeake Bay Maritime Museum, St. Michaels.   Believe it or not, opening an oyster, or "shucking" as it's known in the trade, isn't all that difficult once you get the hang of it. During Oyster Day in early November, we tonged, nipped, and shucked this Chesapeake Bay delicacy. During the annual Crab Day in August, we learned the difference between a "sook" and a "jimmy" and how to "pick" the backfin meat expertly.

Historic buildings display exhibits that trace the history of the bay and its early inhabitants from its Ice Age formation to the present day. Informative sections explain the trading of tobacco with England, the harvesting of crabs and oysters, and waterfowl hunting with flocks of wooden decoys and guns. Having read Michener's *Chesapeake,* we were particularly fascinated by the large punt guns. In the boat shop, our favorite building, we watched skilled shipwrights restore and maintain the museum's collection of wooden work boats.

Climb up inside the 1879 Hooper's Strait Lighthouse to get a feel for the lonely job of the lighthouse keeper. The light, formerly powered by burning lard and now converted to electricity, flashes CBMM (Chesapeake Bay Maritime Museum) at night. At dockside, look at the floating fleet: a log-built bugeye, a skipjack, a Virginia crab dredger, and a buy boat.

This 1879 Hooper's Strait lighthouse is at the Chesapeake Bay Maritime Museum in St. Michaels.

As you wander the grounds, excellent volunteer guides answer questions and spin tales about life on the bay. Do take advantage of their knowledge.

Other highlights of the museum include the propulsion building, which houses more than fifty steam and gasoline engines; the Tolchester bandstand, rescued from a now-extinct Victorian-era amusement park; a small aquarium with rockfish, crabs, and other aquatic life common to the bay; and an excellent museum gift shop with knick knacks, clothing items, an interesting collection of books, and build-it-yourself model boat kits.

For scholars, students, and the intellectually curious, there is a 3,500-volume maritime library.

Open January through mid-March, 10 A.M. to 4 P.M. weekends and holidays; mid-March through December, 10 A.M. to 4 or 5 P.M. daily. During the summer, the museum is open on Saturdays until 7 P.M. Adults, $4; children, $1.50. A quality guided tape tour is available for a $2 rental fee. The museum is located on eighteen acres at Navy Point in St. Michaels. Chesapeake Bay Maritime Museum, Box 636, St. Michaels, MD 21663; (301) 745-2916.

Mount Harmon Plantation, Earleville. This little-known treasure set on a knoll overlooking the Sassafras River is a premier example of an early Colonial tobacco plantation. Visitors reach the grand three-story five-bay Georgian brick structure, which dates from 1730, by driving along a winding two-mile gravel lane under a dense canopy of Osage orange trees. Great care was taken to expertly restore and furnish the house with American, English, Irish, and Scottish antiques from its golden age (1760–1810). Notice the Chinese influence in the house, especially the intricately carved patterns in the stair rails. The only twentieth-century touches added by Mrs. Boden, the former owner who restored the house, are sunken Sherle Wagner tubs in the bathrooms, a special sink in the kitchen to bathe her golden retrievers, and a large swimming pool.

After you tour the house, make sure to go up to the widow's walk for a spectacular view of the river and the plantation's 350 acres of fields, most now planted with corn and soybeans.

The formal boxwood and wisteria gardens bordered by serpentine brick walls have been replanted to reflect the plantation's 1760 to 1810 period. The 200-year-old English yew trees may be the oldest in the United States.

After visiting the house, drive to the edge of the Sassafras River to see the small shed once used for twisting and packing the tobacco into barrels for shipment to England.

The house and property are now owned by the Natural Lands Trust, Inc., a regional nonprofit land conservation organization.

Guided tours are given April through October, Tuesday and Thursday, 10 A.M. to 3 P.M. Tours are also given May 15 through October, Sundays, 1 to 4 P.M. If you would like to see the house during the winter months, a caretaker/guide usually is there on Tuesday and Thursday from November through March, 10 A.M. to 3 P.M. (call in advance, 301–275-8159). $3.75 per person. From Cecilton, go west on Route 282. Turn left on Grove Neck Road and follow signs. Mount Harmon Plantation, Box 65, Earleville, MD 21919; (301) 275-2721.

Historical Society, Easton.   A walking tour of the town conducted by one of the society's knowledgeable guides will introduce you to the town's historic structures.

Following this tour, visit the museum's buildings. Three of the buildings are furnished in the style of their original owners according to probate inventories. The oldest building, called The Ending of Controversy, dates from 1670; next oldest is a 1795 frame dwelling; and finally there is an 1810 Federal townhouse. An award-winning garden, planted in the Federal style by the garden club, is located in the midst of the museum complex. Revolving exhibits from Winterthur (see page 231), the Smithsonian Institution, or other museums are held in the museum headquarters. We enjoyed browsing in the well-stocked museum shop.

Open Tuesday through Saturday, 10 A.M. to 4 P.M.; Sunday, 1 to 4 P.M. Admission, $2. Walking tours are held Tuesday through Sunday at 11:30 A.M. and 1:30 P.M., $2 per person. 25 South Washington Street, Easton, MD 21601; (301) 822-0773.

C&D Canal Museum, Chesapeake City.   The twenty-eight-mile-long canal that connects the Delaware River and the Chesapeake Bay was operated by locks from 1837 to 1927. A powerful liftwheel pumping plant raised and lowered the water level. Of interest to canal enthusiasts is the 1837 stone pumphouse and the original pump. Other displays include a model of the canal and original lock, as well as paintings, drawings, and other archival material that trace the history of the canal.

The museum, operated by the Army Corp of Engineers, is open April 15 through November 15, Monday through Saturday, 9 A.M. to 5 P.M.; Sunday, 10 A.M. to 6 P.M. Located on the south bank of the canal at Chesapeake City, MD; (301) 885-5621.

Academy of the Arts, Easton.   This regional museum, in existence for more than thirty years, has changing exhibits such as paintings by the academy's present and past curators, an Eastern Shore artists show, a children's show, a juried show, and a members' show. Because of its limited exhibition space, the academy also displays works at the local library at the corner of West and Dover streets.

Open Monday through Friday, 10 A.M. to 4 P.M.; Saturday, 1 to

4 P.M. Free admission. South Street, Easton, MD 21601; (301) 822-0455.

Getting Out on the Water

To fully experience the Chesapeake Bay, you have to get out on it. Yachts are available with and without a crew from the many charter agencies located in Oxford, St. Michaels, and Rock Hall. However, we have located other opportunities to experience life on the bay and its tributaries.

Oxford-Bellevue Ferry.   Crossing the Tred Avon River from Oxford to Bellevue and saving twelve land miles in the process is the oldest, free running ferry in the United States, established in 1683. Raise the flag at the dock and a small, six-car ferry will arrive shortly. During the daylight hours, there are crossings every twenty minutes. Operates daily, March 1 through December 24. Fares: car and driver one way, $3.75; round trip, $5.25. Car passenger, 25¢; walk-on passenger, 50¢; bicycles, $1.50.

The Patriot.   This ninety-minute, narrated excursion aboard the sixty-five-foot *Patriot* leaves the docks of the Maritime Museum in St. Michaels and cruises up the Miles River, providing a relaxed introduction to the Eastern Shore waters. You'll see watermen at work crabbing in the summer and tonging for oysters in the fall. You will also see some of the large homes pictured in the real estate offices in Easton, tucked away on the many fingers of land that jut into the Miles River and visible only from the water.

Leaves daily, May through October, 11 A.M., 1 and 3 P.M. Adults, $5.50. Group rates available. Patriot Cruises, Inc., Box 1206, St. Michaels, MD 21663; (301) 745-3100.

Harrison's Sportfishing Center.   For nearly a century, families and groups have summered here and have gone fishing on the bay. Of particular interest to people traveling alone is the Center's buddy plan, which puts six fishers together to make a group. Harrison's fleet of bay-built fishing boats now numbers fourteen. In addition to the fishing, the Harrisons are famous for their large, family-style dinners.

Fifty dollars includes a day of fishing, bait, and tackle; $62.50 includes fishing, bait, tackle, breakfast, and lunch; $104.95–$124.95 per person includes overnight accommodations in one of their motel-type rooms, plus dinner, breakfast, lunch, and a day of fishing. The boats leave from April through November at 7 A.M. and return at 3:30 P.M. Blues run all year; sea trout and weakfish run in July and August. Harrison's Chesapeake House, Route 33, Tilghman, MD 21671; (301) 886-2123.

Rowboats for Fishing or Crabbing.   Rowboats can be rented at East Neck Boat Rental on Route 445 just before the entrance to Eastern Neck Wildlife Refuge south of Rock Hall. Boats are available from June through September. Contact Robert H. Strong, Jr.; (301) 639-7100 or (301) 639-7017.

Charter a Skipjack.   Captain Ed Farley is one of the last remaining watermen still dredging for oysters. His skipjack, *Stanley Norman,* one of nineteen skipjacks remaining, sails out of Tilghman Island. Part of the year he works for the Chesapeake Bay Foundation, taking school groups out on his skipjack. During the summer, he will take groups out for a demonstration of dragging an oyster scrape. Groups have included family reunions, wedding or birthday parties, even a burial at sea. During November, December, and March, he oysters commercially but will consider scheduling a trip to accommodate a group.

Rates are $25 per person, minimum of fifteen, maximum of twenty-four. Trips last from four to six hours, depending on the weather. Box 582, St. Michaels, MD 21663; (301) 745-2717.

Biking or Driving Tours

Although this tour starts in Oxford, it could just as easily begin in St. Michaels. The total round trip is about fifty miles. While this may seem long for one day, bear in mind that the terrain is flat, there are no hills and plenty of places to stop for sustenance. If you are staying in St. Michaels, the trip could be divided in half—going to Oxford one day and out to Tilghman Island on another day.

Starting at the Robert Morris Inn, bicycle along The Strand, then down Mill Street past The Masthead. Poke around the back streets, noting the numerous boatyards and well-maintained homes. Down Pier Street past the Pier Street Marina is a U.S. Bureau of Commercial Fisheries Biological Laboratory doing research on the decline of the oyster catch and discovering how bay fishermen can create oyster "farms." Take a look; you may be interested.

After you've seen Oxford, cross the Tred Avon River on the ferry. The ferry lands in Bellevue. Follow the road for about four miles to Royal Oak, then bear left on Route 33 into St. Michaels. During the War of 1812, according to local legend, the townspeople put lanterns high in the trees and extinguished all other lights, making an approaching British Fleet think that the town was on a bluff. Consequently, the British cannon fire overshot the town and St. Michaels was saved.

In St. Michaels, take the road to Navy Point. Visit the Chesapeake Bay Maritime Museum, gorge on crabs at the Crab Claw, take a cruise on the *Patriot,* and explore the harbor area.

From St. Michaels, the road winds past fields of corn. Five miles out of St. Michaels, turn right on Wades Point Road for a look at the inn and a spectacular view of the bay.

Twelve miles from St. Michaels, you arrive at Knapps Narrows drawbridge, one of the busiest in the east, and the Bay Hundred Restaurant. If you are here in the early afternoon, you can see the watermen returning with their catch.

After crossing the bridge (you are now on Tilghman Island), the road continues for three miles past a skipjack harbor where you can see the last remaining working sailboats in the United States. Continue on to Harrison's Chesapeake House, where you may wish to investigate the possibility of a day spent fishing on the bay.

Bicycle Rentals.   If you haven't brought a bike or your inn doesn't have them, they can be rented at the St. Michaels Town Dock Marina, P.O. Box 398, 305 Mulberry Street, St. Michaels, MD 21663; (301) 745-2400.

Note: An excellent bicycle-touring map showing routes throughout Maryland is available from the county tourist commission offices or at the state information centers on I-95. You can also contact the Office of Tourism Development, 45 Calvert Street, Annapolis, MD 21401; (301) 974-3517.

Historic Towns

Easton.   This is the commercial center and the unofficial capital of Maryland's Upper Eastern Shore. During the past half-century, the area has attracted people of means who have purchased waterfront plantations. Consequently the area is able to support an inordinate number of fine shops and restaurants. The wealth of this area is quickly apparent if you browse the windows of the numerous real estate offices and check the prices of waterfront properties. We feel that the best way to see and appreciate downtown Easton is to take the walking tour offered by the Historical Society (see page 330).

Chestertown.   Fine eighteenth-century homes abound in this former Colonial trading port. Stop by the chamber of commerce for a walking tour map. The interiors of these faithfully restored Colonial homes are open to visitors a few times each year (see *Special Events,* page 326). Even if you are not planning to stay in town, walk into the Imperial Hotel and have a look at the Victorian dining rooms. Then walk across the street to the faithfully restored Colonial Inn's White Swan Tavern and have a cup of tea, served every afternoon from 3 to 5. At the north end of town is Washington College, a small liberal arts school, to which George Washington donated money and his name.

St. Michaels.   Each year that we return to St. Michaels, we find more inns, restaurants, and shops. The Chesapeake Bay Maritime Museum, a must-see, is located here next to the Crab Claw, our all-time favorite crab restaurant. Take a sightseeing boat from here up the Miles River and rent bicycles to explore the area. This picture-perfect harbor is crammed with boats and day visitors during the summer season.

Oxford.   During the past twenty years Oxford has changed little, but the value of its property has multiplied ten times. Located on a narrow peninsula jutting into the Tred Avon River, Oxford is a watermen's community. Boatbuilding and oyster, clam, and crab harvesting are the main industries. Oxford is also home to the Robert Morris Inn. The population of the town swells during the summer season as five marinas attract yachtsmen from throughout the East. A ferry predating the American Revolution crosses the Tred Avon River.

Chesapeake City. The two halves of this town owe their existence to the C & D canal that shortens the water route between Philadelphia and Baltimore by 296 miles. As the canal is part of the inland waterway, thousands of pleasure boats and ocean-going freighters pass by annually. The town is undergoing a renaissance and is fast becoming a tourist destination in its own right.

Off the Beaten Path

Dixon's Auctions, Crumpton. Every Wednesday morning at 9 A.M., rain or shine, Norman Dixon climbs aboard his canopy-topped cart and auctions his way up and down row after row of almost anything imaginable. He makes his way through six large fields, stopping for an average of fifteen seconds to auction off lots that start at $5. Be careful or you might buy an old sofa or set of chairs whether you can use them or not.

We watched, hands in our pockets, as Norman worked his way down a row in field 3: a fine cedar chest went for $35, a not-so-fine coffee table went for $5. Then a momentary hush came over the fifty or so people gathered around the lot as the bidding continued for a full forty-five seconds—an original Gustav Stickley chair went to a New York dealer for $750. Then came an assortment of three dozen potted Alberta spruce trees and a complete Gravely tractor set. Auctions continue all through the day and into the evening until everything is sold. Dealers and individuals come from up and down the eastern seaboard to buy and sell here.

Inside a large building, another fast-talking auctioneer, seated atop a metal platform that is pushed from table to table, auctions off all sorts of bric-a-brac.

The Dixons offer Eastern Shore wisdom for newcomers: "Don't forget to look at it *before* you buy it, not afterwards. We only sell it once. If you get stuck with it, it's your fault not ours.

"If you buy a chest or bureau and you're going to get a car or truck to put it in, make sure someone stays with it until you get back. If you don't, it won't be there."

"No buy bidding. If you have to bid on your own things or get someone else to bid on them, you either paid too much or are selling at the wrong place."

Auction starts at 9 A.M. Wednesdays. Open for consignment Monday through Thursday, 9 A.M. to 9 P.M. Cash or bank reference must be on file in the office. Located at the corner of Routes 290 and 544 in Crumpton. Dixon's Furniture Inc., Box 70, Crumpton, MD 21628; (301) 928-3006.

Wye Mill.   Since 1671, there has been a grist mill on this site. Operating with a fifty-one-acre pond as the water source, the eight-foot-diameter, metal overshot water wheel turns the three-ton milling machinery. The miller, Barton McQuire, grinds locally grown, golden run corn meal, wheat, rye, and buckwheat, which can all be purchased in small quantities at the mill. Corn bread made from freshly ground corn meal has a far superior, nuttier taste than corn bread made from standard supermarket corn meal. We highly recommend that you buy some.

Open Saturday and Sunday, mid-March to just before Christmas, 11 A.M. to 4 P.M. Route 662. Call for further information; (301) 827-6909.

Wye Oak, Wye Mills.   This is the Maryland state tree. At more than 400 years of age and held together with numerous cables, it is the oldest and largest white oak known to exist. The spread of the tree covers more than half an acre. Located on Route 662 in Wye Mills.

Maryland Beaten Biscuits, Wye Mills.   No one knows when or why the first beaten biscuit was made. The most probable reason is that baking powder or soda wasn't available, so some enterprising settler beat air into dough with an ax handle for a good thirty minutes. Today, just one small commercial enterprise carries on this 300-year-old tradition.

People have a love-hate relationship with this strictly Eastern Shore product (if not prepared exactly right, the batch of dough is suitable for use as golf balls). If you're driving by on a Wednesday or Thursday, you'll smell the biscuits baking. We suggest a stop to purchase a couple of dozen for munching on the road, and to see just how owner Ruth Orrell and her eight assistants turn out an average of 1,000 dozen a week.

Look for a small hand-lettered sign just after you pass the Wye Oak tree, going south on Route 662. Biscuits are available here for $2 per dozen. They can also be purchased in area supermarkets or by mail order: Orrell's Maryland Beaten Biscuits, Box 7, Wye Mills, MD 21679; (301) 822-2065.

Remington Farms, Chestertown. We took an interesting self-guided driving tour of this 3,000-acre farm owned by the Du Pont company that is devoted to experimental development and demonstration of practical techniques for the management of wildlife. Drive in, pick up one of the free tour booklets, and follow the signs. You will see how ponds are built and maintained to attract waterfowl; how corn and soybean crops are farmed to provide for soil conservation; and how ducks, geese, rabbits, deer, quail, and songbirds can live off the residue after crops are harvested.

Open February to mid-October during daylight hours. Located off Route 20 south of Chestertown; (301) 778-1565.

THE LOWER EASTERN SHORE OF MARYLAND AND VIRGINIA

Back Road Tours

If you're intrigued by the promise of adventure on back roads, bring your wanderlust to the Lower Eastern Shore. Innumerable roads, lanes, and byways provide a view of this wonderful land that a highway just can't match. Here's a sample from a highly satisfying drive we took on a recent trip to the area.

Hooper Island. From Cambridge, take Route 16 south to Church Creek, then Route 335 to the village of Honga. During oyster season, the tongers—watermen who scoop oysters from the bottom with rake-like metal tongs on long wooden shafts—dock their boats at the retaining wall in Honga and load their catch directly into trucks bound for the shucking houses in Cambridge and Wingate.

Cross the high arching bridge on Hooper Island and navigate along the narrow road with water on both sides, past five crab houses that are scampering with activity from May through October.

Follow this winding drive out to the fishing villages on the island's southern end to catch a glimpse of a lifestyle that depends solely on the whims of wind and water.

Blackwater Wildlife Refuge. Water fowl of all variety—heron, egret, hawk, bald eagle, and dove—share this rich tidal-marsh refuge with raccoons, otters, skunk, red fox, nutria, and deer. After spotting 3 bald eagles we learned that Blackwater is the center of the greatest nesting of bald eagles in the eastern United States north of Florida. We find the months between mid-October to mid-March best for viewing waterfowl, but a drive along the five miles of road meandering through the refuge offers a refreshing retreat any time of year.

Exploring the refuge makes a great continuation of the drive outlined above. From the top of Hooper Island, head along Route 335 to Route 336, then on to a series of crossroad towns, starting with Lakesville. Take a left in Lakesville onto Shorters Wharf Road, through the refuge to Seward, then right on Green Briar Road to Bestpitch Ferry. Make a right on Griffith Neck Road to the draw-bridge, then make an immediate right onto Steel Neck Road into Vienna. Throughout the entire drive you'll see flourishing crops and wildlife, but rarely another car.

Out of Vienna, take Route 50 south to Salisbury, home of Frank Purdue's chicken empire, as well as a most unusual museum (see below).

The refuge is open dawn-to-dusk year round. Hours at the visitors center are Monday through Friday, 7:30 A.M. to 4 P.M.; Saturday and Sunday, 9 A.M. to 5 P.M. except summer weekends, when the center is closed. 2145 Key Wallace Drive, Cambridge, MD 21613; (301) 228-2677.

The Wildfowl Art Museum of the Ward Foundation, Salisbury. Here at one of the finest public collections of American decorative bird carvings, it's easy to forget these incredibly lifelike renderings are not the real thing. It's nearly impossible to accept that each of these birds is an example of a remarkable carver's art, and not taxidermy.

The world championship winners on display are especially astounding. We particularly liked the work of Tan and Jett Brunet from the bayou country of southern Louisiana.

Open Tuesday through Saturday, 10 A.M. to 5 P.M. and Sunday, 1 to 5 P.M. Admission, $1. Salisbury State College, 655 South Salisbury Boulevard, P.O. Box 703, Salisbury, MD 21801; (301) 742-4988.

The Refuge Waterfowl Museum and Local Decoy Carvers, Chincoteague.   The museum features a historical look at the art of decoys. Cigar Daisey, who was the subject of a 1980 *National Geographic* article, often can be found carving at the museum.

The museum and store are open mid-June to Labor Day, 10 A.M.–5 P.M. Hours vary during the rest of the year. Adults, $1.50; children under 12, 50¢. Maddox Boulevard, Chincoteague, VA 23336; (804) 336-5800.

Three of the more than 200 local carvers whose work we've seen on display at the Channel Bass Inn are Walter Oler for cedar decoys, (804) 336-5755; Danny Bowden for songbirds, (804) 336-5745; and Clay Bunting for songbirds, (804) 336-6869. Their work ranges from $100 to $300. Call them directly to visit their homes/shops.

The Pocomoke River Canoe Company, Snow Hill.   Canoeing upstream on the Pocomoke River on a Thursday afternoon without another soul in sight, we could have been scouts for Captain John Smith 300 years ago (except for our modern fiberglass Old Town vessel).

But we were not really alone. We paddled past an osprey nest; a great blue heron flew close by; we spied an eagle in the distance and turtles catching a few rays on logs along the bank. Bald cypress with their knobby knees sticking out of the water were a surprise to see, especially because their usual habitat is far to the south.

Stop by the dock on Route 12, adjacent to the drawbridge, and owner Barry Laws will outfit you for a very peaceful excursion. Note the old red Coke machine—still just a nickel a bottle!

Open weekends in the spring and every day between Memorial Day and Labor Day, 9 A.M. to 5 P.M. Extended hours on weekends and holidays. Rental of canoe, paddles, and life vest (all in very good condition) is $4 per hour, $20 per day, and for an overnight excursion, $30 per weekend (Friday through Sunday). Route 12, Snow Hill, MD 21863; (301) 632-3971.

Julia A. Purnell Museum, Snow Hill. The museum has collected early farm tools, costumes, uniforms, Indian artifacts, kitchen equipment, and other items covering the whole history of the area from the Indian through the Victorian eras. One of the docents will explain the collection and spin a few tales. Smithsonian Tours gave rave reviews to this gem of a museum.

Open weekdays, 9 A.M. to 5 P.M.; weekends, 1 to 5 P.M. Students under 18, 50¢; adults, $1. 208 Market Street, Snow Hill, MD 21863; (301) 632-0515.

Carvel Hall, Crisfield. A division of Towle, Carvel Hall makes its knives here, and sells them for about 50% off the retail price. Other Towle gift items are also for sale at similar discounts. Getting into the spirit of the area, we purchased oyster- and clam-shucking knives. Connoisseur brand wood-handled steak knives cost $5.50 each.

Open Monday through Saturday, 9 A.M. to 5 P.M. Route 413, just north of Crisfield; (301) 968-0500.

SMITH AND TANGIER ISLANDS

When a Eastern Shoreman says he "wouldn't go a peg" for something, he means it's not worth the effort. Your visits to the strangely wonderful Smith and Tangier islands, however, will most certainly be worth the trip.

Perhaps it was the fertile land that drew Captain John Smith to the Chesapeake Bay area—or maybe he was just looking for a shrewd real estate deal, since he purchased Tangier Island from the Indians for the lofty price of two overcoats.

The early islanders were nearly all of British ancestry, and during the 1600s and 1700s Smith Island was a rowdy, lawless place. Then, in 1807, Methodists brought the Great Revival to the island. Hymns and prayers replaced drinking and dancing, and the natives settled down into the same honest maritime culture you can visit here today, some 300 years later.

Spend a few hours strolling in the golden sunshine on Smith or Tangier. Walk past wooden houses weathered to a fine silver, listen to the gentle waves as they lap the shore, and you'll know why we consider these islands and the people who inhabit them a priceless national treasure. Experience the unspoiled lifestyle and culture highlighted in the spectacular National Geographic television special "Chesapeake."

The native waterfolk who live and work on these islands are not actors at a historic re-enactment, nor are they subsidized craftspeople at a "living museum." They are private citizens who ply their trade on the Chesapeake with the same skills and determination—and largely the same types of tools—that their ancestors used for the past three centuries.

You'll find none of the amenities of the usual vacation destination: no luxury hotels, nouvelle cuisine, museums, or theater. But it's for this very reason that we enjoy these islands so much.

Talking with the islanders, we were constantly reminded by the accent and figures of speech that while these people don't live far from the mainland—the land of cable TV and fast food—they inhabit an entirely different world. Crabbing, oystering, and tourism are the only industries here. During the summer, many of these industrious watermen rise at 3:30 A.M. to check their soft-shell-crab floats. Once a crab molts, its soft shell begins to harden in only six hours. To capture this regional delicacy, the watermen must snatch up the molting crabs, pack them in seaweed and ice, and send them off to market immediately.

The people of Smith Island (population 750) live in three villages: Ewell, Rhodes Point, and Tylerton. Boats from the mainland dock at Ewell, largest of the three. From here, you can walk to Rhodes about a mile away. Tylerton is reached by boat.

Tangier, about five nautical miles to the south, is similar except that while Smith is actually three islands, Tangier is a single isle lying across the state line. So, while the 750 residents of Smith Island (which is in Maryland) get to spread out a bit, all 750 living on Tangier (which is in Virginia) find their "huge" population more concentrated. Transportation on the sidewalk-size roads is by golf cart or motorcycles. Look for the above-ground crypts often located in front yards.

These rugged individuals are more than willing to stop, talk, and share their honest, traditional view of life. Slow down and listen to the tales they have to tell. Put on your old Saturday-around-the-yard clothes. Walk or bicycle the roads. Meander through the old cemeteries and notice the Methodist church spires rising out of these very devout working villages. Munch on a soft-shell-crab sandwich as you enjoy the soft bay breezes, and experience a totally different way of life. If you can manage it, spend the night on one or both of the islands (see *Where to Stay,* page 351).

Getting to the Islands

If you can't stay overnight, the cruises let you get the most from a visit in the least amount of time.

For the more adventurous who like to poke about on their own, there's the island mailboat, a rather funky trip of about 40 minutes (to Smith Island). You'll be packed in together with the mail, groceries, and other supplies the islanders have ordered. In season, boxes for soft shell crabs compete with passengers and supplies for space. The day we traveled via mailboat, an old pinball machine was wedged into the stern.

Cruises   *To Smith Island.* Leaves from Somers Cove Marina, in Crisfield, MD. Departure is at 12:30 P.M.; returns at 5:15 P.M. Captain Alan Tyler (301) 425-2771; $13 per person (children 6 to 12 half price), which includes a bus tour of the island. Optional family-style dinner is $9 (children 6 to 12 half price).

Captain Alan Tyler also runs a cruise leaving from the western shore of the bay at Point Lookout State Park. Departure is at 10 A.M.; returns at 4 P.M. $16 per person (children 6 to 12, half price); includes a bus tour of the island. Family-style dinner is optional (adults, $9; children 6 to 12, half price); (301) 425–2771.

To Tangier Island. Captain Rudy Thomas conducts a cruise that leaves from Somers Cove Marina in Crisfield, MD. Departure is at 12:30 P.M., returns at 5:15 P.M. $14 per person (children 6 to 12, half price). Boat ride takes 1¼ hours. Family-style dinners are available at the Chesapeake House on Tangier (adults, $9.75; children 6 to 12, half price); (301) 968-2338.

Mailboats *To Smith Island.* Departs from the Crisfield town dock at the end of Main Street at 12:30 P.M. and 5 P.M., and leaves Smith Island at 8 A.M. and 4 P.M. The round-trip fare is $5. We have found that you can show up at the dock without reservations; the mailboats and cruiseboats run on the same schedule. *Island Belle II:* (301) 425–2201 or (301) 425–3221. Captain Jason: (301) 425-2351 or 4271.

To Tangier Island. Leaves every day at 12:30 P.M. from the town dock and returns from Tangier at 8 A.M. The trip takes 45 minutes. Tickets can be used on either the mailboat or the cruiseboat; the round-trip fare is $14.

THE ATLANTIC COAST BARRIER ISLANDS

If you are looking for resorts and first class hotels, Assateague is not the place to go. Besides the Channel Bass Inn in Chincoteague, deluxe pickings are slim indeed. But if you want to experience nature, read on. Starting at Assateague Island National Seashore in Maryland and continuing on down the Delmarva Peninsula for 125 miles is a wonderful coastal sanctuary that encompasses America's last intact, fully functioning, barrier island ecosystem.

Many of the Virginia Barrier Islands have been purchased by the Nature Conservancy and are part of the Virginia Coast Reserve, the heart of what many consider the most significant natural ecosystem in the eastern U.S. In the past twenty years, as America's coastline has been claimed by resort and residential development (such as Ocean City, MD), the Virginia Coast Reserve has increased markedly in ecological value. What we have today is the last East Coast barrier island wilderness, a wonderful place of salt marshes, bays, and islands where local fishers crab and oyster as their ancestors did. Many of the farms in the area are still in the same families that received the original grant of land from the king of England.

For more information about the Nature Conservancy programs and trips in this area, contact Virginia Coast Reserve, Brownsville Road, Nassawadox, VA 23413; (804) 442-3049.

Assateague

A trip to the thirty-seven-mile-long barrier island of Assateague is an absolute must. Along both sides of this carefully protected, unspoiled island are miles of beautiful beach, about 98% of which are inaccessible by car and 30% of which are closed to the public.

Assateague Island is a magnificent nature refuge with lots to do and see. Unfortunately, the island is divided into a half-dozen or so independent jurisdictions, all running their own programs with no central "bulletin board" or guidebook to sort it all out.

Assateague, Maryland.   Cross the bridge on Route 611 south of Berlin and you enter the Maryland State Park, which offers public beaches, day-use bathhouses, a campground, and food services.

These beaches are a bit more rustic than the ones you'd find in Ocean City or Rehoboth, and more like the dunes the "old-timers" in those beach towns loved so much before the condominiums took over. Lifeguards are on duty in summer.

Immediately to the south, the National Park Service operates a primitive campground, with day-use facilities and naturalist activities. Lifeguards are on duty in summer. If you have a four-wheel-drive vehicle, call ahead for information on obtaining an off-road vehicle permit. The hale and hearty will enjoy the three primitive hike-in campsites, great for a weekend backpacking trip. We have backpacked in from the north for an overnight, and highly recommend it—sleeping under the stars on a pristine beach.

Open dawn to dusk. Day and evening programs are offered; call ahead for details and reservations for the more popular nature walks or the canoe trip. National Park Service Seashore Visitors Center, Route 2. Box 294, Berlin MD 21811; (301) 641-1441.

Chincoteague, VA

Assateague, Virginia (also known, incorrectly, as Chincoteague).   The ponies that live on this Virginia island are known to millions as "Chincoteague ponies," but Misty of Chincoteague actually grew up on Assateague Island (see *Pony Penning,* below).

As you drive across the bridge on Route 175 from the island of

Chincoteague, the first headquarters you come to is the Chincoteague National Wildlife Refuge. Stop here for access to roads, hiking, bicycle paths, and information on programs ranging from bird and marsh walks to evening slide shows.

For more human-centered recreational activities, continue south to the beach operated by the National Park Service.

Our favorite activity here is an early morning walk before breakfast along the four-mile road that circles the Snow Goose Pool. On these walks we've seen Sika deer (a miniature Japanese elk introduced to Assateague in 1923), the famous Chincoteague ponies going about their everyday lives, and countless varieties of birds feeding in and around the pond. Make sure to bring your binoculars. One day as we were leaving, a great blue heron flew directly over our heads, making the morning a soaring success for us.

The park is open dawn to dusk. Snow Goose Pool is open to bicyclists and walkers from dawn to 3 P.M., and to cars from 3 P.M. to dusk. For details on the current schedule of events and to make reservations, call the Chincoteague National Wildlife Refuge Visitors Center, Box 62, Chincoteague, VA 23336; (804) 336-6122, or the National Park Service Visitors Center, (804) 336-6577.

Pony Penning and Carnival Days, Chincoteague. More than 100 wild horses live on Assateague, protected in their natural island home. During the yearly round-up by their caretakers, the Chincoteague volunteer fire department, you can watch them swim the salt-water channel. But be prepared for up to 55,000 people jostling for position along the shoreline and wading out thigh-deep in the surf, cameras aimed to catch a video souvenir. (At least that's what we're told; we haven't been.)

The round-up carnival runs from July 15 through August 1, with the exact date of the pony swim determined each year by the tides. For more information contact Chincoteague Chamber of Commerce, Box 258, Chincoteague, VA 23336; (804) 336-6161.

Guided Wildlife Tours. This superb safari tour on a large bus (complete with screens in the windows) took us through the back roads of the refuge for a close look at the ponies and birds. Our guide was a never-ending font of fascinating information. We observed the ponies in various family groups, and our guide's understanding of the ponies' behavior was marvelous.

The 1½-hour tour runs daily at 10 A.M. during July and August.

In May, June, September, and October, tours are given at 1 P.M. on Wednesday and Saturday and at 10 A.M. on Sunday. Purchase your tickets (adults, $5; children under 12, $2.50) at the Chincoteague National Wildlife Refuge Visitors Center in the Virginia section of the park, (804) 336-5593, or at the Refuge Motor Inn on Maddox Boulevard in Chincoteague, (804) 336-5511.

Evening Cruise on the Assateague.   Catch a breeze with a naturalist on a late afternoon or early evening cruise. On this cruise, you'll see birdlife that many casual visitors would otherwise miss.

The popular 1½-hour guided tour is offered daily at 5 P.M. and 7 P.M. from mid-June until Labor Day, and at 6 P.M. Tuesday, Thursday, and Saturday during early June and September and October. Adults, $8; children under 12, $4.

Oyster Lore

• The shape of an oyster's shell can tell you about conditions at the bottom of the bay where it developed: Oysters growing on softer bottoms tend to be elongated and narrow. Oysters growing on hard bottoms and in calm water tend to be rounded.

• Why are oysters only eaten in months with an R in the name?
1. Lack of refrigeration in earlier times.
2. Biological reasons. Oysters spawn in early summer, during and after which they become thin and watery as they use their stored food reserves to make spawn. As the weather cools, the oysters grow more robust.

WHERE TO STAY

CHESTERTOWN AND CHESAPEAKE CITY, MD

White Swan Tavern, Chestertown

History is ever-present in this museum-quality restoration. The original section, dating back to pre-Revolutionary times, was used as a tannery. Later, as additions were built, the property was operated as a tavern and inn. An archaeological dig, probate inventories, and historical research done in 1977 revealed a paved courtyard, pottery shards, and a listing of furniture dating back to the early 1800s.

The most unusual room, and our favorite, is the original tannery, which later was used as the tavern kitchen and is now a comfortable guest room. The exposed beams, brick floors, and large fireplace reflect the Colonial period, but modern conveniences such as central heating and air-conditioning have been added to remind us that we live in the 1990s.

We adore the Sterling Suite, decorated with canopy queen-size bed and coordinated designer fabrics; it has a small, private sitting room. The second-floor Wilmer Room contains the original wall paneling and floorboards as well as custom-made, twin pencil-post canopy beds. A lavish Victorian suite reflects the tastes of a wealthy merchant who owned the inn in the mid-nineteenth century.

Make sure to take a close look at the extraordinary reproduction of a William and Mary desk, complete with secret drawers, in the Joseph Nicholson sitting room on the first floor.

Afternoon tea and a small plate of sweets is available for purchase by inn guests or visitors.

Six rooms, all with private baths, $75–$100. Children welcome, $25 additional. Continental breakfast included. No pets. 231 High Street, Chestertown, MD 21620; (301) 778-2300.

Brampton, Chestertown

Combining the cordial hospitality of a former Swissair flight attendant with the ingenuity and restoration skills honed on Victorian homes in San Francisco, Danielle and Michael Hanscom have the qualities that spell success in the innkeeping profession. Sharing the dream of working together, the Hanscoms have supplemented good taste with lots of hard work to create a picturesque hideaway. Their 1860 Greek Revival manor house, set on fifteen acres, is listed on the National Register of Historic Places.

Entering the living room, we commented on the difficulty of reaching the books on the top shelves of the twelve-foot-high bookcases. Danielle grinned, pointed to the top shelf where she had stashed a collection of calculus books, and said simply, "I really don't have much need for them." Gravitating toward the pair of matching gray glove-leather Swiss couches set on an Oriental rug next to the fireplace, we relaxed with a pot of tea and plate of buttery, paper-thin pizzelles.

The splendidly solid walnut staircase led up to the two large second-floor bedrooms with eleven-foot ceilings. The fluffy down comforters on the high queen-size beds, the European armoires, wood-burning Franklin stoves, the desks and easy chairs reflect the Swiss penchant for uncluttered sophistication. The third-floor rooms are the same size as those on the second floor, but have nine-foot ceilings. A second-floor three-room suite was in the final stages of completion when we visited.

The first-floor breakfast room is furnished with Swiss antiques crafted in the same period as the house. Breakfast includes fresh-squeezed orange juice, fruit, muffins or coffeecake, and a choice of eggs, sausage, French toast, or possibly a Swiss specialty such as bread-and-butter pudding with strawberry sauce.

The innkeepers live on the property with their daughter Sophie in a converted animal hospital (which we'd happily move into tomorrow).

As an added note, when the inn was renovated, an interior sprinkler system was added.

Four rooms, one suite, all with private baths, $85–$95. Breakfast included. Children permitted with prior arrangements. No pets. Located one mile south of Chestertown on Route 20, RR 2, Box 107, Chestertown, MD 21620; (301) 778-1832.

Widow's Walk Inn, Chestertown

"We raised six kids, so running a four-room B&B is just about right for us," Joanne Toft volunteered as we discussed the complexities of running an inn. "Other innkeepers tell us we pamper our guests too much," said her husband, Don, recently retired from the phone company. "Well, spoil us," we replied.

This 1877 Victorian painted lady, trimmed with maroon awnings and decked out in a new coat of yellow, olive, and brown, has rapidly become a landmark in the center of Chestertown.

The Tofts opened Widow's Walk as a B&B in the spring of 1988, and are bubbling over with plans that include a breakfast garden in the back and period furniture for the spacious living room. The warm feeling and caring attitude of the owners separates this B&B from others.

Our room for the evening, the most elegant, was the Chesapeake Suite: a queen-size bed layered with lace-trimmed pillowcases; white furniture; ceiling fan, air-conditioning, hardwood floors, and a private bath. The other rooms are comfortably appointed with matching curtains and bedspreads, stenciled walls, and a dish of chocolates.

As the Tofts don't want you to leave hungry, a breakfast of omelets, eggs almost any style, or French toast accompanied by sausage, bacon, ham, muffins, and fruit is served in the formal dining room. If you happen to be the only guests, as we were, you can join the owners family-style in the kitchen.

For those of us who like an early morning constitutional before breakfast, the location of this inn in the center of Chestertown is ideal.

Two rooms with private bath, $90; three rooms share two baths, $70–80; midweek $10 less. Breakfast is included. Children over 12 permitted. Third person in room $15 additional. No pets. No smoking. 402 High Street, Chestertown MD 21620; (301) 778-6455.

Imperial Hotel, Chestertown

This skillfully restored 1903 structure, with its double-tiered verandah fronting on High Street, was totally renovated in 1984.

The rooms are decorated in heavy Victorian style with quilted flower-patterned bedspreads and matching flowered draperies; floors are covered with a patterned wall-to-wall carpet. Rooms have king-, queen-, or twin-size beds. Brass table and floor lamps with large translucent globes are in keeping with the opulent era. Towel warmers, color cable television, terrycloth robes, and telephones are found in all of the rooms. Judging from the room we stayed in, we felt that the decor lacked the exquisite attention to detail that is evident in the restaurant. Carla and Albert Massoni purchased the hotel in September 1990 and are planning to lighten up the heavy Victorian decoration of the rooms.

The Imperial is a wonderful contrast to the Colonial White Swan Tavern across the street. If you are thinking of decorating your own home with furnishings from the Victorian or Colonial eras, and are looking for ideas then by all means tour or stay in both.

Eleven rooms, all with private bath, telephone, and television, $110; one-bedroom suite, $210; carriage house suite, $240; two-bedroom suite, $320. Mid-week discount of 20 percent except during the hunting season. Continental breakfast included. Children welcome. Cots $20 additional. No pets, but kennels are available nearby. 208 High Street, Chestertown, MD 21620; (301) 778-5000.

Inn at the Canal, Chesapeake City

We were initially attracted to this town and this inn because we like the thrill of discovering an area before the rush of tourists. This white gingerbread Victorian with a wicker-filled front porch is on the placid main street of this historic canal town.

A large dining/living room is the focal point of activity. Be sure to notice the carpet set *into* the parquet floor and the ornate, as yet unrenovated, painted ceilings that date from the 1870s; a yet-unfinished parlor across the hall has similar features.

We like the back two rooms with views of the large ocean-going ships passing through the Chesapeake and Delaware Canal. All have highly polished pine floors, old quilts, and antique chairs and bureaus that innkeepers Al and Mary Iopollo have collected. Many rooms have a television hidden in a cupboard. New additions include four-poster pencil-post carved queen-size beds in three of the bedrooms and wingback chairs in four of the rooms.

Our favorite bathroom, in one of the back rooms, has a built-in six-foot soaking tub. All the rooms have sinks set into oak bureaus.

Al and Mary also have an antique shop located on a lower level of the inn in the small old brick-floored, low-ceilinged former milking room. We were impressed by the attractive way that the antiques were arranged.

Breakfast is served in the high-ceilinged front room using antique serving pieces. A full breakfast includes an entrée such as French toast with Grand Marnier sauce or stuffed with cream cheese and peaches. In nice weather you can eat on the side porch, which offers a great view of the ships going through the canal.

Six rooms, all with private bath, $65–$95. Full breakfast included. Children over 10 welcome (younger children with permission). No pets. 104 Bohemia Avenue, Chesapeake City, MD 21915; (301) 885-5995.

ST. MICHAELS, OXFORD, AND EASTON, MD

Robert Morris Inn, Oxford

Located along the banks of the Tred Avon River in a town that works awfully hard at staying "sleepy," the pumpkin-colored Robert Morris Inn is a memorable journey's end.

The inn is named after the father of a major financier of the American Revolution who lived here from 1738 to 1750. The history of the inn dates back to Colonial America, when Oxford was a major port in the region. The main inn was built prior to 1710 by ships' carpenters as a private house. Fortunately, much of the original building survives today. You'll appreciate the Elizabethan-period enclosed staircase, the Georgia white-pine flooring in the upstairs hall, and fireplaces made of English bricks brought to Oxford as ballast in trading ships.

If you want to absorb the Colonial flavor while you sleep, reserve a room in the original section of the inn. Though these rooms still retain the feel of a traditional old inn complete with creaky slanting floors, they are gradually being redecorated with the addition of new country-print wallpaper and curtains. No smoking is permitted in the third-floor rooms.

In addition to the main inn there is Sandaway, a large 1875 Victorian waterfront lodge, located one block away. The rooms here are large; some have private porches and most have views of the Tred Avon.

The River Rooms (we liked 109) located next to Sandaway offer great views as well as spacious quarters. A large bathroom with both a clawfoot tub and a separate shower, and a private screened-in porch make these accommodations perfect honeymoon suites.

If you desire a tranquil setting where you can laze away the day on a private porch or on a blanket at the water's edge, we suggest you stay at Sandaway, or in the River Rooms.

Thirty rooms with private bath, $60–$140; three rooms with shared bath, $50–$70. Fifteen Main Inn rooms, $50–$120; two rooms in the River Cottage, $90; eight rooms in Sandaway Lodge, $110–$140; two rooms in River House, $90–$100; four River Rooms, $130; one apartment suitable for a family, $120. Breakfast is available but is not included in the room rate. Children over 10 welcome. No pets. Closed February through mid-March. 312 Morris Street, Oxford, MD 21654; (301) 226-5111.

Victoriana, St. Michaels

"This is my home and then it's an inn," Janet Bernstein told us emphatically. "Keeping house is something I do very well, so having an inn is a natural extension." With more than an acre at the water's edge next to the Maritime Museum and the Crab Claw (see page 371), Victoriana is a spectacular, centrally located spot to spend a few days.

From the vantage point of the enclosed sun porch with floor-to-ceiling windows, we happily relaxed with books from the inn's library and watched the light fade over the harbor. In warmer weather, you would have found us in one of the Adirondack chairs comfortably placed on the lawn.

The house was totally remodeled in 1988. Behind-the-scenes renovations included rewiring the entire electrical system, relining the fireplaces with stainless steel, installing a sprinkler system and individually controlled, exceptionally quiet air-conditioning and heating units, and enclosing and winterizing the sun porch.

Each guest room has color-coordinated, hand-ironed sheets and dust ruffles as well as some of the finest furniture we've seen in any inn on the Eastern Shore. As the weather gets cooler the rooms get dressed for the winter with down-filled comforters and matching sheets. Other touches, such as a music box and fresh flowers in the rooms, are little extras that we noticed.

Our favorite room is Tilghman Island on the first floor with a canopy fishnet bed, water view, and a working fireplace. The four impressive rooms on the second floor share two baths; however, three of these rooms have sinks so there is little congestion.

Breakfast is served buffet style, so each guest can take a tray to a comfortable location. Weekend specialties include creamed chipped beef and corned beef hash with poached eggs.

Besides innkeeping, Janet's other love is Victoriana, or Vicky for short, a friendly golden retriever who sleeps in the kitchen with Janet's stuffed animals.

One room with private bath $135. Four rooms (three with double beds and sink in the rooms, $116; one with twin beds, $95) share two baths. Full breakfast included. Children over 13 welcome. No pets. Box 449, 205 Cherry Street, St. Michaels, MD 21663; (301) 745-3368.

The Parsonage, St. Michaels

Driving down the main street we were intrigued by this unusual all-brick turreted building with gingerbread decorations, wicker furniture, and colorful flowers. The only drawback is that it isn't on the water. Arriving on a brisk day, you'll want to head to the warming fireplace in the front parlor for a cup of afternoon tea and cookies.

The rooms all have king- or queen-size brass beds and individually coordinated Laura Ashley bed linens. Some of the rooms are large enough to accommodate two queen-size beds. Choosing a room is difficult as some have televisions, some have fireplaces, and some have private decks. "You can get two of the three in one room, but none have all three," the innkeeper told us as we deliberated over which room to pick for the evening. The baths were done in good taste with such touches as new tile showers and polished brass faucet fittings on the pedestal shell sinks.

A large continental breakfast is served in the dining room: juice, cereal, fruit salad, yogurt, muffins, bagels, and croissants. After such fortification, we suggest you use one of the bikes the inn makes available free to guests for a ride over to Oxford via the ferry, or out to Tilghman Island over the drawbridge to see the skipjack fleet.

Seven rooms, all with private baths, $78–$84. Three of the rooms have fireplaces. On Friday and Saturday from May through Thanksgiving, there is an additional $10 charge. Breakfast is included. Children permitted by prior approval. No pets. No smoking in bedrooms. 210 North Talbot Street, St. Michaels, MD 21663; (301) 745-5519.

Hambleton-on-the-Harbour, St. Michaels

A view of the harbor and the Maritime Museum is a treat from all of the bedrooms of this finely renovated inn, located on the water next to the Maritime Museum. Built in 1860, this Victorian home was converted to a bed-and-breakfast in 1986 by innkeepers Aileen and Harry Arader.

Discriminating attention has been paid to the details of decorating each of the five guest rooms. On the first floor, the Hearthside Room has a working fireplace. The King's Chambers, also on the first floor, has a four-poster king-size bed and a chaise longue. The two rooms on the second floor, the Queen's Hideaway and the Schooner Room, have easy access to the veranda. The Crow's Nest on the third floor has a bird's-eye view of the harbor and the Miles River beyond. All the rooms have queen- or king-size beds, antique furnishings, and private bath, although in some of the rooms the bath is separated from the room only by a louvered door.

The enclosed porch is the only common meeting space. Coffee, juice, muffins, and coffeecakes are left out for the guests to eat on the porch, outside on the lawn (great in the summer), or back in their room.

Five rooms, all with private bath, $80–$95. Continental breakfast included. Children with advance permission only. No pets. 202 Cherry Street, St. Michaels, MD 21663; (301) 745-3350

The Inn at Perry Cabin, St. Michaels

Sitting in the Morning Room on a cold January afternoon, we watched a flock of several hundred honking Canadian geese land in Fogg Cove. A formally attired waiter set a large tray in front of us that included a pot of tea and another of hot water, along with lemon slices, cream, sugar, and little plates filled with assorted tea sandwiches; scones and accompanying dishes of whipped cream and raspberry jam; banana and nut breads; and assorted cookies. We felt completely relaxed and properly pampered.

STAUFFER

The Inn at Perry Cabin was created to have the look and feel of an English country house hotel.

The inn is owned by Sir Bernard Ashley, co-founder of the Laura Ashley retail empire, and was created according to his vision of an English country house hotel. Over $6 million was spent in expanding and refurbishing the original Colonial Revival waterfront mansion and the surrounding twenty-five acres bordering the Miles River.

The atmosphere at The Inn at Perry Cabin is one of hushed, sophisticated elegance. On the first floor there are three sitting rooms, one with a gas fireplace, that overlook the water. Sofas and chairs upholstered in Ashley fabrics are grouped for ease of conversation; thick carpeting is overlaid with oriental rugs; showcases display such items as English china, teapots, and a collection of oyster plates. Sir Ashley has included marble busts and other items from his home, quantities of antique and reproduction furniture, and small collectibles to give the inn a home-like feel. Guests will find picture books and magazines, baskets of fruit and nuts, fresh and dried flower arrangements, bookshelves filled with English classics, and tables and mantels covered with tin boxes, glass paperweights, and other decorative objects.

Each of the bedrooms, individually decorated with a collection of coordinated Ashley fabrics, is a designer's showcase that combines bright or subtle patterns of polished cottons with antique or reproduction antique furniture. The wallpaper matches or coordinates with the fabrics on the sofas, easy chairs, and quilted comforters. Window treatments get special attention with fabric draperies in fashionable and imaginative styles. Most of the rooms have queen-size beds; a few have twin beds. Fresh flowers, mineral water, and fruit are placed in each room. All the accommodations have telephones, individually controlled heating and air conditioning, and remote-controlled color televisions. Baths have terrycloth robes, hair dryers, English toiletries, and thick towels; most have heated towel racks. Be forewarned that the English-style sinks have separate spigots for hot and cold water.

An additional twenty-two rooms and suites, eight with fireplaces, four with a second-floor sleeping loft, and some with Jacuzzis or terraces are scheduled to be completed in 1991. These rooms will all have excellent water views. The new addition will have a snooker (similar to billiards) room and a conservatory room.

Currently, the bridal suite offers the best views and the best room; it has a private balcony overlooking the water, lots of windows, and a separate sitting room. The deluxe queen-studio suite, underneath the bridal suite, has a doorway that leads to a brick terrace, and to one of the common sitting rooms.

Other rooms have terraces or balconies with views of Fogg Cove or the front of the inn. The least expensive rooms are those with no views.

There are six rooms in the older original section. A number of these rooms and suites have front views overlooking the river, but the windows are smaller than in the newer section; the rooms are darker, and you need to go to the window to appreciate the view.

The inn has bicycles available for guests' use. Afternoon tea, consisting of cookies, sweet breads, tea sandwiches and a beverage, is served only to house guests from 4 to 5:30 P.M.

The extensive breakfast menu includes fresh juices, berries, and melon; buttermilk pancakes with cinnamon, lemon, and brown sugar; Belgian pecan waffles with maple syrup; eggs Benedict with smoked salmon, country ham, or black truffles; crab and potato omelette; or Welsh rarebit.

Nineteen bedrooms and suites: rooms $160–$260, suites $260–$385. An additional twenty-two rooms and suites will be completed in July 1991, $200–$400. Full breakfast and afternoon tea included. Gratuities not included. Children over 10 welcome. No pets. Located on the western edge of St. Michaels. 308 Watkins Lane, St. Michaels, MD 21663; (301) 745-2200 or (800) 722-2949.

St. Michaels Harbour Inn & Marina, St. Michaels

Large rooms with a private balcony overlooking the Maritime Museum and the harbor activity offer dramatic views. Although St. Michaels Harbour Inn is called an inn, it really is a modern hotel on the harbor with a sixty-slip marina, outdoor swimming pool, Jacuzzi, workout room, conference rooms, and full-service restaurant. Each room has a queen-size bed, a phone, and cable TV. Suites are furnished with a wet bar and refrigerator. As coffee drinkers, we appreciated the added touch of fresh beans, an electric grinder, and filter coffee pot in the suites.

This is a top choice for those desiring privacy, spacious rooms, spectacular harbor views, and all of the modern conveniences of a hotel.

Note: We particularly enjoyed the views from the balcony of harbor suite 202.

Forty-six rooms and suites. April through September, $90–$147; October through December, $70–$130; January through March, $50–$110. Breakfast is available but is not included in the room rate. No charge for children under 12. No pets. The inn has a restaurant that serves three meals daily throughout the year. 101 North Harbor Road, St. Michaels, MD 21663; (301) 745-9001.

1876 House, Oxford

Proprietors Eleanor and Jerry Clark restored their nineteenth-century "telescope"-shaped home, furnished it in Queen Anne decor, added Oriental carpets to accent the wide pine floors, and opened three rooms to the public in 1983.

This B&B is the complete antithesis to the thirty-odd room, full-service Robert Morris Inn just down the street.

The living room has ten-foot floor-to-ceiling windows, a fireplace, three comfortable chairs, a couch, dried flower decorations, and books about the area. Breakfast is served in the adjoining dining room.

On the second floor, the January Room is decorated in Country English with twin beds, and shares a bath with the cozy Colonial-style June Room. The October Suite has a queen-size four-poster bed with a private bath and a dressing room.

If you happen to visit in late October, you will have the opportunity to see how the large red maple reflects its autumnal color throughout the front rooms of the house. You start your day with fresh fruit, croissants, English muffins, soft-cooked eggs, and sometimes cold cuts and cheese.

If you need a lift in the area, Jerry also operates a limousine service to all parts of the Delmarva Peninsula, Washington, Baltimore, and the airports.

Three rooms, one with private bath, $75–$86. Tax is included. Two-night minimum stay required on the weekends. Continental breakfast included. Children over 13 permitted. No pets. 110 North Morris Street, Oxford, MD 21654; (301) 226-5496.

Wades Point Inn, McDaniel

Located on a magnificent 120-acre point of land with water views of the bay on three sides, this inn offers as much privacy as you desire. Staying here, you can truly appreciate the beauty of the land and the magnitude of Chesapeake Bay. From the large winterized Bay Room filled with white wicker tables, chairs, couches, and a fireplace, we picked up the field glasses and scanned the Eastern Bay in much the same way that Thomas Kemp, builder of the house and a Baltimore shipwright, scanned the horizon to look for his fleet of Baltimore clipper ships. Thomas Kemp, however, used to climb through a trap door off the Lookout Room on the third floor to a specially designed "room" perched on the roof. Make sure to look for it.

All of the rooms have a relaxed, casual feel. Do not expect coordinated designer rooms. The main house has three rooms that are heated and open all year. A summer wing has six additional small, simply furnished rooms that share three baths. Innkeeper Betsy Feiler showed us her favorite, a corner room, where "you feel like you have your toes in the water." A summer guest house on the property has five additional rooms decorated in "sophisticated Girl Scout" style. The adjoining Kemp building, completed in 1990 and open all year, has some rooms with waterside balconies and kitchenettes.

There is plenty of space to curl up with a good book. In addition to the Bay Room there is a living room with a piano, comfortable couches, and a leather wing chair. Outside are expansive porches, lawn chairs, and a private dock for crabbing.

A continental breakfast buffet of fruit, juices, cheese, croissants, and muffins is served.

Nine rooms in the main house and summer wing, most with shared baths, $60–$90. Five rooms, all with shared bath, in the guest house, $55–$69. Ten rooms in the Kemp house, all with private bath, $95–$135. Children under 12 free. No pets. Discounts on weekdays for senior citizens. Located five miles west of St. Michaels off Route 33. Wades Point Road, McDaniel, MD 21647; (301) 745-2500.

Kemp House Inn, St. Michaels

As you enter St. Michaels, you will find this 1805 inn on the left side of the main street. If you are traveling with a small pet or with young children, take note of this inn—as you won't find many that will accommodate both.

The expression "sleep tight" is especially appropriate to this inn, as all of the rooms have four-poster rope beds; once every two weeks the ropes are tightened with a tool designed for that purpose. Three of the rooms have trundle beds for children. Patchwork quilts, down pillows, and old-fashioned nightshirts are also a part of each room. On a crisp, late fall evening, we particularly enjoyed curling up in bed and watching the flickering of the fire play on the walls. Out back there is a cottage with a high cathedral ceiling.

Since there is no common area, guests take the breakfast plate of fruit, sticky buns, and a cheese wedge back to the room, or outdoors in nice weather.

Two dormer rooms with a washstand and shared bath, $65; two rooms with a washstand, toilet, and fireplace, $80; two rooms with private bath and fireplace, $85; cottage with private bath, $95. $10 less Sunday through Thursday. Continental breakfast included. Children welcome, $10 extra. Small pets allowed. 412 Talbot Street, St. Michaels, MD 21663; (301) 745-2243.

Two Swan Inn, St. Michaels

This bed-and-breakfast inn built in 1790 has a casual, rustic feel. The location—on the waterfront in St. Michaels overlooking the harbor—couldn't be better. You awaken in the morning to a sunrise over the harbor and the smell of coffee and freshly baked breads. On the first floor is a small living room with a wood-burning fireplace.

The best room in the house has a harbor view, private bath, and working fireplace. Two other rooms have harbor views and have washbasins in the room. A fourth room, which we wouldn't recommend, is a small side room. All of the rooms have well-worn pine floors and casual country furniture. Should you arrive by boat, you can dock at the inn.

Breakfast of juice, fruit, muffins, or homemade breads is served outside on the waterfront lawn in warmer weather or by the crackling fire in the winter months.

One room with private bath, $115. Three rooms (two with a sink in the room) share two bathrooms, $75–$88. Sunday through Thursday, $5 less. Tax is included. Continental breakfast is included. Children permitted by prior approval. No pets. No smoking. Carpenter Street, Box 727, St. Michaels, MD 21663; (301) 745-2929.

Tidewater Inn, Easton

Once known as "The Pride of the Eastern Shore," the Tidewater remains the focal point in the region for conferences, weddings, and social events. The four-story brick structure, rebuilt in 1948 after a fire destroyed the original inn, has an ample lobby with several shops, a restaurant, conference rooms, and an outdoor pool.

Most rooms are small, clean, and modestly decorated. They have all the amenities found in a full-service hotel: private baths, television, phone, and room service. We suggest asking for one of the rooms that has been redecorated.

The inn's central location is a plus. We also appreciated the hospitality desk staffed by a knowledgeable hostess.

One hundred thirteen rooms, all with private baths, $69–$84; suites, $165–$235. Ask about special weekend and weekday packages. Children are welcome. Small pets are allowed. Dover and Harrison Streets, Box 359, Easton, MD 21601; (301) 822-1300.

SOUTHERN EASTERN SHORE: SMITH AND TANGIER ISLANDS, SNOW HILL, PRINCESS ANNE

Smith and Tangier Islands

We highly encourage a stay on Smith and/or Tangier islands to experience the traditional lifestyle of the Chesapeake watermen, although the accommodations are not what we'd normally recommend. With that in mind, here are some places to stay.

Bernice Guy, Smith Island. This local resident rents two first-floor rooms of her house (one has air-conditioning). One room has twin beds and the other has a double bed. Dinner and breakfast are served. Dinner includes roast beef or chicken, clam fritters, crabcakes, salad, hot biscuits, and dessert. Breakfast includes preserved figs, bacon or scrapple, eggs, and toast.

Two rooms share one bath, $35 per person. Breakfast and dinner included. Children and well-behaved pets can be accommodated; children under 12 are half-price. Ewell, MD 21824; (301) 425-2751.

Smith Island Motel, Smith Island. This is a basic, low-end type of motel. Bicycles are available free for the guests and $2 per hour for others.

Eight rooms share two baths, $44. Coffee and doughnuts are available in the morning. Ewell, MD; (301) 425-4441.

Chesapeake House, Tangier Island. For the past fifty-one years Hilda Crockett, a descendant of the original Welsh settlers that arrived in 1686, has served sumptuous family-style dinners for cruiseboat passengers as well as locals and overnight visitors. Dinner is served from 11:30 A.M. to 5 P.M. Overnight guests are served at 5 P.M. Dinner, served family style, includes two crabcakes and as much as you want of the clam fritters, Virginia baked ham, pickled beets, potato salad, coleslaw, green beans, hot corn pudding, homemade rolls, and all-butter pound cake.

Chesapeake House also has eight very simply furnished rooms that share three baths. The rooms are air-conditioned; there are no phones or televisions. To experience the peace of the island and to avoid hearing the sounds and smells of meal preparations, we prefer to have dinner here but to stay elsewhere.

Eight rooms share three baths, $35 per person. Dinner and a full breakfast included. Children are welcome: under 6, $7.95; 6 to 12, $15 additional. No pets. If you're not staying overnight, the dinner costs $10.25. Tangier, VA 23440; (804) 891-2331.

Mrs. Grace Brown, Tangier Island.   This is the upscale way to enjoy this remote island. These are the only accommodations on either Smith or Tangier Island that offer rooms with private baths. Each of the five newly constructed cottage units has wall-to-wall carpeting, a queen-size bed, cable television, refrigerator, air-conditioning, and a private bath. For the best view of the bay, stay in the third-floor room that faces west in the main house. This room has its own private balcony. There is a wraparound deck off the second floor of the house, so all the guests can enjoy the water views and get a close-up view of airplanes landing on Tangier Island. On the first floor there is a television room and a large living room exclusively for the guests' use.

The two-mile sand beach is ideal at all times except August, when the waters are typically infested with jellyfish. The owners have immediate plans to construct a swimming pool.

Nine rooms with private bath, $60; two rooms with shared bath, $50. All rooms are air-conditioned. Continental breakfast included. Children are welcome. No pets. Box 156, Tangier, VA 23440; (804) 891-2535.

Mrs. Edna Dize, Tangier Island.   A room for $10 a person? There's nothing fancy here, but at this price you can overlook a lot. Two of the rooms have a double and a twin bed, and the third room has a double bed only. Mrs. Dize will cook breakfast for you ($4 additional) on any day except on Sunday. She also has bicycles for rent. Children welcome, $10 additional. No pets. Box 24, Tangier, VA 23440; (804) 891-2425.

Elmwood Bed & Breakfast, Princess Anne

Situated on a point of land jutting into the Manokin River, a full mile off a quiet country road, this 160-acre estate stands in splendid isolation. Ninety acres are farmed in corn and soybeans. There is a mile of shoreline where you can usually watch the local watermen checking their crab pots in warm weather and tonging for oysters in cool weather.

Built in the late 1700s, the house is one of the outstanding Federal-era buildings on the Lower Eastern Shore. Botanist Norman Taylor, author of the famous *Encyclopedia of Gardening,* lived here for a number of years and designed the landscaping.

Inside the main house you have a choice of four large, handsome, air-conditioned bedrooms with twin or queen-size beds decorated with old quilts and antiques. Guests have use of the expansive drawing room and the porch of this house, which the owners have turned into a showcase that would make any designer proud. We were particularly impressed with the collections of quilts and needlepoint.

Guests who want privacy prefer the two cottages, fully equipped right down to the wine glasses. Both cottages have wood-burning fireplaces. The one-story cottage has a Windsor table and chairs placed by a window that looks out on the river. The saltbox cottage has a view of the water from the second-floor bedroom.

A full breakfast includes this chapter's recipe of Eastern Shore white corn bread (see page 387). A local waterman who crabs the waters that border Elmwood's property gave this recipe to the Monicks, the innkeepers, who now frequently serve it with breakfast.

Four rooms and two cottages, all with private bath, $75–$95. The cottages require a two-night minimum stay, or it rents for $400 a week. From Princess Anne, take Route 363 for five miles. Turn left on Route 627, which becomes Locust Point Road for one mile. Sign for entrance to Elmwood is on right side of road. Box 220, Princess Anne, MD 21853. (301) 651–1066.

Chanceford Hall, Snow Hill

Thelma and Michael Driscoll bought a neglected mid- to late-eighteenth century landmark Georgian-style manor house and have painstakingly restored it to create a magnificent bed-and-breakfast inn. This thirty-by one-hundred-foot house set on over an acre in a quieter residential section of Snow Hill has ten working fireplaces (four are in the guest rooms), a formal dining room, sun room, and five guest rooms. Outside there's a heated thirty-two-foot lap pool that was added to the property about twenty years ago.

Michael, a cabinetmaker by trade, built a number of the pieces of furniture in the home. There are five oversized bedrooms with high ceilings; four have working fireplaces. The master suite has a four-poster queen-size canopy bed, Oriental rugs, fireplace, and couch which can be used if a third person is staying in the room. Never wanting to have a guest run out of hot water or have the water temperature fluctuate as it so often does in older inns, the Driscolls installed individual forty-gallon hot-water heaters for each guest room. The entire building is now fully air-conditioned.

With advance notice, the Driscolls will prepare elegant dinners for their guests. There is no set menu; they prefer to take their cues from their guests. Breakfast is served in the formal dining room.

Five rooms with private bath, $95–$115. Wine and hors d'oeuvres, and a full breakfast, are included. Complimentary use of bicycles. Special rates available for midweek and off-season stays. Not appropriate for young children. No pets. 209 Federal Street, Snow Hill, MD 21863; (301) 632-2231

Snow Hill Inn, Snow Hill

Snow Hill, founded in 1642, is an ideal location for someone interested in canoeing on the Pokomoke River or staying in a quiet Eastern Shore town that's not on the usual tourist route. The town itself, with over 100 historic homes, warrants more than a little exploration. And for anyone digging up their family tree, the library here houses the most complete genealogical section on the Eastern Shore.

The rooms at the inn are nicely decorated with country antiques, brass, and antique double beds. The first-floor living room has a working fireplace. The best room is the Victorian Room on the first floor, which has a massive Victorian bed with a headboard that practically reaches to the ceiling. Families with children are given the third-floor room, which has a double bed and a cot. Rooms with private baths all have showers, while the two shared baths have tubs as well.

Three rooms with private bath, $70.20 and $81. Three rooms share two baths, $50.20. Tax is included. Children welcome in the large third-floor room, no extra charge. No pets. Continental breakfast included. 104 Market Street, Snow Hill, MD 21863; (301) 632-2102.

CHINCOTEAGUE, VA

Note: The best months to visit are May, June, September, and October. We suggest avoiding this area in July and August because of large crowds, excessive heat and humidity, mosquitos, horseflies, and much higher rates.

Channel Bass Inn, Chincoteague

From the outside, this inn will not properly impress you with its magnificence. In fact, if you haven't heard or read about the inn, it's unlikely you would walk in the door: The inn is in an unlikely location, facing a gas station/convenience store. The unassuming exterior of this weathered, white, 100-year-old building blends into this working fishing community and summer vacation spot.

This is a place to get away from the outside world. The rooms are decorated in soft, muted shades of beige. There are no phones or televisions. Room 10, one of the deluxe third-floor rooms, is a favorite: This room has a king-size bed and is called the Reading Room because it features a glass-enclosed bookcase filled with current fiction and nonfiction selections. This spacious room has a sofa and plenty of reading lamps.

Room 4 has a small bedroom with a queen-size bed and a separate sitting room with a mini-bar and two couches. Should you wish to have a private dinner in your room, this is the room you must request (there is a 25% surcharge for room service).

The baths are standard size and include Neutrogena soap and

The 100-year-old Channel Bass Inn blends into the fishing community of Chincoteague.

shampoo as well as Bill Blass terrycloth robes. The deluxe rooms also are stocked with Neutrogena hand, face, and eye cream.

Breakfast here is excellent, but extremely expensive. You won't find breakfasts like these anywhere else: omelets with oysters and a tarragon wine sauce, omelets with shrimp and sauce Espagnol, or souffléed light and fluffy pancakes made with hand-whisked egg whites, French vanilla essence, Irish Cream, Grand Marnier, and Amaretto liqueurs served with whipped cream and fresh strawberries.

Six rooms and 2 suites, all with private bath. May through September: Standard room with queen-size bed, $150; deluxe room with king-size bed, $175; two-room suite with queen-size bed, $200. October through April, rooms are $100, $150, or $175. Breakfast, served 8:30 to 10 A.M. on Saturday and Sunday, is not included in the room rate and must be ordered the night before. For souffléed pancakes with strawberries, fresh orange juice, and coffee, allow about $55 for two, including tax and tip. Dinner is served from 6 to 9:30 P.M. A complete dinner for two with a moderate wine will average about $185. Two-night stay required on weekends. Not appropriate for children. No pets. 100 Church Street, Chincoteague, VA 23336; (804) 336-6148.

Miss Molly's Inn, Chincoteague

Innkeepers Jim and Priscilla Stam own this inn as well as the Little Traveller Inn across the street (see below). Author Marguerite Henry is said to have written her famous children's story, *Misty of Chincoteague* while she was staying in the Blue Room at this inn.

Naturally we wanted to be inspired, so we also stayed in the Blue Room, the largest room and the only one with a private bath. This spacious room has five windows that overlook the street, a king-size bed, an eighteenth-century armoire, petticoat table, and a Victorian loveseat. The Bay Room has a double bed and the best view of the bay. If you are interested in history be sure to talk with Jim, a retired president of a small liberal arts college, who willingly shares his knowledge of the area and its history with interested guests.

Breakfast includes a choice of juice, fresh fruit, and a dish such as apple strudel.

Seven rooms, one with private bath, all with air-conditioning. Summer weekends, $79–$105 per night. Summer midweek, $69–$95. Off-season: weekends, $69–$95; midweek, $59–$85. Afternoon tea and full breakfast included. Children over 12 welcome, $20 additional. No pets. 113 North Main Street, Chincoteague, VA 23336; (804) 336-6686.

Little Traveller Inn, Chincoteague

At afternoon tea, innkeeper Jim Stam told us an interesting local tale about the early history of this building. There were once two gentlemen friends in Chincoteague who built a large house together and married two sisters. Sibling rivalries apparently got out of hand, and the couples parted company—so they split the house in half and moved the front half next door. Today, both buildings are again joined with a large garden room, brick courtyard, and fountain in the middle.

The Witlatch Room, the only one with a private bath (shower only), has a queen-size bed and a view of the brick courtyard and fountain. If you're looking for views of the bay, climb to the third floor Green Room, which has a country feel with a double bed, two window seats, rocker, and antique washstand.

Breakfast is the same as at Miss Molly's Inn across the street (see above).

Six rooms, one with a private bath, all with air-conditioning. Summer weekends: $75–$99. Summer midweek: $65–$85. Off-season weekends, $65–$85; off-season midweek, $55–$75. A full breakfast and afternoon tea, usually served across the street at Miss Molly's, is included. Children over 12 welcome, $20 additional. No pets. 112 North Main Street, Chincoteague, VA 23336; (804) 336-6686.

CAPE CHARLES, VA

Pickett's Harbor Bed and Breakfast, Cape Charles

This bed-and-breakfast inn has an isolated, pristine location at the southern tip of the Delmarva Peninsula on land settled by owner Sara Goffigon's ancestors in the mid-seventeenth century. Both Sara and her husband Cooke have deep roots in the area. Her mother still operates the adjacent farm, and their five children were raised here. In 1976 they built this home. Floor-to-ceiling windows on the back of the house look through the pine and cedar trees to the dunes and the ocean. We walked for several hours along the desolate beach, which is reached by a path through the dunes.

The isolated location of the house requires Sara or Cooke to meet their guests along the main road. When we made our reservation, we were told to go to a corner gas station on Route 13 and call from the phone booth. After traveling past farms down side country roads and turning down a dirt road, we were certainly glad that we deferred to Sara's advice.

The country-furnished living room has a leather chair, rocking chair, sofas, and wood stove. Lots of good reading, especially local books and histories, makes this a wonderful place to stay in any weather. In the late afternoon Sara serves wine, homemade pepper jelly, cream cheese, and crackers. At night the lights of the Chesapeake Bay Bridge Tunnel twinkle on the distant horizon.

We like the large second-floor room that has a private bath, queen-size bed with painted headboard and matching bureau, and a view of the water through the pines. An adjoining bedroom makes this combination ideal for a family. We stayed on the first floor in a large room with a couch, a queen-size bed, and a view through the trees of the bay.

Depending on the number of guests in the house, breakfast is served either in the living room or the country kitchen. Eastern Shore folk like to eat, so breakfast is a hearty affair. We had spicy tomato juice that was served in a silver cup with a stalk of celery, a pineapple filled with cottage cheese, country ham, sweet potato and bran muffins, and mugs of good, strong coffee.

There are several local restaurants that the Goffigons can recommend in the town of Cape Charles, about eight miles north. We enjoyed the local flavor of Rebecca's.

Four rooms with shared baths, $65; two rooms with private baths, $75; and a single, $50. Breakfast is included. Children welcome. Located four miles north of the Chesapeake Bay Bridge Tunnel. Box 97AA, Cape Charles, VA 23310; (804) 331-2211.

WHERE TO DINE

CRAB HOUSES

Our favorite dinner starts with a large order of steamed soft-shell clams served with broth and melted butter. Next, try a dozen or so raw Little Neck or Cherrystone clams, followed by an order of fried whole clams (*not* the strips). The pièce de résistance is a half-dozen spicy steamed jumbo crabs.

Note: Many crab houses have a limited supply of the jumbo crabs. Those in the know (and you are now) call ahead and reserve the jumbos. The added cost is more than offset by the larger quantity of backfin crabmeat.

While all crab houses feature steamed crabs with spicy bay seasoning, they also have an array of selections for those who don't want to work as hard for their dinner. Here is our selection of crab houses where we have dined over the years.

The Crab Claw Restaurant, St. Michaels

Located on the Miles River next to the Maritime Museum, this is one of the first crab houses that we visited some twenty years ago. Although incredibly crowded on summer weekends, it still remains our favorite. Sitting outside on the deck or inside at one of the window tables, we have observed the steady growth and gentrification of this harbor over the years.

In the summer, excursion boats disgorge dozens of hungry day-trippers from the Western Shore onto the Crab Claw's docks. On weekend evenings, the harbor is thick with pleasure craft whose owners eat and drink well into the night.

Try the steamed, spiced crabs served in the traditional way with a side order of cheddar cheese chunks and sweet pickles. Crabs, clams, oysters, and shrimp, mostly fried, are also on the menu. If

An oysterman brings in bushels of oysters to The Crab Claw Restaurant in St. Michaels.

you visit late in the season, you can have a dinner of all the best from the bay: a plate of raw oysters, a bucket of steamers, and a few crabs.

Open daily from early March through December, 11 A.M. to 9 P.M.; until 10 P.M. on weekends. Appetizers, $2.25–$5.75; platters, $9.95–$14.95; sandwiches and salads, $2–$6.75. Crab prices depend on the size and availability. No credit cards. Navy Point, St. Michaels, MD 21663; (301) 745-2900.

The Tap Room, Chesapeake City

Come early, as the line winds around the block on a summer Saturday night at this ordinary-looking crab house, which also serves Italian dishes and pizza. The quality of the food served here more than compensates for the lack of decor and water views.

Regulars at the next table wisely suggested we ask to have our steamed mussels served with the spicier fra diavalo sauce rather than the milder marinara sauce. Stuffed shells, manicotti, and a low-priced Monday night special of spaghetti and meatballs are good alternatives if you don't want crab. The onion rings, thick and meaty with very little breading, along with the crabcake sandwich are good bets. Steamed crabs are served with two dipping sauces: melted butter and a spicy homemade crab sauce. For dessert we asked the waitress to split a tartuffo, a chocolate-coated vanilla and chocolate ice cream ball with a cherry in the middle.

Open Monday through Thursday, 11 A.M. to 9:30 P.M.; Friday and Saturday, 11 A.M. to 10:30 P.M.; Sunday, 1 to 8:30 P.M. Entrées, $5.25–$14.25. No credit cards. Corner of 2nd and Bohemia, Chesapeake City, MD 21915; (301) 885-5973 or (301) 885-2344.

Ebbtide Restaurant, Chester

Instead of racing over the Bay Bridge back to Washington or Baltimore, try this convenient spot for a meal of steamed crabs. Its location, a few miles before the Bay Bridge, couldn't be easier to find—you can see the large sign atop this restaurant as you drive along Route 50. We've stopped here many times over the past twenty years.

You will find a large room where crabs are served on plastic trays. The menu includes the usual assortment of fried platters. On our most recent visit, steamed crabs ranged from $12 a dozen for the small to $25 a dozen for the jumbos.

Open daily, 11 A.M. to 9 P.M.; until 10 P.M. on Friday and Saturday. Entrées, $7.25–$16. Route 50, Piney Creek Road, Chester, MD 21619; (301) 643-6053.

The Red Roost, Whitehaven

A crab feast in an out-of-the-way place guarantees that most of the diners are local residents. Coming from the north, take the road to Whitehaven from Salisbury; from the south, enjoy a free ride on the three-car Wicomico Ferry and follow the signs. Walk through the door of this renovated chicken coop on any given night and you'll find the Palmer family—Frank, Peg, and their four children—serving bushels of crabs and corn to 250-plus faithful customers. Take a seat at one of the long tables covered in brown paper, grab a mallet, and join in. The house special is all-you-can-eat hush puppies, shrimp crisps, fried chicken, clam crisps, and corn on the cob plus steamed crabs or smoked barbecued ribs. If you're very hungry, pay a dollar more and get both crabs and ribs.

Open daily, mid-May through early September, 5:30 to 10 P.M.; Sunday, 4 to 9 P.M.; from early September through October, Thursday through Sunday, 6 to 10 P.M. The line forms early; (310) 546-5443.

The Old Mill Restaurant, Delmar

This family knew a good thing when they saw the Palmer family at The Red Roost. They moved a bit north to an old hardware store, installed steamers, deep friers, tables, and presto—another crab house magically appeared. The Old Mill has the same decor and prices as The Red Roost, but is in a more convenient location. We stopped by on the way back from one of our trips, and blended into the scene with a pile of spicy crabs and a cold pitcher of beer.

Open Monday through Friday, 5 to 9 P.M.; Saturday, 4 to 10 P.M.; and Sunday, 3 to 8:30 P.M. Located at Route 54 and Sharptown Road, Delmar, DE; (301) 846-2808.

Following is a selection of restaurants in geographical order from north to south.

CHESTERTOWN AND CHESAPEAKE CITY, MD

Imperial Hotel, Chestertown

Though the hotel decor is elegant, owners Carla and Albert Massoni want boaters, hunters, travelers, and townspeople to feel that they can dine here without having to wear a tie and jacket, as was formerly the case.

The menu features regional American cuisine. Popular appetizers include grilled oysters served with country bacon; a medley of wild mushrooms served with roasted garlic, tomatoes, and crusty herb bread; a house-smoked plate of salmon, tuna, and bay scallops, served with a cucumber salad and attractively presented in a radiccio leaf; and grilled duck sausage served with wilted greens. The clam bisque with sweet corn is a favorite. Salads are refreshingly different combinations, such as toasted walnuts, tomato, pork cracklings, goat cheese and watercress; or beets, apple, red onion, and Belgian endive.

For the vegetarian there's fresh herb pasta, made at the hotel, served with plum tomatoes, artichokes, and shiitake mushrooms. Other entrées include sautéed filet of rock fish with stewed leeks and chives served with an oyster cream; pan-seared salmon with roasted sweet corn, lime, and cilantro; and grilled breast of duck with toasted shallots. Chef Turgeon likes to prepare vegetables creatively. During our visit, entrées were garnished with roasted corn mixed with red pepper and onions, strips of Swiss chard, carrots julienne, and green beans.

Desserts are sinful. One was a piece of puff pastry cut into a pear shape, topped with slices of poached pears and a caramel sauce, and

served surrounded by a pool of crème Anglaise. Chocolate lovers
will want the chocolate meringue pie, a chocolate shell filled with
a rich chocolate cream, topped with a crunchy meringue and chocolate shavings. The pie is surrounded by a mocha Anglaise sauce.

Lunch entrées include a pizza, such as one topped with grilled
duck sausage and goat cheese, grilled chicken salad, or a hamburger
served with Monterey Jack cheese and salsa. Hunters will be happy
to know that they can still bring their geese to the hotel to be
prepared for their dinner.

Lunch Wednesday through Saturday, 12 to 2 P.M., $5.75–$12.50.
Dinner Tuesday through Saturday, 5:30 to 9 P.M. Entrées
$9.50–$22. Sunday brunch 11 A.M. to 3 P.M., $5–$12.50. 208 High
Street, Chestertown, MD 21620; (301) 778-5000.

Ironstone Café, Chestertown

Ironstone jugs, soup tureens, bowls, and plates line the deep-set
window ledges of this casual café. At a recent dinner we shared an
appetizer of six plump, tender oysters baked on a bed of spinach
and topped with minced Smithfield ham and cream sauce. The fresh
fettuccine had an agreeable bite and was topped with succulent bay
scallops in a delicate shrimp sauce.

The waitress recommended the lowest-priced entrée, a tender
poached chicken breast stuffed with spinach and mushrooms, sliced
and artistically arranged in a fan shape. We were impressed. You
will not easily find a better value than the crabcakes here: two
ample cakes made with a generous portion of lump crabmeat, without filler, lightly seasoned and broiled. Other items on the menu
included filet of beef, sea scallops, boneless breast of duck, and veal
sweetbreads.

Ironstone gets an A+ for the large, individually tossed salad of
fresh, crisp, red- and green-leaf lettuce with a garlic mustard vinaigrette dressing.

Desserts that evening included white sweet-potato pie, moist
Swedish apple cake, and crème caramel.

The lunch menu of spinach, Cobb, and shrimp salads along with
omelets, quiches, and a rare roast beef sandwich with Boursin
sounded enticing enough for a return visit.

Lunch, Tuesday through Saturday, 11:30 A.M. to 2 P.M.; $3.95–$5.95. Dinner, Tuesday through Saturday, 5:30 to 9 P.M. Entrées include a large leaf salad; $10.95–$15.95. 236 Cannon Street, Chestertown, MD 21620; (301) 778-0188.

Bayard House, Chesapeake City

Sitting at a window table, we were startled to see a massive ocean-going freighter pass so close that we were able to read the ship's markings easily. At least fourteen freighters and innumerable smaller boats daily traverse the Chesapeake and Delaware Canal, so a meal here is bound to include views of the passing traffic. At night, the flickering of the candles reflected on the canal adds a touch of romantic magic. When a freighter passes by, the restaurant lights are dimmed to give guests a better view.

On the ground floor there is a brick terrace set with white tables and chairs, a good spot for a leisurely drink. As the weather gets colder you can move inside to an English-style pub. Off the pub is a long dining room with tables that face the canal. Upstairs there are two indoor dining rooms and a glass-enclosed porch. By all means ask to sit at one of the window tables, but if people are outside on the brick terrace we'd opt to sit upstairs and enjoy an obstructed view of the canal.

For lunch we happily nibbled on the deep-fried potato skins that were served with bacon, cheese, and crabmeat. We also enjoyed a bowl of steamed soft-shell clams served with broth and melted butter. The dinner menu has a full range of choices: sea scallops cooked in parchment, grilled peppered shrimp marinated in citrus juices, steak Roquefort, pheasant stuffed with plums, and lobster thermidor. The Bayard House offers a picturesque setting, good continental cuisine, and a small, peaceful town perfect for an after-dinner stroll.

Lunch, Monday through Saturday, 11:30 A.M. to 3 P.M.; $4.95–$6.95. Dinner, Monday through Thursday, 5 to 9 P.M.; Friday and Saturday, 5 to 10 P.M.; Sunday, 1 to 9 P.M. Entrées, $16.95–$23.95. 11 Bohemia Avenue, South Chesapeake City, MD 21915; (301) 885-5040.

Old Wharf Inn, Chestertown

The crab bisque came highly recommended, but when we asked for the recipe, the owner firmly said no. "In fact," she continued, "*Gourmet* has written to us to get it but we won't divulge our secret—it's our calling card." We can understand this attitude after tasting the rich, creamy, crab-filled bisque served with a decanter of sherry.

Located on the Chester River, the Old Wharf Inn is our choice in Chestertown for an informal seafood dinner. In addition to an extensive selection of shellfish, there are a number of entrées for the landlubber. Smaller portions of many of the entrées are available to adults or children at $3 to $4 less than a full-priced entrée. The extensive salad bar comes with the regular size and the petite-portion dinners.

We enjoyed the sautéed backfin crabmeat that was served in a skillet. The crabcakes were the traditional type—deep-fried, with filler and a creamy texture—but we prefer ones that are made with large lumps of backfin and no filler. The petite portion of fried flounder included three large pieces—more than enough for a healthy appetite!

Lunch, Monday through Saturday, 11 A.M. to 4 P.M.; $2.50–$7.75. Dinner, Sunday through Thursday, 4 to 9 P.M.; Friday and Saturday, 4 to 10 P.M. Sunday brunch, 10 A.M. to 3 P.M. Entrées, $8.95–$29.95. Early bird specials, Monday through Friday, 4 to 6 P.M.; $6.95. Foot of Cannon Street, Chestertown, MD; (301) 778-3566.

Lewis' Rainbow's End Restaurant, Tolchester

Without the enthusiastic recommendation of local innkeepers Don and Joanne Toft, we would never have stopped here. This former beer hall is all that remains on the site of the old Tolchester amusement park.

The two dining rooms are clean but currently lack any distinctive personality; future plans include displaying photographs of the Victorian amusement park. (If you're interested, the refurbished bandstand from the Tolchester Park is at the Maritime Museum in St. Michaels.)

Owners Beverly and Lewis Rash dreamed for many years of owning a place that catered to the local population. The portions here are more than ample, in some cases almost gluttonous. We stopped by for the Wednesday night special and stuffed ourselves on thick slabs of perfectly cooked, rare roast beef that literally were draped over the sides of the plates. The restaurant also has daily specials: Tuesday is spiced shrimp; Thursday is 1¼-pound lobsters; Friday is beef and seafood; and Sunday there is a $5 blue plate special. Go to Lewis' for a dinner of plain, home-cooked food at prices that will leave you smiling.

Lunch, Monday through Saturday, 11 A.M. to 3:30 P.M.; $4.75–$6.95. Dinner, Tuesday through Thursday, 4:30 to 9 P.M.; Friday and Saturday, 4:30 to 10 P.M.; Sunday, 12 to 8 P.M. Entrées, $8.75–$14.95 (includes soup). Route 20, Rock Hall, MD; (301) 778-6855.

Andy's, Chestertown

The intimate back room of this popular bar is decorated in casual Victorian, with a working fireplace, wing chairs, coffee tables, stuffed sofas, and Oriental carpets. Andy's has a light menu of tomato seafood bisque, pâté, quiche, and sandwiches (stuffed and baked in French bread). There is live entertainment on Fridays and Saturdays. Make sure to check out the portrait of Andy, the owner, over the bar.

Open Monday through Saturday from 4 P.M. 337 High Street, Chestertown, MD; (301) 778-6688.

ST. MICHAELS, OXFORD, AND EASTON, MD

The Masthead, Oxford

The sign says, "We don't have a crab cooker or a deep fat fryer," and the folks who run this restaurant mean it. Tucked away on a side street in Oxford, where only the inquisitive tourist or a person in the know is likely to tread, The Masthead is one of the more imaginative restaurants of the area. The intimate bar and flower-decked front porch are packed with sailors in season. The tables, arrayed on platforms, and the nautical watercolors give the impression of dining at sea.

Entrées that we have sampled include grilled tuna with orange sauce, shrimp and mussels with spinach fettuccine in a marinara sauce, and grilled chicken breast topped by ancho-pepper-cheddar sauce. Our favorite, the sautéed soft-shell crabs (available in summer only) were prepared with loving care. During cooler weather, try the fresh bay oysters.

If you are planning a picnic, stop in at the Masthead Market next to the restaurant for gourmet take-out items.

Lunch, Monday through Saturday, 11:30 A.M. to 2:30 P.M.; Sunday, 11 A.M. to 3 P.M.; $3.95–$6.95. Dinner, Sunday through Thursday, 6 to 9:30 P.M.; Friday and Saturday, 6 to 10 P.M. Entrées, $11.95–$22.95. In the late fall and winter, lunch is served Friday through Sunday only. 101 Mill Street, Oxford, MD 21654; (301) 226-5303.

Bay Hundred, Knapps Narrows, Tilghman

Overlooking Knapps Narrows drawbridge, one of the busiest in the East, and a working fishing harbor, is a small restaurant with floor-to-ceiling sliding glass doors that serves seafood and continental dishes. Dishes with an Oriental flair reflect the time that the chef spent in Japan: chicken tempura and stir-frys using beef, chicken, shrimp, or vegetables. The crabmeat, prosciutto, and spinach in a delicate brandy cream sauce served over fettuccine did not mask the flavor of the fresh local crabmeat. The soft-shell crabs, Cajun coconut shrimp, and the chutney beef stir-fry are recommended.

We sat by the window for a leisurely lunch of a Havarti and vegetable sandwich and Oriental chicken salad and watched the watermen unload their morning catch of crabs and oysters.

Alas for traditionalists, the winds of change are blowing: A luxury 118-slip marina is under construction nearby, and there are plans to double the size of the restaurant.

Lunch daily, 11:30 A.M. to 5 P.M.; $3.50–$9.95. Dinner daily, 5 to

9 P.M. Entrées, $10.95–$21.95. During the winter, the restaurant may be closed on Monday and Tuesday. Route 33 and Knapps Narrows, Tilghman, MD 21671; (301) 886-2622.

Peach Blossoms, Easton

Your mood is bound to lighten from the moment you walk into this storefront restaurant, decorated with large murals of blossoming peach trees along the three interior walls.

The lunch menu features such sandwiches as smoked turkey and melted Brie with fresh pears and a glaze of spiced plum, or the perennial ham and swiss on pumpernickel. For a change of pace, ask to have the sandwich made with turkey. For the hearty eater, there is a Mexican cassoulet with spicy beans, smoked sausage, and pieces of grilled chicken.

The restaurant takes on a different atmosphere in the evenings. The candlelit tables effectively cast shadows on the large peach-blossom murals. The menu changes monthly. In October, the entrées included a delicately poached salmon with green peppercorns, which was superb. Roast duckling with spiced apple-plum glaze still had more fat than we care for. The evening pasta dish adds crab and peas to fettuccine served with a cream sauce. We also enjoyed the roasted pork loin rolled in chutney. For the traditionalist, veal Marsala with mushrooms was on the menu.

Here you'll find pleasant dining that we enthusiastically recommend for travelers who want fresh ingredients prepared with creative flair.

Lunch, Wednesday through Friday, 11:30 A.M. to 2 P.M.; $5.25–$6.95. Dinner, Wednesday through Saturday, 5:30 to 9 P.M. Entrées, $12.95–$16.95. 6 North Washington Street, Easton, MD 21601; (301) 822-5220.

Inn at Perry Cabin, St. Michaels

When you come to dinner here you are treated as a house guest. You can have a cocktail in one of the three parlors, and discuss the menu with the maitre d'. In the main dining room, a pair of elaborate crystal chandeliers hang from the two-story peaked ceiling. Nine widely-spaced candlelit tables, a large working fireplace, Ashley print wallpaper and tablecloths, crimson upholstered chairs, marble busts, an old English buffet, and a wall of windows overlooking the water make this a beautiful setting. The waiters are attentive and able to explain every selection on the menu with confidence.

We started a four-course winter dinner with tartare of oysters, prepared like traditional steak tartare and presented in three mounds garnished with slivered cucumbers and fresh black truffles. Excellent seared foie gras was sliced and served with glazed apples and a rich port sauce. The mussel soup had a hint of orange and saffron flavor; large salads of baby greens with balsamic vinaigrette or chopped duck confit and hazelnut-and-truffle oil dressing were also available. For an entrée we had loin of lamb served with sweetbreads, lentils, and a grilled tomato. Lemon sole, a lighter entrée, was cooked in a timbale and was served with additional pieces of sole and shrimp in a light sauce. Three other entrée choices included a gratin of lobster and oysters, medallions of salmon, and grilled breast of duck.

Chocolate desserts are a specialty. The most popular is a combination plate with a slice of dense chocolate pâté, a bittersweet chocolate marquise (our favorite) and a small scoop of white chocolate ice cream, beautifully garnished with raspberries, strawberries, and spun sugar. The excellent chocolate mille-feuille was a richer variation of the traditional preparation. Other popular choices include a lemon torte served with lemon ice cream; apple dowdy; pear tart; or shortbread with raspberry coulis. Special touches begin and end the meal: we were served a complimentary appetizer of soft white cheese wrapped in salmon, and a plate of a petit four, chocolate covered strawberry, and cherry was presented along with the check.

Breakfast and lunch are served in the two smaller rooms that adjoin the main dining room. We enjoyed a lunch of creamy corn soup with crabmeat and asparagus. Lunch entrées include stuffed breast of chicken with ratatouille, crab and lobster ravioli, plank roasted cod, grilled leg of lamb with eggplant and goat cheese risotto, and smoked salmon served with potato salad.

The menu changes seasonally. During the busier times of the year, especially summer, the restaurant plans to offer an à la carte dinner.

Lunch, daily 12 to 2:30 P.M., $6.95–$12.95. Tea 4 to 5:30 P.M. Dinner, 6 to 9:30 P.M. Prix fixe dinner $45 or $65. 308 Watkins Lane, St. Michaels, MD 21663; (301) 745-2200 or (800) 722-2949.

Robert Morris Inn, Oxford

Long before the advent of the shiitake mushrooms, exotic pasta dishes, nouvelle cuisine, and high-strung chefs that are here today and gone tomorrow, the Robert Morris made a reputation for its honest cooking. The owners didn't hire chefs with pedigrees then and they don't today.

We can remember when a visit to the Robert Morris started with an Oxford Cooler, a long drink of apricot brandy, cherry brandy, lime juice, and grenadine. This was followed by crab-cakes, a thick slice of prime rib, or baked stuffed shrimp. The menu has remained basically the same for more than twenty years. For the hearty eater, the Robert Morris Special Seafood Platter is a *tour de force* sampling of all the seafood items on the menu: chilled gulf shrimp and crabmeat, deep-fried crabcake, shrimp, scallops, broiled seafood imperial, stuffed shrimp, filet of fish, and more.

At breakfast and lunch, you will be seated in the comfortably casual tavern room with its slate floor, dark wood-paneled walls, and open wood-burning fireplace. At dinner, the same menu is available in the tavern room or, if you've brought a jacket, in the more formal Colonial dining room.

Breakfast, lunch, and dinner served Wednesday through Sunday, Easter through Thanksgiving. Call for winter hours—late November through December, and mid-February until Easter. Breakfast, 8 to 11 A.M. Lunch, 1 to 3 P.M.; $2.95–$17.95. Dinner, 6 to 9 P.M. Entrées, $10.95–$27.95. Children's portions of some entrées are available. Reservations not accepted. 312 Morris Street, Oxford, MD 21654; (301) 226-5111.

The Washington Street Grill, Easton

At this new restaurant across from the courthouse, you are bound to meet most of the Eastern Shore "yuppies" at the long wooden bar, or at the oyster and clam bar, munching veggies during the weekday happy hour. We enjoyed our lunch of burgers on the upstairs balcony, where we could watch the scene below.

An all-you-can-eat Thursday night special of spiced steamed shrimp combined with dance music supplied by a D.J., makes for an entertaining though noisy evening. Tuesday night specials alternate between a Mexican buffet and a seafood buffet. We "pigged out" on the raw clams, oysters, and shrimp.

The lunch menu covers a wide variety of sandwiches, burgers, and salads. Dinner choices include crabcakes, filet, prime rib, boneless chicken, or catch of the day; you can also have a light salad if you don't want a full meal.

Lunch, Monday through Saturday, 11 A.M. to 4 P.M.; $4.25–$5.95. Sunday brunch, 11 A.M. to 2 P.M. Dinner, Sunday through Thursday, 4 to 10 P.M.; Friday and Saturday, 4 to 11 P.M. Entrées, $8.95–$14.95. 20 North Washington Street, Easton, MD 21601; (301) 822-9011.

CHINCOTEAGUE, SNOW HILL, AND CRISFIELD

Channel Bass Inn, Chincoteague

The traveler who is constantly in search of truly fine cuisine quickly learns it's easy to find expensive dining—but very difficult to get an exquisite dinner.

In our three visits here—for breakfast, dinner, and a cooking school lesson in the kitchen—we learned why the food at this out-of-the-way inn is so spectacular, and the prices astronomically high.

Innkeeper and chef James Hanretta, who will celebrate his twentieth year here in 1991, personally prepares each meal with no assistants. He accepts only six reservations per hour, twelve to sixteen guests per evening at seven tables. Those seated in this renovated 100-year-old inn receive a gourmet's gourmet meal, served on Wedgwood china with Waterford crystal and sterling silver.

The menu is heavily influenced by French, Spanish, and Middle Eastern cuisine, as well as an abundance of fresh and delicious local ingredients. We recall, for example, such appetizers as tender little Chincoteague clams in tarragon and white wine sauce, a crab stew thick with crabmeat, and oysters Basque served with chorizo sausage and tomato sauce.

The Caesar salad is made with just the inner hearts of the romaine lettuce. Entrées do not include saffron rice or steamed vegetables, but you may order them separately. The chef's specialty is the broiled seafood Espagnol, a combination of shrimp, lobster, clams, oysters, and chorizo sausage cooked with piquant Espagnol sauce. Flounder stuffed with lump crabmeat imperial, and the chef's version of a crabcake made with sautéed chunks of backfin crabmeat served with saffron rice are other popular choices.

We've witnessed the hand-whisking of the egg whites for the incredibly light chocolate cheesecake, and tasted the results, which have a totally different texture from traditional versions; his is lighter, more aromatic, and redolent of mocha and chocolate.

The restaurant is very expensive. Be prepared to spend an average of $185 for two, including tax and tip.

Dinner by reservation only, 6 to 9:30 P.M. Appetizers and salads, $12–$19; entrées, $30–$39; dessert, $12. 100 Church Street, Chincoteague, VA 23336; (804) 336-6148.

Note: Guests at the inn are given first choice for dinner seatings.

Captain Fish's, Chincoteague

If you want to sample the delicious local seafood without any adornment or atmosphere, head for Captain Fish's on the docks. We slurped oysters and clams while several fishing boats unloaded quantities of black bass to be weighed, sorted, and packed on the spot for trucking to market. This is the place for right-out-of-the-water clams, oysters, and shrimp. Jim Hanretta of the Channel Bass Inn (see page 383), who shops here for his restaurant, readily concedes that you can't beat the Captain's for a fabulous feast of fantastically fresh fish.

Open daily, 11:30 A.M. to 8:30 P.M. during the summer months. Oysters right out of their beds cost $3.95 a dozen, and spicy steamed shrimp cost about $8 a pound. 512 South Main Street, Chincoteague, VA; (804) 336-5997.

Snow Hill Inn, Snow Hill

If you've been canoeing down the Pocomoke or doing a back-road tour, this restaurant is a convenient choice. We had a hefty portion of meatloaf served with traditional fixings of mashed potatoes, green beans, and homemade crabcakes. Other lunch items include quiches, hot roast beef or turkey sandwiches, or a fried oyster sandwich. A good bet for dinner is to stick with the catch of the day. Entrée choices include flounder stuffed with crab imperial, chicken cordon bleu, filet mignon, New York strip steak, and crabcakes. The richest dessert is the three-layer walnut surprise, a black walnut crust with cream cheese filling and pudding on the top.

Lunch, Tuesday through Friday, 11 A.M. to 2 P.M.; $3.95–$5.95. Dinner, Friday and Saturday, 5:30 to 8 P.M. Entrées, $8.95–$14.95. 104 Market Street, Snow Hill, MD 21863; (301) 632-2102.

Aunt Em's, Crisfield

We watched the tourists pack into The Capt's Galley Restaurant (rated by all the reputable guide books as having The World's Best Crab Cake) and headed instead for Aunt Em's, which the rest of the world has yet to discover.

There's no view of the water here, and the fanciest thing on the menu is banana coconut pie, but there is plenty of hearty food and regional color. We enjoyed a very good soft-shell-crab sandwich and one of the best fried oyster sandwiches we'd ever had.

Open daily, 6 A.M. to 10 P.M. Homemade soup and sandwiches under $5. Located on the left-hand side of Richardson Street as you enter town. Crisfield, MD; (301) 968-0353.

Old Salty's, Fishing Creek

Listening to the locals and watching plates of deep-fried regional favorites served to patrons who could care less about fitness, fiber, or undercooked vegetables is an experience in itself. Ample portions of crabcakes, soft-shell crabs, fried oysters, and fried chicken are served with sixteen-ounce glasses of iced tea.

Open Wednesday through Monday, 11 A.M. to 8 P.M. Platters from $5.50. Fishing Creek, MD; (301) 397-3752.

ROADSIDE RESTAURANTS

When you're hungry but don't want a full meal, give one of these places a try.

Money's, near Middletown, DE. This authentic truck stop serves large portions at all hours of the day and night. For the convenience of the truckers, telephones instead of a juke box are located in the booths along one wall. The phones were in constant use while we ate our eggs, scrapple, home fries, and short stack of pancakes. A stop at night for pie and a cup of coffee helps to break up the return trip to points north. A farm market next door sells local produce in season as well as Mrs. Orrell's beaten biscuits (see page 336).

Open daily, 24 hours. Located on Route 301 a few miles south of Middletown, DE.

Twinny's Place, Galena, MD. The smell of fried onions that invaded our olfactory senses as we drove by this local spot persuaded us to stop for lunch. A large lunch crowd fills the small, casual dining room and the take-out counter for subs, sandwiches, and Philadelphia-style cheesesteaks (thin slices of beef smothered with fried onions, hot sauce, and cheese).

Open Monday through Saturday, 5:30 A.M. to 7 P.M.; Sunday, 6 A.M. to 7:30 P.M. Closes at 1 P.M. on Wednesday. Located just north of Galena on Route 213.

Beefeaters, near Wye Mills, MD.   This visually unimpressive roadside eatery should not be given short shrift. The ground top sirloin is marinated overnight and cooked slowly over an open pit, which produces a positively luscious sandwich. Pit-roasted beef (our choice), ham, or turkey can be ordered sliced, with or without barbecue sauce. Or, you can get minced beef or pork with barbecue sauce.

Open May through September. Sandwiches, $2.95–$3.95. Located at the junction of Routes 50 and 213, fourteen miles north of Easton.

Railroad Café, Delmar, DE.   Across the street from an old wooden Pennsylvania Railroad red caboose, you will find this strictly local, friendly family restaurant. This is a good place to sample regional specialties. We happened to stop on a winter Thursday evening when muskrat was being prepared; the flavor was pleasant, but the tiny bones were bothersome. We continued with collard greens, ribs, oyster fritters, and an extra-large dish of rice pudding.

Opens at 5 A.M. for breakfast, Monday through Saturday; lunch, Monday through Friday; early dinner, Thursday and Friday. Dinner entrées from $4.95. Railroad Avenue, Delmar, DE; (302) 846-3687.

RECIPE

Eastern Shore Cornbread

This recipe is standard fare for the waterfolk on the Lower Eastern Shore of Maryland. It was given to Helen Monick at Elmwood (see page 363) by one of the watermen who crabs along the property's waterfront.

2 cups white corn meal
½ cup flour
1 cup sugar
1 teaspoon salt
3 cups boiling water

1 stick margarine
1½ cups cold milk
3 medium eggs, lightly
     beaten

Preheat oven to 375°F.

In a large bowl, mix corn meal, flour, sugar, and salt. Set aside.

In a separate bowl, combine boiling water and margarine; pour over corn-meal mixture. Add cold milk to above and mix. Add eggs and mix. Bake in a greased 9- by 12-inch sheet-cake pan about 40 to 45 minutes at 375°F.

YIELD: About 100 1-inch squares.

ITINERARY

Here's a tour that takes you to the highlights of the entire peninsula.

DAY ONE. Start at **St. Michaels** and visit the **Chesapeake Bay Maritime Museum** for an introduction to the history of the bay and its traditions. Have lunch at **The Crab Claw**. Walk along the waterfront area and browse in the shops. Cruise up the Miles River on *The Patriot* to get a view of the homes from the water. Drive to Bellevue and take the ferry to Oxford. Dine at the **Robert Morris Inn**, an Eastern Shore tradition, or at **The Masthead**.

DAY TWO. Head for **Chestertown**, where we suggest you stop at the **Kent County tourist office** for a walking tour map if you are interested in Colonial architecture. This gracious tree-lined town symbolizes the spirit of the Eastern Shore. Take time to walk the serene streets. If you happen to be in the area on a Wednesday, head to **Dixon's auction** in Crumpton. Otherwise, drive to Rock Hall and stop along the way at St. Paul's Church, the oldest Episcopal church in Maryland (1713) and Remington Farm. Drive out to

Eastern Neck Wildlife Refuge. Lunch at **Lewis' Rainbow's End**, the **Old Wharf Inn**, or **Ironstone Cafe**. A side trip to the **Mount Harmon Plantation** will show you an example of a pre-served Colonial tobacco plantation. Have an elegant dinner at the **Imperial Hotel** or the **Ironstone Café**, or an informal one at **Lewis's Rainbow's End**.

DAY THREE. Head to Easton, the unofficial capital of Maryland's Eastern Shore. Major sights include the **Historical Society** and the **Academy of the Arts**. Have lunch at **Peach Blossoms** or **The Washington Street Grill**. Head north to **Wye Mills** to see the restored, operating grist mill; stop at the **Wye Oak** for a look at the state tree; stop at **Mrs. Orrell's** for some of her beaten biscuits. Return to St. Michaels. Complete the day with a drive out to **Tilghman Island** to see the skipjack fleet, and have dinner at **Bay Hundred**.

DAY FOUR. Head south to explore the **Blackwater Wildlife Refuge** and to drive the back roads to Hooper Island. Have lunch at **Old Salty's** or continue to Snow Hill and have lunch (most weekdays) at the **Snow Hill Inn**. Rent a canoe for an afternoon of paddling on the Pokomoke River. Have dinner in **Snow Hill** or a crab feast at the **Red Roost** in Whitehaven.

DAY FIVE. Drive to Crisfield and take either the mailboat or a cruiseboat out to **Smith or Tangier Island**. Smith Island has more roads to walk; Tangier has a sand beach. Slow down and observe what life is like for a Chesapeake Bay waterman. Bring your bikes, or rent some when you arrive, and explore the roads. Browse in the stores, have soft-shell crabs or oysters direct from the source. There are places to spend the night on either island, or you can take a boat back to the mainland.

DAY SIX. Head to Chincoteague and the beaches on **Assateague Island** to see the **wild ponies** and to walk around the **National Wildlife Refuge**. Have fresh seafood on the dock at **Captain Fish's**. For an elegant, expensive dinner, make reservations at **Channel Bass Inn**.

DAY SEVEN. Enjoy a second day of relaxing on the sand beach, birding, or taking the **guided wildlife tour** or the **evening cruise** around Chincoteague. If the weather doesn't cooperate, visit the **Refuge Waterfowl Museum** in Chincoteague and the **Wildfowl Art Museum** in Salisbury.

Getting to the Area

Easton is about two hours from Washington, D.C., and about three hours from Philadelphia.

From Philadelphia, take I-95 south to Route 896, south to Route 301. Turn left at Route 213 to Route 50. Turn left to Route 50 east to Easton.

From New York, take the New Jersey Turnpike south to the Delaware Memorial Bridge, then to I-95 south and follow directions above.

From Washington, take Route 50–301 across the Chesapeake Bay Bridge to Route 50 east to Easton.

BUDGETING YOUR TRIP

To help you get the most for your money, here are some travel suggestions at three budget levels (cost per day at peak season with two people sharing a room, including tax, 15% gratuity at meals, and service charges). Prices are approximate and intended for planning purposes only. Lodgings are categorized by price. Meal prices at lunch include an average entrée and beverage. Dinner prices include an appetizer, entrée, beverage, and dessert. Wine or alcoholic drinks are not included. Admission prices vary widely based on activities.

Staying and Dining at Expensive Lodgings and Restaurants: From $280 to $570 per day for two.

Lodging: Imperial Hotel (suites) $227–$259; Robert Morris Inn $119–$151; Victoriana $146; Inn at Perry Cabin $173–$416; Channel Bass Inn $157–$209; St. Michaels Harbour Inn $140–$159; Tidewater Inn (suites) $178–$254.

Dining: Breakfast: included except at Robert Morris Inn, St. Michaels Inn, and Tidewater Inn $15; Channel Bass Inn $55. Lunch: about $20 at all of the restaurants. Dinner: Imperial Hotel $90; Inn at Perry Cabin $120; Channel Bass Inn $150.

Admissions: Chesapeake Bay Maritime Museum $8; Mount Harmon Plantation $7.50; Historical Society and walking tour $8; *Patriot* cruise $11; cruise to Tangier Island $30; Assateague safari $10; Assateague evening cruise $16.

Staying and Dining at Moderately Priced Lodgings and Restaurants: From $120 to $180 per day for two.

Lodging: White Swan Tavern $81–$108; Imperial Hotel $119; Parsonage $84; Victoriana $109–$119; Hambleton $86–$103; Brampton $92–$103; Widow's Walk $97; Inn at the Canal $70–$103; Robert Morris Inn $65–$108; Chanceford Hall $103–$124; St. Michaels Harbour Inn $97–$119; Two Swan Tavern $115; Wades Point Inn $103–$146; Kemp House Inn $92–$103; Tidewater Inn $75–$91; Miss Molly's $114; Little Traveller $107; Elmwood $81–$103.

Dining: Breakfast: included except at Robert Morris Inn, St. Michaels Harbour Inn, and Tidewater Inn ($15). Lunch: $20. Dinner: $70 at Bayard House, Masthead, Bay Hundred, Peach Blossoms, or Robert Morris Inn.

Admissions: Chesapeake Bay Maritime Museum $8; *Patriot* cruise $11; cruise to Smith Island $18; Assateague safari $10.

Staying and Dining at Less Expensive Lodgings and Restaurants: From $120 to $180 per day for two.

Lodging: Widow's Walk $76–$86; Robert Morris Inn $54–$76; 1876 House $75; Wades Point Inn $59–$92; Kemp House Inn $70–$86; Two Swan Inn $75–$88; Little Traveller $81; Miss Molly's $86; Snow Hill Inn $50–$81; Pickett's Harbor $70–$81; Bernice Guy $76 (includes dinner); Smith Island Motel $48; Chesapeake House $76 (includes dinner); Mrs. Brown $54–$65; Mrs. Dize $30.

Dining: Breakfast: included except at Robert Morris Inn (go to the Masthead for take-out, $5). Lunch: $10 at Masthead Market, Money's, Twinney's Place, Beefeaters. Dinner: $30–$40 at Crab Claw, Red Roost, Tap Room, Ebbtide, Old Wharf Inn, Lewis' Rainbow's End, Washington Street Grill; $40–$60 at Ironstone Cafe.

Admissions: Chesapeake Bay Maritime Museum $8; mailboat to Smith or Tangier Island $10.

SUGGESTED READING

Chesapeake. James A. Michener. New York: Random House, 1978. This is a marvelous novel of the inhabitants of Maryland's Eastern Shore from 1583 to the present. All of the characters unfold in classic Michener style: you'll meet the hunters, farmers, watermen, craftspeople, and learn about crabs, oysters, geese and much more.

Beautiful Swimmers: Watermen, Crabs and the Chesapeake Bay. William W. Warner, drawings by Consuelo Hanks. Boston: Little Brown and Company, 1976. This excellent resource explains all you ever wanted to know about the Chesapeake Bay blue crab, including the biology of the crab (growth, molting, migration), how crabs are caught, picked, packed, and shipped. The author includes wonderful insights and descriptions about the independent watermen who earn their living catching the blue crab. The detailed drawings are superb.

Maryland: A New Guide to the Old Line State. Edward Papenfuse. Baltimore: Johns Hopkins University Press, 1976. This detailed guide, originally published as a WPA project during the Depression, covers every historical point of interest in thirty-three separate tours. The tours concentrating on Maryland's Eastern Shore are tours twelve through twenty-four. The book was updated in 1976 and contains historical information in driving-tour format for just about every structure along the route. Detailed histories are given for each town along the way. This is a wonderful book for curious souls who want to know about every church and building along the way.

Walks and Rambles on the Delmarva Peninsula. Jay Abercrombie. Woodstock, Vermont: Backcountry Publications, 1985.

Twenty-five hikes, long and short, cover almost every habitat found on the peninsula: upland forests, bottomland swamps, salt marshes, islands, beaches. This guide lists the hiking distance and time as well as detailed maps and instructions to help you reach your destination.

NINE

THE VIRGINIA
HUNT COUNTRY

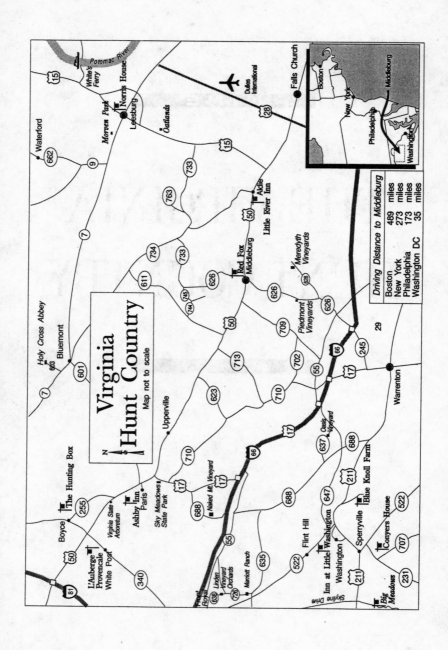

Virginia
Hunt Country
Map not to scale

Driving Distance to Middleburg

Boston	489 miles
New York	273 miles
Philadelphia	173 miles
Washington DC	35 miles

"T*ally-ho!*" The call resounds through the brisk autumn morning.

After *babbling* about all morning in difficult *draw,* the hounds were *cast* once again. One began to *feather,* waving its *stern.* Then it picked up the *line.* Other hounds began *giving tongue.* Now, the huntsman *doubles the horn* and sends thirteen and one-half *couples* away from the *covert* in *full cry.*

Virginia Hunt Country is a world unto itself, with a language all its own. But the description above, or the translation you can build using the glossary on page 399, is nothing compared to the pageantry of sights and sounds of hunters following a red-coated huntsman, his staff, a baying pack of hounds, and—running before them all—their quarry, the cunning and elusive red fox.

Not hunters ourselves, we were hardly unhappy to learn that actually catching a fox is not the goal of the hunt in the United States. In fact, many folks consider "fox chasing" a more apt name for the sport. More than one hunter has had experiences that have left him or her believing the fox is also a wily gamester, leading the hunt on a merry chase to demonstrate who really runs the show.

That would be poetic justice, for the fox deserves a reward—not only in return for the sport it provides, but for being the primary motivating force behind the preservation of *our* quarry: many square miles of prime farmland, wooded countryside laced with scenic country lanes, and quiet historic towns where fine inns and restaurants await.

In contrast, consider the surrounding area of Northern Virginia, which has been developed with a passion. It seems every time we visit there are more strip malls, more office parks, more neon. But drive a few miles beyond the burgeoning suburbs of Washington, D.C., along Route 50 and the shopping centers and housing developments begin to vanish. The countryside is green, the farms expansive, the forests lush. You have crossed into Loudoun County, the home of the fox.

Here the hunt country traditions create prestigious residential addresses. High land values discourage commercial development; at the same time, the residents fight "progress" to save the fox's natural habitat and preserve their sport. Along the way, their country gentlemen's lifestyle has helped to establish many fine shops, inns, and restaurants—and allowed us to experience the distinctive hunting traditions that range far afield from the mainstream of our daily life.

And that's a good reason for discerning travelers to hunt out the haunts of the fox. So while the hunt rarely gets their fox, you ride home from the hunt country of Virginia with a prized travel experience.

Like the watermen of Smith Island, fox hunters have their own vernacular, which may create misconceptions for casual observers. In fact, the average hunter is no more a member of the idle gentry than the Chesapeake tonger is a backwater bumpkin.

Most members of the hunt are families that simply enjoy equestrian sports and are fortunate enough to have a few acres to board their own horses. Riders in the field or the hunt staff at an American hunt are just as likely to be women as men. For them, fox hunting is as much a sport as tennis, golf, or swimming might be to the rest of us, suitable for everyone from teenagers to grandparents. The main things hunters have in common are expert equestrian skills and a love of the outdoors.

Talking with a few participants in the sport quickly gave us a better appreciation for its attractions. What else could give horse lovers a perfect excuse to don hunt costume and play an active role in such a colorful tradition? How else would they gain permission to gallop over miles of private fields and woodlands in the fresh air? Indeed, fox hunting offers the satisfaction of riding and jumping in good form, developing an appreciation for the skill and teamwork of a finely trained pack of hounds, and enjoying the camaraderie of sport with one's neighbors, friends, and family. It didn't take us long to understand the benefits of seeing beautiful countryside, bounded by stone walls and wooden fences, from a saddle in the field instead of a car seat on the road.

Oenophiles will find much to appreciate in the growing number of Virginia vineyards. Lovers of the outdoors will discover dozens of hiking trails, both easy and difficult, many with a sparkling waterfall at trail's end, and it's possible for anyone to get caught up in the fervor of a point-to-point race.

Perhaps you'll want to visit a country fair and craft show. Tour large plantation homes that overlook expanses of fields and formal gardens. Take a scenic motor tour of the Skyline Drive, or explore impressive stalagmite and stalactite formations in underground caverns. Go antiquing, or simply stroll the hushed sidewalks of a secluded historic village.

For everyone who simply desires a quiet getaway, there are plenty of "undiscovered" dining spots, inns of character, unusual shops, indigenous foods, and peaceful back-road drives. In fact, the area offers so much that we can only conclude this introduction to Virginia Hunt Country as we began, with a rousing *Tally-ho . . .* and a cry to let the trip begin!

A Fox-Hunting Glossary

Fox hunters have their own unique language. We have culled the following definitions from various books on the subject to help you understand what's being said if you happen to get into a discussion.

Babbler. A hound that barks simply from excitement rather than from catching the scent of the fox.

Cast. When hounds following the fox lose the scent, this word describes their effort to find it again.

Couple. Two hounds (any sex), for convenience in counting *or* a device for keeping two hounds attached to each other for training (young hound, experienced hound).

Coffee house. To socialize. Riders who spend their time talking instead of paying attention to the hunt are said to be "coffee housing."

Covert (pronounced *cover*). Any area, usually wooded or brushy, in which foxes are accustomed to lie.

Cry. The voices of foxhounds pursuing their quarry.

Draw. What the huntsmen and hounds do when they search every part of a covert for the fox.

Eye for the country. A fox hunter's knowledge of the location of all the roads, lanes, jumpable places and an ability to anticipate the line (or course) of the fox.

Feather. What the hound does when it waves its tail and, with nose to the ground, follows the faint scent of the fox.

Field. All those who follow foxhounds on horseback, other than the members of the hunt staff, are known as the field.

Fixture card. Lists the dates, times, and places where the fox hunt starts.

Foil. When a fox doubles back on its scent trail it is said to run its foil.

Full cry. The moment of the hunt when every hound in the pack cries on the scent of a fox.

Go to ground. A phrase used to indicate that the fox has taken shelter, usually underground.

Hill toppers. Riders who follow hounds on horseback at a distance behind the rest of the field, mostly on lanes and roads, through gates and without jumping.

Holloa (pronounced *Holler*). The high-pitched call of someone who spots a fox breaking covert.

Huntsman. The man who controls hounds in the field, signaling to the hounds where he wants them to draw for the fox.

Line. The scent trail of the fox.

Master or *MFH.* The Master of the Foxhounds. The person in command of the hunt in general, in field and kennels.

Speaks. A hound "speaks" when he finds the line of a fox and announces his discovery by barking, or "throwing his tongue."

Stern. The hound's tail.

Tally-ho. A call indicating that the viewer has seen a fox.

Tongue. A hound is said to give tongue or to throw his tongue when he speaks on the line of a fox.

Whipper-in. A staff member who assists the huntsman in the control of hounds.

Source: Wadsworth, *Riding to Hounds in America.*

Loudoun County Tourist Commission. Located in the restored Market Station shopping complex, Leesburg, VA 22075; (703) 777-0519. Get a county map and additional information here. Open Monday through Friday, 9 A.M. to 5 P.M.

SPECIAL EVENTS THROUGHOUT THE YEAR

Point-to-point races and steeplechase races are held on spring and fall weekends. For a complete day of excitement, organize a group of friends and bring an elaborate tailgate picnic.

Late March. Piedmont Point-to-Point Races, Salem Race Course, Upperville; (703) 592-3304.

Early April. Middleburg Point-to-Point Races, Glenwood Park, Middleburg; (703) 777-0519.

Fairfax Point-to-Point Races, Belmont Plantation east of Leesburg. (703) 777-3805.

Mid-April. Loudoun Point-to-Point Races, Oatlands Plantation; (703) 777-3174.

May through October, second and fourth Sundays. Antique Flea Market. Aldie; (703) 327-4206.

Early May. Gold Cup Point-to-Point Races. Great Meadows, The Plains. This is the biggest of them all; (703) 253-5001.

Late May. Stable Tour: twelve private horse farms are open to visitors. Includes Mellon's Rokeby Farm, Jack Kent Cooke's farm, Foxcroft School, and Paperchase Farm. Hunt Country Stable Tour, Trinity Episcopal Church, Upperville, VA 22176; (703) 592-3711.

Early June. Upperville Colt and Horse Show, the oldest horse show in America; (703) 777-0519.

Mid-September. Fairfax Hunt Steeplechase Races, Belmont Plantation, east of Leesburg; (703) 532-2257.

Early October. Virginia Fall Race Meet, Middleburg; (703) 777-0519.

Morven Park Fall Race Meet, Leesburg; (703) 777-0519.

Waterford Homes Tour and Crafts Exhibit. Old homes open for tours, craft exhibit and sale. Waterford; (703) 882-3018.

Mid-October. Aldie Harvest Festival. Craft demonstrations, music, Civil War encampment. Free admission; (703) 327-4246.

Great Meadows Races, The Plains; (703) 347-2612.

Mid-November to mid-December. Christmas at Oatlands. This historic house is decorated for the holidays and candlelight tours are given; (703) 777-3174.

WHERE TO GO, WHAT TO DO

There are many reasons to visit this lovely locale: wineries, hiking, museums, caverns, fine restaurants, antiquing, and more. But the area's largest claim to fame is that it encompasses the greatest concentration of fox-hunting clubs in America. While we're all familiar with prints of hunting scenes, have used such phrases as "tally-ho" in conversation, or laughed at cartoon depictions of the wily fox tricking the hounds, few of us have ever actually seen, much less participated in, a hunt.

We'd like to help you do just that. First, here is some information on how you can accompany a hunt (whether or not you know how to ride), followed by two hunt-related attractions, and then a town-by-town account of things to see and do in the area.

FOX HUNTING

Fox hunting originated in England to control the population of foxes, serious predators of livestock, and to this day the English hunt is deadly serious.

Fox hunters on the 1,200-acre Morven Park estate.

In America, the hunt is purely for sport. The chase is everything, and no one really wants to catch the fox—because a fox caught is one less to hunt! In any case, foxes are nearly impossible to catch unless they are old, sick, or badly surprised.

Fox hunting was brought to this country by Lord Fairfax, the namesake of Fairfax County outside Washington, D.C., in 1747. Having inherited some 4 million acres from his grandfather, Fairfax started one of the first organized packs of hounds in the colonies.

As a teenager, George Washington worked as a surveyor for Lord Fairfax and gained his introduction to the sport. By the time Washington moved to Mount Vernon he was a fox-hunting enthusiast, and established his own pack of hounds in 1767.

Your image of fox hunting probably relates directly to old English prints. Horses gallop through the countryside, gracefully jump fences, and splash across streams with the hounds leading the way. The image is stirring and fairly accurate. Fox hunting can be quite dangerous if you aren't fit—it requires years of training and expert equestrian skills. It takes a lot of stamina to be able to ride hard at a full gallop, often for long periods of time. In the course of four or more hours, a rider may cover upwards of twenty miles and make thirty jumps.

If you'd like to "ride to hounds" during your visit here, you must be extremely proficient and, in most cases, already a member of another hunt (see below).

But what if you're not an expert rider, or can't ride at all? If you'd like to follow the hunt in a car, we've hunted up ways to do that, too.

Riding to Hounds with a Local Hunt.   If you are a member of a hunt in another part of the country and want to ride in Virginia, we suggest that you contact Cliff and Laura Hunt, who run a B&B called The Hunting Box (see *Where to Stay,* page 428).

Cliff, a whipper-in with the Blue Ridge Hunt, knows the importance of making sure riders are qualified, and he may ask you to come a day early to determine if you fit the bill. Most hunts go out three times a week, and chances are pretty good that from late October to March there will be a hunt in the area almost any day. As you might expect, many more people hunt on the weekends than during the week.

If you bring your own mount, The Hunting Box has stabling facilities for twenty horses, although hirelings are also available. Another option is to call Sandra Cartwright-Brown (The Conyers House; see *Where to Stay,* page 419) a regular rider with the Rappahannock Hunt. She keeps her horse at the inn and may have room for you to keep yours there. Roma Sherman (The Ashby Inn; see *Where to Stay,* page 423) is another source to contact, since she rides with the Blue Ridge Hunt. Roma can answer questions and steer you in the right direction, but doesn't have stabling facilities.

Seeing a Hunt off and Following in a Car.   Most hunts ride three days a week from October to March, except when the ground is frozen. Your innkeeper will be able to help you find out where and when a hunt will be leaving. Anyone can watch the preparations for the hunt; the opening meet, usually around the end of October, and the Thanksgiving meet are two of the more colorful ones to watch. You will see the hunt staff (huntsman, master of the hunt, whipper-in, field master), twenty or thirty hounds (they are always referred to as ten or fifteen couples, and always as hounds, not dogs), plus lots of color and excitement.

Our best suggestion is to look for a photographer in the crowd— they come to most hunts and know where to go for good views of the proceedings. All you have to do is follow the photographer and bring a detailed road map to help you find your way back to more familiar territory.

Road Maps.   Loudoun County maps are available at the Visitor Information Center in Leesburg. However, you will also want Fauquier, Clarke, and Rappahannock County maps in case you are following a hunt through these areas, or plan to do extensive back-roading. It is far easier to write away for all four. Each map is 25¢ plus 4% sales tax, with prepayment required. Make your check payable to Treasurer of Virginia, and write to Department of Highways and Transportation, Information Services Division, 1221 East Broad Street, Richmond, VA 23219; (804) 786-2838.

The Marriott Ranch.   The Marriott Ranch is a large working ranch with 700 head of cattle and 250 horses. Guided trail rides leave four times a day throughout the year until the ground is snow-covered. Rides last one and a half hours and will take you past a mock Western town, through forests, and up and down hilly areas.

More experienced individuals can learn how to move the cattle from one area to another. You will be out about one and a half to two hours.

If you're in the mood for an outdoor barbecue, Amos and Andy, two big draft horses, will pull you out to the Western town in a hay wagon. There you'll find a chuck wagon, barbecued pit-cooked beef, and biscuits cooked over the fire.

Trail rides leave at 10 A.M., 12, 2, and 4 P.M.; $20 per person. If there are five or more in a group, $15 per person. Cattle herding is $35 per person. The barbecue is available for groups only and costs about $40 per person. From Markham exit I-66, take Route 55 west about one mile, then go south on Route 726. Mailing address: Route 1, Box 113, Hume, VA 22639; (703) 364-2627.

VIRGINIA PLANTATIONS

Oatlands. Normally serene and peaceful, the grounds of this Southern plantation come alive with thundering hoofs each April during the annual point-to-point races. A true test of equestrian skill, the races are held here in keeping with the interests of Mr. and Mrs. William Corcoran Eustis, the last private owners, who were active in the local social life and hunt scene.

We found it refreshing to visit a historic estate where the buildings and grounds are in nearly continuous use. Built in the Greek Revival style in the early 1800s, it fell into disrepair during the Civil War. Happily, this estate was saved from the all-too-common fate of many stuffy old national treasures, which seem to be packed with unused period furniture, rarely dusted, and falling apart. Now perfectly restored, with the decor reflecting the period of the early 1900s, it effectively evokes a feel for the life of the wealthy a century ago.

The ceilings on the first floor have spectacular plaster cornices and moldings. Bouquets of flowers from the outdoor cutting gardens and family photos on display contribute to the feeling you are visiting an active plantation rather than a restoration.

Consequently, it is easy to imagine the house as it was in its heyday, when libations would be served on the portico. Strolling through the four and a half acres of terraced formal gardens with their boxwood walk, magnolias, reflecting pool and fountain, tea house, and well-placed garden benches in good repair was a particular joy.

Open from mid-March through late December, Monday through Saturday, 10 A.M. to 5 P.M.; Sunday, 1 to 5 P.M. Adults, $5. Children 12 to 18, $4. Special events include the Loudoun Hunt Point-to-

Point Race on a Saturday afternoon in mid-April. The house is decorated for the holidays from Thanksgiving to Christmas, when candlelight tours are given. Located on Route 15, midway between Route 50 and Route 7. Box 352, Leesburg, VA 22075; (703) 777-3174.

Morven Park. You begin to get a feel for the grand scale of this 1,200-acre estate as you approach from a mile-long, tree-lined gravel drive.

Inside the mansion you'll see a combination of architectural styles, not surprising in a structure that evolved from a 1781 fieldstone farmhouse into a turn-of-the-century mansion. Highlights include a Renaissance great hall, Jacobean dining room, French drawing room, library, four bedrooms, a ballroom, and nine bathrooms.

There was much to see and learn in the Museum of Hounds and Hunting, which is located here. After an excellent twenty-minute videotape explained the origins, rules, and duties of the various people involved in the hunt, we were free to peruse several rooms packed with riding jackets, saddles, buttons, crops, sculptures, and paintings.

A five-minute walk from the main house takes you to a large metal building, not at all in keeping with the estate's character, that houses a collection of about 100 antique horse-drawn carriages.

Open May through Memorial Day and Labor Day to mid-October, Saturday, 10 A.M. to 5 P.M.; Sunday, 1 to 5 P.M. From Memorial Day to Labor Day, open Tuesday through Saturday, 10 A.M. to 5 P.M.; Sunday, 1 to 5 P.M. Adults, $4; children 6 to 12, $2. From Leesburg take Route 7 west to Morven Park Road. Box 50, Leesburg, VA 22075; (703) 777-2414.

Middleburg

Standing on a street corner of this picturesque little town, the unofficial capital of hunt country, we noticed horse vans rolling past with uncommon regularity. As we strolled down the streets, we passed innumerable signs with names like The Iron Jockey, The Chronicle of the Horse, Dominion Saddlery, Finicky Filly, High

Horse Antiques, and Thoroughbreds—leaving little doubt that the horse is king in this part of the country and that Middleburg is the principal town. We found more tourists here than in some of the smaller hamlets, as well as plenty of sophisticated little antique, clothing, and gourmet food shops, along with many purveyors to the horsey set.

Middleburg has been an important town in the area since the early 1700s. The town's name is derived from its early history as the midway stop, the "middle burg," between Alexandria and the frontier town of Winchester. Entwined with the Civil War history of this area is a Confederate general named Mosby, along with his band of 125 raiders. Stories have it that because of him, the homes of the area suffered little damage—which could account for the numerous older structures still standing along the country lanes. Middleburg is where you will find Mosby's Tavern (see *Where to Dine,* page 441).

Following are brief descriptions of the places in town we particularly enjoyed. But first, please note: Speed limits are strictly enforced especially in Middleburg. As we checked out of our inn, we watched another guest writing a check for an $85 speeding ticket.

Emmanuel Episcopal Church.　Take a peek at the interior of this small brick church with unique large, curved, black shutters. Inside this immaculate sanctuary are 120 kneelers bearing needle-pointed scenes which were made by the church's parishioners.

Middleburg Cemetery.　Sometimes you can tell as much about an area's residents from the way they remember their fore-bears as by how they live. You can't miss the cement horse's head or the cemetery plot edged in bricks laid in the shape of a horseshoe. We also noted an original Rodin sculpture on Elizabeth Musgrave Merrill's plot. The cemetery is located just east of town; turn right on Jay Street. Drive to the back of the cemetery, and you'll be treated to a nice view of a pond and horse farm.

The Upper Crust.　Butterscotch Pecan Pies, Mutton Buttons, So-ee-e Pigs, Road Apples, Raspberry Hearts, Lemon Snow-flakes—the names offer just a hint of what you'll enjoy when you try the luscious cookies, tarts, and other pastries available at this small bakery.

Located across from the Safeway grocery store in Middleburg.

Open Monday through Saturday, 6 A.M. to 5 P.M.; Sunday, 7 A.M. to 5 P.M.

The Black Walnut. An ideal spot to pack your gourmet picnic. They will prepare anything from a roast beef and cheese sandwich to a full-fledged tailgate party. We particularly enjoyed the hearty, authentic flavor and texture of the Dimpflmeier rye bread from Toronto. On Wednesday and Friday the store sells fresh baguettes which, combined with a good selection of local Virginia wines, high-quality cheeses, pasta, and pâtés, are sure to satisfy.

Open Monday through Saturday, 10 A.M. to 5 P.M. Route 50, Middleburg; (703) 687-6833.

Service Station. A well-known legend in the area is "Everready" Burns Robertson, owner of the Exxon station in Upperville, who is always ready to help motorists. His station is located on Route 50 in Upperville; (703) 592-3880.

Leesburg

Take a walking tour of Leesburg and you walk into the past. Leesburg is the county seat of Loudoun County, a large historic district that has remained largely unchanged since it was laid out in 1759.

If you enjoy viewing early American architecture, Leesburg offers a nice variety of examples. Union troops controlled this town throughout the Civil War, so there was little war damage. This helped to preserve a wealth of pre-Civil War homes, from an original log house to houses from the mid-1700s to a number of early nineteenth-century dwellings. Take a look at the courthouse and the Ordinary, a tavern on the green, then select one of the many brick sidewalks that lead down picturesque, tree-lined side streets.

Loudoun County Tourist Commission. For a detailed county map or additional travel planning advice, you may want to stop here. Cordial staff spent considerable time delving into the files to answer our every question.

Open Monday through Friday, 9 A.M. to 5 P.M. Located in the restored Market Station shopping complex; (703) 777-0519.

The Loudoun Museum. Stop here to see the audiovisual presentation "A Special Look at Loudoun," and a small collection of Civil War artifacts. The day we visited there was a 200-year-old silk quilt on display as well as a collection of silver flatware made in local workshops between 1780 and 1920. To organize your walking tour, pick up the pamphlet "A Walk Around Leesburg," a bargain at 50 cents.

Open Monday through Saturday, 10 A.M. to 5 P.M.; Sunday, 1 to 5 P.M. 16 West Loudoun Street, Leesburg; (703) 777-7427.

Virginia Mercantile. This store specializes in Virginia products, such as honeys and vinegars, Virginia wines, books, hams, and pottery. If you'd like to take home a few gifts, this is an ideal spot to buy them.

Open Monday through Saturday, 10 A.M. to 6 P.M.; 29 South King Street, Leesburg, VA 22075; (705) 777-3322.

White's Ferry. This is the last operating ferry on the Potomac. The six-car ferry has carried travelers from 6 A.M. to 11 P.M., 365 days a year, since 1836—unless there is a high-water hazard. Confederate General White used this ferry regularly; it was large enough to transport ten cannons or a platoon of cavalry with horses. Today it offers the discerning traveler a change of pace from speeding over a scenic watercourse at 55 mph on a highway bridge.

Honk your horn or flash your lights to attract the attention of the ferry operator. On the Maryland side, boats and fishing gear are available to rent at the general store. Your catch for the day might include smallmouth bass, yellow perch, bluegill, carp, or catfish. You may also want to go hiking or biking along the towpath of the Chesapeake and Ohio Canal.

Ferry operates daily, 6 A.M. to 11 P.M. Located off Route 15, four miles northeast of Leesburg. (703) 777-0519.

Waterford

This is a premier "anti-tourist" destination. There are no shops, no tourists, and no tours—and that's what we like so much about this secluded, serene, historic village. If you like to compare shutter dogs, run your hands over worn paving bricks, and count the number of eight-over-eight versa six-over-six, Waterford may be the highlight of your trip.

This village originally was settled by Pennsylvania Quakers from Bucks County, Pennsylvania, in 1733. The town prospered following the Revolutionary War, and many of the beautiful buildings standing today date from the early nineteenth century.

This small area of old houses, designated a National Historic Site, includes the town's most prominent landmark, the Waterford Mill, built in 1830.

If you visit on the first weekend in October, during the Waterford Foundation Homes Tour and Craft Exhibit, you will have the opportunity to actually visit some of these historic homes. The fair, Virginia's oldest, was first held in 1943 to raise money for renovation and restoration. The town usually hosts more than 100 craftspeople and features thousands of handicrafts for sale, along with music, dance, and the tours.

The fair is held in early October. Tickets may be obtained by writing to the Waterford Foundation, Inc., Waterford, VA 22190; (703) 882-3018.

Washington

This small, peaceful village, home of the famed Inn at Little Washington (see page 431) has had great publicity in recent years. Stretch limos and even the occasional helicopter bring lobbyists from Washington, D.C., to feast and recuperate at the inn. You'll surely notice the coral-colored canopy over its locked entrance, and the wrought-iron fence through which you can peek into the breakfast garden.

This internationally acclaimed country-house hotel, now a member of the exclusive Relais & Chateaux organization from Paris, has been a catalyst for the town, drawing patrons to the many quality galleries and shops that have sprung up here.

We suggest you arrive between Thursday and Sunday, as many of the shops are closed during the first part of the week. You should know, too, that winter hours may vary from what we report here.

Rather than list all the attractions and spoil the joy of making your own discoveries, here are just a few of the places you may want to visit as you wander through the town.

Cabin Fever Books.   This new bookshop is a fine place to browse and purchase local titles. Main Street; (703) 675-1300.

The Rush River Company.   This is a crafts cooperative featuring the designs and work of over twenty artists, with a large selection of craft books and fabrics.

Open Thursday and Friday, 10 A.M. to 4 P.M.; Saturday, 10 to 5 P.M.; Sunday, 11 to 5 P.M. Gay Street; (703) 675-4310.

Kramer and Eiland Woodworking.   Custom furniture is designed and crafted, as are doors, windows, and millwork.

Open Monday through Friday, 8 A.M. to 5 P.M. Gay and Jett Streets; (703) 675-3882.

Country Heritage Antiques and Crafts.   Specializes in American folk art, high-quality handcrafts, country and primitive furniture, and fine antiques. Over 130 craftspeople are represented.

Open Thursday through Sunday, 11 A.M. to 6 P.M.; Main Street; (703) 675-3738.

The Middle Street Gallery.   This artists' cooperative features some of the finest visual arts and crafts in Rappahannock County. Museum-quality paintings, photography, and sculpture. $200 to a couple of thousand. Open Friday to Sunday, 11 A.M. to 6 P.M.; Middle Street; (703) 675-3440.

Sperryville

At the foot of Shenandoah National Park, Sperryville is a sleepy little village with a blinking yellow light marking the main intersection. There are lots of antique and curio shops in and around town, and a plethora of fruit stands along the back roads in the surrounding countryside.

We heartily suggest taking to the back roads hereabouts to explore and discover some of the lovely mountain views and to sample the locally grown produce. In town, you may want to visit the following places:

The Faith Mountain Company.   Sells a wide assortment of dried flowers, herbs, spices, and crafts in a restored eighteenth-century village house. The store is crammed with items, all carefully and attractively arranged. Located in the center of town, (703) 987-8824.

Sperryville Antique Market. Located in an old barn, this expansive emporium covers 20,000 square feet and is broken down into individual shops filled with antiques, crafts, and collectibles for lovers of early Americana. Located in the center of town; (703) 987-8050.

PARKS AND CAVERNS

Shenandoah National Park

We're glad Virginia Hunt Country brushes against the northeastern border of this 195,000-acre national park, as it gives us an excuse to tell you about some of its highlights. Motoring down the Skyline Drive along the mountain tops offers some of the finest scenic vistas anywhere. The park also has hiking trails of all difficulty levels, spectacular fall foliage, waterfalls, nature walks, horseback riding, and more.

Two entrances to the park are accessible from the hunt country. One is at Front Royal, along I-66, and the other at Thornton Gap, near Sperryville, from Route 211. Stop at the visitor center, located at each entrance, and pick up a small booklet on hikes in the park. If you are coming during the busy times, particularly the fall leaf season, you will find a steady stream of cars winding along the roads. However, if you take time to walk the hiking trails even for a few minutes, you may be amazed at what you see. Deer are plentiful and used to being photographed. Black bears are frequently sighted along roads in the park.

Big Meadows. This is the largest stop along the drive, with a restaurant, lodge, campground, and ranger station (see *Where to Stay,* page 426). There are numerous ranger-led nature walks and films. The visitor center is open daily from early March through December and on an intermittent schedule during January and February. For information, phone (703) 999-2266.

Dark Hollow Falls.   This 1½-mile round-trip hike begins just
before Big Meadows as you head south, and rewards the hiker with
a seventy-foot cascading waterfall and rushing brook. An easy walk
down, it takes a little energy to get back to the car.

Old Ragg.   The hike up this mountain, located in the park, is
popular with the college crowd. While we didn't attempt this particular hike, we saw numerous cars at the starting point and have been
told that a large portion of the hike involves clambering over enormous boulders. You can see Old Ragg from Skyline Drive; to get
to the starting point of the climb, follow Route 231 south of Sperryville. Just beyond Route 707, you will see signs on the right pointing
the way.

Luray Caverns.   Year in and out, this is the most popular
cavern in the east. While it is slightly outside of the area properly
known as Virginia Hunt Country, we are including it because of its
fame.

Along the paved and subtly lit walkways, underground lakes
reflect hundreds of stalactites. While we have toured many caves
in places as far away as New Zealand, the effect of The Great
Stalacpipe Organ—made from sixty-four acres of stalactites (solid
pieces of rock) that are hit with rubber-tipped hammers—was truly
impressive. Seated in a subterranean "cathedral," surrounded by
awe-inspiring formations and the sounds of the organ arrangements, one can't help but agree with one visitor's description:
"Man's genius and the hand of God are in perfect harmony there."
Also on the grounds is a historic car and carriage museum that
includes an 1892 Benz (still in running condition), a 1906 Ford, a
1925 Rolls-Royce, and dozens more.

The caverns are open daily, year-round, 9 A.M. to 4 P.M. Hours
are extended to 6 P.M. mid-March through mid-June and from Labor
Day through mid-November; and to 7 P.M. between mid-June and
Labor Day. Adults, $8; children 7 to 13, $4. Located on Route 211.
Box 748, Luray, VA 22835; (703) 743-6551.

Sky Meadows State Park.   Paul Mellon purchased this 1,100-
acre farm in 1973 and donated it to the Virginia Park System. We
thank him, as this is a great stop for everyone who enjoys some
time spent in basking in nature's bounty. There are hiking trails,
weekend interpretive programs, midweek guided trail hikes, and

tours of Mount Bleak, an 1835 house. Picnic and restroom facilities are available, as well as a wooded "hike-in" campground. Access to the Appalachian Trail makes this a good base camp for day or weekend hikes.

Located on Route 17, one mile south of Paris. There is a $1.50 parking fee on the weekends. Route 1, Box 540, Delaplane, VA 22025; (703) 592-3556.

State Arboretum of Virginia. Here at Blandy Experimental Farm, of the Orland White Arboretum, you can drive a three-mile loop road with picturesque views of both. Pick up a guide map at the visitor's parking lot. Highlights include a labeled evergreen trail and a grove of more than 500 ginkgos, one of the largest populations outside of China. A picnic area and restroom facilities are on the grounds.

Open daily from dawn to dusk. Located on the south side of Route 50 just before Route 340. Boyce, VA 22620; (703) 837-1758.

FOODS TO PURCHASE

One of our greatest joys in traveling is to sample an area's indigenous foods. We have some unique tastes to share with you from the hunt country, including a marvelous chutney.

Appleton Farm, Middleburg. The recipe for Appleton Farm chutney comes from Mrs. Skinner, who has canned it for over thirty-five years. You can find the chutney at the B&A Grocery in Middleburg or the Virginia Mercantile in Leesburg, or you can buy it by the case direct from the makers. Mrs. Skinner told us she regularly makes peanut butter and chutney sandwiches, and we will attest that the fresh plums, peppers, ginger, and other spices provide a more mature companion to peanut butter than the usual jelly.

You'll find the cottage where the chutney is made on Route 626 just across the county line, outside Middleburg. Call before visiting, as there is no sign; (703) 687-5678 or (703) 687-3155.

Lowelands Farm, Middleburg. Lemon-thyme, winter spice, wildflower mint, ginger-sage, raspberry, and maple are all flavors of honey that Karen and Rick Lowe make at their Middleburg farm. They also make herbal wine vinegars, culinary sherry, and savory

Worcestershire sauce from their own farm-grown herbs. On weekends from Thanksgiving to Christmas, cars fill the dirt road leading
to their farm as families come to pick out and cut their trees, drink
mulled cider, sample herbal products, take hay rides, and see the
Scottish Highland long-haired cow, sheep, horses, donkeys and
goats. If you'd like to visit before or after the holidays do call ahead,
as this is a working farm. Lowelands Farm products are available
at gourmet and gift shops in the region.

For a free catalog, write Lowelands Farm, Route 1, Box 98,
Middleburg, VA 22117. From Route 50, go north on Route 734,
turn right on Route 733, then left on Route 763; (703) 687-6923.

Merymede Mushrooms, Amissville.   Recent advances in cultivation have made the flavorful shiitake mushroom more common
on restaurant menus throughout the country. Richard and Margaret
Ulf gave us a tour of their collection of 7,000 shiitake logs in the
woods near their home. In the winter when the sap is down, oak
logs are cut, holes are drilled along the bark, and shiitake fungus
is inserted. The holes are then plugged and the logs are left to sit
for up to a year to let the fungus spread through the wood. To start
production, the logs are soaked in water for a day. Mushrooms will
appear in four or five days, and be ready to pick in another few days.
Shiitakes are usually available from May to October on the farm for
$8 a pound. If you'd like to grow your own and your car has a large
trunk, you can also purchase inoculated logs.

Located ten miles west of Warrenton on US 211; turn left on
Route 621. Route 2, Box 473, Amissville, VA 22002; (703) 937-
5478.

Holy Cross Abbey, Berryville.   While you may have seen this
abbey's white or whole-grain bread for sale at the Giant or Safeway
supermarket chains, we enjoyed purchasing the bread directly from
Brother James or Brother Michael at this idyllic 1,200-acre setting
overlooking the Shenandoah River. The Holy Cross fruitcakes,
advertised in the likes of the Smithsonian Catalog and *Yankee*
magazine, are also available here along with foods made at the
seven other U.S. Trappist monasteries: a large variety of jams,
cheddar cheese, flavored honeys, chocolates, and caramels. Visitors are also welcome to attend any of four to six daily religious
services.

Most days services are held at 2, 5:30, and 7:30 P.M. The store is open Monday through Friday, 1:15 to 5 P.M.; Saturday, 10 to 12:30 P.M. Take Route 7 west across the Blue Ridge Mountains and the Shenandoah River; immediately turn right on Route 603 and proceed 1²⁄₁₀ miles to the Holy Cross Abbey; (703) 955-3124.

VIRGINIA WINES

You heard it through the grapevine: The experts said it couldn't be done, but wine grapes are flourishing in Virginia, and the end-products are good. As you drive through Loudoun and Fauquier counties, you'll see signs adorned with a bunch of grapes to indicate a vineyard is nearby.

Here for your edification and tasting pleasure is a little local wine history and our favorite vineyards.

Aspiring Virginia vintners have been dogged by 350 years of frustration in their attempts to produce wine from the European *vitis vinifera* variety of grape. The first settlers in Jamestown tried and were foiled by the cold winters and hot humid summers of the mid-Atlantic region. Thomas Jefferson, acknowledged as the nation's first wine connoisseur, experimented for years at Monticello only to conclude that the vinifera varietals could not be grown in Virginia, and that American hybrids would have to fuel the native wine industry.

Then the French wine industry was almost destroyed by the root aphid *(phylloxera)* epidemic of 1860–1880. The vineyards were saved only after thousands of disease-resistant American root stocks were shipped to Europe and *vinifera* vines were grafted onto them.

Over the next forty years, the French crossed American root stocks with other European root stocks and created new hybrids not susceptible to the root aphid. These French hybrids were first planted in the U.S. in the early 1900s, but only in the late 1960s did Virginians begin to plant the French hybrid grapes of Seyval, Vidal, and Chambourcin.

In 1974, local vintners scorned all the "expert" advice, and again planted the vinifera grapes of Chardonnay, white Riesling and Cabernet Sauvignon. Skeptics say history will repeat itself. We suggest you pay a visit to one or more of the award-winning wineries listed below; speak to the wine makers, and judge for yourself.

Meredyth Vineyards. Virginia's first large farm winery of recent history was started here in 1975 and now has fifty-six acres cultivated with French hybrids and vinifera vines. Its wines have won more medals than any other in the state, and the Seyval Blanc has been served at White House dinners. The grounds also feature a picnic area and a gift shop.

Open daily, 10 A.M. to 4 P.M. Located on Route 628, four miles south of Middleburg. Box 347, Middleburg, VA 22117; (703) 687-6277.

Piedmont Vineyards and Winery. The late Elizabeth Furness planted the first vinifera vineyard since the time of Thomas Jefferson in 1973, at age 75. Now the vineyard covers thirty acres of the 500-acre farm; twenty acres are planted with Chardonnay. Waverly, the Greek Revival main house which was constructed in 1730, is a registered Virginia Historical Landmark. A picnic area and gift shop are also on the grounds.

Open daily from April through December, 10 A.M. to 5 P.M. From January through March, open Wednesday through Sunday, 10 A.M. to 4 P.M. Located on Route 626, three miles south of Middleburg. Box 286, Middleburg, VA 22117; (703) 687-5528.

Naked Mountain Vineyard. Naked Mountain Chardonnay is rated one of the state's best; many innkeepers recommend it, and so do we. A limited output is made here at this small, picturesque 4½-acre vineyard located on a sloping hillside, 1,000 feet above sea level. The site is blessed with thermal inversions, which gives the vines critical protection from frost. There is a picnic area and gift shop.

Tours are given March through December, Wednesday through Sunday and on legal Monday holidays, 11 A.M. to 5 P.M. In January and February, tours are offered on weekends and legal Monday holidays only. Located 1⁷⁄₁₀ miles north of Markham on Route 688, exit 4 off Route 66. Box 131, Markham, VA 22643; (703) 364-1609.

Linden Vineyards and Orchards. This small family operation is situated at 1,400 feet above sea level, with great mountain views. Call ahead to see if your visit will coincide with one of the periodic seminars on grape growing, wine making, and wine appreciation. The grounds also include a pick-your-own apple orchard, featuring historic apple varieties such as Esopus Spitzenburg and Newtown Pippin.

Tours are given March through December, Wednesday through Sunday and on legal Monday holidays, 11 A.M. to 5 P.M. In January and February, tours are given on weekends only. Located on Route 638 two miles south of Route 55, eight miles east of Front Royal. Mailing address: Route 1, Box 96, Linden, VA 22642; (703) 364-1997.

Oasis Vineyard. This large vineyard and winery makes a Sauvignon Blanc wine, as well as champagne using the traditional *méthode champenoise,* and varietals made with Chardonnay and Pinot Noir grapes.

Open daily, 10 A.M. to 4 P.M. From I-66, take Route 647 at the Marshall exit, head south and turn right onto Route 635; the winery is about ten miles west on the left-hand side. Mailing address: Route 1, Highway 635, Hume, VA 22639; (703) 635-7627.

WHERE TO STAY

The Conyers House, Sperryville

Upon arriving at this rambling country inn owned and operated by Sandra and Norman Cartwright-Brown, we found Sandra, an avid fox hunter, washing down her thoroughbred hunting horse named Rachael. You're almost certain to be greeted by Sandra's own little pack of dogs, one a bona fide Jack Russell terrier named Winchester.

"Everything is where it is because it has a purpose," Sandra explained, as we noted the attractively arranged fox-hunting paraphernalia in her tack room that also serves as the inn's foyer. The inside of this comfortable house, which started life as a pre-Revolu-

Conyers House is filled with family memorabilia.

tionary farmhouse, is filled to the brim with family memorabilia. "This is a home, not an inn that has been decorated."

Step down into the living room and drop into the soft leather couches that hug you like old friends. Exposed hand-hewn wooden beams, Oriental carpets, a grand piano, and shelves of books make you feel very welcome indeed. Take the opportunity to wander throughout the premises: through the large dining room with its fireplace, into the charming country kitchen, and out to the wraparound porches—where we enjoyed an alfresco breakfast one beautiful summer morning.

The ground-level Nicholson Room, at thirty feet long, is the largest room in the inn; it has low ceilings with exposed beams, a king-size bed, Franklin stove, and a bathroom with a tub for two. Helen's Room (named for innkeeper Norman's mother) has a fireplace, private balcony, and a sink that, once upon a time, claimed residence in the White House. Uncle Sim's Suite has a high, queen-size 1840 four-poster bed, a fireplace, and an adjoining sitting room. Visit during the week when the inn is less crowded, and take a peek at all the unique rooms.

Two secluded cottages are perfect for romantics. The Hill House is the smaller. It has a single room with a queen-size bed, Franklin stove, VCR, and a double Jacuzzi bathtub. Horse lovers will want to stay in the Spring House because the cottage is in the middle of a horse pasture. The first floor has a porch, living room, and a large bathroom. The second-floor bedroom has a low, slanted ceiling; turn off the VCR on a rainy night and listen to the patter on the tin roof.

Well-suited to their inn's personality, the Cartwright-Browns exude an air of eclectic charisma that puts guests at ease. Norman spent many years as a businessman in Libya. His hobby is his collection of restored 1950s-vintage English cars. Sandra is an experienced fox hunter with the Rappahannock Hunt, and will discuss her sporting passion for hours if you're interested. With advance reservations, Sandra will take guests on a cross-country ride.

The inn is located in Francis Thornton Valley ("F.T. Valley" to the locals) at the edge of the Shenandoah National Park. Sandra, who calls herself the "Chamber of Commerce of Rappahannock County," and Norman will ebulliently steer you to hiking, canoeing, tubing, antiquing, or any other backroading adventure you might seek.

Guests at the inn may arrange ahead of time to have a six-course candlelit dinner here; it is served in front of the fireplace in the formal dining room. Our breakfast, served family style, included an impressive fruit platter, French toast, and bacon.

The inn has five rooms with private bath, $100–$150, and one suite, $195. Two cottages with private bath, $160–$170. Dinner, by prior arrangement only, $125 per couple including four wines and gratuity. Children over 12 welcome in all rooms; younger children allowed in the cottages except during the fall foliage season. Third person in room $25 additional. Small nonshedding dogs are permitted in four of the rooms. From Sperryville, take Route 522 to Route 231, drive south eight miles, make a left onto Route 707 and proceed ⁶⁄₁₀ mile. Route 1, Box 157, Slate Mills Road, Sperryville, VA 22740; (703) 987-8025.

The Inn at Little Washington, Washington

Their "Country House Hotel," as owners Chef Patrick O'Connell and Reinhardt Lynch, maitre d'hotel, like to call this former garage site, is now one of the most luxurious, most expensive, and most written-about country inns on the East Coast. Absolutely no expense is spared here: by either hosts *or* guests.

At this special inn, all your dreams of being pampered in a grand Victorian country house can now be fulfilled: you'll find English antiques, canopied beds, *faux bois* woodwork, luxurious marble baths, heated towel racks, thick terrycloth robes, hair-dryers, fancy soaps, plus flowers in profusion, mints, fruit, expensive books, and a fully stocked refrigerator. A stay here is a little like living theater: during the day, the large staff quietly cleans, polishes, and arranges flowers, somehow managing to keep the whole place in a state of constant perfection.

The rooms themselves are stunning. Interior decorator (or should we say set designer?) Joyce Evans is from London, as are the extravagant fabrics and antique furnishings you see. If you have the wherewithal to stay in a suite, you'll walk from the sitting room with a balcony overlooking the Blue Ridge Mountains up the stairs to your bedroom, Jacuzzi, and *another* balcony overlooking the mountains.

One drawback: Don't expect to have a comfortable evening chat by the fire with the innkeepers—they're busy operating the establishment's famed restaurant (see *Where to Dine,* page 431).

And a final tip if you decide to indulge: Take a superior room with king-size bed, or one of two duplex suites with a Jacuzzi. The standard rooms and intermediate rooms are a bit small for luxuriating in the "ultimate experience."

Eight rooms and two suites. Standard rooms have a queen-size bed and a bath with shower, $210. Intermediate rooms have a queen-size bed and a bath with a bathtub and shower, $250. Superior rooms have a king-size bed, bath with a bathtub and shower, and a private balcony, $300. Suites have a king-size bed, Jacuzzi bath and separate shower, and a lower and upper balcony, $410. Friday, Saturday, Sunday, holidays, and throughout October there is a $80 per room surcharge. Continental breakfast is included; full breakfast is extra. Children over 10 welcome. No pets. Overnight guests are guaranteed dinner reservations at the restaurant. Box 300, Middle and Main Streets, Washington, VA 22747; (703) 675-3800.

The Ashby Inn, Paris

After a day's hunt, where will many riders, trainers, and breeders go to sip a sherry and commiserate? Why, Paris, of course.

Paris, VA (population 60), is where John Sherman and his wife, Roma, an avid fox hunter, have lovingly remodeled this 1829 residence into a convivial country inn and English pub, complete with dart board.

When we first stayed here several years ago, John was commuting to Washington, D.C., working long hours as a top Congressional assistant. Today, he commutes from his log house a few doors down, where he continues to write major speeches—like the keynote address for the 1988 Democratic National Convention—and can be more attentive to his guests.

The Shermans continually strive to make each aspect of the inn "just a little bit better." But the Ashby Inn already is close to our ideal, a friendly establishment where everyone makes you feel at home the minute you walk through the door.

The English pub downstairs is a good example. During the day, the fully stocked bar is open to guests on the honor system—a dream come true for every closet bartender. Just step behind the bar, concoct your favorite poison, jot down what you've made, and enjoy.

Upstairs, the six bedrooms are furnished with antiques and country furniture the Shermans have collected across the mountains in the Shenandoah Valley. Oriental carpets and rag rugs soften polished wood floors, and hunt prints evoke Roma's passion for the sport. Our room for this stay was the Victorian Room, with a high cannonball bed and primitive, painted armoire. On a previous visit we slept in the larger Fan Room, which features a private balcony and is named for its Palladian window. All the rooms overlook a picturesque hillside, grazed by Black Angus cattle. Look closely and you may see deer browsing early in the morning, or spot a fox hunt pass by in season.

Head downstairs early in the morning and you'll be greeted by the comforting aroma of bread baking for the evening meal. We had our breakfast of just-from-the-oven muffins, poached eggs, cereal, juice, and coffee on the patio. The scent of fresh hay in adjacent fields prompted us to linger for a moment and contemplate settling in this idyllic village.

Four rooms, with private bath, $90–$115. Two dormer rooms share an adjacent full bath and water closet, $80. Saturday night there is a $15–$20 surcharge for a one-night stay. Full breakfast included. Children over 10 welcome. No pets. Located just off Route 50 on Route 759 (just after Route 17). Route 1, Box 2/A, Paris, VA 22130; (703) 592-3900.

Little River Inn, Aldie

Arriving here for our night's lodging, we were greeted only by a "baaing" flock of sheep, a braying mule, a goat, and a "henny" (a unique mule bred to protect sheep from wolves and coyotes). We found the back door open, with a note asking us to phone the antique shop down the road. A cordial voice answered and invited us to grab a cold drink from the fridge and make ourselves at home. Less than five minutes later, the manager arrived to show us our room and make us feel genuinely welcome.

During your stay, talk with Tucker Withers—definitely a one-of-a-kind host, innkeeper, antique dealer, fellow traveler, tour guide, chauffeur, restaurateur, and unofficial mayor of Aldie, Virginia.

If you want to buy an antique, attend an auction, or check out an estate sale, just ask Tucker. He has traveled extensively up and down the coast collecting pieces for his shops, and he knows where to look. He works one night a week at an auction and is glad to take guests.

And if it's lodging you want, ask Tucker. Each time we stop here, it seems Tucker has added another antique building to his "Inn Complex," which is scattered along both sides of Route 50. All are nicely (but not overly) decorated with period furniture and a fine collection of Currier and Ives prints.

The main house, a nineteenth-century home, has five guest rooms furnished in antiques and quilts. Guests are free to help themselves to the refrigerator, which is stocked with cold beer, wine, and fresh lemonade, as well as cheese and crackers.

Next door is an authentic log cabin with living room, fireplace, bedroom, bath, and additional sleeping loft. On the same site is the Patent House. Constructed in the late 1700s to the dimensions required by original landgrants, it has a living room with fireplace, small sleeping area, and bath.

Down the road apiece, the elegant circa 1870 Hill House sleeps up to six and sits on two very private acres complete with boxwood and herb gardens. For those on a budget, Tucker recently acquired Woodbyrn Guest House, a three-acre property with an in-ground pool, which he lovingly refers to as "The No Frills Inn." While not as elaborate as the other properties—it's furnished in a collection of "grandma's attic" furniture, has limited maid service, and offers juice and coffee only in the A.M.—the price is lower.

Breakfast here is a treat. The taste of the special Dutch Apple Baby Pancake, fresh apples, cinnamon, and pecans baked in a puffed pancake and smothered with confectioners' sugar, lingers for hours.

If you'd like a tour after breakfast, Tucker's deluxe London Sterling cab or restored 1948 Dodge are available for hire with driver at $35 per hour for the first two hours, $30 per hour thereafter. For a discerning insider's view of Washington, D.C., we suggest hiring Tucker Withers and his cab for a day of touring the nation's capital in style.

At the Main House: two rooms with private bath, $90; three rooms with shared bath, $80–$85. The log cabin is $135; $20 per additional person. The Patent House is $120 a day. The Hill House is $210 per double; each additional person, $20. Woodbyrn: three rooms, with private bath, $75. Full breakfast and beverages are included, except at Woodbyrn. Children over 10 welcome, $20 additional. No pets. Swimming pool. Located on Route 50. Box 116, Aldie, VA 22001; (703) 327-6742.

L'Auberge Provençale, White Post

It is indeed a special pleasure to savor a superb dinner of French cuisine prepared by fourth-generation master chef Alain Borel (see *Where to Dine,* page 430), enjoy a bottle of fine wine, relax over a snifter of fine Cognac, then simply ascend the stairs to your bedroom in this circa 1753 stone country house, with no concern over the ride home.

Then after a fine evening's rest, you awake refreshed to gaze out your window onto farmland, alive with sheep and cattle. You dress for breakfast in your room—perhaps in one of the two large ones in the main house, decorated in Victorian-era blues or greens, with modern baths and fireplaces, or in a similar room, without a fireplace, in the adjacent building.

Upon arriving in the dining room once again, you'll partake of a gourmet breakfast. Ours included fresh-squeezed orange juice; a beautiful fruit plate with poached pear slices arranged as a fan, decorated with fresh raspberries and bunches of tiny Champagne grapes; freshly made croissants with butter and an assortment of jams. Shenandoah mountain trout in a light batter, lobster mousseline with crabmeat and cottage fries, homemade veal sausage, lobster claws with tarragon maple syrup, and other items are also served for breakfast.

Nine rooms, five with fireplaces, and one suite, all with private bath, $120–$175. An additional charge of $25 per room on Saturday nights. Gourmet breakfast included. Closed the month of January. Children over 10 welcome, $20 additional. Third person in room $40 additional. No pets. Located on Route 340 just south of Route 50. Box 119, White Post, VA 22663; (703) 837-1375.

Big Meadows, Shenandoah National Park

We found this stone and timber lodge, built by local mountain men in the 1930s, very reminiscent of the National Park lodges in Yellowstone, Yosemite, or Grand Canyon. By staying in the park, we could enjoy the full complement of National Park services, from day hikes and horseback riding to evening campfire talks.

There is a wide range of accommodations here, from small rooms in the main lodge, to motel-type rooms with balconies overlooking the valley, to large, log cabin–type, one- and two-bedroom cottages, some with fireplaces. We stayed in a room with a view—and we were not disappointed. In the morning, from the windows of our room in the lodge situated 3,400 feet above sea level, the Shenandoah Valley spread out below us, with a beautiful silver ribbon of river meandering through farmlands and villages—quite an inspiring wake-up sight. We slept well, too; even in the sweltering summer months, the temperatures were about fifteen degrees cooler here than in the valley below.

If you stay here, you will most likely eat in the park. Do not expect gourmet dining, as this is basic family fare. A meal in the large dining room with magnificent wooden chestnut trusses spanning the ceiling, servers scurrying to and fro, and a noise level a few decibels higher than we'd prefer is typical of our experiences at other national parks. You don't make reservations; just get in line if you wish to dine early, or wait and relax a little more at a later sitting.

Big Meadows, milepost 51 on the Skyline Drive, is open from April through November. Rates, $45–$135. You might also try Skyland Lodge at milepost 41, open from March through New Year's. Rates, $45–$140. Both lodges are operated by ARA Virginia Sky-Line Co., P.O. Box 727, Luray, VA 22835; (703) 743-5108. Direct lines for reservations: Big Meadows (703) 999-2221; Skyland Lodge, (703) 999-2211. Or call 800-999-4714 (central switchboard).

Norris House, Leesburg

Take a step out the front door of this 1806 house and you've just begun your walking tour of the Leesburg historic district. This stately home is also conveniently located for a visit to Morven Park, Oatlands, and Waterford.

A pleasant porch along the side of the house and the landscaped yard behind it are available for guests' use, as is the library, which features a fireplace, wideboard pine floors, and a working 1880s pump organ originally built for a small church. Our room on the second floor was comfortably furnished with fireplace, Victorian couch, baskets filled with magazines, quilts on the wall, and a four-poster bed with a white coverlet and lace canopy overhead. The matching, stenciled lamp shades, curtains, and dust ruffle were a nice touch.

Breakfast was an elegant "family affair," with all the guests seated together at a candlelit table. Our breakfast was fresh fruit salad, a variation of eggs Benedict, and freshly baked muffins. Chamber music played softly in the background.

Five rooms share three baths: second-floor fireplace rooms, $85 and $95; third-floor rooms, $55 and $65. Two suites, with private bath, and a fireplace, $115 each. Full breakfast included. Children over 12 welcome. No pets. 108 Loudoun Street S. W., Leesburg, VA 22075; (703) 777-1806.

The Hunting Box, Boyce

Located on a horse farm in the Blue Ridge Hunt territory, this inn produces a brochure that has nearly as many photos of the stables as it does rooms for its two-legged guests!

And no wonder, as avid fox hunters Laura and Cliff Hunt operate their establishment within an hour's drive of eleven area hunts. This means you have access to fox hunting every day from late October to the end of March, as well as riding facilities and lessons throughout the year. The Hunts offer care, tack, and stabling for twenty steeds, vanning to the hunt, grooms quarters, and an indoor rink, so it's the perfect place to bring your own horse. If you are an experienced rider and can prove it, hirelings are available. The motel-style rooms are comfortably furnished. A heated, outdoor swimming pool is open from April through November. Breakfast is provided before hunting, with a large lunch and cocktails afterward. *Tally-ho!*

Five rooms, all with private bath: $80 for one, $120 for two. Includes breakfast, lunch, and cocktails. Stabling, $20–$35. Horse rental (hunting), $100; hacking, $15 per hour; vanning, $15–$30;

capping fees, $50–$100. Box 226, Boyce, VA 22620; (703) 837-2160.

The Red Fox Inn, Middleburg

Travelers who long for a historic inn (actually more of an elegant, small hotel) with random-width pine floors and walls a bit out of plumb from several hundred years of settlement, but who can't be without the twentieth-century conveniences of a color television, a direct-dial phone at your bedstead, and a private bath, look no more.

This historic landmark in the center of Middleburg is a convenient central base from which to explore hunt country. Because The Red Fox is a large complex (restaurant, inn, art gallery, catering department, facilities for small meetings and banquets) the feel, while friendly, is more businesslike than at some of the other inns we list.

The inn complex of four buildings features authentic eighteenth-century decor. Many of the rooms and suites have fireplaces, canopy beds, fine antiques, and Oriental rugs. All of the accommodations offer fresh flowers, thick cotton robes, *The Washington Post* outside your door, and continental breakfast in your room if requested. The Red Fox can also arrange riding lessons, shooting and ballooning trips.

Twenty-three rooms and suites, spread among four buildings, all with private bath, $125–$225. Continental breakfast included; full breakfast extra. Children of all ages welcome, no additional charge; rollaways, $25, and cribs, $10. No pets. 2 East Washington Street, Box 385, Middleburg, VA 22117; (703) 687-6301.

Blue Knoll Farm, Castleton

We studied the state map in vain trying to find Castleton, and were we relieved when innkeepers Richard and Joy Cartwright-Brown informed us that Castleton wasn't marked. Because the local kids play pranks with the signs on the road, it is important to get directions to the inn before venturing down the attractive but confusing back roads. The directions on the inn's brochure make it all very clear. Persevere, as you're in for a treat.

The nineteenth-century blue house with both a front and back porch sits surrounded by fields near a newly constructed pond, where we spied a blue heron doing a bit of fishing. We felt immediately welcome when, upon walking in, we were shown a table laden with such goodies as fresh peach pie, cherry pie, double chocolate cake, and a pitcher of lemonade—all ready and waiting whenever guests wanted something sweet. We kept this in mind and planned our dinner to save room for a late-night dessert with coffee and a cordial on the front porch.

The house reflects Joy's style as a talented interior decorator and Richard's skill at renovating old buildings. Rooms are coordinated with fine fabrics and appointments, yet have lots of family mementos scattered about to give the inn a warm, home-like feel.

In the winter we'd choose the first-floor Library Room. The queen-size bed has a feather bed on top of the mattress. A wood-burning fireplace, Oriental rug, antique desk, shelves of books, and a wingback chair with an ottoman invite you to escape for a quiet afternoon. The bath is private, but is not attached to the room. At other times of the year we'd choose Meadowview, which has a king-size bed covered with layers of lacy pillows, along with antique crewel bedspread, dressing table, and lots of details: a wall of old family photographs, decorative boxes, perfume bottles, an old-fashioned evening purse, and formal gloves.

All of the guests eat breakfast together at 9 A.M. in the formal dining room. Places are set with fine china, sterling flatware, and lace napkins. A platter of cantaloupe slices, peeled orange slices, strawberries, grapefruit, and kiwi was attractively arranged. The breads were orange muffins and banana bread; the main course was baked eggs with cheddar cheese, ham, and mushrooms.

Four rooms, all with private bath (some are private hall baths), $95–$115. $20 extra for Saturday night only. Full breakfast is included. Not appropriate for children. No pets. Take Route 211 through Warrenton to Benvenue. Turn left on Route 729 for 4½ miles to T junction. Continue left for 2 miles to Route 676. Turn right onto second gravel road, ½ mile to inn. Route 676, Castleton, Virginia 22716; (703) 937-5234.

WHERE TO DINE

FINE DINING

The Inn at Little Washington, Washington

"When we first opened, we couldn't get any suppliers to come out this far for deliveries—now we can't keep them away," said Chef Patrick O'Connell. He loves to tell this story, and with good reason. He and co-owner Reinhardt Lynch have built their business into one of the most written about, most exclusive, and most expensive country restaurants in the East.

In the beginning, Patrick and Reinhardt relied on local residents to staff the kitchen and serve the guests. Then as now, they worked with farmers in the area to grow the finest produce, cure the tastiest hams, harvest the freshest trout, and bring in the best mushrooms (including a spring harvest of morels). Their demand for perfection has trained a corps of dedicated professionals who have begun to move out and cook at other area inns and restaurants. The excellent staff is now recruited from throughout the United States; having The Inn at Little Washington on one's resume is said to be an almost certain guarantee of landing a job in any of this country's finest kitchens.

With that kind of introduction, you shouldn't be surprised to learn that a meal here is simply amazing. The food-critic elite have all eaten here, and each one has rhapsodized over the experience much more eloquently than we ever could. But we can at least give you an idea of what to expect. How about starting with lobster gazpacho, a salad of goose foie gras with lobster and green beans in a tarragon vinaigrette, or homemade boudin blanc? You might continue with an extravagant filet of beef with oyster cream and oysters wrapped in bacon; a loin of baby lamb with black-eyed peas, wilted greens, and garlic mayonnaise; the finest soft-shell crabs from Smith Island, delicately browned in beer batter; grilled duck breast with red currants and wild rice; or veal with Calvados, apples, and cider from Sharps' Mountain Green Farm just down the road. Suffice it to say that no matter which extraordinary entrée you choose, you'll find it beautifully prepared and exquisitely presented.

The desserts are extravagant. In early spring the rhubarb mousse is special, but we wouldn't feel right if we didn't also recommend the strawberry dessert and the unusual grapefruit pecan chocolate tart.

Open for dinner, Monday and Wednesday through Friday, 6 to 9:30 P.M.; Saturday, seatings 5:30, 6, 9, 9:30 P.M. for people not staying at the Inn. House guests may be seated at any time. Sunday, 4 to 9:30 P.M.. Prix fixe for appetizer, entrée, ice or salad, dessert, and coffee is $68 per person ($88 on Saturday night). Washington, VA 22747; (703) 675-3800.

L'Auberge Provençale, White Post

We arrived at L'Auberge Provençale in the late afternoon and found preparations well underway for the evening meal. Owner/chef Alain Borel (the fourth generation of a fine French restaurant family to don the toque) was at the stove and, as usual, juggling three tasks at once: finishing wild rice to stuff the quail he was boning, preparing the stock for a duck consomme, and taking reservations for the evening meal. Nearby, the pastry chef arranged blueberries and fresh apricot halves in crème Anglaise and prepared fresh raspberry sorbet in a remarkable Swiss ice cream machine. An assistant was out in the garden, cutting herbs and harvesting tiny haricots verts.

While Alain is working magic in the kitchen, his wife, Celeste (who until the birth of their young son worked as pastry chef), greets patrons, offers suggestions, assists in the selection of an appropriate wine, and acts as all-round major-domo.

Everyone looked so busy that we decided the healthiest thing to do was to leave the kitchen and sip our complimentary drink (we each had a glass of Naked Mountain Chardonnay) while we discussed which of three dining rooms to choose for our meal later in the evening. Alas, even that task proved more difficult than we anticipated, as they all are lovely. Original Picasso, Matisse, and Dufy prints and drawings hang in the Blue Room. In the Green Room, a large Bernard Buffet painting and an attractive assortment of antique copper pots and cooking utensils from Alain's great-grandmother's restaurant create a unique ambience. In the bright, airy Peach Room, a 1½-story bank of windows offer a wonderful vantage point for viewing the countryside. Each is decorated with coordinating handblocked fabrics purchased from the south of France and made into draperies, tablecloths, and napkins. We finally decided it doesn't matter where you sit, as long as you get the chance to savor the wonderful food here.

Throughout the menu, which changes with the seasons, extensive and creative use is made of fourteen different herbs from the garden. Celeste will be delighted to tell you what was picked fresh from the garden that day. *Boeuf* fans should try the filet mignon with sweet Vidalia onions, sage, and red pepper strips. Lobster lovers, especially those who don't like the challenge of dismantling the whole crustacean, will appreciate the delicate medallions of lobster with crab mousseline and fresh rosemary sauce. We found one advantage to ordering the tiny, boned quail with cherries and tarragon is that you will have room for one of the luscious desserts, now prepared by an alumna of The Inn at Little Washington. During the warmer months, you might try the puff pastry with fresh citrus sorbets served with strawberry coulis and fresh berries. In cooler weather, the extra calories consumed from the white chocolate mousse cake with dark chocolate glaze are worth every mouthful.

Dinner, Wednesday through Saturday, 6 to 10:30 P.M.; Sunday, 4 to 9 P.M.; closed January through mid-February. Appetizers, $6.75–$13; entrées, $19.50–$26.50; desserts, $6.50–$7.50. Located on Route 340, just south of the intersection of Route 50. Box 119, White Post, VA 22663; (703) 837-1375.

The Ashby Inn, Paris

John and Roma Sherman have successfully re-created the atmosphere of a relaxed yet refined English country inn and pub in Virginia Hunt Country. Loved by its local patrons, the inn radiates the feeling that once you walk through the door, you've been welcomed as part of an extended family.

In warmer weather, we suggest sitting out back on the patio, which overlooks the perennial gardens framed by fields of grazing cattle and the foothills of the Blue Ridge Mountains. In cooler weather, stay in the tap room by the fire with a pint of ale or a glass of wine and try your hand at darts. Of the three intimate dining rooms, our favorite is the one with painted wooden booths.

On our visit, we stopped to chat with the chef while he cut sage from the herb garden for a Marsala sauce, to be served that evening over sautéed fresh calf's liver. As we spoke, a truck arrived packed with fresh crabs and bluefish from the Lower Eastern Shore. The menu was immediately changed to include both crabcakes and bluefish. (If you think bluefish is mundane, try having it broiled with

There is an English pub at the Ashby Inn, located in Paris, Virginia (population 60).

roasted red peppers, olives, sun-dried tomatoes, and fresh basil—
wonderful!)

Mushroom lovers must try the succulent sautéed shiitake, pleu-
rotte, and button mushrooms with prosciutto, garlic, and cream
served on a garlic flan. We also recommend the yellowfin tuna
smoked at the inn, thinly sliced and served with marinated cucumbers and a watercress-horseradish mayonnaise. For a main course,
if you are a fan of the Chesapeake Bay blue crab and it's in season,
order the jumbo lump crabcakes—no filler here, just the real crabmeat broiled in sweet butter.

You'll find John and Roma take their wines seriously, traveling
personally to the California vineyards to select the wines that will
ultimately appear on their reasonably priced wine list. Virginia
wines, including local Naked Mountain Chardonnay, are also available. For a special occasion, the Champagne list is exceptional.

Dinner, Wednesday through Saturday, 6 to 9 P.M.; Sunday
brunch, 12 to 2:30 P.M.. Appetizers, $3.25–$6.95; entrées,
$13.95–$22.95. Sunday brunch, $17.50. Paris, VA 22130; (703)
592-3900.

Four and Twenty Blackbirds, Flint Hill

Heidi Morf was the pastry chef at The Inn at little Washington
before opening a small bed-and-breakfast inn with her husband,
Vincent Deluise. They served dinners to a maximum of twelve
guests in the inn's dining and living room. Realizing that they
enjoyed the cooking more than the innkeeping, they recently
opened their own restaurant in the center of one of those small
crossroads towns where if you blink you might drive right
through.

On the first floor there are about half a dozen tables and three
booths. The windows have lacy café curtains and the walls are
decorated with Audubon elephant folio prints. The intimate room
downstairs has low ceilings, stone walls, and a small service bar.
We claimed the last portion of the day's special soup, chilled gazpacho decorated with small mounds of red and yellow peppers,
cucumbers, shrimp and crabmeat, corn kernels, and pieces of olive-

oil-soaked bread. A second appetizer of fettuccine carbonara with fresh rosemary was tantalizingly good.

A salad of tender greens with chilled slices of Lutz beets comes with dinner. Entrée choices included eggplant carriage wheels, which were slices of eggplant filled with a ricotta mixture, rolled, sliced and served with linguine. Other choices were grilled shrimp with sun-dried-tomato aioli, steak au poivre with Maytag Bleu cheese and local shiitake mushrooms, grilled chicken with Oriental plum sauce and toasted walnuts, and broiled salmon with creamy tomato-basil sauce served with roasted potatoes and vegetables. The menu changes every three weeks. But what we hope won't change are the spicy, homemade, chewy breadsticks.

Desserts the night we dined included ricotta cheese tart with raspberry caramel and local berries, plum upside-down cake, and frozen chocolate mousse with mint crème Anglaise.

If you can't come for dinner, plan your meanderings through the beautiful countryside to include a lunch stop. Sandwiches and salads include a smoked turkey sandwich with sweet and sour cabbage, poached salmon salad, creamy tomato basil soup, and a club sandwich with pesto mayonnaise.

Open Wednesday through Saturday. Lunch, 11:30 A.M. to 2 P.M. $4.50–$6.25. Dinner, 5:30 to 9 P.M. Entrées, $10.95–$16.95. Sunday brunch, 10 A.M. to 2 P.M. Flint Hill, Virginia 22627; (703) 675-1111.

Oliver's, Front Royal

Richard and Lynn Mahan, who formerly cooked gourmet low-cost dinners at the Village Café in Washington, Virginia, have renovated a Victorian house restaurant in Front Royal. It opened in July 1990. Both Richard and Lynn are chefs with experience cooking at The Inn at Little Washington and L'Auberge Provençale. Their maitre d' also came from The Inn at Little Washington.

The main dining room is octagonal, with gray carpeting and matching tablecloths. Other dining rooms have peach- or cassis-colored walls, and a fourth has a long banquette. Richard calls his cooking style new American with ethnic touches, particularly from Southeast Asia or the Mediterranean. His aim is to cook the dish using the correct principles but to modernize it and add his own creative touches. The menu changes seasonally.

For an appetizer, start with Oriental spring rolls, lobster and pork pot stickers (fried wontons), mussels served with red pepper butter, strata of smoked salmon layered with spinach and caper lemon butter, or marinated and grilled beef and pork skewers served with tomato salsa.

The house salad, included with the dinners, is served with a raspberry or blueberry vinaigrette and a local goat cheese. Entrées include American bouillabaisse of scallops, shrimp, catfish, and lobster in tomato saffron broth with aioli; steamed crab and salmon packets flavored with mint and melon served with mustard shallot sauce; grilled swordfish with rosemary tomato cream; veal scallopine with shiitake, pleurottes, and wild mushroom port sauce.

Lynn used to make the desserts at L'Auberge Provençale (see page 432), so you can imagine the treat you'll get here. Try the dark-chocolate mousse cake with praline and chocolate caramel sauce, frozen white-chocolate hazelnut parfait with raspberry sauce, old-fashioned blueberry crisp with pecans and cinnamon crème Anglaise, or a crème brulée with raspberries.

Open for dinner, Wednesday through Sunday from 6 P.M. Entrées, $13.95–$16.95. 108 South Royal Avenue, Front Royal, Virginia; (703) 635-3496.

Jordan's, Leesburg

Across the street and around the corner from the courthouse, in a Victorian brick building with flower boxes out front, is one of the finer restaurants in the area. As you enter the restaurant, which may remind you of a French bistro, you will be greeted by owner Peggy Jordan. Smoking is permitted only on the first floor at the marble-topped bar. "This is an eating bar where people who want a couple of appetizers or singles come. If you're by yourself, it's ever so much nicer to be able to talk with the bartender than to read a book," chef Kim Jordan told us.

On the second floor there are two dining rooms, one seating about twenty-five and the other forty. For an appetizer we started

with cold seafood salad—shrimp, lobster, scallops, and calamari—
that tasted very similar to one we had in a first-rate trattoria on
fashionable Via Montenapoleone in Milan. The crabmeat and corn
soup was thick with sweet crabmeat. Our entrées nicely demonstrated the depth and variety of chef Kim Jordan's experience. The
West Indian chicken curry was filled with tender chunks of meat
and suffused with an authentically spicy flavor. The delectable calf's
liver with shallots and balsamic vinegar is prepared by deglazing the
pan with the vinegar, reducing the liquid, and adding brown sugar
and softened butter.

As for dessert, Kim likes to work with chocolate—so be sure to
try the evening's special concoction. Our night was topped off with
a dense chocolate mousse full of hazelnuts, covered with whipped
cream, lady fingers, and shaved chocolate. If you've no room for
such decadent delights you still won't go dessert-less, as each guest
is served a butter cookie and a delicate chocolate truffle at meal's
end.

Dinner, Monday through Saturday, 6 to 9:30 P.M. Entrées,
$13.25–$19. 2 West Market Street, Leesburg, VA 22075; (703)
777-1471.

Tuscarora Mill, Leesburg

Upon walking into this restored 1899 grain mill and seeing the
grain bins, old belts, and pulleys hanging from the fifteen-foot
ceiling (not to mention the Fairbanks grain scale, which still works),
you might think we've erred and sent you to one of those chain
establishments where decor is 90% of your tab. Rest assured, it
simply ain't so.

Oenophiles drive from D.C. just to sample the large selection of
reasonably priced wines—about a dozen are available each evening
by the glass, and that has an appeal all its own. But having lunched
here recently, we know the attraction goes beyond the wine.

For example, we thoroughly enjoyed a large portion of grilled,
marinated chicken kebob with peanut sauce. The chicken was moist

and the sauce sweet, with just a hint of spice. The salads are large and artfully arranged, and the chili is thick and spicy. Chilled California gazpacho proved an excellent choice for a hot summer day. Our meal was a delicious bargain, and offered a chance to explore the menu—which does get quite a bit more expensive in the evening. If lunch is any indication (and we don't know why it wouldn't be), this restaurant seems to be a fine choice for dinner if you're in the area.

Note: Leesburg is the county seat, and the cadre of local legal folk can crowd the rooms during the week. To be safe, reserve a table when you decide to go.

Lunch, Monday through Saturday, 11:30 A.M. to 2:30 P.M.; $5–$9. Dinner, 5:30 to 9:30 P.M. (to 10 P.M. on Friday and Saturday); Sunday, 12 to 8 P.M. Entrées, $14–$19.50. Located in the restored Market Station shopping complex. 203 Harrison Street S. E., Leesburg, VA 22075; (703) 771–9300.

The Red Fox Inn, Middleburg

"The Fox" is placed squarely in the middle of the beaten path, and has been well promoted in most guidebooks. But while it attracts its share of tourists, the two downstairs dining rooms with their heavy dark beams, flickering candles, pewter and copper plates, and hunt prints on the walls are the epitome of what we imagine a hunt country tavern should be.

The menu is wide-ranging and changes with the seasons. In early spring the shad is excellent. In cooler weather, we have lunched on a green salad and black bean and sausage soup made with fresh herbs—an attractive and delicious presentation.

Note: The restaurant has seven dining rooms; when you dine here be sure to reserve a table in one of the two downstairs rooms, as they have the cozy atmosphere we appreciate so much. If you visit in winter, you'll find a welcome fire roaring in the Pub Room.

Open daily. Breakfast, 8 to 10:30 A.M. Lunch, 11 A.M. to 3 P.M.; $4.95–$6.95. Dinner, 5 to 9:30 P.M. (to 8 P.M. on Sunday). Entrées,

$14–$21. 2 East Washington Street, Box 385, Middleburg, VA 22117; (703) 687-6301 or (800) 223-1728.

INFORMAL DINING

Coach Stop, Middleburg

This is the locals' place. The horse enthusiasts stop by for breakfast after their early morning workouts, after the hunts or point-to-point races. Coach Stop has been a fixture in Middleburg for years. The atmosphere is rather like a high-class diner, but you can get anything from a hamburger to a lobster, and everything is nicely prepared with fresh ingredients. The quality of the food notwithstanding, this is *the* spot if you are a people-watcher. As owner Mike Tate said, "It's like coming to a party every day."

We like to come in for a rare burger and an order of onion rings (these are made fresh, not prepackaged). When asked what were the best things on the menu, Mike agreed on the onion rings and also suggested the crabcakes and liver.

Open Monday through Saturday, 7 A.M. to 9 P.M.; Sunday, 8 A.M. to 9 P.M. Lunch, $3.95–$14.50. Dinner entrées, $8–$18.95. *Note:* Selected items from the lunch menu are available at dinner. 9 East Washington Street, Middleburg, VA 22117; (703) 687-5515.

Boyce's Station, Boyce

This authentic railroad station was built by the Norfolk & Western in 1913 and it is now a reasonably priced, family restaurant.

That this rather large building is in a rather small village on the edge of the Blue Ridge Mountains gives you an accurate idea of how important the railroad was in the early twentieth century. Today, the outside of the building is a bit shabby, and although a sign states it is undergoing restoration, the inside is much the same as it was when constructed. The walls are paneled with long-leaf,

Georgia yellow pine, and memorabilia abounds: old photos, timetables, china from the dining cars, the telegrapher's desk. This is still an operating freight line, so railroad buffs may be treated to a train rumbling past as they dine.

The small menu features large portions of basic American fare. We sampled the fresh, deboned Virginia trout and enjoyed two thick slices of properly salty Smithfield ham served with sweet potatoes. Children's portions are half-price. Pies and bread pudding round out the dessert menu.

Open Tuesday through Saturday. Lunch, 11:30 A.M. to 2 P.M., $4.50–$7. Dinner, 5:30 to 9:30 P.M. Entrées, $7.75–$9.65. Sunday breakfast, 8:30 A.M. to 1:30 P.M. 117 East Main Street, Boyce, VA 22620; (703) 837-1500.

Mosby's Tavern, Middleburg

This is a large and attractive spot for lunch if you are shopping and touring in Middleburg. Up front, there's a long bar with beer and ale on tap, two televisions, ceiling fans, hanging baskets filled with healthy plants, tile and old pine floors, wooden tables, and stenciled ceilings. In the rear, there's a more intimate dining room with large, colorful contemporary sporting scenes of the horse set by Frank Ashly.

The menu leans toward a variety of burgers and Tex-Mex entrées. We suggest the chicken fajitas served with two kinds of cheese, picante sauce, guacamole, tomatoes, and lettuce. Tuesday through Thursday from 5 to 9 P.M. there are specials. On Tuesday, all burgers are half price; on Wednesdays, the New York strip steak is $7.95; on the last Wednesday of the month, everything on the menu is half price; and on Thursday, all Tex-Mex entrées are $5.95. A young, somewhat noisy crowd fills Mosby's in the evenings.

Open daily for lunch and dinner (brunch on Saturday and Sunday), 11 A.M. to 10 P.M. (to 9 P.M. on Sunday). Lunch entrées, $4–$9; dinner entrées, $7.95–$12.95. 2 West Marshall Street, Middleburg, VA 22117; (703) 687-5282.

RECIPE

A Hunt Breakfast: Venison Stew

After a few hours of riding to the hounds in the late fall or winter, hearty appetites welcome the traditional hunt breakfast. The term "breakfast" bears no relation to the time of day the meal is served—it may be noon or mid-afternoon, whenever the hunt is over. Members of the hunt take turns hosting these festive meals. Roma Sherman served this version of a hearty venison stew at her inn, The Ashby Inn, after an invigorating morning riding to the hounds. (*Note:* Beef can be substituted for venison.)

Marinade:

2 cups red wine
3 or 4 garlic cloves, crushed
1 or 2 bay leaves
1 onion, chopped
1 or 2 tablespoons chopped
　　fresh parsley

3 pounds boneless
　　venison, cut into 1½
　　inch cubes

flour, for dredging meat
salt and pepper, to taste
4 tablespoons oil, for
　　sautéing meat

2 or 3 bay leaves
1 onion, chopped
2 or 3 tomatoes, peeled, seeded,
　　chopped
½ teaspoon thyme
1–2 cups wine or beef broth

1 pound button
　　mushrooms
2 or 3 tablespoons butter

18 pearl onions, peeled
2 tablespoons oil
1 bay leaf
¼ teaspoon thyme
1 cup red wine

Mix the marinade ingredients together in a large bowl and marinate the venison overnight in the refrigerator.

Dry the venison between paper towels. Flour and season the venison with salt and pepper. Brown in oil. Add bay leaves, chopped onion, tomatoes, and thyme. Cover with wine or beef broth. Bring to a simmer on the stove, then bake in a casserole dish at 350°F for 1½ hours.

While the meat is cooking, sauté mushrooms in butter and set aside.

In another pan, brown pearl onions in oil with bay leaf and ¼ teaspoon thyme. After onions are browned, add 1 cup of wine and simmer until tender.

Just before serving, add the mushrooms and the onions to the casserole. Serve with noodles or with boiled potatoes.

YIELD: 8 servings

ITINERARY

As you drive in the area, notice the miles and miles of fencing and stone walls—several of the largest farms employ crews of stone-wall builders to maintain them. Start on Route 50 west of Middleburg; using this as your beginning and ending point.

DAY ONE. Start the morning getting a feel for the beauty of hunt country by touring the territories of the Orange and Piedmont hunts, two of the area's most prestigious. (It is with these hunts that famous folk such as Jackie Onassis ride.) Go south on Route 623, known to the locals as Mellon Road. You will pass Herron-wood, the estate of Charles Smith (the developer of Washington's Crystal City), and Rokeby, Paul Mellon's estate, whose famous stables are open at the end of May. On the left side of Route 623 is Mellon's private air strip. Turn left on Route 710, then left again on Route 713. This is known as Atoka Road. Senator John Warner, ex-husband of Elizabeth Taylor, has his residence here.

Now turn right at Route 50, take your next right on Route 709, turn left on Route 55 and left again on Route 626. As you head north on Route 626, take a right turn on Route 628 to **Meredyth Vineyards**. Return to Route 626 and continue to **Piedmont Vineyards**. Our suggestion is to visit just one of these vineyards today. If your stomach is rumbling, go into Middleburg and pick up a picnic at **The Black Walnut** or **Upper Crust**, which you can enjoy at

Meredyth Vineyards. Or, continue north on Route 626 to Middleburg where you can lunch at **Mosby's Tavern, The Red Fox Inn**, or the **Coach Stop**.

Following lunch, pick up your tour at Route 734, just west of Aldie. Turn left onto 734. To get to **Lowelands Farm**, turn right at Route 733 and left onto Route 763 for 4/10 mile. Retrace your route to 734, where you will make a right turn. Follow Route 734 for about nine miles to Bluemont. Stop in at the Snickerville General Store (you can't miss the potbellied stove on the front porch) to buy homemade donuts, ice cream, a sandwich, or just to look around. Continue on Route 734 to Route 7. Cross the Shenandoah River; make an immediate right on Route 603, which you will follow for about a mile to get to the **Holy Cross Abbey**.

After crossing the Shenandoah River, turn right onto Route 601. This road passes the entrance to the "underground city" where the President of the United States and top government officials would be taken in the event of a national emergency. Turn right on Route 50, then right again on Route 255 to Millwood, where you can tour the restored mill. Return to Route 50; if you'd like to visit the **University of Virginia Arboretum**, turn right on Route 50 and then left at the Arboretum. For dinner you might make reservations at **The Ashby Inn** or **L'Auberge Provençale**, check out the fare at the less expensive **Boyce's Station**, or head back to your inn.

DAY TWO. This drive will take you to the northeastern part of Virginia Hunt Country. From Route 50, east of Aldie, turn north on Route 15. About seven miles up the road on your right is **Oatlands**. From here continue to Leesburg, where you may want to walk around and perhaps have lunch—our suggestion is **Tuscarora Mill**. Then take Route 7 west from Leesburg to **Morven Park** for a tour of the mansion, **Museum of Hounds and Hunting**, and the carriage barn. If you are getting a bit tired, take a slight detour to Route 9, then to Route 662, which will bring you to the relaxing, historic hamlet of **Waterford**. An alternative for this afternoon is to take Route 15 from Leesburg to **White's Ferry** on the Potomac for a ferry ride, picnic, and hike. Head back to Leesburg for a very elegant dinner at **Jordan's**.

DAY THREE. Head south and west to the famous Skyline Drive. From Route 50, just east of Paris, go south on Route 17. On your

right is **Sky Meadows State Park**. On your left is Route 710, a
dirt road down which Willard Scott, the famous TV weatherman,
lives. Turn right onto Route 688. Stop in at **Naked Mountain
Vineyard** for a tour and a taste. Then continue south on Route
688. Just before you get to the Markham interchange of I-66, you
will see signs for Hartland Orchards, a pleasant spot to pick cherries, peaches, apples, or pumpkins. If you want to continue on a
winery tour you can make detours to **Oasis** or **Linden vineyards**. Otherwise, continue on Route 688; turn right on Route 647,
then left on Route 522 to Route 211. The turn-off to **Washington**
is here. Have lunch at **Four and Twenty Blackbirds** in Flint Hill.
Continue on Route 211 to **Sperryville**. From Sperryville you can
continue on Route 211 to the **Skyline Drive**; at this point, it is
thirty-one miles north to the Front Royal entrance. **Luray Caverns** can be reached by staying on Route 211. If you're feeling
affluent, plan to have dinner at the tony **Inn at Little Washington**.

Getting to the Area

To reach Middleburg from Washington take Route 66 West to
the Winchester Route 50 exit near Fair Oaks Mall. Continue on 50
west for 26 miles passing through Aldie into Middleburg.

To reach Little Washington, Virginia and Sperryville from Washington D.C. take Route 495 to Route 66 west, then exit on 29 south
to Warrenton, where you turn west on Route 211 and continue to
Washington and Sperryville.

BUDGETING YOUR TRIP

To help you get the most for your money, here are some travel
suggestions at three budget levels (cost per day at peak season
with two people sharing a room, including tax, 15% gratuity at

meals, and service charges). Prices are approximate and intended for planning purposes only. Lodgings are categorized by price. Meal prices at lunch include an average entrée and beverage. Dinner prices include an appetizer, entrée, beverage, and dessert. Wine or alcoholic drinks are not included. Admission prices vary widely based on activities.

Staying and Dining at Expensive Lodgings and Restaurants: From $270 to $625 per day for two.

Lodging: Inn at Little Washington, $218–$428; Conyers House, $167–$209; Little River Inn, $140–$220; Red Fox Inn, $234.

Dining: Breakfast: included. Lunch: $20 at Tuscarora Mill or Red Fox Inn. Dinner: Inn at Little Washington, $170; L'Auberge Provençale, $100.

Admissions: Oatlands, $10; Morven Hall, $8; Shenandoah Park, $5.

Staying and Dining at Moderately Priced Lodgings and Restaurants: From $160 to $240 per day for two.

Lodging: Red Fox Inn, $130–$151; Ashby Inn, $94; L'Auberge Provençale, $125–$183; Norris House, $120; Big Meadows, $146; Hunting Box, $125; Conyers House $105–$157; Ashby Inn, $94–$120; Blue Knoll, $99–$120.

Dining: Breakfast: included except at Big Meadows. Lunch: about $15 at Mosby's Tavern, Coach Stop, Boyce's Station. Dinner: about $70 at Ashby Inn, Jordan's Tuscarora Mill, Four and Twenty Blackbirds, Olivers.

Admissions: Oatlands, $10; Morven Hall, $8; Shenandoah Park, $5.

Staying and Dining at Less Expensive Lodgings and Restaurants: From $125 to $180 per day for two.

Lodging: Ashby Inn, $84; Little River Inn, $78–$89; Norris House, $57–$99, Big Meadows, $47.

Dining: Breakfast: included. Lunch: about $10 at the Village Café, take-out at Black Walnut, Upper Crust. Dinner: about $35–$40 at Boyce's Station, Mosby's Tavern, Coach Stop.

Admissions: Oatlands, $10; Morven Hall, $8; Shenandoah Park, $5.

SUGGESTED READING

Riding to Hounds in America. William Wadsworth. The Chronicle of the Horse, Inc. Mailing address: Box 46, Middleburg, VA 22117. 301 West Washington Street, Middleburg. (703) 687-6341. $2.50. William Wadsworth, a master of the foxhounds, presents the basics of fox hunting in an easy-to-understand format. We suggest reading this before you go, or purchase a copy at Chronicle of the Horse when you arrive.

Virginia Wine Country. Hilde G. Lee and Allan E. Lee. White Hall, Virginia: Betterway Publications, 1987. $11.95. This book explores the history of the Virginia wine industry, followed by chapters on the different regions in Virginia. The history of each vineyard, hours of operation, and recipes using the wines are included in each chapter. If you are doing a tour of the vineyards this book is particularly recommended.

Virginia, A History and Guide. Tim Mulligan. New York: Random House, 1986. $9.95. The strength of this guide is the historical background and the personal and very readable style in which the author describes the things to do in each area of Virginia. The Places to Stay and Eat section, however, is of limited value.

Virginia: Off the Beaten Path. Judy and Ed Colbert. Chester, Connecticut: Globe Pequot Press, 1988. $8.95. This guide is especially useful for learning about out-of-the way places or little known facts about the popular tourist destinations. The book is organized by region and county. There are a number of books in the "Off the Beaten Path" series; we feel this is one of the best.

TEN

ROMANTIC HIDEAWAYS OF THE MIDDLE ATLANTIC STATES

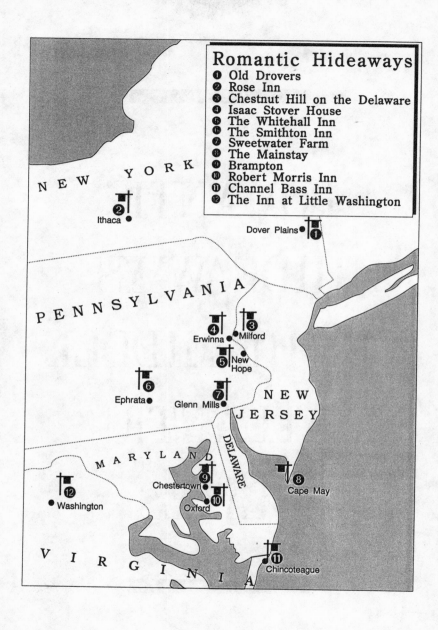

Close your eyes and imagine your ideal romantic hideaway. To some, this means a small inn, warm and cozy with a working fireplace, crisp linens, plush pillows, and a canopy bed. To others, it is formal elegance with expansive rooms, a panoramic view of the mountains, and a formal dinner. Others see a quiet porch with rocking chairs and a red sunset over the water; still others relish sleeping late, luxuriating in a Jacuzzi, and enjoying a gourmet breakfast served in front of the fireplace. Still others look for a remote location, preferring more primitive facilities and the undeveloped splendor of thick forests and untouched shorelines.

As we begin the last decade of the century, many travelers are deciding that less is better than more. The prominence of the "grand hotel" has been discarded by travelers who have discovered the joys and unequalled pleasures of the country inn.

Creating a truly great inn is a continuing process. It's not just a package of amenities, a list of ingredients mixed and spread in certain proportions. There are intangible as well as tangible aspects of an inn that make it a unique experience. At its best, innkeeping is a commitment, an ideal, a striving for perfection, a dream. Many of the "intimate" hostelries described in this chapter are virtual museums of treasured antiques and artifacts—the result of years of passionate collecting.

The pace of life in these bucolic settings becomes an integral part of a truly great getaway; time can almost stand still. Sharing a few days with someone special is time and money well spent. The gift of time, of love, of caring is one of the most meaningful gifts

Close your eyes and imagine your ideal romantic hideaway.

you can give. An experience that you and your loved one have shared can never be taken away from you.

That is what this chapter is all about: a gift to you of twelve romantic hideaways where you can create lasting memories.

Each of these hideaways is unique in its own way. From fairy-tale homes and charming cottages to restored, elegant farmhouses, all have picture-perfect settings that are sure to nurture the soul.

No matter where you live or when you plan to go, you're sure to find that unique haven, that romantic hideaway right for you. Choose one, or visit all twelve of our romantic choices.

Old Drovers Inn, Dover Plains, New York

Almost 250 years of continuous use has imparted a warm glow of welcome to this historic inn. The dark, low-ceilinged, wood-beamed tap room with its great stone fireplace is one of the coziest and most intimate dining spots we've seen. Four gracious guest rooms beckon travelers to stop and rest. For a romantic getaway, especially in cold weather, this is ideal.

Innkeepers Alice Pitcher and Kemper Peacock have admirably preserved this museum-quality gem. On the first floor there is a quiet, formal library. The mate to the shell cabinet is in the American Wing at the Metropolitan Museum of Art. The front-hall lounge has a wood-burning fireplace across from a down-filled couch and an array of international magazines. While sitting on the couch, notice the antique chest that appears to be level but whose legs have had to be drastically altered to compensate for the sagging floor. The building reminds us of a cultured old aristocratic lady whose slight idiosyncrasies have become part of her charm.

Three of the four guest rooms have working wood-burning fireplaces. The largest and the most sumptuous is the Meeting Room, which has a barrel-shaped ceiling, two double beds, a fireplace, and two wingback chairs. An antique writing desk, bureau, and window seats that were filled with more than a dozen current upscale magazines create a cozy, inviting retreat.

The second-largest room is the Cherry Room, which has much

JANE STAUFFER

Two hundred and fifty years of continuous use have given a warm glow of welcome to Old Drovers House.

larger windows than those in the Meeting Room along with two double beds, lined chintz draperies, a fireplace, and two wingback chairs. The third most romantic room is the Sleigh Room with a double sleigh bed, fireplace, and two easy chairs. We appreciated the thick terrycloth robes as well as the high-quality soap, shampoo, and conditioner in the baths. Be forewarned that all of the baths have tubs only except for the Meeting Room, which has a combination tub and shower. The evening turndown service includes a plate with an apple, chocolate thin mints, chocolate truffles, and an old glass milk bottle filled with cold water.

A thermos of juice and freshly brewed coffee is set out for early-rising guests in the first-floor Federal Room, where breakfast is served starting at 9 A.M. The walls of this room are decorated with murals painted in 1941 of the inn, West Point, and Hyde Park. Start with a glass of freshly squeezed orange or grapefruit juice and homemade breakfast breads. This is followed by a choice of omelets with wild mushrooms or cheddar cheese, French toast ba-guette, Belgian malted waffles, shepherd's eggs on hashed browns, or Southern-style grits. Bacon, sausage patties, and Canadian bacon are also served.

Both lunch and dinner are served to inn guests as well as to the general public under the watchful eyes of Charlie Wilbur (who has been an Old Drovers tradition for the past twenty-five years) in the low-beamed tap room with its massive fireplace that oozes atmosphere. Lighting is supplied mainly by candles set inside etched hurricane lamps. The inn is justly famous for the double-size drinks served in hand-blown Lenox crystal glasses, accompanied by stuffed eggs and hickory-smoked salt, cheddar cheese soup, and browned turkey hash. The blackboard menu is hung on hooks by your table. We started with gravlax attractively formed into a large rose shape and poached sea scallops in a light cream sauce served with crisp potato baskets.

The lamb chops are in a class by themselves. Two double-thick chops trimmed of excess fat were perfectly grilled and served with Charlie's tomato chutney. Other house specialties are breast of Muscovy duck, grilled veal chop, and the traditional browned turkey hash served with mustard sauce.

For dessert we'd stick with the peppermint-stick-candy ice cream, specially made for Old Drovers at a local dairy, or with traditional favorites such as pecan or key lime pie.

Open all year. Four rooms, all with private bath, $110–$170. 15% service charge. A full breakfast is included. Lunch Monday, Thursday, Friday, Saturday, 12 to 3 P.M.; $7.70–$15. Sunday brunch, 12–2 P.M. Dinner Monday and Thursday, 5:30–9 P.M.; Friday, 5:30–9:30 P.M.; Saturday, 3–10 P.M.; Sunday, 2–8:30 P.M. Entrées, $15.50–$26.50. Located off Route 22, about seventy-five miles north of New York City. Old Drovers Inn Road, Dover Plains, NY 12522; (914) 832-9311.

What to Do. The inn is ideally situated for day trips in a number of different directions. In Lenox, Massachusetts, just over an hour to the north, is Tanglewood, where the Boston Symphony Orchestra performs for thousands during July and August. An hour to the west is Hyde Park, home of the Franklin Delano Roosevelt National Historic Site, the grand Italian Renaissance Vanderbilt

Mansion, and the Culinary Institute of America, all with grand views of the Hudson River. Nearby, there are vineyards, antique shops, parks, and scenic roads.

For detailed information about this area, refer to Chapter 1.

How to Get There. From New York City take the Metro North train to the Dover Plains station, where the innkeepers will pick you up. Driving from New York City, take the Saw Mill River Parkway to I-684 to Route 22. The inn is located just off Route 22 between Wingdale and Dover Plains.

Rose Inn, Ithaca, New York

Innkeepers Charles and Sherry Rosemann are consummate professionals. Unlike many other innkeepers, Charles was trained in hotel management schools in Germany and managed five-star hotels in the United States before joining Sherry in running their own inn. Their teamwork, attention to details, and constant striving for perfection is most commendable.

For a romantic getaway, what could be better than a spacious, luxuriously appointed room with a Jacuzzi big enough for two and dinner in a private dining room? Of the three rooms with Jacuzzis at the Rose Inn the ultimate is the bridal suite, which has a double

For a romantic getaway at the Rose Inn, the bridal suite has a Jacuzzi and Palladian windows that overlook the garden.

Jacuzzi surrounded by fan-shaped Palladian windows overlooking the gardens, a stand of white pines, a fifty-year-old apple orchard, and fields of corn beyond. The fireplace is clearly visible from the king-size bed, from the Eames chair, or the love seat.

A ground-floor suite has a living room with French doors leading to a flower garden. The king-size bed is in the same room but gives the impression of greater privacy, as it's on a level four steps higher than the rest of the room. There is also a large bath with a double Jacuzzi and a separate shower. Note the eighteen-inch-tall carved white falcon: the Air Force Academy liked this model of its mascot so much that it commissioned a duplicate.

The third room with a double Jacuzzi has a skylight, king-size bed with an ornate brass headboard, and an old-fashioned, large white porcelain sink. On a slightly smaller scale are twelve additional well-decorated rooms, which are clustered around two sitting areas where the telephones are located. One of the sitting areas has a refrigerator stocked with wines and Champagne. Items out-of-the-ordinary in the rooms include French soap and other toiletries, thick bath sheets, terrycloth robes, adjustable shower heads, and padded satin hangers.

After you're thoroughly relaxed, dress for dinner and descend the Honduran-mahogany circular staircase—the centerpiece of this 1850s Italianate mansion that sits, along with several classic eighteenth-century barns, on twenty acres of photogenic farmland just outside of Ithaca.

If you appreciate fine dining, this is an experience you should not miss. Do a Few Things Perfectly is the motto that Charles and Sherry strictly adhere to as they plan their dinner selections. The policy at this country inn that you select both your appetizer and entrée before arriving for dinner. Diners are seated in the center hall, in the parlor, or in one of two intimate dining rooms. Fine linens, fresh flowers, candles, china, and silver flatware frame your meal.

As a first course, try the sinfully rich, intensely flavored lobster bisque made with chunks of lobster and heavy cream. The artichoke-heart strudel served on puréed tomato is excellent and somewhat lighter than the bisque. A third appetizer, which melts in your mouth, is the smoked oysters in beurre blanc sauce served in a flaky puff-pastry shell. The salad, one of the best we've had, is an artistic presentation that includes Boston lettuce, radicchio, artichoke hearts, hearts of palm, red and yellow peppers, tomatoes, and sprouts.

If you like duck tender with no excess fat, it is always available as a special request. The grilled rack of lamb, veal chops, and fish dishes are cooked outdoors year-round on several charcoal grills. The veal chop is served with a classic Madeira sauce and topped with sliced, sautéed wild mushrooms. The lamb chops are marinated in garlic and herbs. The scampi is sautéed with tomato, curry, and cream, and flambéed with brandy. The harmonious colors of the steamed broccoli, cauliflower, and slivered carrots artfully arranged in a crisp potato basket is the ultimate vegetable dish. The small, thoroughly researched, reasonably priced wine list is designed to complement the entrées. Dessert may be a rich chocolate pot de crème or a cornucopia-shaped pizzelle filled with local raspberries set on crème Anglaise.

The elegant attention to detail continues at breakfast. You may start with a mixture of fresh-squeezed Israeli blood oranges and California Valencias. During the fall season, a glass of apple cider made from the inn's apples is served. The coffee is a mixture of Kona, Colombian, and Amaretto. A fruit dish might include raspberries and blueberries served with crème fraîche and brown sugar. An entrée could be salmon arranged in the shape of a rose, served with bagels and cream cheese or German apple pancakes served with the inn's own apple butter.

Twelve rooms, all with private bath, $100–$150; three suites all with a Jacuzzi for two, $165–$220. A full breakfast is included. Children over 10 welcome. No pets. Two-night minimum stay on weekends. Dinner is served Tuesday through Saturday at 7 P.M.; 24-hour advance reservations required; $50 per person prix fixe. No tipping. Located on Route 34, nine miles north of the city. 813 Auburn Road, Route 34, Box 6576, Ithaca, NY 14851-6576; (607) 533-7905.

What to Do.   The Finger Lakes wineries are well worth visiting. Cornell University is nearby. Take a walk along the gorges in nearby Buttermilk Falls State Park, Taughannock Falls State Park, or Robert Tremain State Park.

How to Get There. From New York City, take I-87 north to I-84 west. When you reach Scranton, take I-81 north to Cortland, Route 13 to Ithaca, and Route 34 north to the inn.

For detailed information about this area, refer to Chapter 2.

Chestnut Hill on the Delaware, Milford, New Jersey

Sitting in the wicker chairs on the Country Cottage's private Victorian porch overlooking the Delaware River, we couldn't help but think that this is the perfect private retreat—a place for rejuvenation or an idyllic honeymoon. The ornate nineteenth-century porch has been painstakingly stripped and painted in eight Victorian colors—shades of green, beige, a touch of cranberry and a thin strip of gold leaf. The living room has a stereo, TV, couch, and easy chairs. A corner stove adds to the country atmosphere. Glass doors open from the living room to the bedroom where a queen-size, four-poster bed has an unobstructed view of the river. The kitchen is stocked with eggs, bread, juice, fruit, and coffee. Innkeeper Linda Castagna brings freshly baked goodies over each day.

Our second favorite hideaway is found next door in the main inn. The entire third floor, the bridal suite, is called Teddy's Place—a private retreat filled with one hundred and forty teddy bears at last count (many sent as presents by former guests). We felt as though we were tucked away as, once we opened a door on the second floor and climbed a steep flight of stairs, a large private space was there for us to enjoy.

Teddy's Place is a two-bedroom suite, the Teddy Bear Room and Hearts and Flowers. The beds are made with crisp, lacy, white cotton designer sheets. There are monogrammed toothbrushes in the private bath. Make sure to read the room diary, replete with passages from honeymoon couples—then add your own. Teddy's Place is also a good choice for families, since there are two bedrooms. Note: Linda never rents the suite to two couples who don't know each other.

The second floor has three stunning rooms. Pineapple is a large room decorated in a yellow pattern with a private bath. The Bayberry Room, decorated in blues and grays, shares a bath with

Peaches and Cream. For budget-minded romantics, the two rooms that share a bath are some of the nicest for the money that we've seen.

Downstairs, the informal parlor has a wood-burning fireplace. In the winter, return from a bracing walk or cross-country skiing on the old Delaware Canal towpath to hot-mulled apple cider or hot chocolate. Curl up with a book by the fire or sit in the High Victorian Eastlake–furnished parlor with a working pump organ, a piano, and a mannequin dressed in formal Victorian attire. In warmer weather, take a cool drink out to the porch and watch the changing reflections on the river.

Breakfasts are special. Sitting in the formal dining room, we enjoyed a leisurely candlelit breakfast of freshly squeezed juice served in crystal Champagne glasses, fresh fruit salad, homemade muffins, and crispy German apple pancakes. Another breakfast favorite is eggs with mushrooms, tomato, garlic, and picante sauce.

You may be interested to know that Rob, Linda's husband, has patiently restored the inn, the Country Cottage, and two additional houses in the small town of Milford. After completing the Victorian porch, and not being one to rest on his achievements, Rob has begun to create a second suite in the Country Cottage.

The Country Cottage, $125; Teddy's Place, $95 for two, $145 for four. Three additional rooms, $75 with shared bath, $85 with private bath. Two-night minimum is requested on the weekends. Breakfast included. 63 Church Street, Milford, NJ 08848; (201) 995-9761.

Where to Dine. *EverMay on the Delaware.* If you are here on a Friday, Saturday, or Sunday night, reserve a table for an elegant, prix-fixe, seven-course dinner at EverMay on the Delaware. A set, superbly presented meal, with a choice of entrée, is served each evening. For romance, this restaurant is our first choice. EverMay is on Route 32 in Erwinna, PA, about a fifteen-minute drive from Milford; (215) 294-9100.

The Frenchtown Inn. Imaginatively prepared gourmet French food is served here Tuesday through Sunday for dinner and Wednesday through Friday and Sunday for lunch. It's located three miles south of Milford; (201) 996-3300.

What to Do. The towpath along the Delaware Canal is sixty miles long; you may enjoy hiking or bicycling on it. In the summer, you can rent tubes for a leisurely float down the river. For shoppers, there are countless high-quality outlets (Royal Doulton, Calvin Klein, Anne Klein, Harvé Bernard) in Flemington, just about twenty minutes away. New Hope and Lambertville, two enticing towns, are thirty minutes to the south. Antiquing, shopping, museums, or backroading are other options.

How to Get There. Milford, New Jersey, is approximately 1½ hours from both New York City and Philadelphia. From New York, take I-78 to Clinton, Route 513 south to Frenchtown, Route 29 north to Milford.

From Philadelphia, take I-95 to the exit after Yardley on the New Jersey side of the river. Take Route 29 north to Milford.

For detailed information about this area, refer to Chapter 4.

Isaac Stover House, Erwinna, Pennsylvania

What happens when a successful television talk-show host decides to buy a historic French Second Empire brick house, spares no expense to decorate it in nineteenth-century High Victorian elegance using the finest French hand-printed wall coverings, faux marbling, glass etching, exquisite draperies, and fills it with a superb collection of Victorian-era antiques, art, and artifacts collected on trips throughout the world? You have an expensive, eclectically romantic hideaway strategically situated in the pristine, unspoiled part of Bucks County, Pennsylvania, with excellent vistas of the Delaware River and the surrounding countryside.

You might be greeted with a "hello, hello" from Lord Rum Bottom, the large green resident parrot, or more likely from innkeeper Sue Tettemer, who enthusiastically operates the inn for owner Sally Jessy Raphael. The guest parlor is elegantly furnished in Renaissance Revival furnishings. The swag of the lacy window treatment and the wide band of wallpaper that encircles the top of the room echoes the cresting section of the maroon sofa. A pair of crystal chandeliers (one in the living room and another in the breakfast room) reflects in the mirror over the couch. Crystal table lamps are on the end tables, and the floor is covered with Oriental carpets. The walls are adorned with items that Sally has brought back from her travels: Balinese puppets, heavy gold-embroidered wall hangings from Burma, and baskets from Nepal.

A greenhouse room, where the parrot's cage is located, is a more informal lounge where wine and juice are set out in the late afternoon. A filled cookie jar and a bowl of fresh fruit are always available for snacking.

The six guest rooms are filled with decorative and often whimsical objects. The two-room bridal suite is the most expensive accommodation. The bedroom has a good view of the Delaware River. The white iron double bed faces the fireplace, and is covered with a down duvet and lots of lacy pillows. A photograph of the stars of "The Honeymooners" is prominently displayed, showing Jackie Gleason in one of his classic poses. In this room there is a wicker settee covered with miniature pillows made from old quilts, an antique crib filled with stuffed animals, and a collection of thirty Norman Rockwell plates on the walls. In the sitting room is a television, bamboo chairs, and a convertible sofa.

The sign in the Emerald City Room proclaims, "Gee, Toto, I don't think we're in Kansas anymore." This room transports its guests to the world of Oz. The Tin Soldier and the Scarecrow welcomed us from the mantel of the fireplace. Bits and pieces of Oz memorabilia are on the shelves of the dresser. The wallpaper is emerald green with a gold design. The only thing missing is the yellow brick road; instead, this room has a plush beige carpet. There is also a cradle filled with stuffed animals, which sits at the foot of the double bed. A life-size panda sprawls in the corner. A stumpf fiddle is next to the fireplace. The windows look out over the back of the house and the fields, where Sally's private residence is located. This room has a large, private hall bath.

History buffs may want to stay in the third room on the second floor, the Loyalist Royal. Decorations include a framed certificate from the Daughters of the American Revolution, a chart of the kings and queens of England, and a book entitled *George Washington's Expense Account* on the dresser. The double bed faces the fireplace, and a sofa is in one corner. Two windows in the bedroom and a third in the adjoining private bath face the river.

On the third floor, the Amore and Cupid's Bower rooms each have a very small private bath, while Secret Garden shares the spacious hall bath with Shakespeare and Company. Amore has a Victorian carved-walnut bed and shirred rose-colored curtains surrounding the edge of the ceiling. We liked this room's view of the sun reflecting on the rapids. Cupid's Bower has lavender plush carpeting and a matching set of a flower-decorated dresser, double bed, and two end tables. Framed photographs of Sally Jessy Raphael and her family are found throughout the inn.

Breakfast is served by the fireplace. It includes juice, fresh fruit, granola, home-baked breads and muffins, and a Stover House egg specialty such as the potato-cheese frittata served on the day we were there.

Four rooms with private bath, $175; 2 rooms with shared bath, $150, one bridal suite, $250. A full breakfast and afternoon refreshments are included. Children over 12 welcome, $15 additional. No pets. Two-night minimum stay on the weekends. The inn is located on Route 32, thirteen miles north of New Hope. Box 68, Erwinna, PA 18920; (215) 294-8044.

Where to Dine. Without question, the best restaurant in the area is EverMay, located on the adjacent property. If you should come during the week, try the Frenchtown Inn for elegant dining, or the Race Street Café in Frenchtown or the Mill Ford Oyster House in Milford for less formal fare (EverMay is open weekends only).

What to Do. The towpath along the Delaware River is perfect for hiking. In the summer you can rent tubes for a leisurely float down the river. Drive through the woods and farmland of Bucks County, head to New Hope for craft stores and antiques, or go to Flemington to shop at discount outlets.

How to Get There. From New York City, take I-78 west to Clinton. Go south on Route 513 to Frenchtown, cross the bridge and go south on Route 32 two miles to Erwinna. From Philadelphia, take I-95 to the Yardley exit. Follow Taylorsville Road to Route 32 north.

For detailed information about this area, refer to Chapter 4.

The Whitehall Inn, New Hope, Pennsylvania

The grandfather clock chimed nine. The two white-linen-covered tables were set with stemmed glasses, Villeroy and Boch (flower-pattern) china, and ornate Victorian sterling flatware.

Lighted tapers were on the table; side buffets were adorned with lighted candles of varying heights and pots of bright red poinsettias. Sunlight sparkled through the seventy-seven panes of the large window overlooking the Bucks County countryside. What followed was an extraordinary 1½-hour breakfast.

Beverage Course

Whitehall's Special Blend of Coffee
Selection of thirty English and Herbal teas
Freshly Squeezed Tangelo Juice

Bread Course

Cinnamon Streusel Coffee Cake
Raised Buckwheat Biscuits served with Raspberry Jam and Butter

Fruit Course

Individual Phyllo Shell filled with Kiwi, Strawberries, Pineapple, and Oranges over a Ricotta-Honey Sauce

Soup Course

Warm Granny Smith Apple Bisque

Main Course

Individual Holiday Breakfast Tart with Swiss Cheese, accented with Red and Green Peppers
Bucks County Sausage

An Appropriate Ending

Chocolate Peanut Butter Cremes

Go ahead, indulge yourself—you only live once! We savored this breakfast on a recent cold January morning. Innkeepers Mike and Suella Wass beautifully orchestrate the meal: Suella happily bakes, sautés, and souffés in the kitchen while Mike elegantly serves and chats with the guests. Each morning the menu is different. In fact, the Wasses keep your menu on file so that you'll never get a repeat (unless you make a special request).

When you return to the inn at 4 P.M., the aromas of Suella's baking and the smell of freshly brewed tea make you forget that you resolved not to eat another thing all day. Sitting by the fire on a recent visit, we enthusiastically sampled peach tea, orange and currant scones, gingered-cream sandwiches, chocolate cookies, and red grapes.

The living room is warm and inviting: comfortable couches, rocking chairs (including original Shaker chairs), Oriental carpets, a wood-burning fireplace, sconces with lit candles, and Suella's fine needlepoint samplers. Guests can also sit in the plant-filled entrance porch and try their hand at one of the puzzles that are always temptingly left half-finished.

For a romantic stay, we recommend the Albert Hibbs Room. The lacy, ecru-colored, Court of Versailles 250-count hand-ironed sheets on the queen-size bed are some of the finest made. There are at least six pillows on each bed, so you can have firm pillows for reading and choose between down and Quallofil for sleeping. Slip into the velour robe, light the fire, and open the bottle of Vidal Blanc (from nearby Buckingham Vineyards). The large bath is thoughtfully stocked with Ralph Lauren towels, Crabtree & Evelyn colognes, talcum powder, shampoo, conditioner, and custom-blended bath salts, plus a selection of individually wrapped soaps. At night, when your bed is turned down, two handmade truffles with a Whitehall "W" are placed on your pillow.

Next door is the equally spacious Gerald Gimsey Room with Williamsburg potpourri wallpaper, a fireplace, and a queen-size bed made with lacy sheets. This room shares a bath with one other room. However, all of Whitehall's guests are pampered with a bottle of wine, truffles, bath soaps, and colognes.

The smaller Phineas Kelly Room is popular, as it is adjacent to the living room. In the late evening, guests like to don the inn's velour robes and curl up in front of the wood-burning fireplace.

In warmer weather, guests spend time relaxing around the outdoor swimming pool, playing tennis, and feeding the horses.

You'll discover thoughtful touches throughout your stay: flannel sheets in winter, sherry in the evening, a personal note when you leave. And if you return . . . there's a surprise in store for you.

Three rooms with private bath, two with fireplaces, $120–$160 on the weekend, $110–$150 midweek. Two rooms, both with fireplaces, shared bath, $120–$140 on the weekend, $110–$130 midweek. Breakfast and afternoon tea are included. No smoking. Children over 12 welcome. No pets. Two-night minimum on the weekends. RD 2, Box 250, Pineville Road, New Hope, PA 18938; (215) 598-7945.

Special Theme Weekends:

Presidents' Day Weekend. Celebrates Valentine's Day and includes a special romantic breakfast.

Chocolate Lover's Weekend. Includes a chocolate high tea, chamber music, chocolate breakfast, and a talk by a chocolate expert. Held the weekend after Easter.

Baroque Tea Concert. Quartet performs baroque music at an afternoon high tea in late March.

Holiday Picnic Weekends. Memorial Day, Independence Day, and Labor Day. Great picnics are served on the grounds.

Strawberry High Tea. Chamber music followed by high tea. First weekend in June.

Champagne Candlelight Concert. Chamber music, champagne and hors d'oeuvres. New Year's Eve.

Where to Dine. For truly romantic, elegant, expensive dining, we suggest La Bonne Auberge in New Hope (215-862-2462). About thirty minutes up the river is EverMay on the Delaware (215-294-9100), open weekends only, where an excellent, set-price seven-course meal is served. New Hope and Lambertville also have many fine restaurants.

What to Do. Fine galleries and shops are just a few minutes away in Peddler's Village, New Hope, and Lambertville. The Mercer Museum and the Michener Museum are in Doylestown. Outdoor enthusiasts can hike or bike along the Delaware Canal towpath.

How to Get There. From Philadelphia (approximately one hour), take I-95 north to Newtown exit, Route 332 west to Newtown. Take Route 413 north to Pineville. Go right at the Pineville Tavern on Pineville Road.

From New York (approximately 1½ hours), take NJ Turnpike south to exit 10, Route 287 north to Route 22 west and Route 202 south. Take Route 202 south to Lahaska. Turn left on Street Road. Turn right on Stoney Hill Road. Turn left on Pineville Road.

For detailed information about this area, refer to Chapter 4.

The Smithton Inn, Ephrata, Pennsylvania

Candlelight danced on the walls of our room. The fireplace glowed as flames flickered. The full-length velvet canopy draped gently around the edges of the bed. Chamber music played softly in the background. After soaking in the whirlpool, we donned the handmade, room-coordinated, flannel nightshirts and slipped into the caressing comfort of the feather bed. Propped up with down pillows and covered with a collector-quality quilt, we felt utterly pampered.

This was our introduction to Smithton, located in the heart of Lancaster County, Pennsylvania, home of the Amish. Here you can combine a stay in a romantic hideaway with a look at an authentic, early-American lifestyle as practiced by the Plain People of Lancaster County.

Innkeeper Dorothy Graybill, along with partner Allan Smith, lavish attention on the impeccable details of this 1763 stone house. They have incorporated numerous decorative influences from the nearby Ephrata Cloister into the design of the inn. Notice the Cloister-inspired wooden door hinges, the hand-planed floors, the handcrafted dining room buffet, and the inn's emblem of two doves.

The accommodation of choice is the South Wing Suite, actually a small apartment, which is a luxurious study tour of eighteenth-century furnishings. Enter through the authentic "Indian door" (designed with a sliding wooden panel to protect settlers from Indian attacks). Notable furnishings include the rust-colored leather wing chair, a corner table, and a Pennsylvania Dutch split-chevron barn door hung with handmade strap hinges. A modern kitchen is stocked with cold sodas, juices, and snacks for nibbling. In warm weather, sit on your private screened porch; in the cooler seasons, light a fire in the living room and curl up on the black leather couches.

Upstairs, the queen-size bed is made with one of the most beautiful Amish quilts we have seen: a meticulously detailed tree-of-life pattern. Encasing the head of the bed are notably fine, hand-woven blue hangings. An enclosed, twin Dutch bed, constructed with wooden pegs, provides an unusual sleeping alternative. A large bathroom features a stall shower as well as a whirlpool tub.

Another favorite of ours, secluded in the back of the inn, is the Gold Room. Gold velvet draperies match the full canopy of the queen-size bed. The colorful quilt, designed by Allan, and the tin and copper cut-out lampshades, made by Dorothy, were inspired by Ephrata Cloister drawings. Notice the hand-painted blanket chest, the gleaming hand-pounded copper sink, the black leather couch, and the fireplace strategically situated at the foot of the bed.

The third floor with its exposed beams, slanted roof with sky-lights, and wood stove is a favorite with guests who want a large, private loft space in which to hibernate.

On the second floor are slightly less expensive rooms. Dorothy tells us that guests have a difficult time deciding between the Red Room with a step-up Jacuzzi, red and white quilt, and red stenciling on the walls, or the Blue Room with a full blue-velvet canopy bed so high that a step-stool is needed.

In the dining room, the exquisite sideboard, designed by Allan, was made by a master Amish craftsman. Pennsylvania redware plates and handmade quilts, both available for purchase, decorate the walls. A full breakfast is served either in the dining room or in the privacy of your room. It might include blueberry waffles or blueberry pancakes, fresh fruit, pastry, and juices.

Six rooms, all with private baths, fireplaces, and handmade flannel nightshirts. One room has a Jacuzzi. $65–$95 midweek, $95–$115 weekends and holidays. South-wing two-story suite, $140 midweek, $170 weekends. If you'd like a featherbed, request it when you make your reservation. A full breakfast is included. A two-night stay is required on weekends. Mannerly children and pets are welcome. 900 West Main Street, Ephrata, PA 17522; (717) 733-6094.

Where to Dine. *Accomac Inn.* A river setting, high-quality formal French food and service spell romance at the circa 1775 Accomac Inn in Wrightsville, a thirty-minute drive from Smithton. Open for dinner seven days a week. Take the first exit off Route 30, after you cross the Susquehanna River. Turn right and follow the signs. Wrightsville, PA; (717) 252-1521.

Stouch's Tavern. Drive out in the country to this authentic 1785 family-run restaurant for excellent American cuisine in a historic Colonial tavern setting. Ask to be seated in the main dining room, which has a large open fireplace and exposed wooden-beam ceiling. From Smithton Inn (about thirty minutes away), Route 322 west. Go north on Route 419 to Womelsdorf; (215) 589-4577.

Shopping Tip. On your way to Stouch's Tavern, stop at Lester Breiniger's house to have a look at his impressive collection of Pennsylvania redware. Commission a custom-designed piece (birthday, anniversary, wedding) as a remembrance of your special weekend stay at Smithton. Call ahead; (215) 693-5344. 476 South Church Street, Robesonia, PA.

How to Get There. From Philadelphia (approximately 1½ hours), take the Pennsylvania Turnpike to exit 21. Take Route 222 south to the Ephrata exit. Turn west on Route 322 for exactly 2½ miles. The inn is at the corner of Main Street (Route 322) and Academy Drive.

From Baltimore (approximately two hours), take I-83 north to York. Take Route 30 east to Lancaster, then north on Route 222 to the Ephrata exit.

For detailed information about this area, refer to Chapter 5.

Sweetwater Farm, Glen Mills, Pennsylvania

Turning in the circular drive, off a narrow country road dotted with private estates, we arrived at a large eighteenth-century field-stone manor house. A flag fluttered above the front door; the brick walkway was lined with bright flowers; graceful, majestic trees told us that skilled arborists had been at work. Sweetwater is far more than an elegant inn: Along with cottages and a swimming pool, it is set on a fifty-acre working farm with sheep and horses grazing in the fields, rows of corn and flowers, and chickens in the hen house. This idyllic retreat in Pennsylvania's Brandywine River Valley (made famous by Andrew Wyeth's paintings) is the epitome of gentleman farm living.

The library, with its wall of books, is a comfortably casual room where guests can sit by the fireplace engrossed in the Sunday papers. A sunny formal parlor is decorated with candles, a spinning wheel, and a basket of subtly dyed skeins of wool spun from the farm's sheep. In warm weather, the terrace overlooking the fields and swimming pool is a favorite spot.

Our selection of romantic rooms begins with the Hideaway Cottage, the ultimate in privacy and romance. On the first floor is a cozy living room with a wood-burning fireplace, a corner cupboard of china pieces, and a full kitchen. The upstairs bedroom has a four-poster bed with a fishnet canopy, a glass-topped dressing table, and a private bath. A private sitting area, with furniture made from unfinished tree branches, overlooks a horse rink.

The Fan-window Suite on the third floor is a favorite with honeymooners. The room is white with pink roses: white plaster walls, white wicker couches, white chairs, and a white headboard for the queen-size bed. The small bathroom has a white claw-footed tub that adds to the charm of this room.

Across the hall is the Loft Room with both a queen-size and a double bed. This room reminds us of Wyeth paintings, with dark woods, a large spinning wheel, a basket of skeins of yarn, and a staircase that once led to the attic. In contrast to the bath next door, this one is large and modern.

For those on a budget who want the romance of a fireplace room and don't mind sharing a bath, we find the Georgian Room on the second floor fits the bill. The room has large windows and a high four-poster queen-size bed with a fishnet canopy.

New innkeeper Guillermo Pernot knows that after a day of sightseeing, guests often don't want to leave the inn to go out to a restaurant. On weekends he will cook a prix-fixe five-course dinner for up to ten house guests. A sample dinner might include corn bisque, a green salad with a crabcake, homemade pasta tossed with fresh herbs served with a filet of salmon, medallions of veal, and a fruit cobbler or strawberry shortcake.

Breakfast is served in the country kitchen: fresh eggs, country sausage, fresh fruit, juice, homemade bran muffins as well as cereal and hot oatmeal.

Note: If you plan to spend daytime midweek summer hours at the farm, be aware that there is an active quarry (audible but not oppressive) beyond the trees.

Seven rooms with private bath, $130–$140. Three rooms with shared bath, $120. Four cottages, $120–$165. A country breakfast is included. There are phones in all and TVs in most of the rooms. Children under 18, no charge; third adult in room, $25 additional. Pets permitted in the cottages. Box 86, Sweetwater Road, Glen Mills, PA 19342; (215) 459-4711.

Where to Dine.   The closest restaurant is Pace One (215-459-3702), serving excellent food at moderate prices. For romantic dining we suggest the candlelit Dilworthtown Inn (215-399-1390). On a Friday or Saturday night, visit Wilmington, a thirty-minute drive, and dine in elegance in the exquisite Green Room at the Hotel du Pont—perfect for more formal special occasions (302-594-3156).

What to Do.   The world-renowned Longwood Gardens is an absolute must. There are 350 acres of outdoor gardens and woodland trails and six acres of indoor conservatories. Winterthur is one of the country's premier museums of American decorative arts: 83,000 objects are on display in nearly 200 room settings dating from periods covering 1640 to 1840. The Brandywine River Museum houses paintings by three generations of Wyeths.

How to Get There.   Sweetwater Farm is approximately 2½ hours from New York and Washington, D.C., and less than an hour from Philadelphia, about a half-hour drive from the Philadelphia airport.

From New York, take the New Jersey Turnpike south to exit 2. Take Route 322 west. Go north, a right turn, on Route 452. Turn left and drive one mile on Route 1. Turn right at Valley Road (Franklin Mint intersection). At the end of the road, turn left and immediately right. Continue ¾ mile to Sweetwater Road. Turn left and drive for ½ mile to the farm.

From Washington, take I-95 north to Wilmington. Take Route 202 north to Route 1. Turn right on Route 1 for five miles to Valley Road. Then follow the preceding directions.

For detailed information about this area, refer to Chapter 6.

The Mainstay Inn, Cape May, New Jersey

Sitting on the grandest Victorian veranda in Cape May, with iced tea and a plate of assorted sweets in hand, surrounded by a manicured lawn, gardens, and fountains, and listening to the horse-drawn carriages passing by the front of the inn, we couldn't imagine a better spot to soak up the Victorian era. The atmosphere of the expansive 14-foot-ceilinged first-floor living room, parlor, and dining room is impressively elegant. Veteran innkeepers Tom and Sue Carroll have taken this 1872 men's gambling and entertainment club and created a museum-quality environment that accurately reflects the Renaissance Revival style. While the inn is maintained to perfection, Tom and Sue definitely do not want guests to feel as though they need to tiptoe and talk in hushed tones.

The interior of the main inn is furnished with fine antiques; many are original to the house, such as the massive twelve-foot mirror in the entrance hall and the eight-foot-long brass chandelier over the dining room table. On the ground floor are two formal parlors with floor-length windows framed by heavy swag draperies, and the dining room, where elegant breakfasts are served in the cooler months. For a view of the town in a room only large enough for two, climb the steep stairs to the Belvedere, which is furnished with a circular couch and a ceiling that's painted blue with silver stars.

All of the rooms in both the main inn and in the cottage next door are decorated with extreme care. Here are a few that evoke the most romantic mood. The Decatur Suite in the cottage takes up most of the third floor and has windows on four sides of the house. The sitting area is a ten- by twelve-foot room furnished with an Eastlake parlor set and a nineteenth-century walnut writing desk. The adjoining bedroom has a carved Victorian queen-size bed (*note:* the bed is the width of a queen-size, but is not as long).

In summer, the Bret Harte Room on the second floor of the cottage is popular for its private veranda that wraps around three sides of the room, where you can spend the day lazing in the hammock or in a rocker. This bedroom, about fourteen feet square, has a massive nine-foot-tall headboard with a carving of Shakespeare. The headboard towers over a queen-size bed, a matching dresser, and a rosewood parlor set. The bed is extraordinarily large, however, the bath is one of the smaller ones at the inn.

The Cardinal's Room in the main inn is located on the second floor at the back of the house. In this corner room you'll find a double bed with an eight-foot-tall headboard and a matching nine-foot-high dresser. There is also a matched pair of armoires with wooden fronts, and a large bath. The Stonewall Jackson Suite, also in the main inn, is an extraordinarily large room with a sitting alcove. A king-size bed with a brass and iron headboard, wicker furniture, and nine windows that wrap around three sides of the inn create a breezy feel. If you prefer a large bath, this room has the largest in the inn.

During the spring and fall, a full breakfast of a hot or cold fruit dish, an entrée such as strawberry French toast or English muffins with cheese and bacon, and homemade coffeecakes is served in the formal dining room. Up to fourteen guests can sit around the dining room table at the 8:30 or 9:30 A.M. breakfast seating. During the summer, the feeling at the inn is more casual. Cereals, yogurt, fresh fruit, juices, and coffeecakes are set out on the veranda for guests to help themselves. Each afternoon, tea and assorted pastries are served As a memento you may want to add Sue's cookbook, *Breakfast at Nine, Tea at Four,* to your collection.

Note: A stay at The Mainstay, particularly during July, August, and during Victorian Week in October must be planned well in advance. Reservations for these months are accepted beginning in January, and guests tend to ring in the New Year with a call to reserve their favorite rooms.

Open April through mid-December. Ten rooms and two suites, all with private bath; During the summer and other peak times, $115–$140; other times, $85–$125. A full breakfast is included except during the summer, when there's a continental buffet. Afternoon tea is included. Three-night minimum on weekends and during the summer. Children over 12 welcome. Third person in room $20 additional. No pets. 635 Columbia Avenue, Cape May, NJ 08204; (609) 884-8690.

Where to Dine. Within walking distance of the inn is a wide range of dining choices during the peak season. Top romantic choices include Maureen's, Washington Inn, 410 Bank Street, Water's Edge, Es-Ta-Ti, and the Virginia Hotel. The Virginia Hotel, the Washington Inn and the Lobster House remain open throughout the year.

What to Do. During the spring and fall, Cape May Point is a birder's paradise. The New Jersey Audubon Society has an office here and sponsors special weekends. In summer, the beach is of major interest to most visitors. Throughout the year there are tours of the exterior and interior of the restored Victorian buildings.

How to Get There. From New York City or Philadelphia, take the Garden State Parkway south to the end. Take Lafayette Street to the mall, turn left on Ocean Street and left on Columbia Street.

For detailed information about this area, refer to Chapter 7.

Brampton, Chestertown, Maryland

In the heart of Maryland's Eastern Shore, two miles from the center of Chestertown on fifteen acres of woodland and farmland is this 1860 Greek Revival manor house that's listed on the National Register of Historic Places. Combining the cordial hospitality of a former Swissair flight attendant with the ingenuity and restoration skills honed on Victorian homes in San Francisco, Danielle and Michael Hanscom have the qualities that spell success in the innkeeping profession. Sharing the dream of working together, the Hanscoms have combined good taste and lots of hard work to create a picturesque hideaway.

With its twelve-foot ceilings the living room has an airy, uncluttered feeling. When we commented on the difficulty of getting books down from the bookcases that reached to the ceiling, Danielle pointed to the top shelf where she had stashed a collection of calculus books and said, "I really don't have much need for

Brampton, an 1860 Greek Revival manor house, sits on fifteen acres in the heart of Maryland's Eastern Shore.

them." The focal point of the room is the pair of matching sensuous glove-leather gray couches that Danielle brought from Switzerland. These face each other on an Oriental rug next to a fireplace. On the other side of the room is an ornate Victorian couch.

The solid walnut staircase leads up to two large second-floor bedrooms and a suite with eleven-foot ceilings. We were glad to learn that an interior sprinkler system had been installed when the inn was renovated. The most romantic room in the house is the Yellow Room with a curly maple, queen-size, lacy canopied bed, fluffy down comforter, European armoire, desk, comfortable easy chairs, and a working fireplace. We liked the romance of lying in bed under the down duvet and watching the soft glow of the embers. Equally attractive is the Blue Room on the second floor, which has twin beds with white duvet covers. Danielle indicated that these can be made into a king-size bed if requested. The placement of the two easy chairs is ideal for reading by the working fireplace. A second-floor three-room suite with a lower ceiling includes a four-poster pencil-post double bed as well as a twin bed and a television, but no fireplace. *Note:* This is the only room that has a television.

The third-floor Red and Green rooms are the same size as the second-floor rooms, but have nine-foot ceilings and wood-burning Franklin stoves instead of fireplaces. Each room has a desk and two reading chairs. The furnishings reflect the Swiss penchant for uncluttered sophistication. The Green Room is a bit more romantic, as there is a lacy canopy over the queen-size bed and a large armoire with a mirrored door.

A plate of fresh fruit is in each room. Danielle offers refreshments in the afternoon and sherry or wine after dinner. We enjoyed the buttery, thin, crisp cookies.

The large first-floor breakfast room is furnished with Swiss antiques crafted in the late nineteenth century. Breakfast includes fresh-squeezed orange juice, fruit, muffins or coffeecake, a choice of eggs, sausage, French toast, or possibly a Swiss specialty such as bread and butter pudding with strawberry sauce.

Danielle and Michael live on the property with their daughter Sophie in a converted animal hospital. Also wandering the premises are two friendly dogs, a chocolate-colored labrador and a white mutt. There's plenty of room for the dogs and guests to roam.

Four rooms, all with private baths, $85–$95. One suite, $95. A full breakfast is included. Children permitted with prior arrangements. No pets. One mile south of Chestertown on Route 20, RR 2, Box 107, Chestertown, MD 21620; (301) 778-1832.

Where to Dine.   One of the most popular restaurants in Chestertown is the casual, moderately priced Ironstone Café. For elegant, expensive dining in Chestertown we'd recommend the Imperial Hotel. If you enjoy spicy hard-shell crabs, you can spend a couple of glorious hours by the water enjoying the view and picking the crabs. The closest crab house is in Rock Hall.

What to Do.   Stroll around Chestertown, making sure to walk along the streets of restored Colonial homes by the river. Farther south you may want to visit Oxford and St. Michaels. The area is very flat and there are plenty of back roads, so bicycling in this area is a lot of fun.

How to Get There. From Washington, D.C., take the Bay Bridge, then take Route 301 north to Route 213. From Philadelphia, take I-95 south. Exit at Route 279, then take Route 213 to Chestertown.

For detailed information about this area, refer to Chapter 8.

Robert Morris Inn, Oxford, Maryland

Located along the banks of the Tred Avon River on Maryland's Eastern Shore, Oxford is a sleepy little town that has worked to maintain the feel of a bygone era, when time was measured by the coming and going of sailing ships. Here you'll find no fast food, no supermarkets, and no shopping centers. But for a couple looking for a shaded porch, spectacular sunsets over the water, a friendly community, and traditional Eastern Shore seafood, the Robert Morris Inn may be the perfect place.

The main inn was built prior to 1710, when Oxford was a major port in the region. It is named after the father of one of the major financiers of the American Revolution, who lived here from 1738 to 1750. Fortunately, much of the original inn survives today. If you want to absorb the Colonial flavor, you can reserve a room in the original section complete with creaky, slightly slanting floors and handmade wall paneling. You'll appreciate the Elizabethan-style enclosed staircase, the Georgia white-pine flooring in the upstairs hall, and fireplaces made of English bricks brought to Oxford as ballast in trading ships. On the second floor, are the original rooms, 1 and 2, with side views of the river; on the third floor, also with side views of the river, are rooms 15 and 17.

We prefer to stay in the Victorian Sandaway Lodge, about a block from the main inn, or the recently constructed River Rooms that overlook the Tred Avon River. Here, in a quiet, tranquil setting, you can laze away the day sitting on your private porch or on a blanket at the water's edge.

At Sandaway, each room is designed with slight variations.

Room 105 has a large bathroom with gold Sherle Wagner fixtures, a king-size canopy bed that was once in Washington, D.C., at the Blair House; it has a side view of the river. Three riverfront rooms, 101, 102, and 202, have either a queen-size canopy bed or a king-size four-poster. Each room has a private balcony perfect for warm-weather relaxing. On the third floor, which is reserved for non-smokers, room 301 is a riverfront room with a sitting room, large bathroom with both a tub and a shower, and a king-size pencil-post bed.

Next door, the non-smoking River Rooms have a private, screened-in porch, a large picture window overlooking the water, a spacious bathroom with both a clawfoot tub and a shower, and a king-size four-poster bed.

For meals, the pumpkin-colored inn is a pleasant stroll away. At breakfast and lunch we were seated in the comfortably casual tavern room with its slate floor, dark wood-paneled walls, and open wood-burning fireplace. Adjoining the tavern room is the formal dining room. Of note are the impressive murals made from 140-year-old wallpaper samples. The original wallpaper of this design is in the reception room of the White House.

The menu has remained basically the same over the twenty years in which we have frequented the Eastern Shore. Robert Morris made its reputation by serving honest food cooked by chefs without pedigrees. The menu is straightforward with dishes such as fried shrimp, scallops, or crabcakes, broiled seafood imperial, stuffed shrimp, filet of fish, and prime rib.

Thirty rooms with private bath, $60–$140; three rooms with shared bath $50–$70. Accommodations: fifteen rooms in the main inn, $50–$120; two rooms in the River Cottage, $90; eight rooms in Sandaway Lodge, $110–$140; two rooms in River House, $90–$100; four River Rooms, $130; one apartment suitable for a family, $120. Breakfast is available but not included in the room rate. Children over 10 allowed. No pets. Closed February through mid-March. 312 Morris Street, Oxford MD 21654; (301) 226-5111.

What to Do. Bring some books and relax by the water. Walk around the quiet streets of Oxford. This is a great area for bicycling, as there are no hills and little traffic. An ideal day's outing takes you across the Tred Avon River on the historic ferry. From there, visit the Maritime Museum and have a lunch of hard-shell crabs at the Crab Claw in St. Michaels.

How to Get There.   Oxford is about two hours from Washington, D.C., and about three hours from Philadelphia.

From Philadelphia, take I-95 south to Route 896 to Route 301. Turn left on Route 213 to Route 50. Turn left to Route 50 east to Easton. Turn right to Route 322 (Easton bypass); then right to Route 333 to Oxford.

From New York (about five hours) take the New Jersey Turnpike south to the Delaware Memorial Bridge then to I-95 south. Then follow directions above.

From Washington, take Route 50-301 across the Chesapeake Bay Bridge to Route 50 east to Easton. Then follow directions above.

For detailed information about this area, refer to Chapter 8.

Channel Bass Inn, Chincoteague, Virginia

While the dining experience at the 100-year-old Channel Bass Inn is one-of-a-kind, the unassuming exterior of the weathered white building blends into this working fishing community and summer vacation spot. The inn is a five-minute drive from the 27-mile-long Assateague Island Wildlife Refuge and National Seashore. Here we've spent exhilarating hours hiking the wild beaches in almost total solitude, with only the crashing waves of the Atlantic Ocean and the cries of the gulls and geese breaking the silence.

As you bicycle the paved roads and hike the natural trails of the refuge, you may encounter the famed Chincoteague ponies as well as members of the large herd of Sika deer that roam the refuge. Assateague Island is a paradise for birders, as Chincoteague is a prime wintering spot on the Atlantic flyway. Bring your scope and binoculars for hours of birding.

This rare combination of a preserved natural setting, the plush modern comforts of a first-class inn, and the gastronomic delights that start and finish each day make the Channel Bass part of a completely romantic destination.

The rooms are decorated with thick beige wall-to-wall carpeting, queen- or king-size beds, reading chairs, comfortable couches, and tastefully selected antiques. Enter any of the rooms, and you are gently transported to a slower, more genteel way of life. No telephones, television, or young children will intrude on your privacy. Just relax, take a long soak in the tub, and anticipate the rest of the evening. Room 10, one of the deluxe third-floor rooms, is a favorite. This room has a king-size bed and is called the Reading Room for its glass-enclosed bookcase filled with current fiction and nonfiction selections. This spacious room has a sofa and plenty of reading lamps.

Room 4 has a small bedroom with a queen-size bed and a separate sitting room with a mini-bar and two couches. Should you wish to have a private dinner in your room, this is the room you must request (there is a 25% surcharge).

Two of the small rooms were recently converted into a suite, which has a private deck and a bath with a single Jacuzzi.

The baths are standard size, and include Neutrogena soap and shampoo as well as Bill Blass terrycloth robes. The deluxe rooms also have Neutrogena hand, face, and eye cream.

Make your dinner reservations when you book a room, as only twelve to sixteen guests are served each evening, no more than six each hour. Chef-owner James Hanretta personally attends to all of the buying, preparation, and cooking of the food. He travels throughout the region, selecting his ingredients from only the most reliable local sources: the freshest fish, jumbo lump crabmeat, oysters, clams, produce, and herbs. This is a restaurant for the food connoisseur who knows and appreciates fine ingredients prepared with distinction and is willing to pay a high price. As a result, the Channel Bass is very expensive.

In the dining room, the seven tables are widely spaced; the service is ever so correct without being snobbish; the place settings include shell-patterned Wedgwood china, Waterford crystal stemware, and silver flatware. Jim feels so strongly about his food that he asks guests to refrain from drinking hard liquor, as it dulls the palate. (Where else have you seen a restaurateur request patrons not to have a drink?) Jim feels that wine complements the food, and has carefully selected his cellar.

We started a recent meal with prime littleneck clams simmered in a delicate tarragon white wine sauce. Our second appetizer was a thick, rich tomato-based crab stew.

Entrées emphasize the shellfish that the Lower Eastern Shore is noted for. We recommend the seafood Espagnol, a combination of shrimp, lobster, clams, oysters, chorizo sausage, bacon, and spices served with sauce Espagnol. The sautéed medallions of backfin crab are formed into a patty and lightly sautéed. After a meal of these medallions, all other crabcakes bear no comparison. The rich, light crab soufflé is a signature dish that guests return for year after year.

For dessert, try the cheesecake. Instead of the usual heavy, creamy New York style, this one is light and feathery with semisweet chocolate drizzlings laced over the top.

Breakfast here is unlikely to resemble any meal you've eaten before. You won't find omelets with truffles and mushrooms or with caviar and salmon anywhere else. Each serving of the souffléed pancakes are whipped to order, as the egg whites need to be folded in at the last minute. These fluffy pancakes are made with Irish Cream, Grand Marnier, and Amaretto liqueurs. The pancakes are served with Vermont maple syrup, chopped pecans, or fresh strawberries and whipped cream.

Six rooms and two suites, all with private bath. May through September: Standard room with queen-size bed, $150; deluxe room with king-size bed, $175; two-room suite with queen-size bed, $200. October through April, rooms are $100, $150, or $175. Full Breakfast is served on Saturday and Sunday, 8:30 to 10 A.M.; it is not included in the room rate and must be preordered the night before. For souffléed pancakes with strawberries, fresh orange juice, and coffee, allow about $55 for two. Dinner, 6 to 9:30 P.M. Continental breakfast most other days. A complete dinner for two with a moderate wine will average about $185. Two-night stay required on the weekends. Not appropriate for children. No pets. 100 Church Street, Chincoteague, VA 23336; (804) 336-6148.

Note: The best months to visit are May, June, September, and October. We suggest avoiding this area in July and August because of large crowds, excessive heat and humidity, mosquitos, horseflies, and much higher rates.

How to Get There. From Philadelphia (approximately 3½ hours), take I-95 south to Route 13 (just below Wilmington, DE). Just beyond the VA state line, take Route 175 east to Chincoteague. From Washington, approximately three hours, take Route 50 to Salisbury, then take Route 13 south. Route 175 east to Chincoteague.

For detailed information about this area refer to Chapter 8.

The Inn at Little Washington, Washington, Virginia

What is the chemistry that causes a couple to willingly pay an extra $80 to $120 to dine and lodge on a Friday or Saturday night in a tiny Virginia town? What is so extraordinary to cause the flurry of articles, the five-star Mobile award, the AAA Five Diamond Award, and designation as the only "Relais Gourmand" hotel in the U.S.? What is the reason that a stream of limousines, even the occasional helicopter, brings well-heeled patrons to The Inn at Little Washington?

We think it's the very real possibility that the inn will fulfill your romantic dreams of being pampered in a grand Victorian English country home.

If you are going to invest in this experience, we suggest you choose one of the two duplex suites. (The standard and intermediate rooms are stunning, but just too small for this "ultimate romantic extravagance.") You'll walk from your sitting room, with a balcony overlooking the Blue Ridge Mountains, up the stairs of the duplex to your luxuriously appointed bedroom with another balcony.

We really didn't want to leave: the rooms included English antiques, canopied beds, *faux bois* woodwork, luxurious marble baths including a Jacuzzi, heated towel racks, thick terrycloth robes, hair-dryers, fine soaps, as well as flowers in profusion, mints, fruit, expensive coffee-table books, and a stocked refrigerator.

A stay here is living theater: During the day, the large staff quietly cleans, polishes, arranges flowers, and somehow manages to keep the whole place in a quiet, hushed state of constant perfection.

With that kind of introduction, you shouldn't be surprised to learn that dinner here is simply superb. You can start with lobster gazpacho, a salad of goose foie gras with lobster and green beans in a tarragon vinaigrette, or homemade boudin blanc. Now you must make a difficult choice of entrée: a filet of beef bathed in oysters and cream; a loin of baby lamb with black-eyed peas, wilted greens, and garlic mayonnaise; the finest Chesapeake Bay soft-shell crabs delicately browned in beer batter; grilled duck breast with red currants and wild rice; or tender white veal with Calvados, locally picked apples and pressed cider. No matter which extraordinary entrée you choose, you'll find it beautifully prepared and presented.

The desserts are equally extravagant. In early spring the rhubarb mousse is special, but we wouldn't feel right if we didn't also recommend the very unusual grapefruit pecan chocolate tart.

Since every item on the menu is so good, we suggest you make arrangements for the tasting dinner (an extra course). Make your wishes known when you make your dinner reservation.

Eight rooms, standard rooms $210, intermediate rooms $250, superior rooms $300. Two duplex suites, $410 each. Friday, Saturday, holidays, and the month of October, $80 surcharge per room— but even at these rates, weekends are booked two to three months in advance. Continental breakfast is included; full breakfast is extra. Overnight guests have guaranteed dinner reservations at the restaurant, which opens for dinner Monday and Wednesday through Friday, 6–9:30 P.M.; Saturday, 5:30–10:30 P.M.; Sunday, 4–9:30 P.M. Prix fixe for appetizer, entrée, ice or salad, dessert, and coffee, $68 per person ($88 on Saturday night). Middle and Main Streets, Washington, VA 22747; (703) 675-3800.

What to Do. Stroll around the village and visit the high-quality craft, art, antique, and custom-furniture galleries. Taste Virginia wines at local vineyards. The following are nearby and have regular tasting hours: Naked Mountain Vineyards in Markham, Linden Vineyards in Linden, and Oasis Vineyard in Hume. Visit the 195,000-acre Shenandoah National Park with hiking trails, nature walks, waterfalls, and some of the finest scenic vistas in the East. Trail rides are available at the Marriott Ranch. Or, follow the back roads in Middleburg and Fauquier counties to see the panoramas enjoyed by the fox hunters.

How to Get There. From Washington, D.C., just over one hour, take the Beltway I-495 to I-66 west to Exit 10-A Gainesville. Follow Route 29 south to Warrenton. In Warrenton, take Route 211 west. Turn right on 211 Business to Washington, Virginia.

For detailed information about this area, refer to Chapter 9.

INDEX

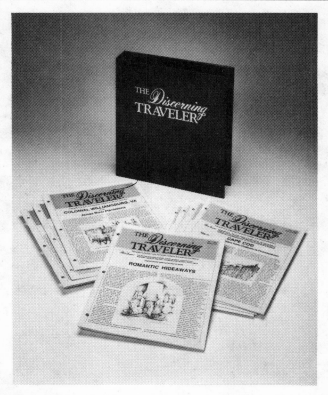